Windows® XP
VISUAL™
ENCYCLOPEDIA

by Kate Chase, Jim Boyce

Windows® XP Visual Encyclopedia™

Published by
Wiley Publishing, Inc.
111 River Street
Hoboken, NJ 07030-5774

Published simultaneously in Canada

Copyright © 2006 by Wiley Publishing, Inc.,
Indianapolis, Indiana

Library of Congress Control Number: 2005938258

ISBN-13: 978-0-471-75686-6

ISBN-10: 0-471-75686-5

Manufactured in the United States of America

10 9 8 7 6 5 4 3 2 1

Trademark Acknowledgments

Contact Us

For general information on our other products and services please contact our Customer Care Department within the U.S. at (800) 762-2974, outside the U.S. at (317) 572-3993, or fax (317) 572-4002.

For technical support please visit www.wiley.com/techsupport.

WILEY
Wiley Publishing, Inc.

Sales

Contact Wiley at (800) 762-2974 or fax (317) 572-4002.

CREDITS

Project Editor
Jade L. Williams

Acquisitions Editor
Michael Roney

Product Development Supervisor
Courtney Allen

Copy Editor
Marylouise Wiack

Technical Editor
Allen Wyatt

Editorial Manager
Robyn Siesky

Business Manager
Amy Knies

Manufacturing
Allan Conley
Linda Cook
Paul Gilchrist
Jennifer Guynn

Book Design
Kathie Rickard

Production Coordinator
Adrienne Martinez

Layout
Beth Brooks
Jennifer Heleine
Amanda Spagnuolo

Screen Artists
Ronda David-Burroughs
Cheryl Grubbs
Lynsey Osborn
Jill Proll

Illustrator
Cheryl Grubbs

Proofreader
Lisa Stiers

Quality Control
Leeann Harney

Indexer
Joan Griffitts

Special Help
Microsoft Corporation

**Vice President and Executive
Group Publisher**
Richard Swadley

Vice President and Publisher
Barry Pruett

Director of Composition Services
Debbie Stailey

ABOUT THE AUTHORS

Kate J. Chase (Woodbury, VT) has more than three dozen references for Windows operating system, Microsoft applications including the Microsoft Office Suite, Web design and publishing, and the Internet. She has previously written *Norton Desktop Reference For Dummies* and *Build It Yourself Visually: Windows Media Center PC*. A general freelance writer as well as a columnist and journalist, Kate also works on science, medical, political, and other topics. She is perhaps best known as PC Kate (www.pckate.com) from America Online and the Microsoft Network where she led thriving technical communities for more than a decade and is a Microsoft MVP (Most Valuable Professional).

Jim Boyce (Rothsay, MN) has authored/co-authored 50 books on computer software and hardware. His more recent titles include *Outlook 2003 Inside Out*, *Windows 2003 Server Bible* (with Jeffrey Shapiro), *Windows XP Power Tools,* and *Absolute Beginner's Guide to Microsoft Office 2003*. He is a former contributing editor and columnist for WINDOWS Magazine and has contributed to several publications including PC Magazine, Connected Home, Cadence, CADalyst, InfoWorld, Home PC, and others. He is also a frequent contributor to techrepublic.com and WatchIT.com, and he writes daily Windows 2000 Professional and Windows 2000 Server TechMails for techrepublic.com. He has also authored white papers and reports for techrepublic.com and developed content for online training and white papers for Microsoft.

PREFACE

Do you look at the pictures in a book or newspaper before anything else on a page? Would you rather see an image instead of read about how to do something? Search no further. This book is for you. Opening *Windows XP Visual Encyclopedia* allows you to read less and learn more about the application.

Who Needs This Book

This book is for a reader who has never used the Windows XP operating system. It is also for more computer literate individuals who want to expand their knowledge of the different features that Windows XP has to offer.

Book Organization

This book consists of sections, all listed in the book's table of contents. A *section* is a set of steps that show you how to complete a specific computer task.

Each section, usually contained on two facing pages, has an introduction to the task at hand, a set of full-color screen shots and steps that walk you through the task, and a set of tips. This format allows you to quickly look at a topic of interest and learn it instantly.

What You Need to Use This Book

To perform the tasks in this book, you need a computer with these specific requirements:

Windows XP Home or Professional Edition

128 MB RAM (256 MB or greater is recommended)

PC with 300 MHz or greater CPU

1.5 GB of available hard disk space

CD or DVD drive

Keyboard and pointing device such as a mouse

SuperVGA display capable of a resolution of 800x600 or greater

Internet connectivity strongly recommended

The Conventions in This Book

A number of typographic and layout styles have been used throughout *Windows XP Visual Encyclopedia* to distinguish different types of information.

Bold

Bold type indicates text and numbers that you must type into a dialog box or window.

Italics

Italicized words introduce a new term and are followed by a definition.

① Numbered Steps

You must perform the instructions in numbered steps in order to successfully complete a section and achieve the final results.

Indented Step Text

You do not have to perform these steps; they simply give additional information about a feature. Indented step text tells you what the application does in response to a numbered step. For example, if you click a certain menu command, a dialog box may appear, or a window may open. Indented step text may also present another way to perform a step.

Notes

Notes give additional information. They may describe special conditions that may occur during an operation. They may warn you of a situation that you want to avoid, for example, the loss of data.

 You can easily identify the tips in any section by looking for the TIP icon. Tips offer additional information, including tips, hints, and tricks. You can use the TIP information to go beyond what you have learn learned in the steps.

Table of Contents

W

Part II: Techniques 95

A

B

C

INTRODUCTION

We are long time users, technicians, and experts in Windows operating systems as well as other Microsoft programs. We feel that Windows XP, especially when upgraded with the security patches available in Service Pack 2, is the most stable Windows version available for both consumer and professional platforms. Service Pack 2 also makes Windows considerably more secure from outside threats. If you have not already upgraded to Service Pack 2, please do so. It is our hope that this is your experience as well, especially once you employ this book to take advantage of all that this operating system offers to you.

Because Windows XP Home or Professional Edition is so comprehensive and encompasses so many different tools and features, this subject lends itself extraordinarily well to an encyclopedia. Instead of reading countless pages of text on a particular topic, you can use this book to easily look up a feature by alphabetic entry and find all the steps you must perform.

The moment you can master many of the basics of file management, Internet and other network connectivity, as well as hardware and software installations, you can control far more over your desktop workspace. This book, with its steps and visual presentations, helps you to do just that quickly and efficiently. Once mastered, you can move on to your real work of enjoying the Internet and all the digital world and its ever-changing revolution can provide to you. This includes your ability to run applications, transfer files to and from your system, and play today's top PC games.

Windows XP Visual Encyclopedia is divided into two parts.

Part I is a comprehensive A to Z reference of tools. Tools can be icons found in palettes, panes, or toolbars. Tools can also be specific commands accessed from the menu bar. A named dialog box, window, or panel that is used to accomplish a specific task can also be a tool.

Within Part I, you learn about key components such as the Windows Firewall engineered to protect your network and Internet connections, and My Computer and Windows Explorer, the two core file management tools. There is also Registry Editor to aid you in viewing and making careful changes to your master Windows index called the Registry. You will also read about Accessibility Options designed to help you work in Windows if you have special physical or cognitive challenges. In addition, you can explore tools that will enable you to work remotely from home to the office, or between different computers on your home or small office network, such as Telnet or Remote Desktop Connection.

Part II is an alphabetical reference of techniques, including basic operations as well as advanced, solutions-based effects. Techniques represent results from an operation that may involve the use of one or more tools.

Inside Part II, you will find useful techniques, such as how to secure your files or share them with others. You will also see how to adjust Windows Security options like Windows Updates and the Windows Firewall, as well as step through the various wizards available to you. These wizards include Network and Wireless Network Setup, Fax Configuration and Send Fax, and troubleshooting aids. Screenshots and callouts assist you throughout your efforts to get the right results the first time you try, which is the beauty of a visual encyclopedia.

Kate J. Chase
S Woodbury, VT, 2006
kate@pckate.com

Jim Boyce
Minnesota, 2006
jim@boyce.us

Windows XP Visual Encyclopedia

Part I: Tools

Most people use Windows XP for both work and personal enjoyment. Regardless of how you use it, Windows XP offers you many tools that can help you do your work more quickly, easily, and accurately, and enhance your personal computer experience.

The first part of this book describes tools that empower you to do just about anything that you want with your Windows XP computer. These tools help you to communicate with your office network or set up a home network, send e-mail or receive a fax, browse the Web, or transfer files from your system to another computer. You can also play the latest games, produce a family movie, create a custom audio CD to play in your car, or use a special compatibility wizard to help you to run older software.

Whether you are an Administrator or a rookie, a computer enthusiast or an occasional user, the tools in Windows XP offer a range of options and features to help you master your system, add, remove, and use your peripheral devices, and successfully run your programs.

ACCESSIBILITY WIZARD

Windows XP includes several accessibility features that can assist people with physical challenges to use their computer more easily and more effectively. You can use any or all of these features to improve your Windows experience. Some may assist you even if you do not have a physical limitation but want to do something in a different way.

Windows XP includes accessibility features such as the Magnifier, Narrator, and On-Screen Keyboard. The Magnifier expands an area of the desktop to make it easier to read. The Narrator reads items such as dialog box options from the screen. The On-Screen

Keyboard allows a user to type text on the screen rather than with a keyboard.

Although you can configure each of these accessibility features separately, Windows XP also provides a wizard to help you configure them. The Accessibility Wizard allows you to activate and configure these three tools, along with other related features, such as the desktop and window font size, and input options for the keyboard and mouse.

See also>>   **Accessibility Wizard**

❶ Click Start.

❷ Click All Programs.

❸ Click Accessories.

❹ Click Accessibility.

❺ Click Accessibility Wizard.

The Accessibility Wizard opens.

ADD HARDWARE WIZARD

A

If the operating system does not automatically detect new devices when you install them, then you can use the Add Hardware Wizard to force Windows to seek them out. This wizard specifically steps you through the process to install new devices that Windows cannot find through its standard hardware detection scheme.

Windows XP automatically searches for new hardware and then usually installs the needed drivers with little or no input from you. However, sometimes Windows does not recognize hardware that you have added to the system. This may

happen for many reasons, for example, nonstandard hardware and its drivers or hardware not specifically designed for Windows XP.

You can use the Add Hardware Wizard that is included with Windows to easily add new hardware. It is important to have any disks that came with your new device nearby so that you can insert them into the appropriate drive when prompted to do so, or when you click the Have Disk option in the wizard.

See also>> **Add Hardware Wizard**

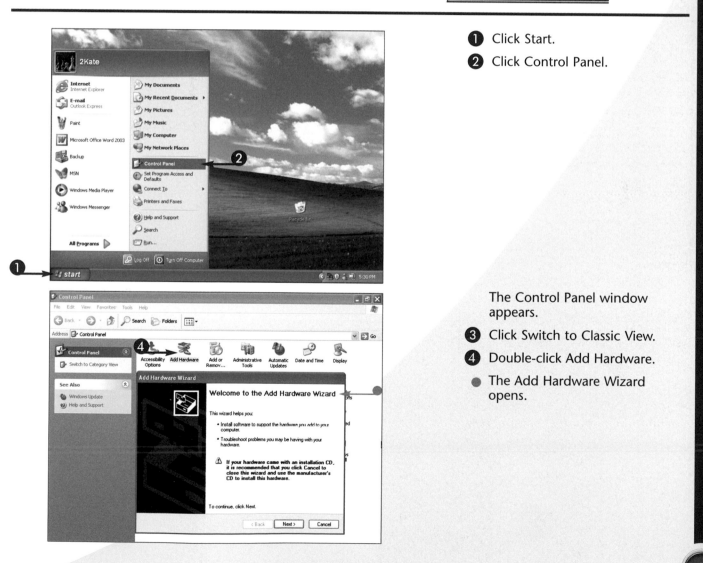

① Click Start.

② Click Control Panel.

The Control Panel window appears.

③ Click Switch to Classic View.

④ Double-click Add Hardware.

● The Add Hardware Wizard opens.

3

ADD NETWORK PLACE WIZARD

You can use the Add Network Place Wizard to link to a store of files or to another resource that is located on your home or small office network.

The Add Network Place Wizard helps you to add these types of shortcuts to your My Network Places folder. In addition, the wizard also helps you to connect to other types of network storage resources. For example, you can subscribe to space on MSN Communities to share files with other MSN users, or add Web or FTP sites where you can store your files.

When you add a network resource to My Network Places, a unique icon represents the resource to indicate the type of resource for easy identification.

A network environment uses a network server to store documents that people can access and share. Although you can browse for documents on the network, you can simplify access to those documents when you add a shortcut icon in the My Network Places folder. You can then access a folder simply by double-clicking the icon.

See also>>   **Add Network Place Wizard**

1. Click Start.

2. Click My Network Places.

   If you do not see My Network Places from the Start menu, then click Control Panel. From the panel, double-click Network Connections, and then click My Network Places from the Other Places pane.

   The My Network Places window appears.

3. Under the Network Tasks section, click Add a network place.

   ● The Add Network Place Wizard opens.

ADD OR REMOVE PROGRAMS

You can use the Add or Remove Programs tool in the Control Panel to easily install or uninstall software, as well as additional Windows components that did not apply to your setup when you first installed Windows. Normally, when you insert the disk for a new program, Windows automatically launches the setup software for it. However, when you need to modify a program installation or remove a program, you can run the Add or Remove Programs applet to accomplish this. For example, you may want to use a completely different program to open a document or an image than the software that loads by default with it.

The Add or Remove Programs window displays a list of all of the installed programs. Each entry includes the total disk space that each program uses, how frequently you use the program, and when you used it last. This information helps you to identify seldom-used programs that you can remove to recover disk space.

See also>> Add or Remove Programs

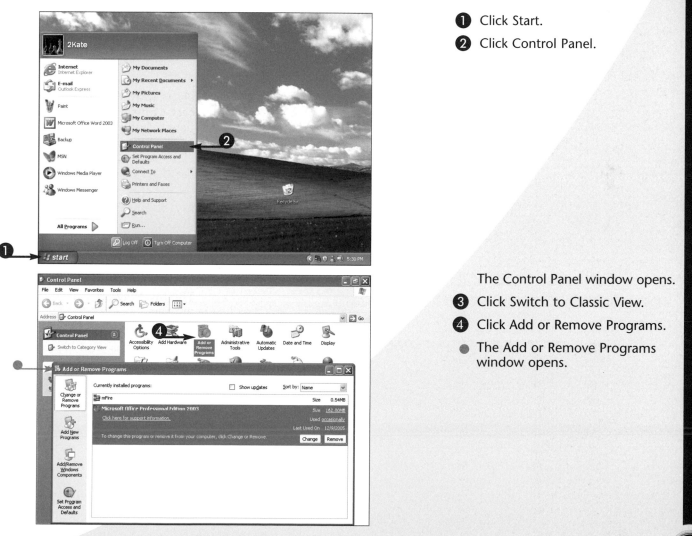

❶ Click Start.

❷ Click Control Panel.

The Control Panel window opens.

❸ Click Switch to Classic View.

❹ Click Add or Remove Programs.

● The Add or Remove Programs window opens.

ADD PRINTER WIZARD

You can add a printer to your computer quickly and easily by using the Add Printer Wizard. This wizard is an all-inclusive tool to locate, add, and configure a printer for use with your Windows desktop or associated network. You may need the disk that accompanies a new printer to complete the wizard.

With many of today's newer printers, you do not need to use the Add Printer Wizard. For example, when you connect a printer that uses a hot-pluggable interface such as USB, IEEE 1394, or infrared, Windows automatically detects and installs it. However, you

can use the Add Printer Wizard to add printers that connect to an LPT or COM port on your local computer, as well as printers that are shared by other computers on the local area network.

The Add Printer Wizard can detect many printers and install the appropriate printer driver. Keep in mind that you must turn on the printer before you run the wizard.

See also>> **Add Printer Wizard**

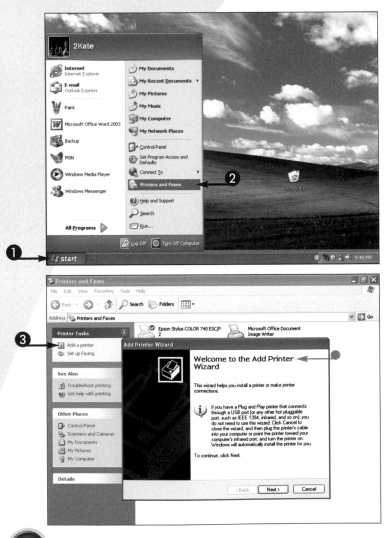

① Click Start.

② Click Printers and Faxes.

The Printers and Faxes window appears.

③ In the Printer Tasks section, click Add a printer.

● The Add Printer Wizard opens.

ADDRESS BAR

You probably use the Internet Explorer Address Bar all of the time. This is a text box in which you type the location of a resource such as a Web page, network share, or local folder or file.

Although you can use the Address Bar within Internet Explorer, you can also use it outside of Internet Explorer to access these types of resources quickly. For example, you can add the Address Bar to the Windows taskbar, to navigate to Web pages quickly, local folders, network folders, and even network printers. The Address

Bar also appears at the top of the My Computer and Windows Explorer windows. You can use it to navigate either to a Web or other Internet site or to a different folder or drive on your system.

Regardless of where you access the Address Bar, you must type a URL and then press Enter, or click the Go button.

See also>> **Address Bar**

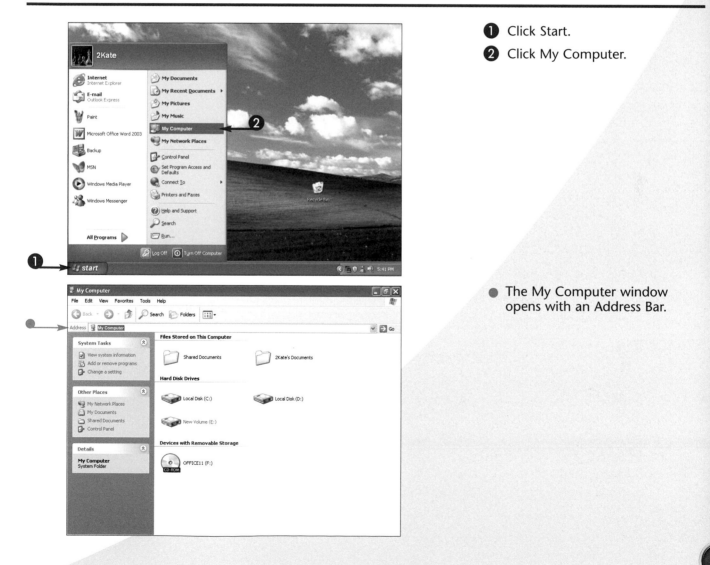

1 Click Start.

2 Click My Computer.

● The My Computer window opens with an Address Bar.

ADDRESS BOOK

One of the most common tasks that people perform on a computer is sending and receiving e-mail. To send an e-mail, you must know the e-mail address of the message recipient. You can use the Windows Address Book to store contact information, including e-mail addresses.

The Windows Address Book offers a great way to keep track of addresses, phone numbers, e-mail addresses, and other important contact information. For example, the Address Book offers fields for a contact's first and last name, birthday, instant messaging address, and Web page. You can even click the View Map button in the Home or Business tabs of a contact's properties to perform a search at expedia.com and display a map showing the location of the contact.

Windows Address Book is available directly in Windows, where you can conveniently view and manage contact information. When you use Outlook Express, it uses Windows Address Book to store its contact information. As a result, you can use a single address book for both programs.

See also>>   **Address Book**

① Click Start.

② Click All Programs.

③ Click Accessories.

④ Click Address Book.

If this is the first time that you open Address Book, then Windows asks if you want to use it as the default vCard viewer. For now, click No.

The Address Book opens.

AUTOMATIC UPDATES

Because Windows XP is a complex operating system that requires security updates and patches against new threats, you need to update your system to protect it. Microsoft constantly develops and publishes updates for Windows to make it work better and to be more secure and reliable.

To safeguard your computer without extra effort on your part, you may want to use Automatic Updates to download these patches and updates. For example, you can schedule Automatic Updates to automatically download and install updates on a regular basis, such as every day at 2:00 A.M. You can also configure Automatic Updates to

download the updates but not install them until you direct it to do so. This option offers the advantage of automatic updates and notification, as well as control over when Windows applies these updates.

You can manually obtain updates and patches from the Windows Update Web site, located at http://update.microsoft.com. However, you must perform manual updates yourself, which may be difficult to remember to do.

See also>> **Automatic Updates**

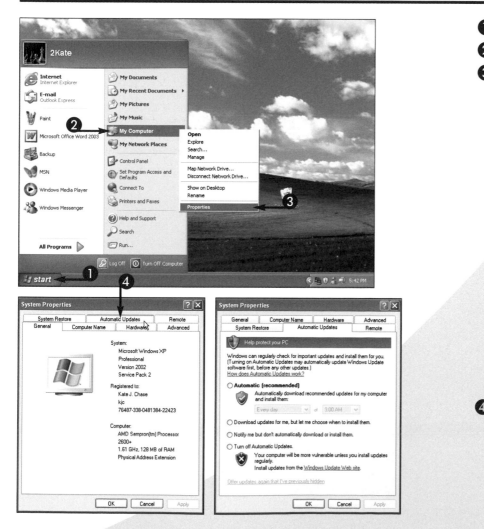

❶ Click Start.

❷ Right-click My Computer.

❸ In the sub-menu, click Properties.

The System Properties dialog box appears.

You can also open the System Properties dialog box through the System icon in the Control Panel.

❹ Click the Automatic Updates tab.

The Automatic Updates panel appears.

BACKUP

Backup is a tool that you can use to protect yourself and your files from many kinds of disasters that can happen to your computer. This tool allows you to make a copy of either specific or all primary files and store them as a single master file in another location, such as a secondary hard drive.

You can then call upon this master file later to restore your system in the event of an emergency or when you change either to a different computer or to a new hard drive. When you create your backup, you have duplicates of key files on your hard drive, if you need them. This saves you from having to recreate or redo crucial files and folders that are lost to a system emergency. You can restore your entire setup or just individual files and folders from the backup that you make.

When you launch Backup, the Backup and Restore Wizard opens to guide you through the process. You can also opt to run the tool in Advanced mode without the simple wizard.

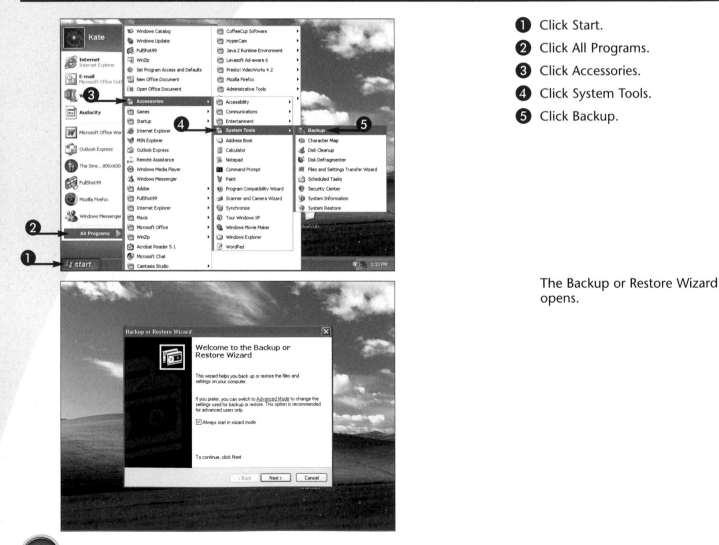

① Click Start.

② Click All Programs.

③ Click Accessories.

④ Click System Tools.

⑤ Click Backup.

The Backup or Restore Wizard opens.

BRIEFCASE

When you work on more than one computer, you often need to synchronize your files. *Synchronizing* is the process by which different versions of the same file are reconciled between two or more computers. You can use the Windows Briefcase feature to do this. As a result, only one file version remains among the computers.

For example, you may want to move documents between a desktop computer and a notebook without creating different versions of the same document. Ultimately, you want the two computers to have the same file version, where each reflects

the changes that you have made to a file on one of the computers. Briefcase allows you to facilitate this action.

You can create a Briefcase on either a removable disk, such as a floppy disk or a shared external drive, or on a hard drive. In either case, you can direct Briefcase to synchronize files either automatically or manually.

See also>> **Offline Files**

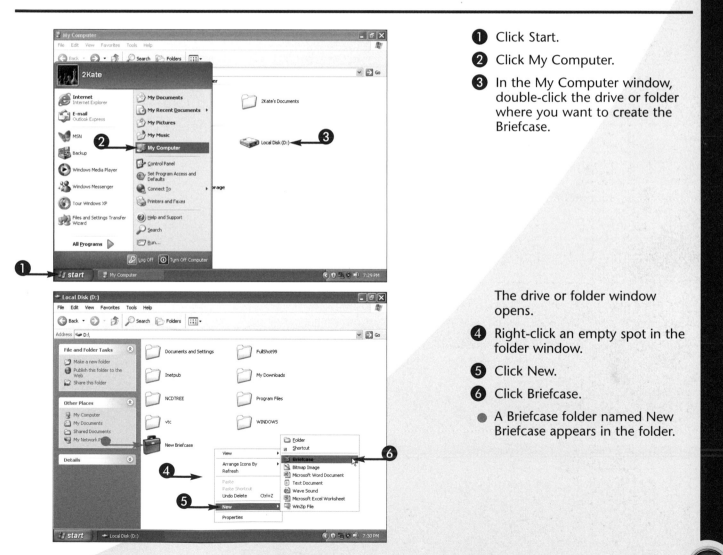

❶ Click Start.

❷ Click My Computer.

❸ In the My Computer window, double-click the drive or folder where you want to create the Briefcase.

The drive or folder window opens.

❹ Right-click an empty spot in the folder window.

❺ Click New.

❻ Click Briefcase.

● A Briefcase folder named New Briefcase appears in the folder.

CALCULATOR

When you need to add some numbers together or calculate costs, you can use Calculator, a virtual desktop tool that Windows XP provides as a standard accessory. With it, you can perform both basic and advanced math tasks.

Calculator works very much like a handheld calculator, with the advantage of always being on and ready to use. You simply click your mouse rather than press a button when you perform your calculations. To enter numbers for calculations, you can either use the numeric pad on your keyboard or click the corresponding numeric key within the calculator. Specific calculator keys perform a math function: the asterisk key (*) allows you to multiply, the plus key (+) to add, the minus key (-) to subtract, and the slash key (/) to divide.

An important difference between the Windows XP calculator and a regular calculator is that the Windows version supplies two modes of operation. You can use the standard mode for all basic calculations, and the scientific mode to handle complex mathematical formulas and statistics. By default, Calculator is set to standard mode.

❶ Click Start.

❷ Click All Programs.

❸ Click Accessories.

❹ Click Calculator.

Calculator opens on the desktop.

CD WRITING WIZARD

The CD Writing Wizard allows you to easily record CDs — filled with music or other files — on a computer with a record-capable CD drive. With the wizard, you can easily store copies of important files from your computer's hard drive to save space and reduce drive congestion. When you create copies of files from the hard drive, you also protect yourself against the loss of these files in the event of a drive failure.

When you insert a blank CD into the drive, Windows XP detects it and asks you what you want to do. You can choose to open a writeable

CD folder, select the files that you want to copy to a blank CD, and then launch the CD Writing Wizard.

Once the wizard asks you to type a name for the blank CD, it begins to back up your files. This means that the wizard checks through the files that you want it to copy, verifies that the blank CD is ready to use, and then begins the file-copying process.

See also>> **CD Writing Wizard**

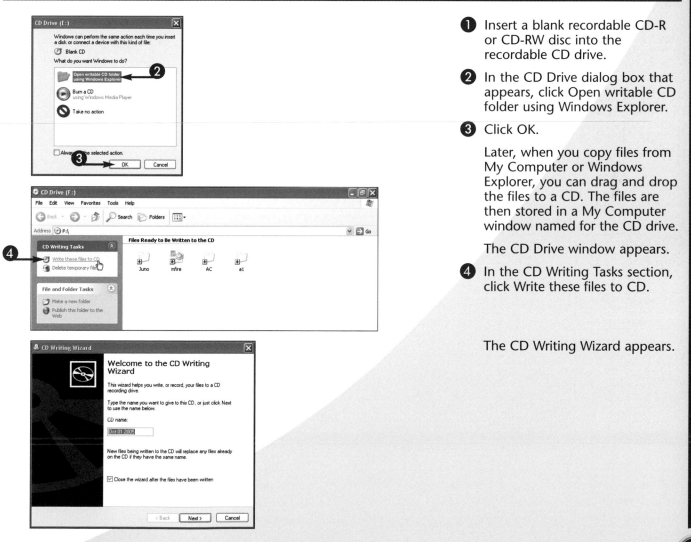

1 Insert a blank recordable CD-R or CD-RW disc into the recordable CD drive.

2 In the CD Drive dialog box that appears, click Open writable CD folder using Windows Explorer.

3 Click OK.

Later, when you copy files from My Computer or Windows Explorer, you can drag and drop the files to a CD. The files are then stored in a My Computer window named for the CD drive.

The CD Drive window appears.

4 In the CD Writing Tasks section, click Write these files to CD.

The CD Writing Wizard appears.

CLIENT FOR MICROSOFT NETWORKS

Whenever you install a home or office network with Windows, or create an Internet access account for use with a new computer, you must verify that the Client for Microsoft Networks is installed in Windows. Without the client, you cannot perform basic network communications or access the Internet or other online services. If you experience difficulties, then you should always check immediately to ensure that the client is installed.

This client is a package of *drivers,* which provide software support for hardware, and *protocols,* which

offer support for standard network communications and functions. There are also utilities to check for proper two-way network data transfer. Together, these drivers, protocols, and utilities supply the computer with what it needs for you to work on a network in your home or small office, or the Internet.

Many new computers ship with this client already installed as part of Windows to facilitate networking and Internet access. Even if it is not installed, Internet or network software that you add will probably install this client automatically.

1 Click Start.

2 Click My Network Places.

The My Network Places window opens to display a list of network resources.

3 In the Network Tasks section, click View network connections.

4 In the Network Connections window, click a network connection.

5 Click Change settings of this connection.

The Connection Properties dialog box appears, displaying your type of network connection.

● The Client for Microsoft Networks check box is selected.

CLIENT SERVICE FOR NETWARE

If your computer connects to a network using Novell NetWare, then you must ensure that a package of tools called Client Service for Netware is installed on your system. Otherwise, your computer will not be seen by, or be able to communicate with, the rest of the computers and services on the Novell-based network.

The client includes a number of files that offer Novell networking services. These include drivers that are needed by network hardware and diagnostic tools to check network operation.

As you work, you must read and follow instructions that are included with your Novell NetWare setup to determine what else you need to configure a

new computer as a Novell network workstation. For example, this client alone will not set up your Novell network; you must run the network setup software after you make your physical network connections. However, you only need this client if your network is Novell-based; Microsoft networking requires the Client for Microsoft Networks instead.

See also>>

Client for Microsoft Networks

Network Setup Wizard

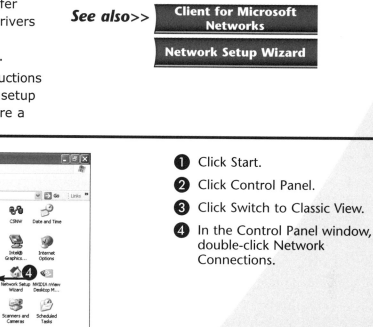

① Click Start.

② Click Control Panel.

③ Click Switch to Classic View.

④ In the Control Panel window, double-click Network Connections.

The Network Connections window appears.

⑤ Right-click the network connection that you want.

⑥ Click Properties from the sub-menu.

● The Properties dialog box appears, displaying the General tab where Client Service for NetWare is selected.

COMMAND PROMPT

If you are comfortable with a command-line interface — where you type commands rather than clicking to run programs or open files — then you can use the Command Prompt, also called the Command Console. The Command Prompt is a separate window that opens on the desktop. Within the console, you can type commands through your keyboard; your mouse does not function, and there is nothing to click.

You may sometimes need the Command Prompt to run certain troubleshooting programs as well as very old utilities and software. For example, some Windows XP and network diagnostics can only run

from the Command Prompt. Other commands that you can type allow you to open tools that you can also run from the graphical interface.

One of the most important Command-only utilities is the Windows Recovery Console. This is a Windows XP emergency repair service that is available from the Windows XP setup CD for use when your computer does not boot into Windows.

See also>> **Recovery Console**

Command Prompt

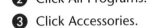

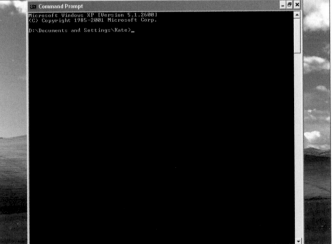

① Click Start.

② Click All Programs.

③ Click Accessories.

④ Click Command Prompt.

The Command Prompt window appears on your desktop.

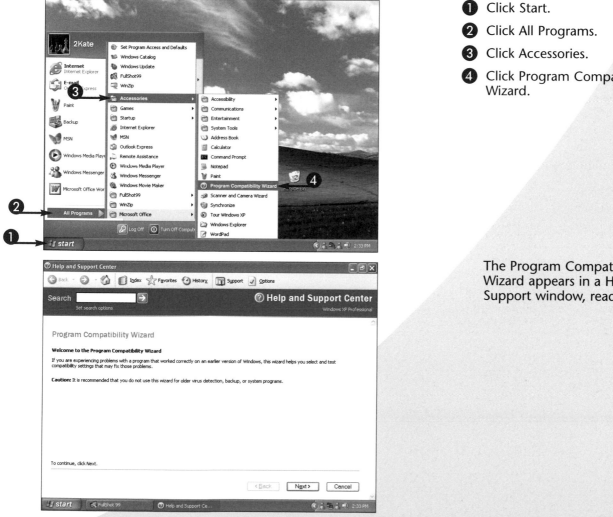

COMPATIBILITY WIZARD

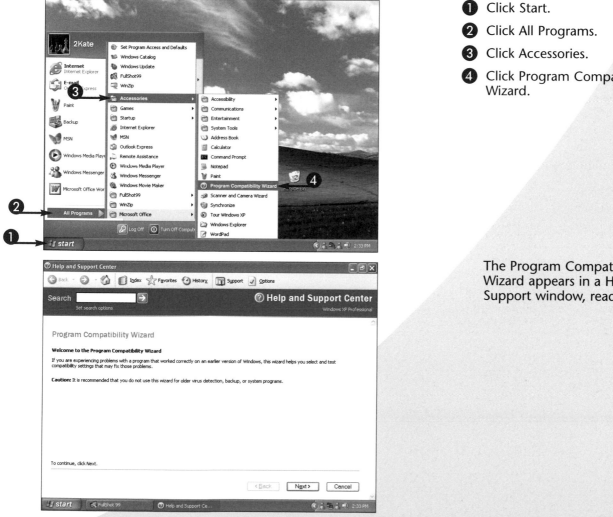

If you have trouble when you attempt to run an older program in Windows XP, then you can use the Compatibility Wizard — also called the Program Compatibility Wizard — to try to run the software. Once the wizard loads, it checks both your Windows XP configuration and the requirements of the program that you want to run. The wizard then tries to create an environment that makes it easier for the software to execute. You can also choose options such as which previous Windows version you want to emulate for the software.

Although the wizard cannot successfully launch every old program, this feature offers you an option to try when no others are available. Keep in mind that it may take more than one pass through the wizard to find the right environment for the software to launch. This means that you may need to run the wizard two or more times, and then try to run the program between each wizard attempt.

See also>>   **Program Compatibility Wizard**

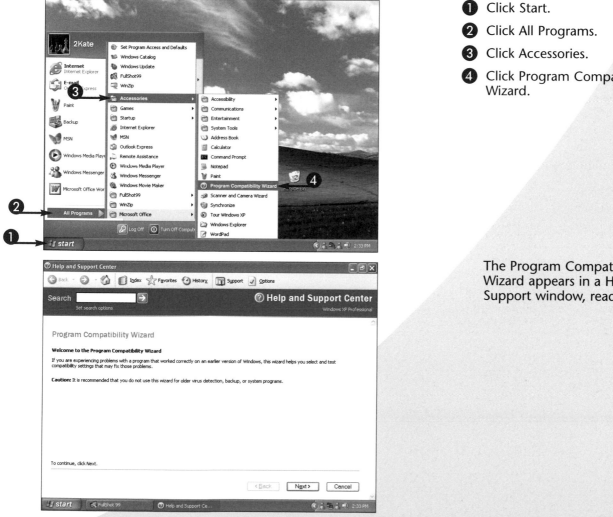

① Click Start.

② Click All Programs.

③ Click Accessories.

④ Click Program Compatibility Wizard.

The Program Compatibility Wizard appears in a Help and Support window, ready to run.

COMPUTER MANAGEMENT MMC SNAP-IN

You can use the Computer Management MMC Snap-In to manage your system and adjust user settings. The snap-in is a window console from which you can check your computer setup and change options.

The Computer Management console allows you to easily access individual tools from different administrator software from one location. From the console, you can view details such as which users are connected to a computer, and which services are currently running. You can also start and stop services, manage programs, and monitor system events such as when someone logs on or off, or when a problem occurs on the computer that is being watched.

The settings and choices in the Computer Management Snap-In go well beyond those that you can modify under the options that you find in the Control Panel. This tool is designed for professional-level system management. You can and should use this snap-in only if you have Administrator access and advanced experience in Windows.

See also>>   **Control Panel**

❶ Click Start.

❷ Click Control Panel.

The Control Panel window appears.

❸ Click Switch to Classic View.

❹ Double-click Administrative Tools.

You can also start this tool by clicking Start, right-clicking My Computer, and selecting Manage.

The Administrative Tools window appears.

❺ Double-click Computer Management.

The Computer Management window appears.

If you do not see Administrative Tools in the Control Panel, click Start and then click Help and Support. Type **Computer Management** into the search window and then click the white-on-green arrow. When search results appear, click Computer Management and then click the option in the article to open it.

CONTENT ADVISOR

You can enable and use Content Advisor when you want to limit the types of content that open in your Microsoft Internet Explorer Web browser. Content Advisor restricts access to designated material, based on criteria that you specify.

Once a user types or copies a Web address — called a *uniform* or *universal resource locator* or URL — within the Web browser, Content Advisor checks the Web address. If the information found on that site — referred to as the site content — violates a rule that you set, then Content Advisor

prevents the Web page from opening. This feature is primarily intended to keep young children from viewing mature or objectionable material while still allowing them access to the Web.

When you use Content Advisor, you set a supervisor password, which you need to provide each time you modify settings or when you want to disable the control mechanism. No one else should be able to adjust the advisor settings without that password.

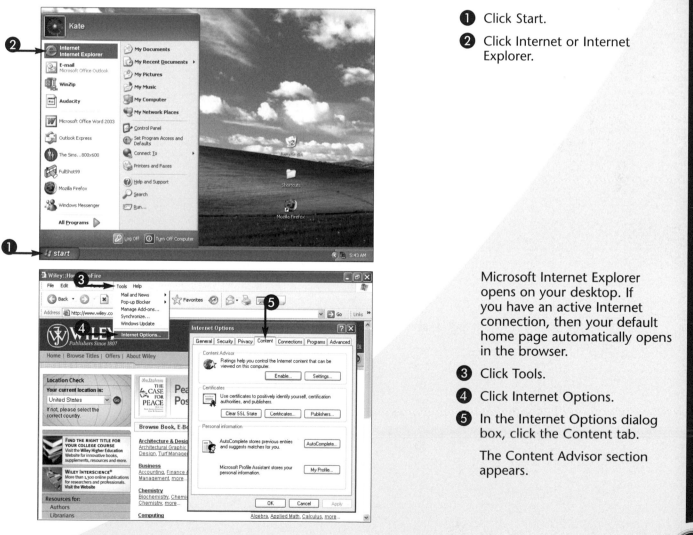

① Click Start.

② Click Internet or Internet Explorer.

Microsoft Internet Explorer opens on your desktop. If you have an active Internet connection, then your default home page automatically opens in the browser.

③ Click Tools.

④ Click Internet Options.

⑤ In the Internet Options dialog box, click the Content tab.

The Content Advisor section appears.

CONTROL PANEL

Control Panel acts like a master computer console and provides you direct access to the hardware, settings, and services that are installed on your computer. You can double-click an icon in Control Panel to display information about a device or service.

You can view, add, remove, or edit settings for devices such as your keyboard and mouse from Control Panel. You can also add and remove programs, hardware, and Windows XP components, tweak your sound and display settings, and inspect,

change, or troubleshoot individual devices installed in the system.

You can choose between two Control Panel views: Category view lists options by type, and Classic view divides the categories into individual components such as Printers and Fax as well as System.

You may notice that Control Panel does not always appear identical in different Windows XP systems. This is because various options that are installed on your computer may place new icons in the pane, changing or rearranging the icons that are listed.

❶ Click Start.

❷ Click Control Panel.

Control Panel opens on your desktop in Category View.

DATE AND TIME

You can determine the time or the date by using features on your Windows desktop. You can view the Windows clock and calendar through the Date and Time Properties feature, which is available in the Control Panel. You can also find the current time in the System Tray at the bottom-right corner of your desktop, at the far right of the taskbar. Although the time is usually visible, you can see the date when you open the Date and Time window or when you pause your mouse over the time in the System Tray.

Thanks to a small battery found on your motherboard called the CMOS battery, both your computer and Windows keep track of the time and

date automatically for you. For example, if you turn off your computer on Tuesday evening and do not turn it on again until Friday morning, then your system knows the time and reports it properly. Windows XP also synchronizes your computer with an official Internet-based clock to keep highly accurate time.

See also>>   **Date and Time**

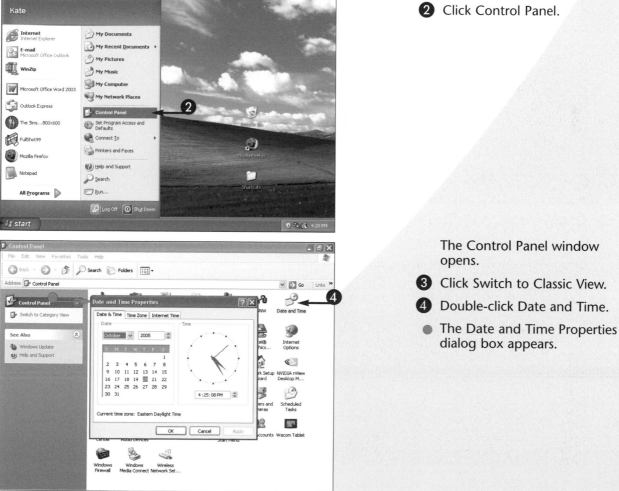

❶ Click Start.

❷ Click Control Panel.

The Control Panel window opens.

❸ Click Switch to Classic View.

❹ Double-click Date and Time.

● The Date and Time Properties dialog box appears.

DESKTOP CLEANUP WIZARD

When your Windows desktop becomes cluttered with files and the icons of shortcuts that you rarely use, you can run the Desktop Cleanup Wizard to remove those icons that you no longer need. This wizard allows you to keep your desktop organized and saves time that you would otherwise spend removing desktop icons manually.

There are three different ways that you can use the Desktop Cleanup Wizard. First, by default, Windows sets this wizard to run automatically every 60 days. Second, at the end of the 60 days — or whenever

Windows detects a large number of unused icons on your desktop — you see a notification window. This window appears as a pale yellow balloon over your System Tray at the bottom-right corner of the desktop. When you click this message, the wizard loads to guide you through the cleanup. Third, you can run the wizard manually at any time.

See also>> **Desktop Cleanup Wizard**

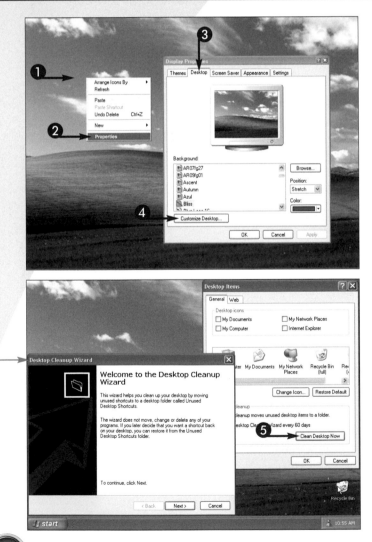

1 Right-click an empty area on your Windows desktop.

2 In the sub-menu, click Properties.

The Display Properties dialog box appears.

3 Click the Desktop tab, if not selected.

4 Click Customize Desktop.

The Desktop Items dialog box appears.

5 Click Clean Desktop Now.

● The Desktop Cleanup Wizard opens.

DEVICE MANAGER

Device Manager is a key resource within Windows that you can consult about the hardware and *drivers* — software that is associated with a device to help it communicate with Windows — that are available on your computer. Device Manager serves as an inventory of different, mostly hardware, components, and allows you to check device status, run troubleshooting wizards, and install driver updates. Although not all hardware attached to your PC may display within Device Manager, core components should be listed. Always consult Device Manager when you begin to use a new PC.

When you open Device Manager, you can view a listing of hardware by device type, such as drives, your graphics board, or display adapter, as well as add-on boards. These add-on boards, also called adapters, are the printed circuit boards that you can install on your motherboard to add system functions like a modem, a network card, or a sound card.

See also>> 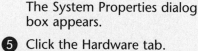 **Device Manager**

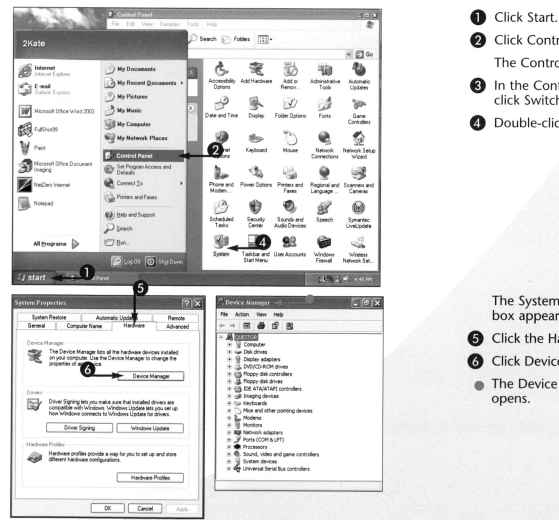

① Click Start.

② Click Control Panel.

The Control Panel opens.

③ In the Control Panel section, click Switch to Classic View.

④ Double-click System.

The System Properties dialog box appears.

⑤ Click the Hardware tab.

⑥ Click Device Manager.

● The Device Manager window opens.

DISK CLEANUP WIZARD

The Disk Cleanup Wizard helps you to identify and remove old, temporary, or unnecessary files from your system. You can use the wizard weekly or monthly as part of your standard computer maintenance.

You can also run the wizard to perform quick disk cleanups. For example, a low disk space warning may appear in a yellow balloon over the System Tray at the bottom-right corner of your desktop. When you click this balloon, Windows asks if you want to run the Disk Cleanup Wizard to free up space on the disk.

You may also need to perform additional disk cleanup manually by using tools such as My Computer or Windows Explorer to remove the low disk space warning.

The files that the wizard targets for removal include temporary files that are created as you work in a program, files that are left over from Web browsing, and setup files that remain after the installation of some applications. Any file that is listed within the wizard once it runs is usually safe to purge.

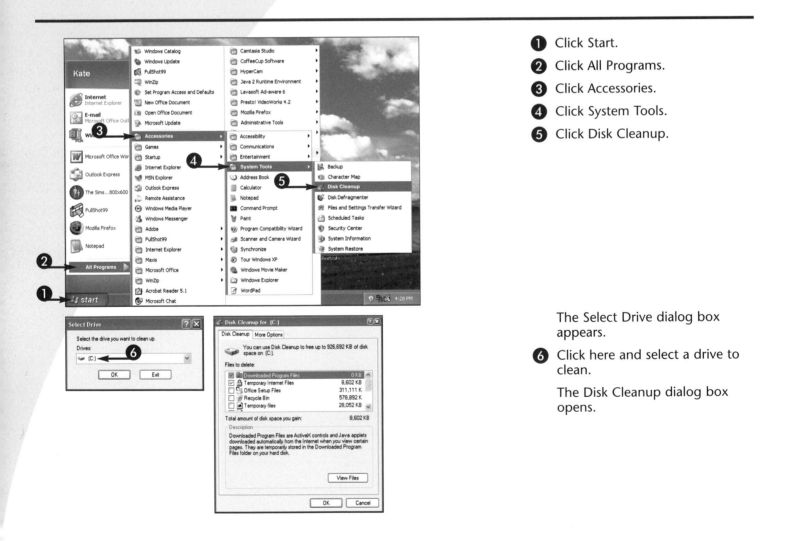

① Click Start.

② Click All Programs.

③ Click Accessories.

④ Click System Tools.

⑤ Click Disk Cleanup.

The Select Drive dialog box appears.

⑥ Click here and select a drive to clean.

The Disk Cleanup dialog box opens.

DISK DEFRAGMENTER

If you notice that your computer takes longer to open files or that the hard disk seems to make more noise than usual, then you should immediately run Disk Defragmenter in Windows XP. Disk Defragmenter is designed to reorganize files that are written to your computer hard disk. You should run this tool on a regular basis, such as once a week or once a month, as part of standard system maintenance.

Over time, as you work with your computer, you may experience system crashes, or you may have to exit a program that does not close normally.

Each time an incident like this occurs, it can interrupt the proper writing of files to the drive, and the files themselves can become fragmented. As fragmentation builds, it takes longer for Windows XP to find and load a file or program.

See also>>

Scheduled Tasks

Disk Defragmenter

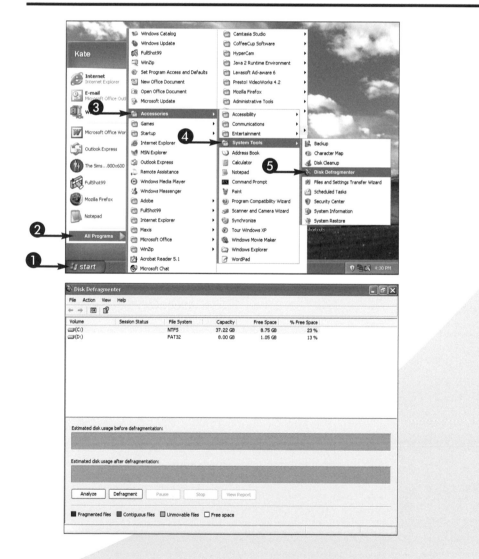

❶ Click Start.

❷ Click All Programs.

❸ Click Accessories.

❹ Click System Tools.

❺ Click Disk Defragmenter.

The Disk Defragmenter window opens.

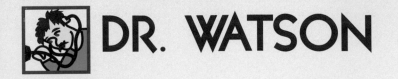

DR. WATSON

Dr. Watson is a system diagnostic tool that you can use to monitor your Windows computer, such as when you begin to troubleshoot a suspected problem. When you run Dr. Watson, the tool remains in the background, out of sight, as it records details about your Windows operations along with any device or service failures that it detects. You can then review the log file that Dr. Watson creates to see if you can spot the source of the trouble.

This tool has long been part of the Windows system and is widely recommended in help articles on computer and Windows troubleshooting. You can find many articles in the Help and Support Center that recommend using Dr. Watson, along with the types of entries that you should look for in the log that it creates.

See also>> **Help and Support Center**

Help and Support Center

1 Click Start.

2 Click Run.

The Run dialog box appears.

3 Type **drwtsn32**.

4 Click OK.

The Dr. Watson for Windows dialog box appears.

EVENT VIEWER

One of the best ways to monitor your system and troubleshoot problems that arise is to check details about what happens on your computer. When the Windows operating system or a Windows application detects an action or occurrence, it treats this occurrence as an event. For example, if a service fails to launch when Windows starts, then this situation generates an event that your system records. You can use the Event Viewer to view these events.

By default, Windows records events and sorts and stores them into three different event logs: Application, System, and Security. The Application log stores events that are generated by programs; the System log stores events that are generated by Windows; and the Security log stores security-related events that are generated by both Windows and applications.

You can also consult Event Viewer to determine which programs and services run regularly. Scheduled tasks such as backups also appear as events.

See also>>   Event Viewer

① Click Start.

② Click All Programs.

③ Click Administrative Tools.

④ Click Event Viewer.

The Event Viewer window opens.

FAX CONFIGURATION WIZARD

After you set up Windows XP to send and receive faxes through the installation of the Microsoft Fax Service, you can configure how faxes are sent and received to and from your computer by running the Fax Configuration Wizard. Until you install the service and run this wizard, you may not be able to successfully receive or transmit faxes to or from your Windows desktop. This wizard guides you through the full fax setup process, by specifying all of the necessary information to use the fax feature, such as your name, company name, and fax number.

To configure and use the fax service, you must have a fax-capable modem installed on your computer or be willing to use a subscription fax service. You can find information about subscription services once you install and configure the fax feature. These services offer you full fax options, either for a set monthly fee or on a per-fax or per-page basis.

See also>>

> **Fax Console**

> **Fax**

❶ Click Start.

❷ Click Printers and Faxes.

The Printers and Faxes window opens.

❸ Double-click Fax.

● The Fax Configuration Wizard opens.

Note: If the Fax icon does not appear in the Printers and Faxes window, then you need to install the Microsoft Fax Service. For more information, see "Fax Configuration Wizard: Install the Microsoft Fax Service in Techniques."

FAX CONSOLE

Once you install and configure the Microsoft Fax Service, your Fax Console serves as your central fax communication command center. Through the console, you can check, send, or receive faxes, as well as modify your fax service settings.

You can manage and review almost every aspect of your computer-based fax service from the Fax Console, as well as read, print, and delete incoming faxes. The console also allows you to run the Fax Configuration Wizard again to make changes to your fax settings. For example, this is necessary if you change your fax number or need to use a different name as the fax sender.

The first time you double-click the Fax icon in the Printers and Faxes window after you install the service, the Fax Configuration Wizard launches. Thereafter, when you double-click the Fax icon, the Fax Console appears.

If the Fax icon does not display in the Printers and Faxes window, then you need to install the Microsoft Fax Service. If the Fax icon appears and a wizard opens instead of the Fax Console when you click the icon, then you need to reconfigure the Fax Configuration Wizard.

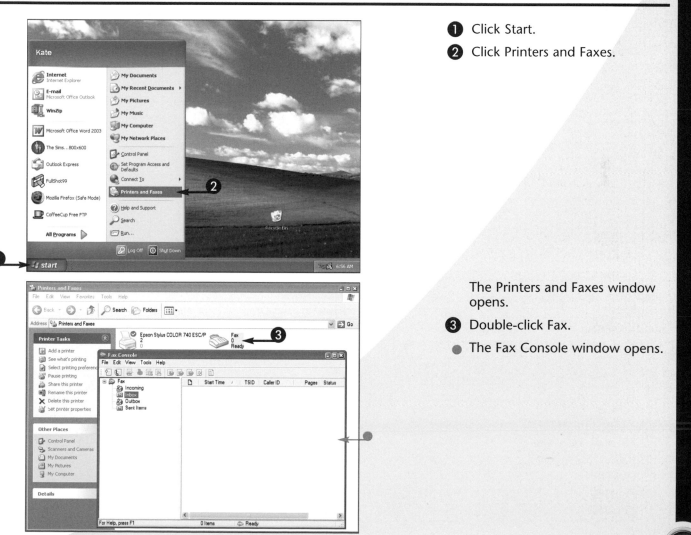

❶ Click Start.

❷ Click Printers and Faxes.

The Printers and Faxes window opens.

❸ Double-click Fax.

● The Fax Console window opens.

FILES AND SETTINGS TRANSFER WIZARD

The Files and Settings Transfer Wizard makes moving important files and settings between two computers a relatively simple task. For example, you can use the wizard to copy important files as well as customized settings when you acquire a new computer and want to mirror these files and settings from an existing computer to the new one.

Without the wizard, you face more of an ordeal as you struggle to identify, locate, and move important files as well as re-create specific settings between computers. This can be both time-consuming and

frustrating, leading you to abandon the effort and then waste time recreating information that already exists elsewhere.

The Files and Settings Transfer Wizard is specifically designed to bridge your old computer setup with your new system. You can also use it to set up two or more existing computers to share the same settings and files. The wizard copies basic settings, as well as those used for e-mail, configuration of the Microsoft Internet Explorer Web browser, desktop display, and folder and taskbar options.

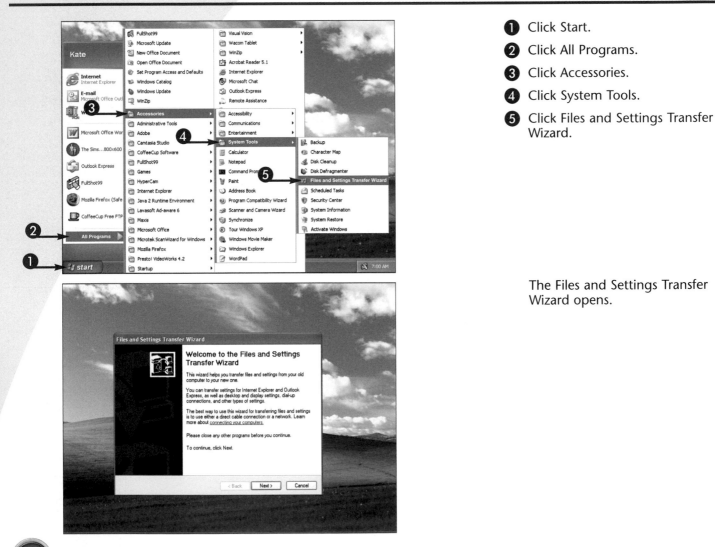

1. Click Start.
2. Click All Programs.
3. Click Accessories.
4. Click System Tools.
5. Click Files and Settings Transfer Wizard.

The Files and Settings Transfer Wizard opens.

FILTERKEYS

If you experience difficulty as you type, either due to a physical limitation or an issue with the keyboard, then you can use the FilterKeys accessibility feature. When you enable FilterKeys, you can adjust the overall responsiveness of your keyboard when you press a key. Once you configure the FilterKeys feature, your typing accuracy should improve along with your speed.

FilterKeys is useful if you have a physical problem that causes you to accidentally press a single key for a prolonged period of time. FilterKeys forces Windows to ignore this input so that your typing

is not affected. Otherwise, special windows may open, or a program that you are using at the time may respond with an error message. This can interrupt your Windows session or cause problems in documents that you currently have open. FilterKeys can also be useful when your keyboard has a sticky key.

See also>> **Accessibility Wizard**

1 Click Start.

2 Click Control Panel.

The Control Panel window opens.

3 In the Control Panel section, click Switch to Classic View.

4 Double-click Accessibility Options.

● The Accessibility Options dialog box appears, displaying several tabs.

FORGOTTEN PASSWORD WIZARD

You can use the Forgotten Password Wizard to create a special recovery disk to help you access your system if you forget your Windows logon password. This is extremely useful when you have to manage many passwords. For example, if you use a Windows logon password, then without it, you cannot access the system to do your work. You can use the Forgotten Password Wizard to protect against this problem. Rather than disable your user password, you can use this wizard and the disk that it creates, so that you can maintain system security.

Passwords that you assign are actually stored in special parts of your operating system and application files where, if you knew how to locate and read the files, you could find them yourself. The Forgotten Password Wizard circumvents the need for this expert knowledge. Instead, it allows you to insert the disc that you make through the wizard to access Windows. You must immediately access the User Accounts option from the Control Panel to set a new password. You also need to run the Forgotten Password Wizard again to configure the new password.

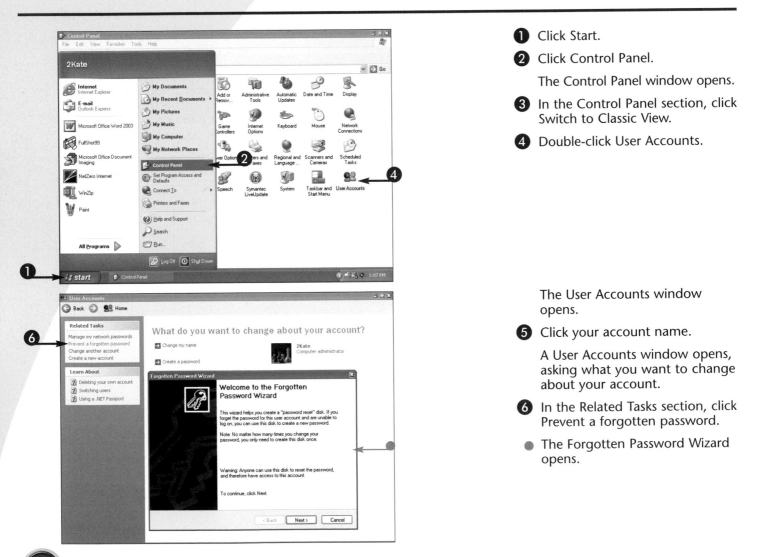

❶ Click Start.

❷ Click Control Panel.

The Control Panel window opens.

❸ In the Control Panel section, click Switch to Classic View.

❹ Double-click User Accounts.

The User Accounts window opens.

❺ Click your account name.

A User Accounts window opens, asking what you want to change about your account.

❻ In the Related Tasks section, click Prevent a forgotten password.

● The Forgotten Password Wizard opens.

FOUND NEW HARDWARE WIZARD

You can use the Found New Hardware Wizard when Windows cannot automatically install software by itself. Available in the Windows Control Panel, this wizard guides you through the successful installation of a hardware device, as well as the software that comes with it.

When you install new hardware in your system with the computer off and then restart it, the Found Hardware Wizard appears. It may also appear when you plug in a new USB or IEEE 1394 device, such as a camera or external drive, while your computer is on. The wizard appears when

Windows cannot automatically process hardware installations.

When it cannot perform an installation, Windows displays the Found New Hardware Wizard to alert you and ask for your help. You should keep any disks that accompany new hardware nearby in case Windows cannot locate the files that it needs to support the device. These files include drivers, special software that helps Windows to communicate with the hardware.

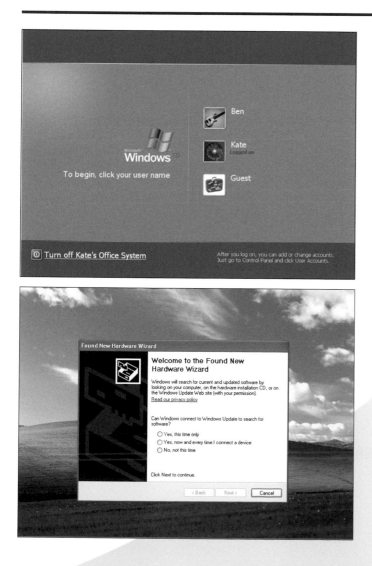

❶ Install your new hardware device according to the instructions that come with it.

❷ Restart your computer so that Windows rechecks your hardware to detect the newly installed device.

After Windows loads, a yellow balloon appears over the bottom-right corner of the desktop, stating that new hardware has been found.

The Found New Hardware Wizard opens.

GROUP POLICY SNAP-IN

The Group Policy Snap-In allows you to set standard rules for how Windows appears and operates, as well as the features that are available to a group. This tool is called a snap-in because it opens through the Microsoft Management Console, or MMC, window in which you can open and edit many snap-ins.

Through the snap-in, you can change the Windows configuration for a group, choose which features are available for a particular group to use, specify the setup and use of System Restore to make a copy of your system at a specific point in time, and set

password management. You can also tweak options for overall security, file and folder management, and network connections.

To change group policy through the snap-in, you must log on with your Administrator-level user account. If you are online with a limited account instead, log off and then log on again with the Administrator account.

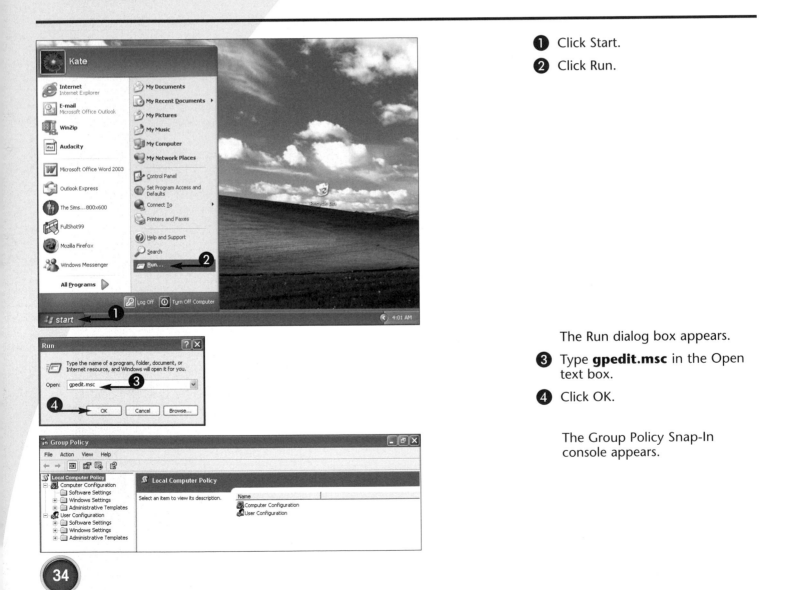

1 Click Start.

2 Click Run.

The Run dialog box appears.

3 Type **gpedit.msc** in the Open text box.

4 Click OK.

The Group Policy Snap-In console appears.

GUEST ACCOUNT

Are you ready to allow others to temporarily share your computer, but without the same amount of access or control that you have? If so, then you may want to allow them to use the Guest account in Windows.

The Guest account is a limited account type, which means that it has restricted ability to view advanced settings or to modify the Windows configuration or support files. However, a person with Guest access can browse the Internet, play computer games, and use accessories like Notepad and WordPad.

By default, Windows automatically sets up a Guest account. However, keep in mind that when you have the Guest account available, it reduces overall Windows system security because it allows someone without a user account on the computer to use the system and open files. If you leave this account enabled, whenever you arrive at the Windows Welcome screen, at least two accounts display there: yours and the Guest account.

See also>> **System, Secure Accounts**

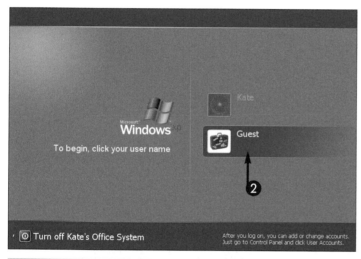

❶ Start your computer.

❷ When the Welcome screen appears, click Guest Account.

Windows opens to an empty desktop.

HELP AND SUPPORT CENTER

The Windows XP Help and Support Center is your first and fastest avenue for expert assistance and step-by-step instructions. You can open this resource whenever you have a question or a problem, or when you want to customize your setup. Many of the tools that you can refer to in this book have detailed entries within the Help and Support Center, such as Remote Assistance and System Restore.

The Help and Support Center includes access to help files that are stored on your drive, as well as to those found online within Microsoft Web sites such as the Microsoft Knowledgebase, a database of problems

and solutions for all Microsoft products. From the toolbar, you can choose from help Web pages that you have already visited, look at help from an index view, or click Support for additional aid options.

If your computer is connected to the Internet when you open the center, then you can search for online articles and Microsoft Web support resources.

See also>>   **Remote Assistance**

Windows Update

❶ Click Start.

❷ Click Help and Support.

The Help and Support Center opens.

LANGUAGE OPTIONS

You can access the Regional and Language Options window through the Control Panel to configure the languages that are used by Windows, as well as to add support for additional languages. For example, if you want to create or view documents in more than one language, then you can add support for those languages.

As more companies share information with users in different countries, documents and files need to be exchanged in an increasing number of languages. As a result, Windows offers many ways in which you can customize your operating system to add support for multiple or alternative languages that you need, as well as to adjust for regional differences in information formatting.

In the Control Panel, you can access the Regional and Language dialog box, where you can specify how information displays, based on regional differences, such as currency, time, and date. The choices that you make based on language and region are reflected throughout Windows. For example, currency may appear differently in Microsoft Word documents that you create.

See also>> **Regional and Language Options**

① Click Start.

② Click Control Panel.

The Control Panel window opens.

③ In the Control Panel section, click Switch to Classic View.

④ Double-click Regional and Language Options.

● The Regional and Language Options dialog box appears.

⑤ Click the Languages tab.

The Languages section enables you to view or change the language you use to enter text.

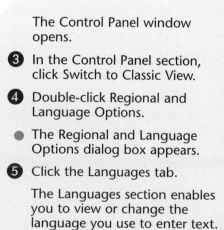

LOCAL SECURITY POLICY

The Local Security Policy is a roster of security settings that you can use to specify who can access your local computer, and what resources, such as drives and tools, are available to them. You can use the policy to configure Windows for stronger security than the standard Control Panel options allow.

The security settings that you can change through the Local Security Policy include options to enforce password rules. For example, you can tell Windows to lock a user out if they cannot type the correct account password within three attempts.

Local Security Policy also allows you to review current security settings to help you to determine where the system may be vulnerable. For example, through the User Rights Assignment option, you can ensure that only Administrators can access tools that may affect computer operation.

See also>>   **Group Security Policy**

Security

① Click Start.

② Click Control Panel.

The Control Panel window opens.

③ In the Control Panel section, click Switch to Classic View.

④ Double-click Administrative Tools.

The Administrative Tools window opens.

⑤ Double-click Local Security Policy.

● The Local Security Settings console opens.

MAGNIFIER

M

Do you have difficulty seeing or reading parts of your Windows desktop? If so, then you can take advantage of one of the Accessibility features, called Magnifier, to help. This feature uses a magnifying glass tool to increase the size of a particular part of your screen to help you read it. You can also drag the Magnifier around the desktop to see other sections.

Magnifier is designed to help anyone with visual challenges to work in Windows. You can also customize to it to be more useful to you, and you

can combine it with other Accessibility options such as Narrator, which is a screen reader.

Magnifier is useful as a temporary assistant when you work with a much smaller monitor. It can also help you when you are working with an older screen with low resolution, where you cannot see part of an image or text adequately.

See also>>

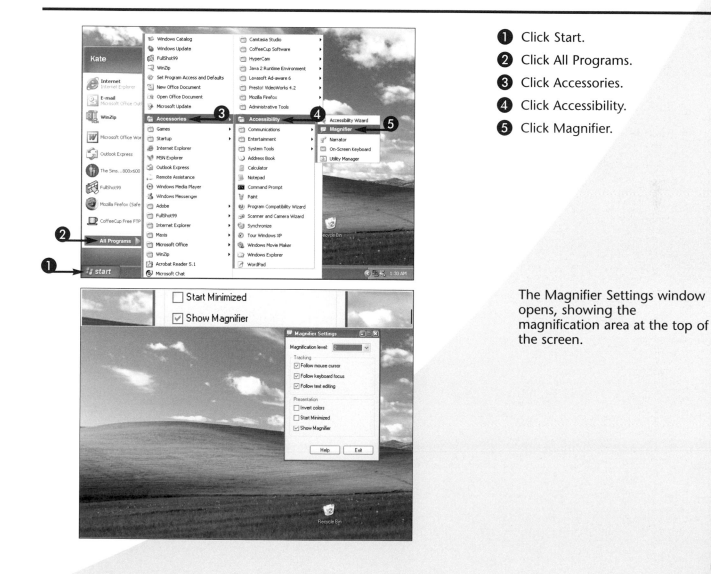

① Click Start.

② Click All Programs.

③ Click Accessories.

④ Click Accessibility.

⑤ Click Magnifier.

The Magnifier Settings window opens, showing the magnification area at the top of the screen.

39

MEDIA LIBRARY

You can create your own Media Library from the audio and video files that you have stored on your hard disk, such as movies, MP3s, and other multimedia files. Media Library is part of Windows Media Player. It allows you to easily access all of your files so that you can play them whenever you want or store them on a recordable CD.

When you first use Media Player, you can begin to populate your library by launching Media Library and scanning your system for multimedia files. Media Player searches through the files that are available

on your disk drives and then links compatible media file types to the library. You can then launch a media file from Media Player, rather than searching your hard disk to find it.

You can also use Media Library and Media Player to create unique categories called playlists of your favorite songs or other audio files taken from your amassed library. You can later edit or delete your playlists.

See also>> | **Media Player**

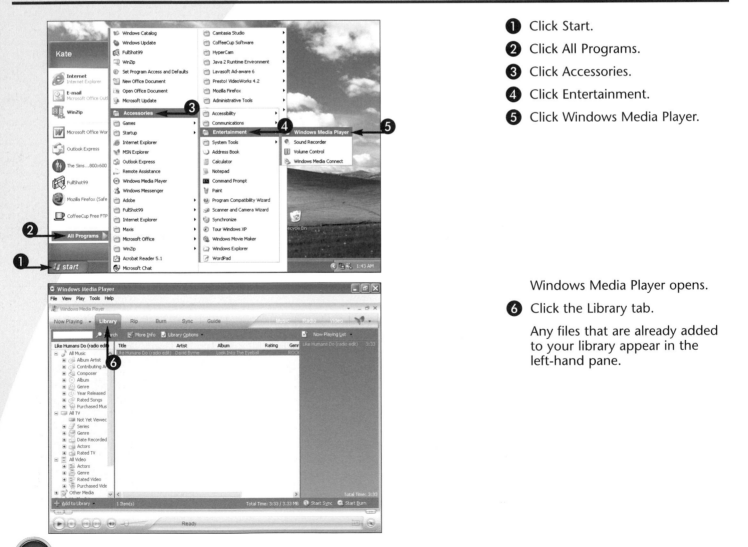

❶ Click Start.

❷ Click All Programs.

❸ Click Accessories.

❹ Click Entertainment.

❺ Click Windows Media Player.

Windows Media Player opens.

❻ Click the Library tab.

Any files that are already added to your library appear in the left-hand pane.

MEDIA PLAYER

Windows Media Player allows you to listen to an audio CD, or play a movie that you have downloaded. You can also turn a collection of MP3s into a custom CD that you can play in the car or send to your portable audio device, such as an iPod. Windows Media Player can also play streaming audio and video such as from an Internet radio broadcast site.

Media Player recognizes most of the popular media formats, including AVI movies and MP3 audio files, and offers easy-to-use playback tools to allow you to watch DVD movies from your

desktop. Keep in mind that not every graphics adapter — the part of your computer that draws what you see on the monitor screen — is capable of playing DVD movies.

In addition to playing media, Media Player offers management tools such as the Media Library, which searches your system for media files to add to the library. Media Player also allows you to transfer files from your computer to a recordable CD or personal audio player.

See also>> **Media Player**

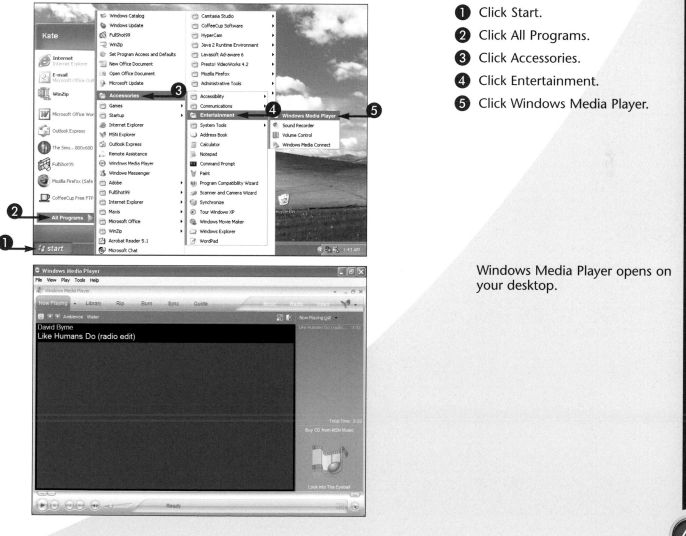

1 Click Start.

2 Click All Programs.

3 Click Accessories.

4 Click Entertainment.

5 Click Windows Media Player.

Windows Media Player opens on your desktop.

MESSENGER SERVICE

The Windows Messenger Service offers you instant messaging directly from your desktop. You can use it to chat with friends, family, and colleagues at work, and to exchange files over the Internet.

There is more than just a social component to the Messenger Service. For example, some Windows XP utilities and applications use Messenger to notify you when a specific event happens, such as a hardware failure or a service shut-down. You can also configure

Messenger to receive and display continuous news headlines, which are called alerts.

If you use the Windows Firewall or any other type of *firewall* — which is a special software or hardware that is designed to protect your local network or computer from attempts by others to access your data — then you may need to adjust your Windows Messenger settings. Otherwise, you may be blocked from using certain features or functions.

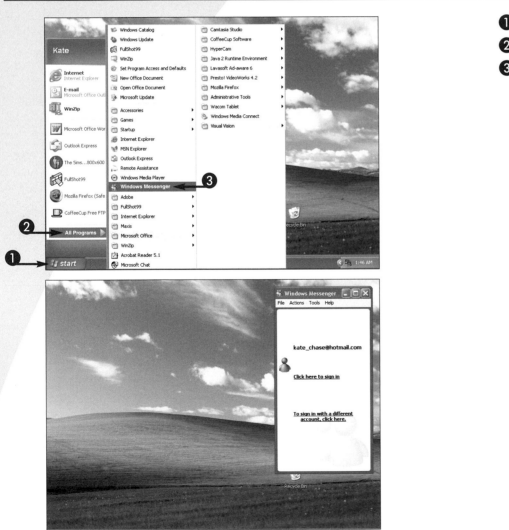

❶ Click Start.

❷ Click All Programs.

❸ Click Windows Messenger.

The Messenger window opens in the upper-right corner of your desktop.

MOUSEKEYS

If you find it physically difficult to use your mouse, then a feature called MouseKeys allows you to turn your keyboard into your mouse. This allows you to perform mouse functions directly from the keyboard without needing to use a mouse or other pointing device. It should also provide you with the added benefit of better speed and accuracy as you work.

MouseKeys is one of the Windows Accessibility options that are designed to help people with special physical challenges work more easily on their desktop. For example, MouseKeys turns the numeric keypad on your keyboard into a

navigation console to give you an alternate way to move the mouse pointer. You can use this console to move up or down and left or right, by pressing the appropriate arrow key.

MouseKeys allows you to drag, click, and double-click all functions that are normally performed with a mouse. You can also customize MouseKeys to make it work better for you. For example, you can adjust the speed or acceleration of the mouse pointer, and specify whether you want to use the NumLock key to turn on the feature.

❶ Click Start.

❷ Click Control Panel.

The Control Panel opens.

❸ In the Control Panel section, click Switch to Classic View.

❹ Double-click Accessibility Options.

The Accessibility Options dialog box appears.

❺ Click the Mouse tab.

❻ Click the Use MouseKeys option.

❼ Click OK.

Windows enables MouseKeys.

43

MOVIE MAKER

Windows Movie Maker allows you to create a movie from images on your hard disk, from a digital video camera, or from an older *analog*, or non-digital, videotape. To work with a camera that you attach to your computer, your *graphics adapter* — which is the chipset devoted to drawing the images that appear on the monitor screen — must support the type of connections that you are using.

Tips appear in the Movie Maker window to guide you through capturing video that you want to add to your movie, as well as editing clips and adding transitions

and other special effects. How professional your results will appear really depends on how good your video and audio sources are, as well as how you modify them.

Once you create a movie, you can share it with others by sending it as an e-mail attachment or publishing it to a Web site. If you do the latter, then you can send the Web address to others so that they can view the results.

See also>> **Movie Maker**

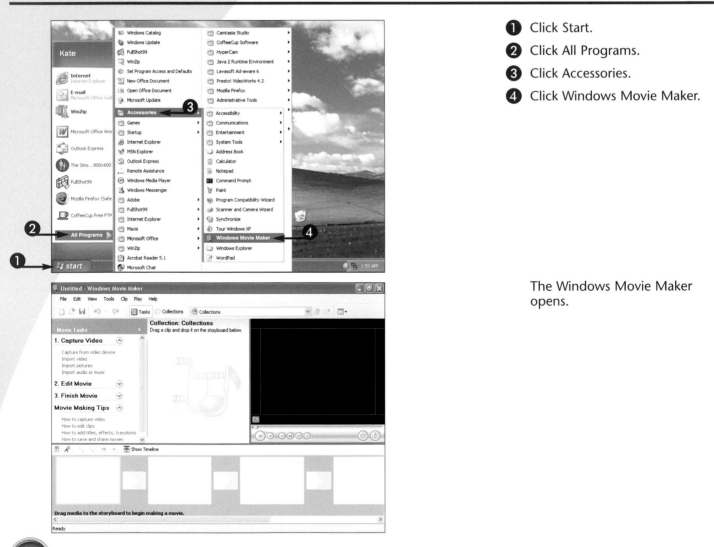

❶ Click Start.

❷ Click All Programs.

❸ Click Accessories.

❹ Click Windows Movie Maker.

The Windows Movie Maker opens.

MY COMPUTER FOLDER

Through the My Computer folder, you can quickly access all hard disks or other storage drives that are installed on your system, as well as the files and folders contained within each drive. You can then double-click a drive in the My Computer window to explore its contents.

Storage drives for Windows include hard disks, CD or DVD recording drives, a floppy drive if you have one in your computer, and any special or external drives that you install.

In addition to storage, My Computer also shows the My Documents folder for each user with an

account on that computer if the folder is *shared*. To share a file or folder, you can edit the file or folder properties so that it can be accessed by anyone on your network.

Other designated storage areas may also appear in the My Computer window, depending on how you configure your system. For example, you can set up certain special folders to display here.

See also>>

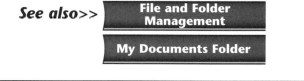

File and Folder Management

My Documents Folder

---

1 Click Start.

2 Click My Computer.

The My Computer window opens.

A left-hand task pane points you to other options such as file and folder tasks.

MY DOCUMENTS FOLDER

The My Documents folder on your computer is the default folder where you store many of the files that you save as you work or browse the Web. These can include word processor files, spreadsheets, and Web pages.

If you use Microsoft Office, then by default, all newly created files that you save to disk are saved to the My Documents folder. You can change the default folder under program options so that you do not end up with a hopelessly cluttered folder.

My Documents also becomes the home of other specialized sub-folders that are unique to each user with an account on the computer, and each user has their own My Documents folder. These folders include My Downloads for files that you transfer to your computer over a network or the Internet, My Music for downloaded audio files, and My Pictures for files that you transfer from your digital camera or scanner.

See also>>   **My Recent Documents**

① Click Start.

② Click My Documents.

The My Documents folder opens for the computer user who is currently logged on.

You can also open the My Documents folder by clicking Start and then clicking My Computer. At the top of the window, choose the Documents folder for the current user.

MY DOWNLOADS FOLDER M

You can use your My Downloads folder to easily store and retrieve files that you have transferred to your system from an online storage location. When you download files from a network or over the Internet, the default location for storing these files on your computer is in the downloaded programs file folder. This folder is usually labeled My Downloads, although some customized Windows installations may not create this folder, or they may vary the name slightly.

Although you can choose an alternate location for your downloaded files, it may be easier to retrieve and organize them if you use the designated

folder. For example, if you download files into many different folders, then it can become much more difficult to find these files later or identify what they are.

If you use a virus scanner, then it takes far less time to scan one folder than the entire system. Between full system scans, you can simply set the scanner to exclusively examine the My Downloads folder.

See also>> **My Documents Folder**

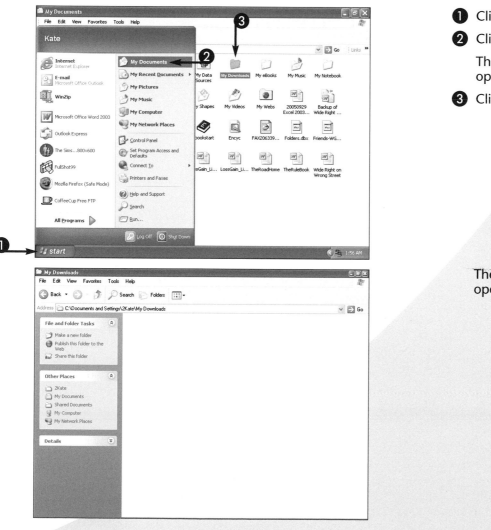

❶ Click Start.

❷ Click My Documents.

The My Documents window opens.

❸ Click My Downloads.

The My Downloads window opens.

MY NETWORK PLACES FOLDER

When you need to quickly access all network resources that are available to you, you should first go to the My Network Places folder. Every network option that is currently available to you appears there.

Listings within My Network Places are divided between Local Network, which displays shared folders and printers on your home or small office network, and The Internet, which displays a list of FTP sites or other Web sites.

To open a network resource from My Network Places, you can simply double-click it. You may be prompted to supply your user account name and password; this depends on whether a password is required when a folder is shared or made available to others on the network.

The left-hand Network Tasks section contains many options to view and modify your network connections, such as View workgroup computers or Add a network place. To locate more details about a listed network resource, you can right-click the resource and then click Properties.

See also>> **Network Setup Wizard**

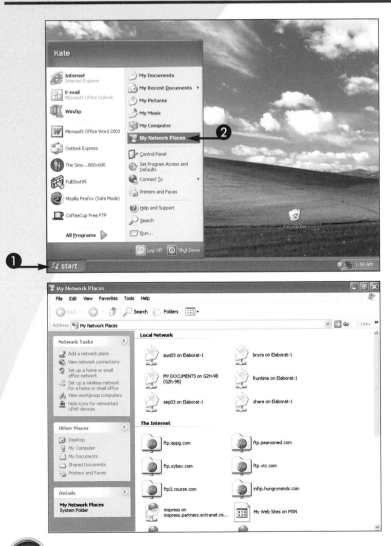

① Click Start.

② Click My Network Places.

The My Network Places window opens on the desktop, displaying the available resources.

MY PICTURES FOLDER

You may want to check the My Pictures folder if you are having trouble locating the pictures that you have transferred from your digital camera to your computer hard drive.

My Pictures is a sub-folder within the My Documents folder, and acts as a central repository for digital image files. For example, when you use the Scanner and Camera Wizard, many digital cameras store their files to the My Pictures folder by default. You can also move images from elsewhere to the My Pictures folder so that you do not have images spread throughout your file system.

You can click within the Picture folder inside My Pictures to display the left task pane where you can perform actions related to images. These tasks include Get pictures from camera or scanner — which launches the Scanner and Camera Wizard — and Print pictures, which loads the Photo Printing Wizard.

See also>>

Photo Printing Wizard

Scanner and Camera Wizard

① Click Start.

② Click My Pictures.

The My Pictures window opens.

MY RECENT DOCUMENTS

To locate and open the most recently accessed files on your system, you can consult your My Recent Documents listing. This listing can contain up to ten items, including documents, graphics, Microsoft Office files, and spreadsheets. This feature helps you to save time by limiting your search for a particular file only to those that you have created, read, or modified within the last several days.

Although Windows keeps track of these files automatically to determine which files are listed under My Recent Documents, you can reset the display at any time. Windows creates a fresh view, which is temporarily empty until the next time that you start or open a file.

Users with an account on the computer have their own separate My Recent Documents listing. If they reset their list, it does not affect the display for other users. Windows also allows you to turn off the feature so that the option no longer displays from the Start menu. This can save some space in a crowded menu, and prevents others from viewing your file list.

See also>> **My Recent Documents**

① Click Start.

② Click My Recent Documents.

③ Click a document to open.

The file opens in its associated program on your desktop.

NARRATOR

Narrator is an Accessibility option that helps visually impaired users to work on a Windows computer. Narrator is a text-to-speech tool. It reads what is written on the screen and speaks it aloud to you through your computer sound system when you cannot read it yourself.

You can customize the voice options in Narrator. For example, you can modify the text-reading speed, the voice pitch, and the overall volume.

Narrator is an example of adaptive or assistive technology because it bridges the gap between those with a disability and their computers. However, Narrator provides only basic assistance. If you find that Narrator is too limited for your needs, then you may want to consider other, more robust text-to-speech tools. You can find a list of these tools at www.microsoft.com/windows/reskits/websources.

See also>> **Accessibility Options**

① Click Start.

② Click All Programs.

③ Click Accessories.

④ Click Accessibility.

⑤ Click Narrator.

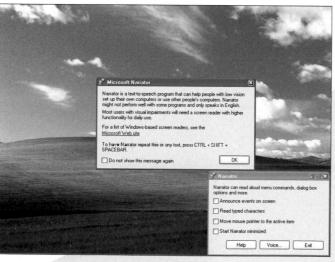

The Narrator window opens on your desktop.

NETWORK IDENTIFICATION WIZARD

You can use the Network Identification Wizard to identify and configure various devices that are on your network. Every network component, including connected computers, notebook computers, and printers, must have a unique identity. It is this identity that helps you to distinguish a component from others on the network. The Network Identification Wizard helps you to view, set, or change a network device identity.

The Network Identification Wizard can help you to join a computer to a *domain*, which is a group of computers and network devices that function together. This network-based wizard guides you

through the choices that you must make and the information that you need to supply as part of the domain connection procedure.

Most basic home and small office setups do not use a domain because they are workgroup-based. For this type of network, you do not need to run the Network Identification Wizard.

See also>> Network Setup Wizard

Network Setup Wizard

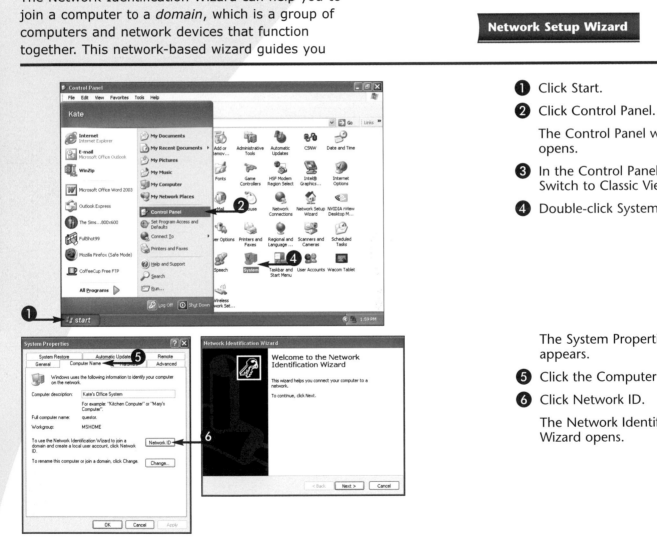

❶ Click Start.

❷ Click Control Panel.

The Control Panel window opens.

❸ In the Control Panel section, click Switch to Classic View.

❹ Double-click System.

The System Properties dialog box appears.

❺ Click the Computer Name tab.

❻ Click Network ID.

The Network Identification Wizard opens.

After you install the necessary hardware to set up a network between two or more computers in your home or small office, you can run the Network Setup Wizard to quickly configure Windows to recognize and establish a basic network. The wizard takes care of the detail work in setting up the network, which saves you both the time and frustration of manual configuration, especially if you have no experience in network setup.

When you launch the wizard, Windows locates and identifies network hardware and resources, and then configures them for use, based on the

choices that you make through the wizard. The wizard also offers you a checklist where you can determine that you have all of the necessary equipment to connect and use a network.

During configuration, the wizard also prompts you to specify whether other computers will need to connect to your computer to reach the Internet, or whether your computer shares the Internet connection with another network computer.

See also>>   **Network Setup Wizard**

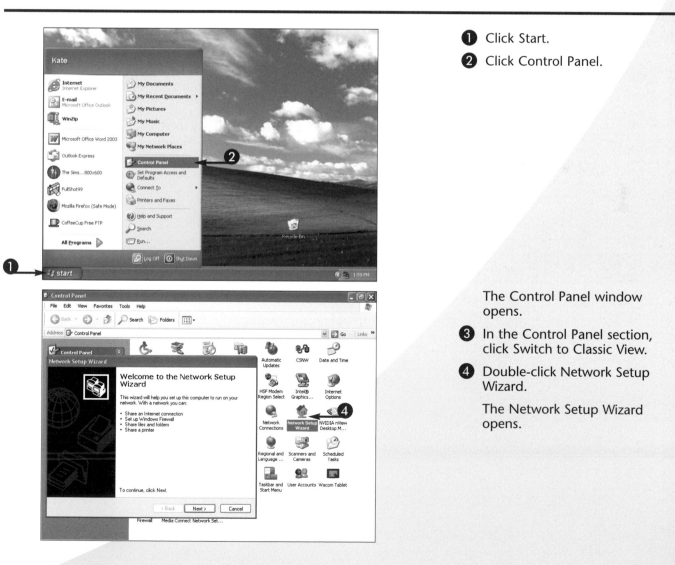

① Click Start.

② Click Control Panel.

The Control Panel window opens.

③ In the Control Panel section, click Switch to Classic View.

④ Double-click Network Setup Wizard.

The Network Setup Wizard opens.

NEW CONNECTION WIZARD

You can use the New Connection Wizard to create a new connection to a network. This wizard works for either a home or small office network, or the Internet, which is a master network of millions of smaller networks. For example, you should run this wizard when you create a new Internet access account, such as when you change Internet service providers, or ISPs, or add an additional Internet account.

You can also use the wizard to set up a connection to a private network or a *virtual private network.* The latter is a special two-way, secure communication

tunnel between two computers, similar to the one that you may have at your workplace.

The wizard guides you through the process where you can choose options that you want to create the connection. For example, you can specify whether the computer that you set up connects directly to the Internet, or uses Internet connection sharing to connect online through a different computer on a home or small office network.

See also>> **Virtual Private Networking**

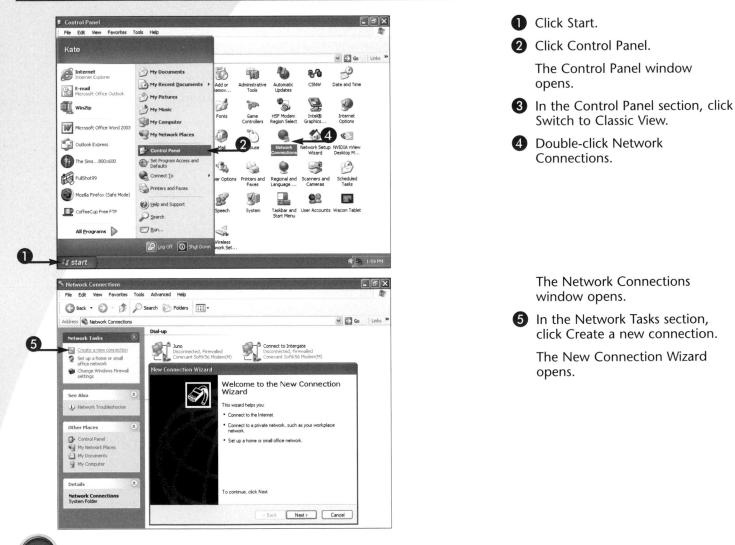

❶ Click Start.

❷ Click Control Panel.

The Control Panel window opens.

❸ In the Control Panel section, click Switch to Classic View.

❹ Double-click Network Connections.

The Network Connections window opens.

❺ In the Network Tasks section, click Create a new connection.

The New Connection Wizard opens.

NOTEPAD

Notepad is one of the simplest, most straightforward text editors that you can use. It is ideal when you need to create, read, or edit short, text-only documents. In fact, Notepad allows you to read and create files that can be read on almost any other computer or hand-held communications device, such as a Web-enabled cell phone.

Unlike word processors that offer customized formatting to make text appear in a certain way — such as all bold or centered — Notepad only works with unformatted text. You cannot apply any fancy styles. However, plain text is an advantage for

you when you need to create a document that can be opened on virtually any type of computer, regardless of what programs are installed on that computer.

All of the Notepad options are available through the menu bar near the top of the window. The size of the files that you can open or create in Notepad is limited to about 32K, which corresponds to a few pages of text. You can open larger files through an alternate program such as WordPad, or a word processor such as Microsoft Word.

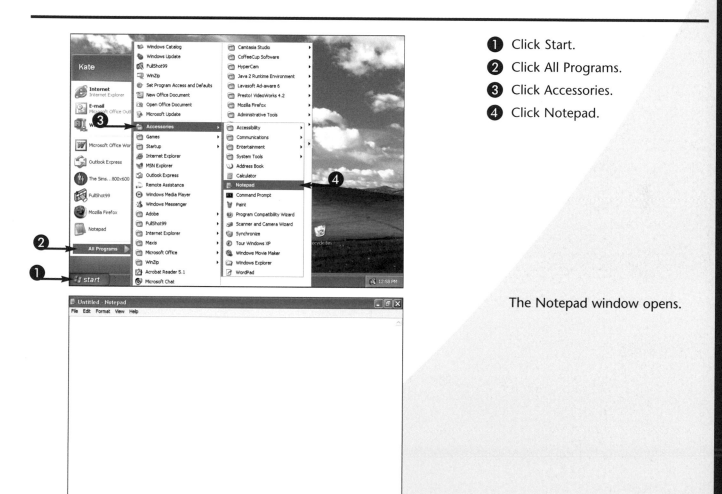

❶ Click Start.

❷ Click All Programs.

❸ Click Accessories.

❹ Click Notepad.

The Notepad window opens.

ON-SCREEN KEYBOARD

You can enter text through the graphical interface by using the On-Screen Keyboard, a virtual keyboard that opens on your desktop. Windows includes this accessibility tool to assist those who cannot type through a standard keyboard due to a physical challenge. If you use a special tool to work in Windows, such as a joystick or pointer, and you want to be able to type as well, then you should consider using the On-Screen Keyboard, which allows you to point to a key to type it.

The On-Screen Keyboard displays a virtual desktop keyboard through which you can type in one of three ways. The clicking mode enables you to type when you click an on-screen key with your pointing device. The scanning mode works with some forms of alternative input devices, such as a toggle switch, to provide extra help when you type. The hovering mode enables you to hold a pointing device over a key and have that key recognized as if you actually pressed the key.

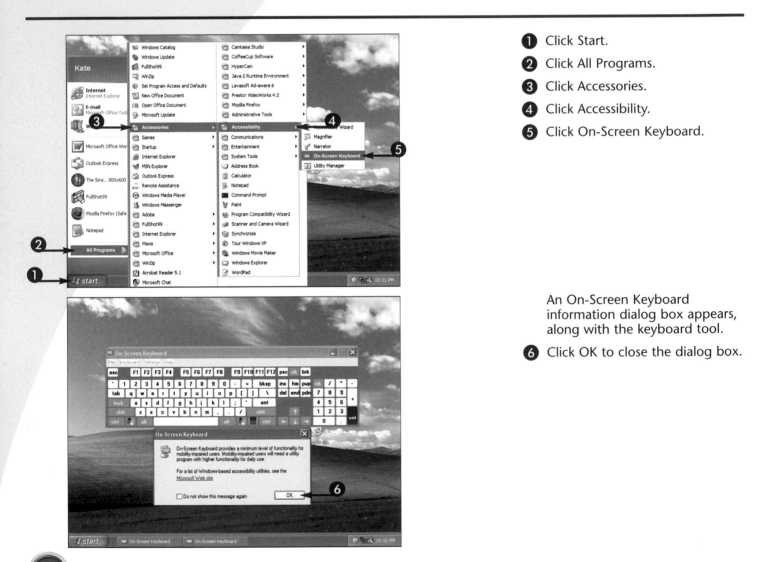

1. Click Start.
2. Click All Programs.
3. Click Accessories.
4. Click Accessibility.
5. Click On-Screen Keyboard.

An On-Screen Keyboard information dialog box appears, along with the keyboard tool.

6. Click OK to close the dialog box.

OPEN DIALOG BOX

Windows XP offers a number of ways to open documents and other types of files. For example, you can double-click a filename in Windows Explorer or My Computer to open that file, along with the program that is needed to read or run the file. Many popular Windows programs offer the standard Open dialog box to help you browse, locate, and open files.

The far-left section of the Open dialog box displays the Places Bar, a list of five of the most commonly used folders and other file storage

areas, such as the My Documents folder. If the file that you want to open is not listed in the current folder in the Open dialog box, then you can click one of these alternate folders to search for the file.

You can click the drop-down Look in list box and click a different drive, folder, or sub-folder. This allows you to locate a file that is not stored in one of the pre-set folders.

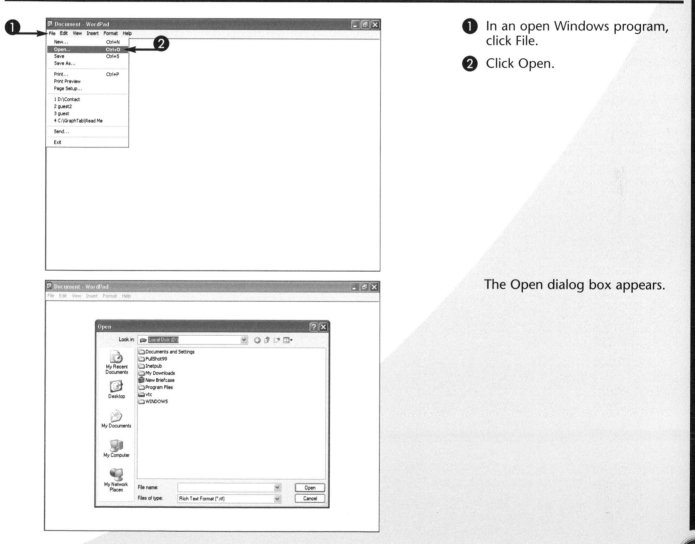

① In an open Windows program, click File.

② Click Open.

The Open dialog box appears.

PERFORMANCE MONITOR

You can use Performance Monitor to measure your system speed. If you are concerned that your computer is operating less than optimally, then Performance Monitor is an Administrator tool through which you can observe different key system characteristics, such as the amount of time your CPU spends idle or how much memory is available.

Performance Monitor consists of a series of counters. These counters are divided into categories and then by individual elements that impact system performance, such as data transfer speeds. You can also see an encapsulated view of Performance Monitor through the Windows Task Manager.

You usually need to be logged in as an Administrator to use Performance Monitor. You should also understand how various factors could affect your system performance.

Once you have monitored your system, you can review the results to see how well different system elements are performing. This information can tell you whether you need to upgrade memory, your CPU, or other hardware.

See also>> **Task Manager**

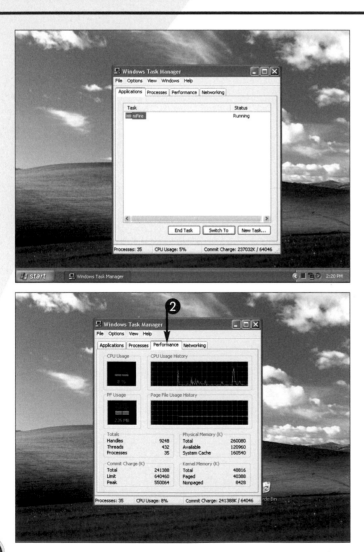

① In Windows, press Ctrl+Alt+Del.

The Windows Task Manager appears.

② Click the Performance tab.

This tab displays counters for central processing unit usage, page file usage, physical and kernel memory usage, and commit charge.

PHONE AND MODEM OPTIONS

You can open Phone and Modem Options in the Control Panel to review information about the modem and telephony options that are installed on your system. This feature serves as the major configuration and support center for phones, fax modems, and voice over Internet protocol, or VOIP.

The Phone and Modem Options dialog box displays three different tabs. The Dialing Rules tab allows you to adjust how your computer dials out over a modem. In the Modems tab, you can check the properties of the modem. The Advanced tab displays the special services and providers that are available to your make and model of modem.

The Phone and Modem Options dialog box displays basic configuration details along with dialing rules that you can establish to save on long-distance costs or to dial around an internal phone system, such as those that are found in hotels that use PBX switchboards.

If you want to test and troubleshoot the working status of your modem, then you can use the Device Manager.

See also>>   **Device Manager**

① Click Start.

② Click Control Panel.

The Control Panel window opens.

③ In the Control Panel section, click Switch to Classic View.

④ Double-click Phone and Modem Options.

The Phone and Modem Options dialog box appears, displaying three tabs.

PHOTO PRINTING WIZARD

The Photo Printing Wizard makes it easy for you to print pictures that you acquire through your digital camera or a scanner that is attached to your Windows XP computer. Although your printer should have little difficulty printing out a standard word processor document, it may not provide the best results when you use it to print a color photo from your digital camera. In this case, the Photo Printing Wizard can help you achieve the best print reproduction.

You can access the wizard from the My Pictures folder or through the Help and Support Center. Once

it is launched, the wizard attempts to optimize the conditions for a well-balanced image printout.

Ultimately, the printout quality depends on the starting image as well as the printer, the print format, and the paper that you use. For the best results, you should follow the recommendations for paper and ink that are provided in your printer manual.

See also>> **My Pictures Folder**

Printers and Faxes

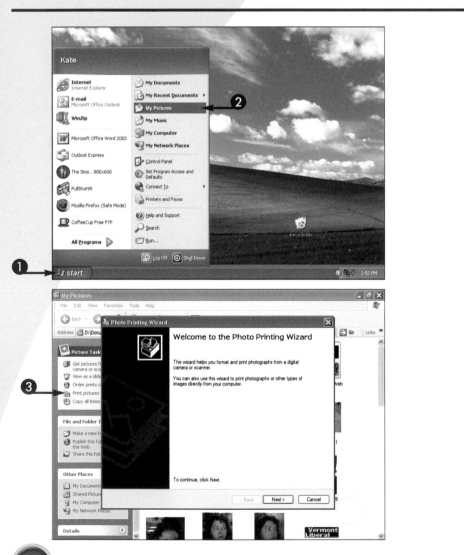

① Click Start.

② Click My Pictures.

The My Pictures window opens.

③ In the Picture Tasks section, click Print pictures.

The Photo Printing Wizard opens.

PRINTERS AND FAXES

The Printers and Faxes folder displays the printers and fax services that you have installed in your system. All fax services and previously set up printers — whether attached to your computer or through a network — display in the folder window.

If the folder displays a Fax icon, then the Microsoft Fax Service is already set up and available. From this folder, you can also specify the printer that you want to use, as well as change the default printer.

You can check a printer and perform diagnostics on it by using the Windows Print Manager. You can also add and remove printers and fax services

to and from this folder. If you have Microsoft Fax Service installed, then when you click the Fax option, Windows launches the Fax Console to allow you to send, receive, read, and manage faxes.

See also>>

| Fax Configuration Wizard |
| Fax Console |
| Photo Printing Wizard |

1 Click Start.

2 Click Printers and Faxes.

The Printers and Faxes window opens.

61

RECOVERY CONSOLE

Recovery Console is a powerful repair and restore feature that resides on your Windows XP setup CD. You can use it to troubleshoot and fix a problem with your Windows installation, for example, when Windows does not boot and fails to respond to other attempts to recover. You can use the Help and Support feature in Windows XP to learn about the commands that are available in Recovery Console.

Recovery Console works only outside of normal Windows operations. Although you can install it to your hard disk as shown here, Recovery Console is normally only available from the Windows CD, which

you can use to boot your computer. Once you start the console, you must type commands from the command line or prompt, or in the Run dialog box. Windows offers online help through the Help and Support Center, including the commands and switches that you can use.

See also>>

> **Command Prompt**
>
> **Help and Support Center**
>
> **Recovery Console**

---

① Insert the Windows XP setup CD into your CD or DVD drive.

② Click Start.

③ Click Run.

The Run dialog box appears.

④ Type **D:\i386\winnt32.exe /cmdcons**.

⑤ Click OK.

⑥ Click Yes to proceed.

⑦ Follow the on-screen instructions to copy Recovery Console.

When you are done, Windows copies Recovery Console to the hard disk, and it becomes available as a Startup option. You are prompted to restart Windows before you use the console.

RECYCLE BIN

The Windows Recycle Bin is a virtual wastebasket that resides on your desktop. You can drag and drop files into it from other folders, or you can delete a file to send it automatically to the Recycle Bin where it stays until you empty the Recycle Bin basket.

When you delete files from your drives, these files remain on the disk, in the Recycle Bin, and you can still restore them to their previous location and condition. You can use the Recycle Bin to look through these files, and empty the Recycle Bin when you want to make more disk space available.

Keep in mind that the Recycle Bin cannot contain very large files. For example, when you delete a file that is larger than 2GB, you receive a message that states that the file is too large and asks if you want to delete it immediately.

See also>>   **Recycle Bin**

① Double-click the Recycle Bin.

The Recycle Bin window opens.

REGIONAL AND LANGUAGE OPTIONS

The Regional and Language Options in the Control Panel allow you to check and modify settings that specify the language that you want to use in Windows. For example, you can change the language that is used in menus and dialog boxes. They also allow you to set regional options that determine how time, date, currency, and other numbers should display.

Even if you normally use just one language, such as English, you may need to add support for other languages if you receive and edit documents in a second language. Windows programs such as Notepad and WordPad allow you to create and

modify documents in various languages. Many other applications support multiple languages as well.

Several common languages are available. These include Arabic, French, German, Hebrew, Japanese, Korean, and Spanish. When you add a different language, you also install keyboard support for that language. Keep in mind that you may need your Windows XP install CD to add more languages.

See also>>

① Click Start.

② Click Control Panel.

The Control Panel opens.

③ In the Control Panel section, click Switch to Classic View.

④ Double-click Regional and Language Options.

The Regional and Language Options dialog box appears, displaying three tabs.

REGISTRY EDITOR

R

There are times when you may need to adjust the Windows Registry, a master information index that stores almost every detail about Windows. To edit the Registry, you need a special editor called the Registry Editor, or REGEDIT.

The Registry Editor allows you to search for, view, and modify the many different categories of information that are stored within the Registry, such as specifics about a program or an installed hardware component. The editor opens into a console view of major categories — such as local

user, local machine, and current configuration — which you can expand to display individual registry entries, called registry keys.

Before you modify the Windows Registry, you should back up your system. If you use System Restore, then you should create a new restore point. Even then, you should only edit the Registry if you know exactly what to do and you are prepared for a problem with Windows if the system crashes because of your change.

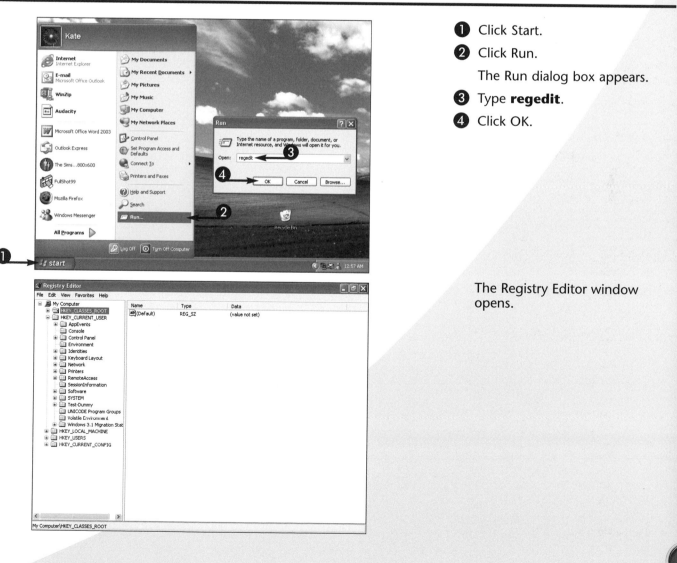

① Click Start.

② Click Run.

The Run dialog box appears.

③ Type **regedit**.

④ Click OK.

The Registry Editor window opens.

65

REMOTE ASSISTANCE

You can use Remote Assistance to allow someone in a remote location to access your computer. For example, you can use it to seek assistance with a Windows problem from the Windows XP online support area. When you do this, someone may offer to connect to your computer through Remote Assistance to check and troubleshoot your system. You can also use this tool to assist another person.

This service works only if you and the other person have Windows XP and use either Windows Messenger or Outlook Express e-mail software. You must also both be connected to the Internet, and have Remote Assistance enabled.

Once you identify the person that you want to connect to, you can send this person an invitation to visit your computer. When that person accepts your invitation, they can connect to your system and view it. Both of you can chat with one another, and the other person can make changes to your system.

1 Click Start.

2 Click Help and Support.

The Help and Support Center opens.

3 Click the Invite a friend to connect to your computer with Remote Assistance link.

Windows launches Remote Assistance, after which you can send an invitation to a specific person to visit your computer remotely.

REMOTE DESKTOP CONNECTION

With Remote Desktop Connection, you can connect to another Windows XP desktop and work from it as if you were at the keyboard and mouse of that remote system. This is useful when you want to work on another computer on your network without being physically present at the other system. You can also connect with a remote system at work to run programs and access files.

To connect remotely, you need to install the Remote Desktop Connection component to Windows, as well as Internet Information Services, which is a Web publishing server. These components must be installed on the system that you plan to access

remotely. Neither of these two components is automatically installed with Windows XP.

The remote connection actually runs on the Web server, where you connect to it similar to other Web pages over your Internet connection using Microsoft Internet Explorer. The Internet address, or URL, that you use is for the remote desktop connection that is running on the Web server.

See also>>

Remote Assistance

Internet Options

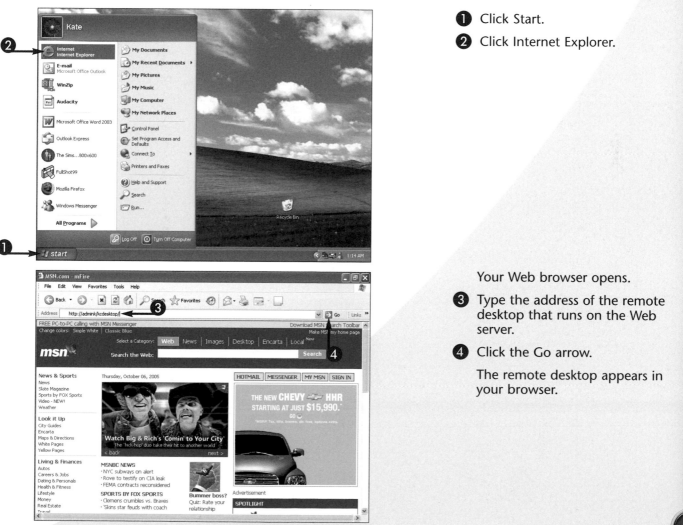

① Click Start.

② Click Internet Explorer.

Your Web browser opens.

③ Type the address of the remote desktop that runs on the Web server.

④ Click the Go arrow.

The remote desktop appears in your browser.

SAVE DIALOG BOX

The Save dialog box appears whenever you save a new file for the first time. It displays options such as how and where to save your file. This dialog box appears when you click the File menu and click Save, when you press Ctrl+S on your keyboard, or when you click the Save icon in the toolbar in most programs. Many Windows applications use the same standard Save box for consistency.

From the Save dialog box, you can type a name for the file, choose a file type, and then save the file with its new name. You can also specify a different folder or drive in which to store the file, rather than the default location. The left side of the box displays alternate storage locations such as Desktop or My Network Places. You can also click the drop-down list box next to Save in and click to choose a different location.

See also>> **My Documents Folder**

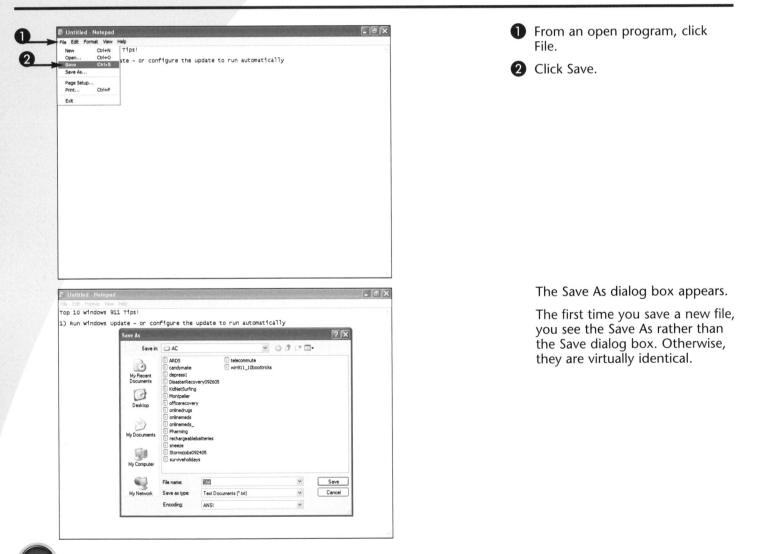

① From an open program, click File.

② Click Save.

The Save As dialog box appears.

The first time you save a new file, you see the Save As rather than the Save dialog box. Otherwise, they are virtually identical.

SCANNER AND CAMERA WIZARD

You can launch the Scanner and Camera Wizard to help you to bring photos or other file types into your computer through a digital camera or scanner — a process called acquiring files. The wizard guides you through the process to transfer the images into your computer and to store them on your system, such as in the default My Pictures folder.

Once Windows detects a camera or scanner that you have installed, the wizard appears every time you connect the camera or scanner to your computer. You can also launch the wizard

manually at any time, such as when you want to scan a document.

With a scanner, you can set options for color, quality, and layout. For cameras, you can choose which images you want to transfer before the wizard copies the files and deletes them from the camera. You can also choose to delete selected files from your camera directly through the wizard, without having to delete them manually.

See also>> My Pictures Folder

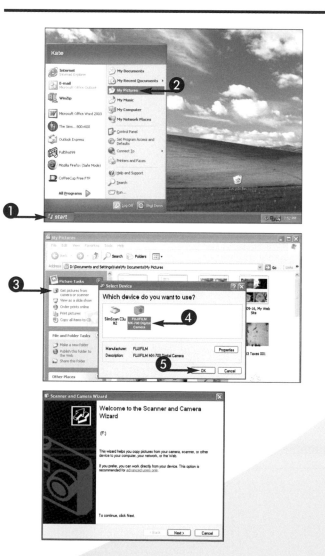

① Click Start.

② Click My Pictures.

The My Pictures folder opens.

③ In the Picture Tasks section, click Get pictures from camera or scanner.

The Select Device dialog box appears.

④ Click the device that you want to use.

⑤ Click OK.

⑥ Follow the on-screen instructions for the device that you chose.

The Scanner and Camera Wizard opens.

SCHEDULED TASKS FOLDER

When you schedule a task to run at a certain time and day, an entry appears for that task in your Scheduled Tasks folder. You can open the Scheduled Tasks folder to display its contents whenever you want to know what is on your computer chore calendar.

You can view a log of tasks that have to run, add more tasks, or edit existing ones. Each task in the folder lists certain details, such as its next and most recent run times.

You can configure the Scheduled Tasks folder to notify you when a particular task does not successfully run. For example, this can happen when your computer is turned off at the scheduled time, or if you close the task once it starts. Once you establish that a task did not run, you can launch it manually so that Windows performs the maintenance.

See also>> **Scheduled Tasks Wizard**

① Click Start.

② Click All Programs.

③ Click Accessories.

④ Click System Tools.

⑤ Click Scheduled Tasks.

The Scheduled Tasks window opens.

SCREEN SAVERS

Screen savers are the most common way that users customize their computers. A screen saver is a special type of file or collection of files that display animation on your desktop after a period of inactivity. You can add a screen saver to conceal whatever is on your desktop when you are away from your computer, or simply to add a colorful display to the monitor.

Although Windows XP includes many screen savers, you can also find many more on the Web. These often-colorful animations, which can even include optional sound, are some of the most commonly downloaded files on the Internet.

At one time, screen savers were almost mandatory — if you left a single image on the screen for too long, then some of those features could actually become burned permanently into the screen. The monitors of today do not really have this problem; instead, a screen saver is used as a creative or pleasant customization and a privacy feature to hide open files from others.

See also>> **Display Properties**

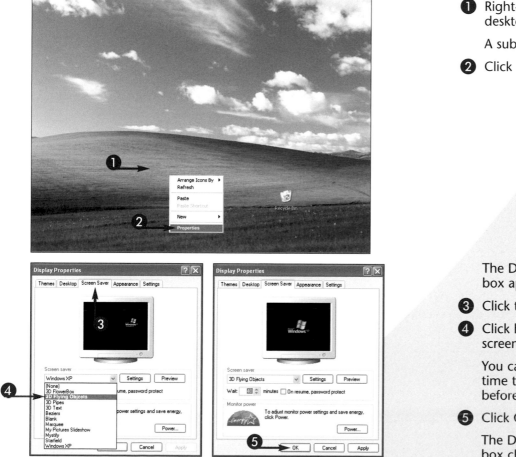

① Right-click a blank spot on your desktop.

A sub-menu appears.

② Click Properties.

The Display Properties dialog box appears.

③ Click the Screen Saver tab.

④ Click here and select a screensaver.

You can change the length of time that Windows should wait before the screen saver appears.

⑤ Click OK.

The Display Properties dialog box closes, and Windows enables the screen saver.

SEARCH COMPANION

The Search Companion allows you to scan the drives on your computer to locate files, such as documents and images. This tool is useful when you save or move files outside of the default folders and then cannot remember where the files are.

Search Companion offers several options to customize your search. For example, you can search by time period to locate and identify all files that you have modified, such as in the past day or week. You can set many variables for your search. These variables can include a word or phrase in the file, part of a

filename, when you last worked with the file, and both where and how many layers of folders the Search Companion searches for a file. The more variables that you set, the more likely you are to target the exact file or files that you want.

As Search Companion identifies a search match, the file displays in the right-hand Search results pane. You can also stop an active search and go back to refine your options.

❶ Click Start.

❷ Click Search.

The Search Results window opens, displaying the Search Companion.

SECURITY CENTER

The Windows Security Center — new with Windows XP Service Pack 2 — provides you with a central location where you can view and configure security options for your system. You can review which security measures are on and which safety issues need to be addressed through the Security Center. You can also use it to manage security settings for Windows Firewall, Internet Options for your Internet connection and Web browser, and Automatic Updates that you control through Windows Update.

With this feature, you can take a proactive approach toward protecting your computer and

Internet connection, as well as customizing how security affects the operations on your system. If this is the only firewall and Internet security package that you use, then you can configure these options to protect both your computer and your Internet connection. But you do not need to double up with packages.

The Resources window in the Security Center keeps you informed about new system protection problems such as newly released viruses — you can simply click the provided links to find out more.

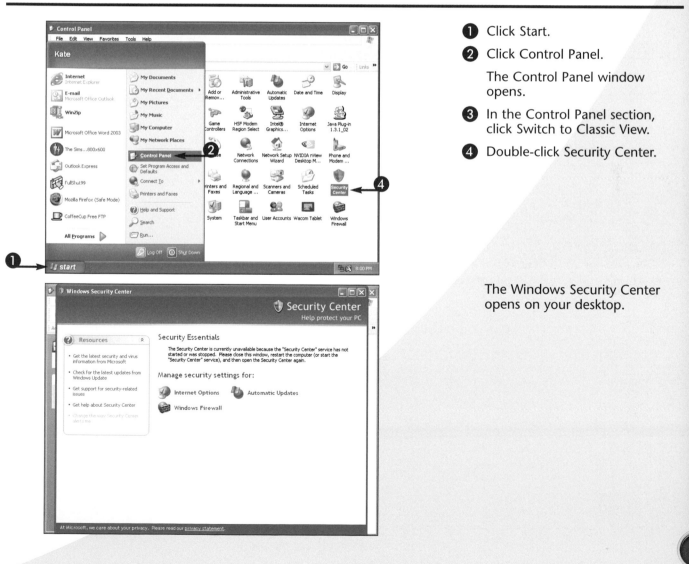

❶ Click Start.

❷ Click Control Panel.

The Control Panel window opens.

❸ In the Control Panel section, click Switch to Classic View.

❹ Double-click Security Center.

The Windows Security Center opens on your desktop.

SERIALKEYS

If you cannot work with a standard computer keyboard or mouse, then the SerialKeys feature may be able to help you. SerialKeys allows you to use an alternative input device to register mouse-clicks and key presses on the Windows desktop. This tool is part of the Accessibility options, which are designed to help you overcome physical challenges as you work with Windows.

Some of the *assistive devices* — devices that help people with physical limitations to access a computer — that are compatible with SerialKeys

include the *puff and sip*, or head-mounted gear that allows you to control the mouse and keyboard by breathing through a straw. Another device is the *single switch*, where limited body movements can trigger a switch for computer input.

Once you enable SerialKeys, you typically need to adjust device settings to properly match a specific device to this Accessibility tool.

See also>> **Accessibility Options**

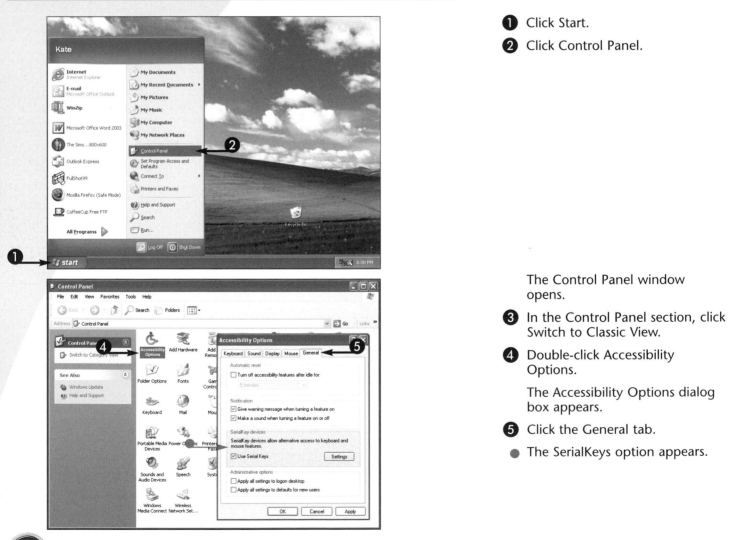

1 Click Start.

2 Click Control Panel.

The Control Panel window opens.

3 In the Control Panel section, click Switch to Classic View.

4 Double-click Accessibility Options.

The Accessibility Options dialog box appears.

5 Click the General tab.

● The SerialKeys option appears.

SERVICES MMC SNAP-IN

When you want to know what services run on your Windows desktop in the background, you can use the Services MMC Snap-In console to see a list of these services. You can also stop and start these services from the same console window. These services include Internet Information Services, a Web server for Windows, and Windows Messenger.

You can click one of the services that appear in the right side of the console to view a description

of the role that this service plays. To see more details about a service, you can right-click the service name and click Properties. Depending on the service, a multi-tabbed Properties dialog box appears where you can select settings.

Above the description, you can click links to stop or restart the service. Tabs at the bottom of the Services MMC Snap-In Console allow you to move between standard and extended services.

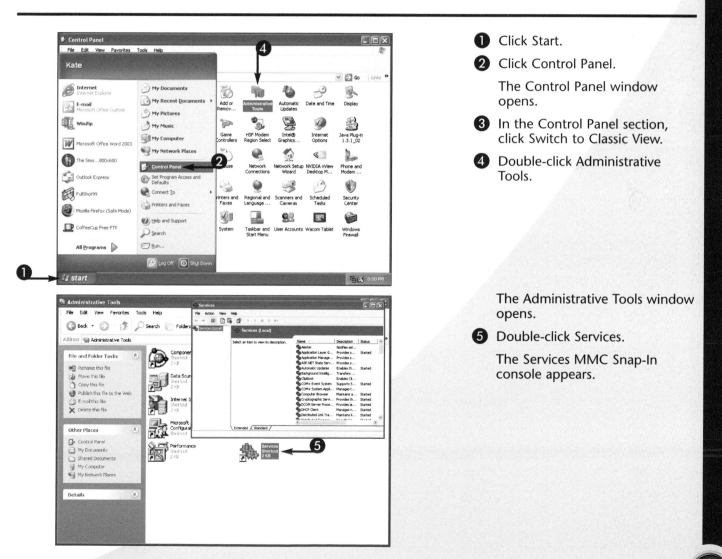

① Click Start.

② Click Control Panel.

The Control Panel window opens.

③ In the Control Panel section, click Switch to Classic View.

④ Double-click Administrative Tools.

The Administrative Tools window opens.

⑤ Double-click Services.

The Services MMC Snap-In console appears.

SHARED DOCUMENTS FOLDER

You can use the Shared Documents folder to copy and share files with other people who have user accounts on your computer. This feature separates the Shared Documents folder from other types of shared folders where you allow other users on a network to access and modify the files that they contain.

You can use My Computer or Windows Explorer to drag and drop files from other folders into the Shared Documents folder. You can also use the options listed in the task pane in My Computer to copy or move selected files. Whichever method you choose

depends on your personal preference, although you can use either method at any time.

Windows automatically creates the Shared Documents folder whenever more than one user account is added to the system. This folder is found within the My Documents and Settings folder, along with your My Documents folder.

See also>> **My Documents Folder**

File and Folder Management

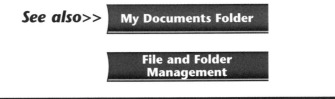

① Click Start.

② Click My Computer.

The My Computer window opens.

③ Double-click Shared Documents.

The Shared Documents folder opens.

The Shared Pictures folder makes it easy for you to place images in a folder that others with a user account on your computer can find and access with minimal fuss. When you import images into your computer through a scanner or camera and you want to share these images with others, you can place them into the Shared Pictures folder, which is found within the Shared Documents folder.

You can use the Shared Pictures folder to organize and protect your image collection. For example, you can keep your private photographs in the My Pictures folder, and copy or move only those pictures that you want to share into the

Shared Pictures folder. This is usually a better idea than sharing your entire My Pictures folder.

The Shared Pictures folder also offers a much better option than storing images throughout your system where you may forget where you have put them.

See also>>

> My Pictures Folder

> Shared Documents Folder

> File and Folder Management

① Click Start.

② Click My Computer.

The My Computer window opens.

③ Double-click Shared Documents.

The Shared Documents window opens.

④ Double-click Shared Pictures.

The Shared Pictures window opens, displaying the folder contents.

SHOWSOUNDS

You can use ShowSounds to display on-screen text to accompany the audio that plays through your computer sound system, similar to closed captions that display on your TV. Although this Accessibility tool is intended for users with hearing impairment, you can also use ShowSounds when you want to use Windows with the audio off.

If you use ShowSounds, then speech and certain other sounds appear on your screen in the form of text captions or information icons. You may not always see the full context of the audio presentation, but you should be able to achieve some understanding of what is said or played.

Keep in mind that not every program or tool that you run will support the ShowSounds feature. As a result, you may not know when speech or other sounds play.

See also>> SoundSentry

Accessibility Options

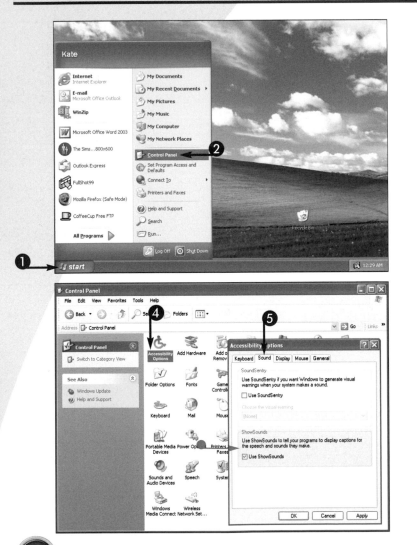

① Click Start.

② Click Control Panel.

The Control Panel window opens.

③ In the Control Panel section, click Switch to Classic View.

④ Double-click Accessibility Options.

The Accessibility Options dialog box appears.

⑤ Click the Sound tab.

● The ShowSounds option display.

SOUNDS AND AUDIO DEVICES

When you want to view, set up, or configure sound and audio accessories on your computer, you can do this through the Sounds and Audio Devices option in the Control Panel. From here, you can adjust your speaker and microphone recording volume without needing to adjust the actual hardware.

Keep in mind that a sound adapter is required to provide sound and to record through a microphone. If you have not installed a sound adapter, then most of the options in this window are not available.

As you move through the five tabs in the dialog box, you can see that several of the tabs focus on specific components of your computer audio system such as Sounds and Voice. The remaining tabs combine features or display audio support details, such as in the Hardware tab.

The options that you have available within the Sounds and Audio Devices Properties dialog box depend entirely on what hardware — and to some degree, software — you have on your computer. For example, if you do not have any speakers attached, then you will not see options to control them.

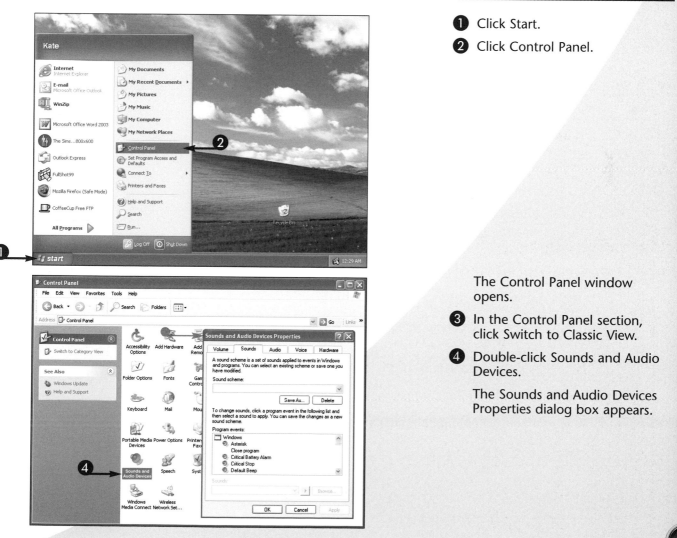

1 Click Start.

2 Click Control Panel.

The Control Panel window opens.

3 In the Control Panel section, click Switch to Classic View.

4 Double-click Sounds and Audio Devices.

The Sounds and Audio Devices Properties dialog box appears.

SOUNDSENTRY

If you or someone who uses your computer is hearing impaired or you do not have sound enabled, then you can configure Windows to turn sound alerts into on-screen warnings and messages. To do this, you can use SoundSentry, which is one of the Accessibility options.

By default, Windows produces sounds to alert you to certain problems or errors that may occur as you work with your computer. However, if you are hearing-impaired or you have the sound disabled, then these alerts cannot attract your attention.

When you use SoundSentry, Windows displays a visual warning on your screen to notify you of whatever situation warrants the alert. SoundSentry also provides a good companion for the ShowSounds tool, which displays text as an alternative to program sounds or speech.

See also>>

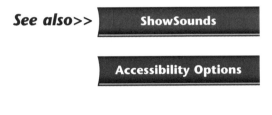

ShowSounds

Accessibility Options

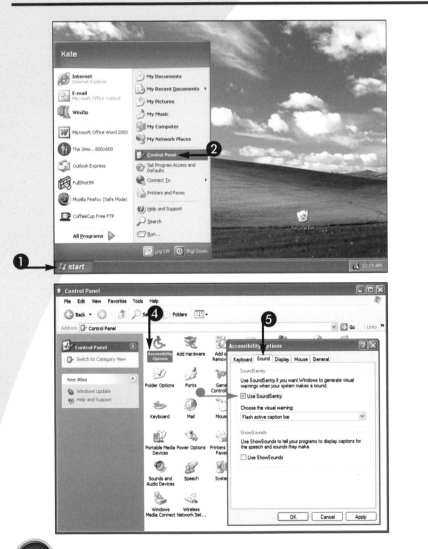

① Click Start.

② Click Control Panel.

The Control Panel window opens.

③ In the Control Panel section, click Switch to Classic View.

④ Double-click Accessibility Options.

The Accessibility Options dialog box appears.

⑤ Click the Sound tab.

● The SoundSentry options display.

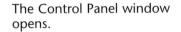

STICKYKEYS

If you have a physical disability that makes it difficult to work in a graphical user environment like Windows, then you can use StickyKeys to assist you. Some users cannot easily hold down two or more keys simultaneously, which is necessary to perform some operations or to use *keyboard shortcuts*, which are key combinations that are used instead of clicking an icon or choosing from a menu. As with other Accessibility options, you may find StickyKeys useful for this purpose, even if you do not have a physical challenge.

With StickyKeys active, when you press and release the Control, Alt, Shift, or Windows logo key on your keyboard, Windows reacts as if you are holding the key down while you press another key. For example, if you want to use the keyboard shortcut Ctrl+S to save a file, then you can press and release the Ctrl key and then immediately press and release the S key. Windows behaves as if you pressed these keys in unison, and completes the task.

See also>> **Accessibility Options**

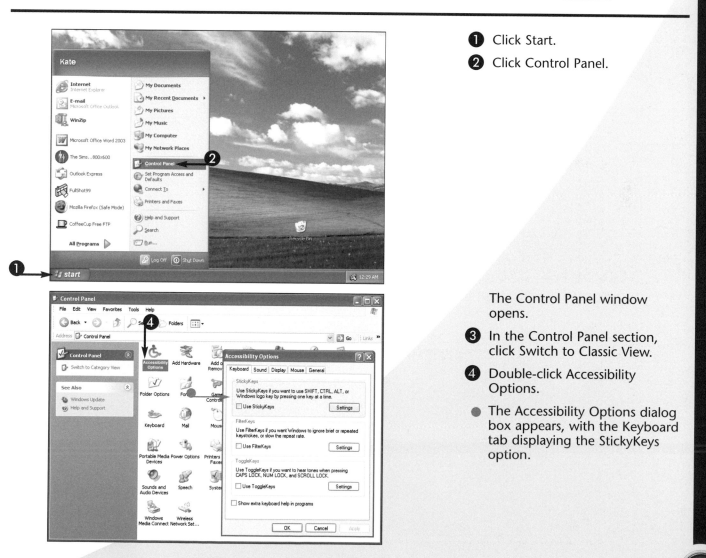

❶ Click Start.

❷ Click Control Panel.

The Control Panel window opens.

❸ In the Control Panel section, click Switch to Classic View.

❹ Double-click Accessibility Options.

● The Accessibility Options dialog box appears, with the Keyboard tab displaying the StickyKeys option.

SYSTEM INFORMATION

You can use the System Information utility to quickly view specific details about your computer at a glance. Sometimes called SysInfo, this utility collects and reports on various aspects of your Windows XP computer and makes this information available for you to view.

Details such as Hardware Resources, Software Environment, and Internet Settings are listed by category under System Summary. If you have Microsoft Office installed, then that category also appears. When you open the System Information window, the right-hand pane displays a profile of your computer that includes the exact Windows version, processor type, and amount of available memory.

You can use the System Information tool when you need to troubleshoot a problem with your system. You can also use it to review the effects of changes that you make through an upgrade. Technical service representatives may also ask you to use this utility to obtain details about your system or an application when you make a call to a customer support line.

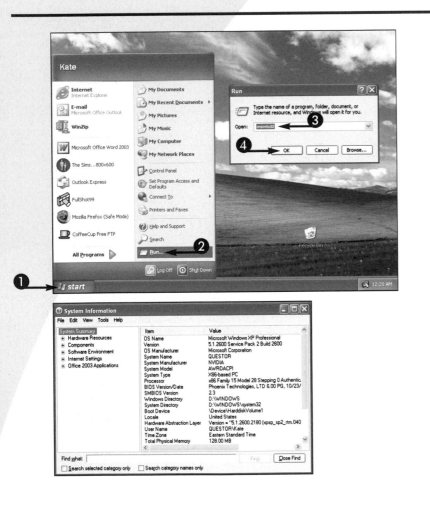

1 Click Start.

2 Click Run.

The Run dialog box appears.

3 In the Open text box, type **msinfo32**.

4 Click OK.

The System Information window opens.

SYSTEM RESTORE

System Restore is a disaster recovery utility that you can use to restore your system to the way it worked at a certain time before your computer encountered problems. This gives you a buffer to undo a catastrophic change to your system or to revert to a time before you opened a virus-infected file or deleted a critical file.

There is an important difference between System Restore and the Backup tool in Windows. When you use System Restore, you create a copy of your Windows setup, called a *restore point*, which saves to your hard disk. If a problem incapacitates

Windows, then it may also disable access to System Restore. By comparison, the Backup tool can store a copy of all of your files — or just those that you select — to another hard disk or to another drive. If the hard disk crashes, then you can restore the Backup copy on the replacement disk.

See also>>

Backup

System Restore

① Click Start.

② Click Control Panel.

The Control Panel window opens.

③ In the Control Panel section, click Switch to Classic View.

④ Double-click System.

The System Properties dialog box appears.

⑤ Click the System Restore tab.

The System Restore option and settings appear.

TASK MANAGER

You can use Task Manager to check your system, close a program that you cannot exit normally, or do a quick check of overall system performance. Task Manager provides you with multiple options through a multi-tabbed window, each tab displaying a label for the information or services that it allows you to view or perform. These tabs include Applications, Processes, Performance, and Networking, although additional tabs may appear, based on your Windows setup. More options are available from the menu bar, such as opening a new task.

Just as its name implies, Task Manager watches all open programs that you can see in the Applications

tab. Task Manager also lists services that run invisibly in the background, which you can view from the Processes tab.

You can use the Networking tab to see what is presently occurring on your network, just as you can view real-time performance through the Performance tab. You can use the Shut Down option when Windows refuses to restart.

See also>> **Task Manager**

1 In Windows, press Ctrl+Alt+Del.

The Windows Task Manager dialog box appears.

TASKBAR

You can do more with the Taskbar that appears across the bottom of your desktop than click the all-important Start button. For example, with multiple programs open, you can click their entry in the Taskbar to move swiftly from one program to another, as well as to re-open a program that you have minimized.

The right end of the Taskbar displays the System Tray — also known as the Windows Notification area — where you can check the time and view system messages. You can also click to open icons for programs that are listed there.

You can customize the Taskbar through the Properties dialog box, which you can access by right-clicking the Taskbar. You can also drag the Taskbar to another position or hide it until you need it. You can expand its depth so that you have access to more open programs. You can also add the Quick Launch bar to the Taskbar to gain faster access to the tools and tasks that you frequently use.

See also>>

Quick Launch Bar

Taskbar

➊ Right-click a blank area of the Taskbar.

A sub-menu opens.

➋ Click Properties.

The Taskbar and Start Menu Properties dialog box appears.

TELNET

If you need to log onto a network over the Internet from a remote location, then you can use a tool called Telnet to communicate with the network and even run programs remotely. You may already use this feature if you telecommute to work from home or otherwise need to operate from a location other than where the physical network resides. If you have not used Telnet before, then you should check with your network or system Administrator to confirm that Telnet is compatible with your network for remote work and access.

Telnet is short for telecommunications networking, and has two main components: Telnet client and

Telnet server. A client is a program that you run to connect with a server, while a server is special software that you configure to act as a host for connections. You can use the Command Prompt-run Telnet client to log on to the network, or you can set up a Telnet server to allow you or others to communicate with your network through the Telnet client.

See also>> **Telnet Client**

Launch the Telnet Client

1 Click Start.

2 Click Run.

The Run dialog box appears.

3 Type **telnet**.

4 Click OK.

The Command Prompt console appears, with Microsoft Telnet Client loaded.

TOGGLEKEYS

ToggleKeys is an Accessibility option that can produce audio cues whenever you press a keyboard key that can lock, such as the NumLock, Scroll, and Caps Lock keys. The ToggleKeys features help to prevent problems that arise when a feature has been turned on without your knowledge.

If you have visual challenges or difficulty in concentration, then this cue alerts you to key presses that may affect how you work. For example, when you select NumLock, you cannot use the navigational arrows or other keys on the numeric keypad of your keyboard until you

deselect it. If you press Caps Lock and leave it on inadvertently, then everything that you type appears in capital letters. If you do not usually look at your keyboard, then you may not notice the problem.

ToggleKeys uses different sounds to alert you to different situations. For example, a high-pitched beep means that a key is locked, while a lower-pitched signal tells you that the key is now unlocked.

See also>> | Accessibility Options

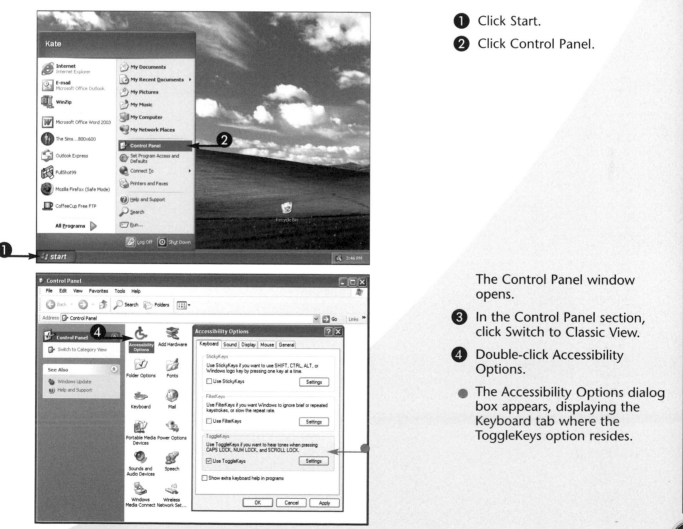

1 Click Start.

2 Click Control Panel.

The Control Panel window opens.

3 In the Control Panel section, click Switch to Classic View.

4 Double-click Accessibility Options.

● The Accessibility Options dialog box appears, displaying the Keyboard tab where the ToggleKeys option resides.

WEB PUBLISHING WIZARD

If you have access to a Web site on the Internet or an *intranet* — a network-based Web site — then you can use the Web Publishing Wizard to help you work. Through the wizard, you can expedite the transfer of new or updated Web pages, documents, or folders to that site.

The wizard prompts you for specific information, such as the network or Internet address of the Web site where you want to publish. This can also be an FTP site or a company intranet that you have available

through work. Once the wizard collects the necessary details from you, it uses your network or Internet connection to contact the Web server and transfer your files.

The Web Publishing Wizard offers an easier way to upload your files than through *file transfer protocol,* or FTP, tools. However, the wizard is a basic tool with limited options. It does not compete with Web management packages such as Microsoft FrontPage or Macromedia Dreamweaver.

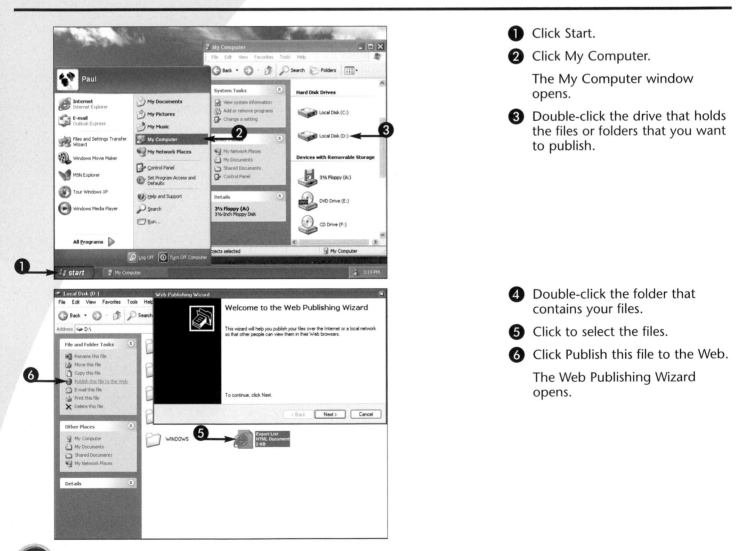

① Click Start.

② Click My Computer.

The My Computer window opens.

③ Double-click the drive that holds the files or folders that you want to publish.

④ Double-click the folder that contains your files.

⑤ Click to select the files.

⑥ Click Publish this file to the Web.

The Web Publishing Wizard opens.

WINDOWS EXPLORER

You can use either Windows Explorer or My Computer to manage files and folders in Windows XP. Through Windows Explorer, you can see your drive contents listed by drive, folder, and sub-folder. If you find that the folder-based interface of My Computer requires too much screen space or is difficult to manage, then you can perform file and folder management through Windows Explorer instead. The tool that you use depends on your personal preference.

From Windows Explorer, you can use the left-hand organizational tree, where you can click the plus sign to expand a drive or folder to see its contents. These files and folders then appear in the right-hand pane.

You can use commands from the menu options as well as the toolbar to perform operations such as searching for files, as well as deleting and renaming files. When you right-click a file or folder in the contents pane, a sub-menu appears, from which you can also perform file actions.

See also>>

My Computer Folder

File and Folder Management

❶ Click Start.

❷ Click All Programs.

❸ Click Accessories.

❹ Click Windows Explorer.

My Documents window opens in the Windows Explorer.

WINDOWS FIREWALL

You can configure and use Windows Firewall to protect your computer from unwanted privacy intrusions or other problems when you connect to a network or the Internet. The Windows Firewall software is designed to act as a barrier between your private computer files and outside connections.

When you enable Windows Firewall, it monitors all programs that either access the Internet from your computer or try to communicate with you from an external source. You should enable the firewall if you do not have a third-party program like Norton Internet Suite, which provides this protection.

Once you enable Windows Firewall, it automatically acts to block certain programs that may compromise the security of your system. These programs can include instant messaging tools such as Windows Messenger or AOL Instant Messenger. When the firewall detects a potential problem, it pops a message up onscreen asking what you want to do. You can choose to either continue blocking the software or stop blocking it.

See also>>

Security
Windows Firewall

1 Click Start.

2 Click Control Panel.

The Control Panel window opens.

3 In the Control Panel section, Click Switch to Classic View.

4 Double-click Windows Firewall.

The Windows Firewall dialog box appears, displaying multiple tabs.

WINDOWS PICTURE AND FAX VIEWER

With the Windows Picture and Fax Viewer, you can display images, such as those that you import from your digital camera. As its name states, this tool also allows you to read faxes that you receive through your computer, such as when you install the Microsoft Fax Service.

The viewer performs other functions, as well. For example, you can rotate images and perform an automatic correction for brightness and contrast. You can then save your changes to the image or discard them when you close the viewer.

When you click a fax that is listed in the Fax Console — which is part of the Microsoft Fax Service — the same viewer opens to display the contents of the fax. Using options in the viewer, you can zoom in to read text that is very small. You can also choose to print a fax to a printer that is installed to your computer or network.

See also>> **My Pictures Folder**

Fax

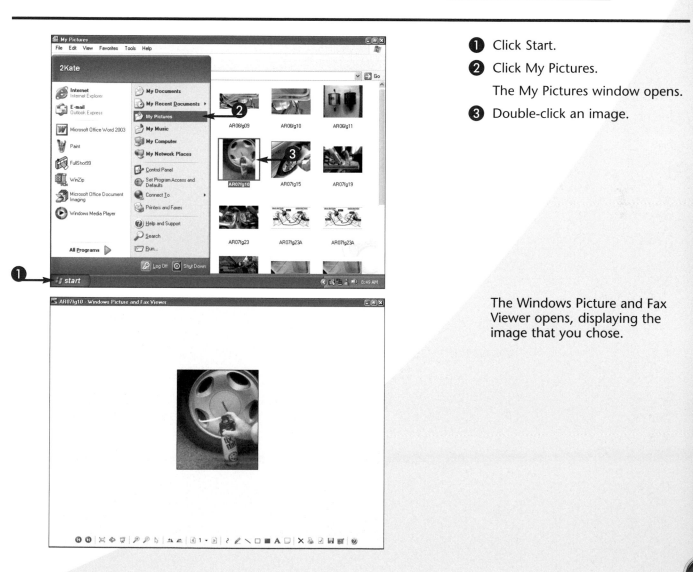

❶ Click Start.

❷ Click My Pictures.

The My Pictures window opens.

❸ Double-click an image.

The Windows Picture and Fax Viewer opens, displaying the image that you chose.

((•)) WIRELESS NETWORK SETUP WIZARD

You can use the Wireless Network Setup Wizard in Windows XP when you install the hardware components that you need for a cable-free network in your home or small office. This wizard helps you to set up system support for the equipment, often more easily than the software that ships with the equipment.

This tool can reduce your installation time, and it can also ensure that you will successfully configure your wireless network on the first try, compared with manual setup.

To begin, you first install the hardware, by following the instructions in the manufacturer documentation.

You may need to run software that is included with your network hardware as part of the setup process.

You can now run the Wireless Network Setup Wizard. The wizard guides you through the setup, helping you specify the wireless components that you have and what type of network you want to establish.

See also>> **Help and Support Center**

Network Setup Wizard

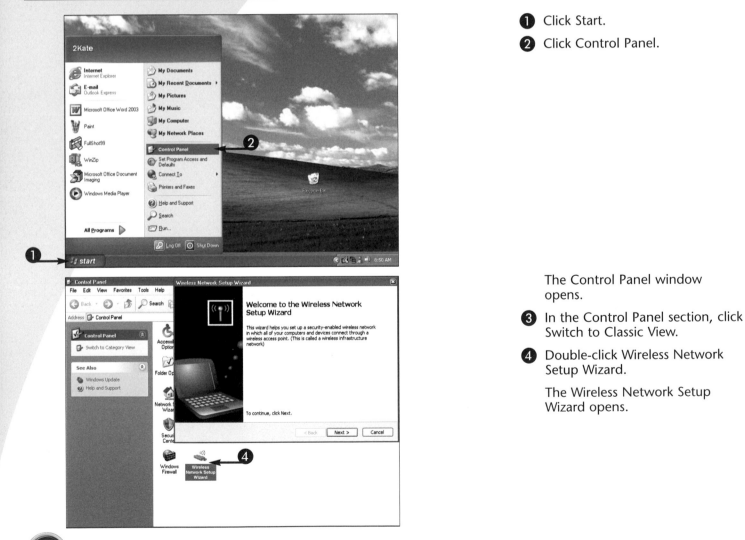

1 Click Start.

2 Click Control Panel.

The Control Panel window opens.

3 In the Control Panel section, click Switch to Classic View.

4 Double-click Wireless Network Setup Wizard.

The Wireless Network Setup Wizard opens.

WORDPAD

WordPad is a basic word-processing tool that is built into Windows XP. You can use WordPad to write letters, keep a text list, type an address to print on an envelope, or read a document. You can also copy information from a Web page and paste it into an open WordPad document where you can save it to disk for later reference.

While Windows Notepad allows you to create and view only plain-text files, WordPad works with several types of formats. These include the document, or DOC, format and rich text format, or RTF, which shows more stylized text features than a plain-text file.

You can also write Web pages with WordPad if you save them with the .htm file extension. You can find a list of extensions in the drop-down list box next to the File Type option in the Save As dialog box. WordPad can also create and open some other file types, such as Microsoft Word and Web files.

See also>> Notepad

1 Click Start.

2 Click All Programs.

3 Click Accessories.

4 Click WordPad.

The WordPad window opens on the desktop, displaying a blank document.

Windows XP Visual Encyclopedia

Part II: Techniques

Many of the features in Windows XP are available from the Start Menu. For example, a quick tour of the Control Panel displays a variety of many new features. Although Windows XP offers a lot of powerful tools and features, it may not be immediately clear how you can use them — at least, not until you arrive at the second part of this book.

From Accessibility options to working with media files, the Techniques section walks you through some of the most frequently used tasks that you can perform with the tools and features in Windows XP. You will also discover new options that you may not have thought possible without needing to purchase third-party software. For example, Windows XP allows you to copy or move files directly to a recordable CD or DVD drive; you no longer need to install special software to do this.

If you share your computer with others, you can configure individual user accounts. If children use your system, then you can enable and configure Content Advisor — the parental control option that is available in the Internet Explorer Web browser — to restrict the sites that they can open.

ACCESSIBILITY OPTIONS:
Set Up Features without the Wizard

When you add Accessibility options to Windows XP, tools become available that can help you, or others who share your computer, to work in the Windows graphical environment. These tools serve as a bridge between the system and any users who have physical challenges such as visual or motor limitations. Although all Accessibility tools come with pre-configured settings, individual needs can differ greatly. As a result, you may need to manually adjust each tool to suit your needs.

For example, with Narrator, you can modify the way in which the tool reads the screen to you. You can

also adjust the way that you use On-Screen Keyboard to fit the assistive device that you use to type when you cannot work with a standard keyboard.

See also>>

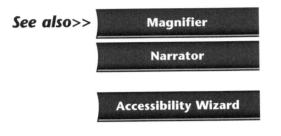

Magnifier

Narrator

Accessibility Wizard

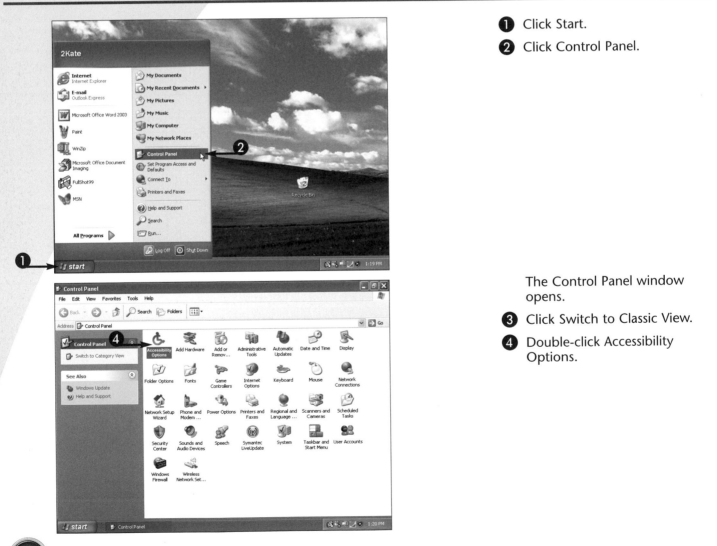

① Click Start.

② Click Control Panel.

The Control Panel window opens.

③ Click Switch to Classic View.

④ Double-click Accessibility Options.

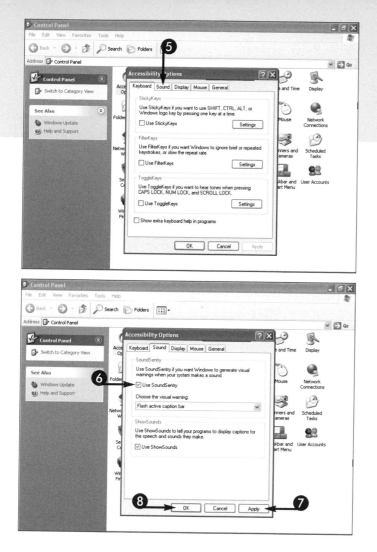

The Accessibility Options dialog box appears.

5 Click the tab that corresponds to the Accessibility feature that you want to modify.

If a user needs Accessibility options turned on to use Windows, someone else would need to perform this action for the user.

6 Click to select the options that you want to enable, or deselect the options that you want to disable.

7 Click Apply.

8 Click OK.

Windows applies your changes, and the Accessibility Options dialog box closes.

TIPS

Did You Know?
Some Accessibility features may turn on automatically if Windows detects certain behavior that may indicate a need for the tool. For example, if you press and hold a key for too long, then ToggleKeys may enable by itself, followed by on-screen notification. However, you can turn this feature off again at any time.

More Options!
You can go back and adjust the settings for active Accessibility features, as well as enable additional features at any time. You can do this through Accessibility Options in the Control Panel.

Important!
For best results when you need to use assistive devices in Windows, ensure that the devices that you obtain are fully compatible with Windows XP.

ACCESSIBILITY WIZARD:
Configure Usability Features

Accessibility Options, which you can configure through the Accessibility Wizard, gives you a way to work with Windows even when you may have physical or cognitive challenges. Such challenges can otherwise make normal use of the keyboard, mouse, or your display difficult. Windows XP includes several different Accessibility features that correspond to various motor skill or other challenges you may encounter to use your operating system more easily and more effectively.

The Accessibility Wizard allows you to activate and configure the Magnifier, Narrator, and On-Screen Keyboard, along with other related features, such as the desktop and window font size, and input options for the keyboard and mouse. You can use one, two, or more of these options, dependent on your specific needs.

The Magnifier expands an area of the desktop to make it easier to read. The Narrator reads items such as dialog box options from the screen. The On-Screen Keyboard allows a user to type text on the screen rather than with a keyboard.

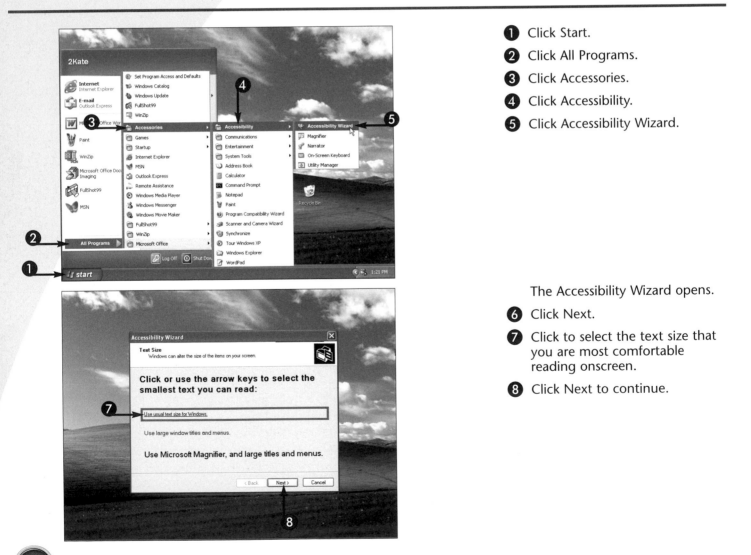

❶ Click Start.

❷ Click All Programs.

❸ Click Accessories.

❹ Click Accessibility.

❺ Click Accessibility Wizard.

The Accessibility Wizard opens.

❻ Click Next.

❼ Click to select the text size that you are most comfortable reading onscreen.

❽ Click Next to continue.

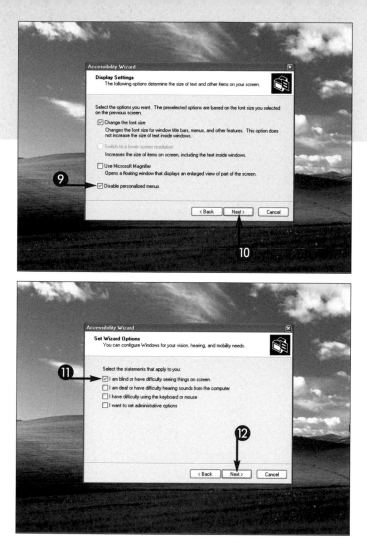

If you choose certain features, then a dialog box may appear where you can specify additional options.

Note: See Magnifier for details on configuring and using the Magnifier. See Narrator and On-Screen Keyboard for additional features.

9 To have Windows display full menus in all applications, click to select the Disable personalized menus check box.

10 Click Next.

11 Click to select the options that you want.

12 Click Next.

The pages that the wizard displays from this point on depend on which options you choose. The following screens appear in groups that reflect your choices in the previous screen.

TIPS

Attention!

If something interrupts your Windows session as you run the wizard or otherwise configure Accessibility Options, you may need to run the wizard again. For example, if your PC locks up or the power goes out, any changes made before the wizard closes prematurely will not save. You also have the option of terminating the wizard by clicking Cancel when it first appears.

Important

If you use physical assistive devices to help you work through Windows, always consult the documentation for such products before you configure Accessibility Options. Such devices include hardware designed to help you manipulate the keyboard or read text aloud to you. This hardware may have specific requirements or associated software that may be of more assistance to you than Accessibility Options offer.

ACCESSIBILITY WIZARD:
Configure Usability Features (Continued)

You can use the "I am blind or have difficulty seeing things on screen" option to control the size of window scroll bars, desktop icons, and pointers. You can also control a selection of high-contrast desktop color schemes, cursor width, and blink rate.

The "I am deaf or have difficulty hearing sounds from the computer" option displays a visual warning when the computer makes a sound, as well as captions for speech and sounds.

The "I have difficulty using the keyboard or mouse" option controls the following: the ability to press key combinations one key at a time and to ignore repeated keystrokes; playing a sound when you press the Caps Lock, Num Lock, or Scroll Lock keys; using the numeric keypad to move the mouse; changing the mouse cursor size; switching between right-hand and left-hand mouse; and changing the mouse pointer speed.

The "I want to set administrative options" option allows you to specify whether accessibility features are turned off automatically after a set idle period, and whether to save the settings for all users or only the current user.

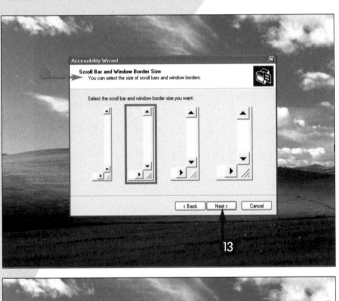

- If you previously selected the "I am blind or have difficulty seeing things on screen" option, then the next five wizard pages display options for scroll bar size, desktop icon size, desktop color scheme, pointer and cursor size, and cursor width and blink rate.

⑬ Click Next to continue.

- If you previously selected the "I am deaf or have difficulty hearing sounds from the computer" option, then the next two wizard pages allow you to set options for visual warnings of system events and to display captions for speech and sounds.

⑭ Click Next.

A

- If you previously selected the "I have difficulty using the keyboard or mouse" option, then the next eight wizard pages allow you to choose options for key combinations, to ignore repeated keystrokes, to play a sound when certain keys are pressed, to display additional keyboard help, to use the numeric keypad to control the pointer, and to set pointer size, left-hand or right-hand mouse, and mouse pointer speed.

⑮ Click Next.

If you previously selected the "I want to set administrative options" option, then the next two wizard pages allow you to specify if accessibility features turn off after a certain idle period, and if settings should be applied to all users or only the current user.

⑯ Click Next to continue.

A screen appears, stating that you have completed the wizard.

⑰ Click Finish to close the wizard.

TIPS

Did You Know?
You may need to experiment with various Accessibility options as well as the individual settings for each option. Although some features may not seem very useful at first, you can adjust them to become more suitable to your needs. You may also need to use two or more Accessibility features to increase the effectiveness of the tools.

More Options!
Some of the Accessibility features can assist more users than those with a physical impairment. For example, some of the keyboard alternatives can work for those who work with keyboards whose keys may stick or which are too sensitive to pressure.

ACCOUNTS:
Access the Administrator Account

Whenever you want to make changes to Windows XP that affect either the system or features for other users, you must log on as an Administrator. An *Administrator* is the most powerful type of user account — someone who can add and remove other accounts and change virtually anything about the system or the network. You also need to log on with the Administrator account before you can use many of the tools and techniques provided in this book, such as the Recovery Console and other advanced system tools.

An Administrator account is created when you install Windows XP. The setup prompts you for a username and password to assign to the Administrator account. You can use this same name and password to log on as an Administrator.

If you are not already an administrator, you have two options. Either you must have someone with an administer account perform these tasks for you or you need to request that an existing administrator upgrade your account to administrator status.

See also>> **User Accounts**

1 In the Welcome screen, click the name of your Administrator account.

Note: If you do not use the Welcome screen, then the Log On to Windows screen should appear. If it does not, then press Ctrl+Alt+Del to open it. You can type your username and password.

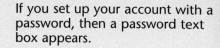

If you set up your account with a password, then a password text box appears.

② Type your password.

③ Click the arrow button or press Enter.

The Windows desktop appears.

ACTIVATION:
Activate and Register Windows

After you first install Windows XP, you have 30 days in which you can activate the operating system. You must activate it before the time limit expires or you lose the ability to log on to Windows. With activation, you connect directly with Microsoft servers through your Internet connection to verify your Windows installation, or call a phone number provided on your Windows screen.

When you activate Windows, you can also register your operating system. Registration means that you provide your name and mailing address to Microsoft,

the same as you would register other products that you buy. This is another way that Microsoft identifies you as a user of their products. Unlike activation, registration is optional.

If you do not activate Windows immediately after you install it, then a Key icon appears in the System Tray — also called the Notification Area — at the bottom-right corner of the desktop, at the far right of the taskbar. You also receive reminders to activate Windows each time you log on.

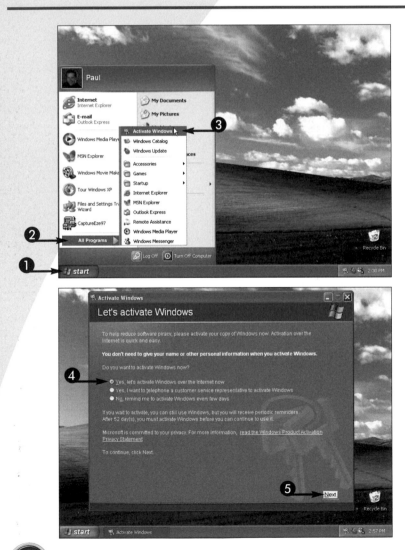

1 Click Start.

2 Click All Programs.

3 Click Activate Windows.

If the Key icon appears in the System Tray, then you can click this icon to go directly to the Let's activate Windows screen.

If you have previously activated Windows but did not register, then you can click the Key icon in the System Tray.

The Let's activate Windows screen opens.

4 Click the Yes, let's activate Windows over the Internet now option.

5 Click Next.

If you do not have Internet access, then click the Yes, I want to telephone a customer service representative to activate Windows option.

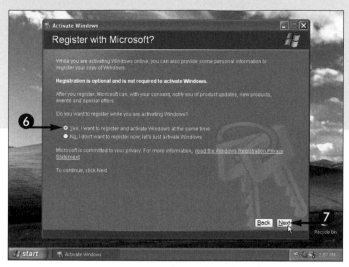

The Register with Microsoft? screen appears.

Registering with Microsoft is optional. You can still activate your copy of Windows without registering.

⑥ Click the Yes, I want to register and activate Windows at the same time option.

⑦ Click Next.

A Thank You! screen appears, stating that your activation was successful.

⑧ Click OK.

TIPS

Attention!

After you let the time period expire without activation, you will be unable to log on until you activate Windows. If you have a high-speed, always-on Internet connection, then you can do this directly through Windows. However, if you use dial-up access or do not have Internet access on your system, then you must dial the provided phone number to proceed.

Did You Know?

If you reinstall Windows, then you must re-activate the product. Microsoft limits the number of times that you can reinstall Windows to prevent the chance that you may install the same copy to many computers. Once you reach the reinstall and activation limit, you must call the number provided through the Activate Windows screen.

ACTIVE DESKTOP:
Add Dynamic Content to the Desktop

Your Windows desktop can consist of more than icons and a background wallpaper. You can also add *dynamic content* — material, usually from the Internet, that changes your desktop as the material does — to the desktop through the Active Desktop feature. You can then add any page on the Web to your desktop or choose from a special desktop gallery of items. For example, you can place your personal Web page there or the Web address for a site you use regularly, such as a news or financial Web service.

This feature allows you to display your own Web page, that of your favorite news or financial reports site, or virtually any Internet resource to which you have access. As the page updates, so does your desktop.

For this feature to work properly, you need a dedicated, always-on Internet connection such as with a broadband service — either DSL or cable modem. If you only have a dial-up connection, then your desktop cannot display active content all of the time.

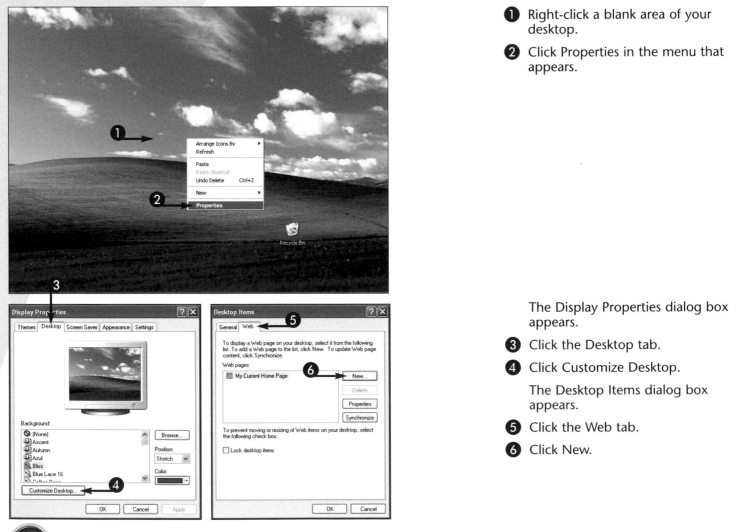

① Right-click a blank area of your desktop.

② Click Properties in the menu that appears.

The Display Properties dialog box appears.

③ Click the Desktop tab.

④ Click Customize Desktop.

The Desktop Items dialog box appears.

⑤ Click the Web tab.

⑥ Click New.

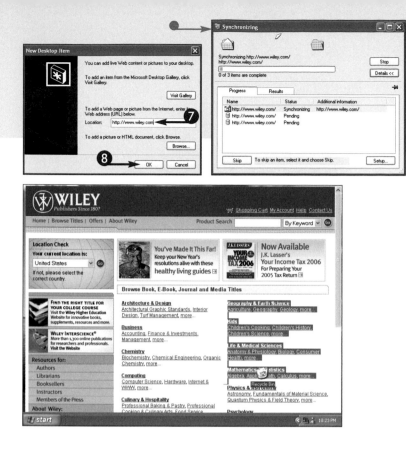

The New Desktop Item window opens.

⑦ Type the Web address, or URL, of the Web site that you want to use.

⑧ Click OK.

● A window opens to show the synchronizing progress. This window closes automatically when you are done.

⑨ Click OK to close all of the dialog boxes.

The Web page that you chose appears on your desktop.

TIPS

Did You Know?

If your computer does not have a constant connection to the Internet such as with high-speed DSL or cable modem services, then the page that displays is based on the version that was available the last time you connected online.

More Options!

If the content does not display properly, then right-click a blank area and click Refresh. Windows redraws the desktop screen.

Try This!

You may find that some Web pages work better than others as active content on your desktop. For this reason, you may want to experiment with a few different Web pages before you decide on one. For example, as you work, determine whether the content allows you to easily see icons on your desktop.

ADD HARDWARE WIZARD:
Add Unrecognized Hardware to the Computer

Windows XP automatically searches for new hardware and can usually install needed drivers automatically with little or no input from you. However, sometimes Windows does not recognize hardware that you have added to the system. You can use the Add Hardware Wizard, which is included with Windows, to easily add that new hardware.

You can start the Add Hardware Wizard from the Control Panel. The wizard searches your computer for new hardware that has been physically added but for which no drivers or other required supporting software has been installed.

In most cases, the wizard successfully locates the new hardware and installs the necessary drivers, prompting you to insert the driver CD, if required. If the wizard is unable to locate the hardware, then you can identify the hardware type manually and specify the location of drivers or other required software. Regardless of whether the wizard locates the hardware automatically, you can manually specify the location of the drivers or other software to be installed with the hardware.

See also>>   **Device Manager**

Note: *Most USB devices require you to install software before you connect the device.*

1 Click Start.

2 Click Control Panel.

3 In the Control Panel window, click Switch to Classic View.

4 Double-click the Add Hardware icon.

The Add Hardware Wizard opens.

5 Click Next.

The wizard searches for hardware that has been connected to the computer but not yet installed.

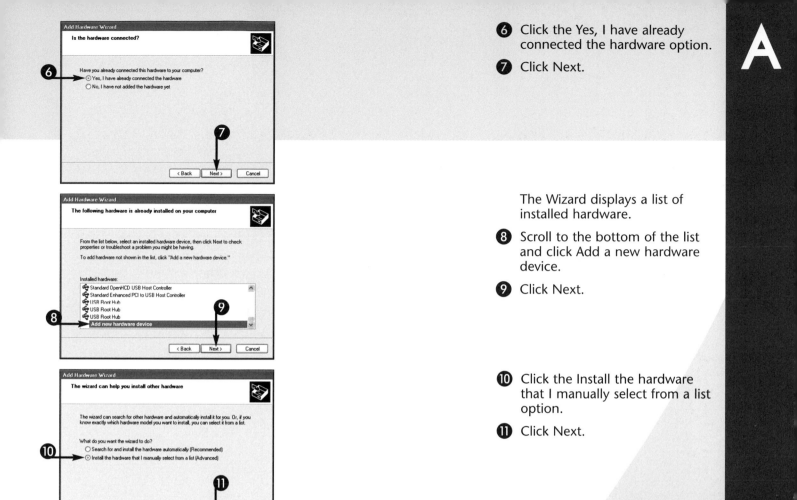

6 Click the Yes, I have already connected the hardware option.

7 Click Next.

The Wizard displays a list of installed hardware.

8 Scroll to the bottom of the list and click Add a new hardware device.

9 Click Next.

10 Click the Install the hardware that I manually select from a list option.

11 Click Next.

TIPS

Did You Know?

If you are unsure of which drivers Windows Update can update automatically for you, then keep in mind that Windows Update can only handle hardware that is specifically designed to work with Windows XP, or other versions. These drivers are submitted for approval to Microsoft. You should always use Windows XP-approved hardware.

Try This!

It is a good idea to check your manufacturer's Web site frequently to look for updated drivers, even before you install a particular piece of hardware for the first time. This ensures that you have the most up-to-date driver — and perhaps associated software — to use with your hardware, which may not otherwise be available from Windows Update.

ADD HARDWARE WIZARD:
Add Unrecognized Hardware to the Computer (Continued)

The Add Hardware Wizard displays a list of available hardware types from which to choose. The types listed by the wizard are generic, and may not match the type of hardware that you are installing. If you do not see your hardware type in the list, then you can choose the Show All Devices item in the Common Hardware Types list. When you click Next, the wizard displays all available manufacturers and devices.

When the wizard prompts you to choose a hardware type, your choice only determines which manufacturers and devices it displays in the next

page. For example, if you choose Modems from the list, then the wizard only displays modem manufacturers and modems in the resulting page. If you choose Show All Devices, then the wizard includes all manufacturers and device types in the resulting page.

If you install a non-plug-and-play device, then you may have to change the hardware resources — such as IRQ — that are used by the device. Plug and play enables Windows to automatically see and install support for new hardware as it is installed.

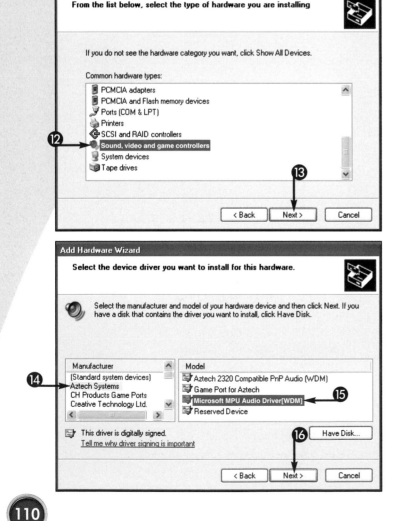

The wizard displays a list of hardware types.

⑫ If the list displays the type of device that you are installing, then click the device type in the list.

⑬ If the list does not display the device type, or you have already selected it, then click Next.

The wizard displays a list of manufacturers and devices.

⑭ Click the manufacturer in the left column.

⑮ Click the device in the right column.

⑯ Click Next.

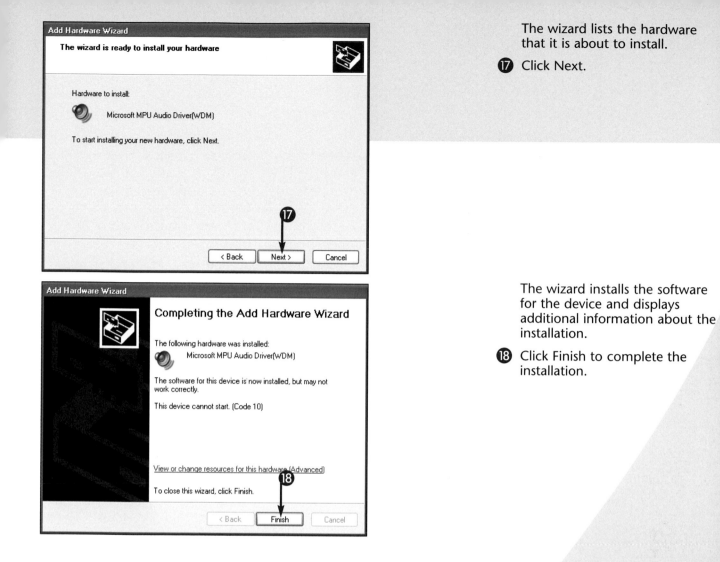

The wizard lists the hardware that it is about to install.

⑰ Click Next.

The wizard installs the software for the device and displays additional information about the installation.

⑱ Click Finish to complete the installation.

TIPS

Did You Know?

In some situations — particularly when you install a very new device — the Add Hardware Wizard does not include the device in its list, even if the manufacturer is listed. You can click the Have Disk button when the wizard asks you to choose a device, browse to the location where you have the driver, and click Open.

More Options!

New hardware that you physically install may not appear in the wizard and, even when you point to the driver, Windows may not recognize the device. When this occurs, you should recheck the installation. It is most likely that the device is not properly installed, that you have not turned on the power, or that the cable or other connector that attaches to the computer is loose or defective.

ADD NETWORK PLACE WIZARD:
Add Online Network Storage to the Computer

If your Windows computer operates as part of a network, then you can add online network storage to your list of drives on which you save and retrieve files. This online network storage can include a drive that is located on another computer or a drive that is located on a system that acts as a server to the rest of the network for file storage. You can add this storage through the wizard, to make it easier and faster to work with files that you want to store on a separate resource.

You should use this option when the hard drive on your computer is nearly full or when you want to be able to share files with others.

After you add the network storage, it appears on your list of resources, which is available in the My Network Places window. This list is also available in the Open and Save dialog boxes. The first part of the wizard allows you to make basic selections.

See also>>

Open Dialog Box

Save Dialog Box

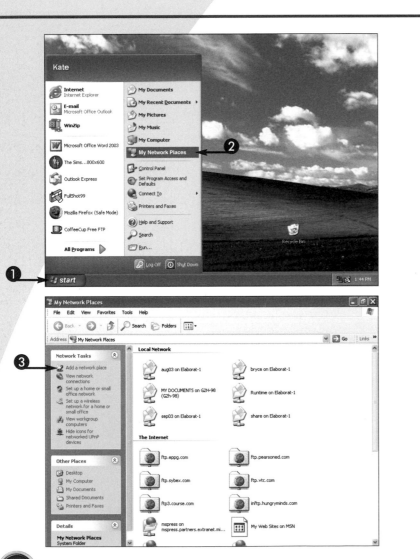

1 Click Start.

2 Click My Network Places.

The My Network Places window opens.

3 Click Add a network place.

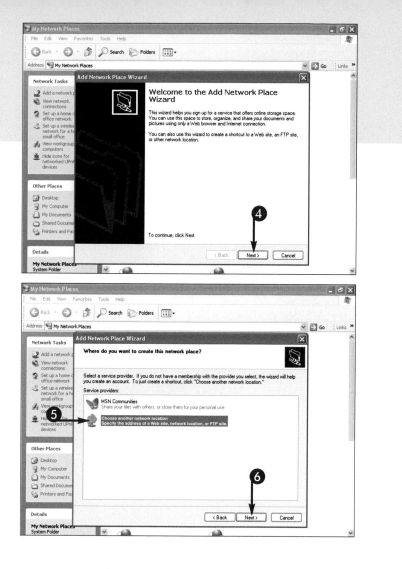

The Add Network Place Wizard opens.

④ Click Next.

⑤ Click Choose another network location.

⑥ Click Next.

TIPS

Attention!
If you experience difficulty when you try to add a network resource to your system, then it may be because the resource that you want to add is not shared.

More Options!
You can add a Web or FTP site as a network resource through the Add Network Place Wizard. To do this, type the Web or FTP site address instead of the network address in Step 7 on the next page.

Try This!
If you have problems when you add the network place, then start with the source to correct it. If you have an Administrator account on the computer or server where the network resource is located, then you can ensure that the resource is shared on that system. For more information, see File and Folder Management: Share a Folder.

A

ADD NETWORK PLACE WIZARD:
Add Online Network Storage to the Computer (Continued)

Before you add a network place, you need to know the exact address or location of the network storage that you want to add. This location may be a drive and folder location or a pre-designated network address such as QUESTOR\\SHARE.

If you operate as part of a professional network in a corporate-type office setting, then you may have to consult your network Administrator for additional information before you proceed.

The label that you apply to the new network place is intended to help you readily identify it when you open My Network Places. The more network places that you designate, the more important it becomes to identify each location clearly. You should use a label that is easy to recognize, and that distinguishes the location from other network places that you have already set up. For example, if you set up a frequently used FTP or Web site as a network place, then you must identify the location type as part of the label to avoid confusion.

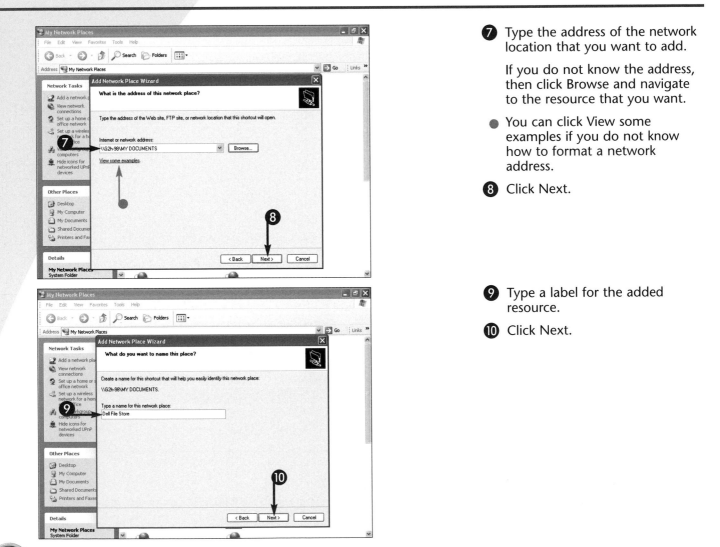

⑦ Type the address of the network location that you want to add.

If you do not know the address, then click Browse and navigate to the resource that you want.

● You can click View some examples if you do not know how to format a network address.

⑧ Click Next.

⑨ Type a label for the added resource.

⑩ Click Next.

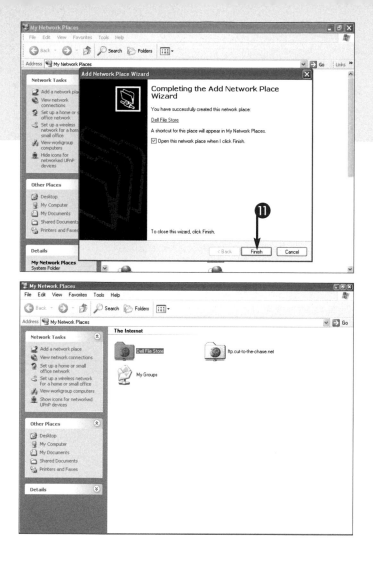

The wizard creates the network place.

⑪ Click Finish.

The network resource is now available in the My Network Places window.

ADD PRINTER WIZARD:
Add a Printer to the Computer

One of the easiest things that you can do with a computer is to add a new printer. This is true both when you physically connect the printer to the computer and when you install the software that supports the printer in Windows. The Add Printer Wizard makes it even faster and easier to bring a printer online.

Your first step is to physically connect the printer, which you should do by following the instructions that came with it. As soon as the printer is connected, Windows should recognize it and install support drivers for it; you may see a prompt asking you to supply the CD that came with the printer.

As part of the installation process, Windows may automatically add your new printer to the Printers and Faxes window. If not, then you can run the Add a Printer Wizard to do this for you.

See also>> Printers and Faxes

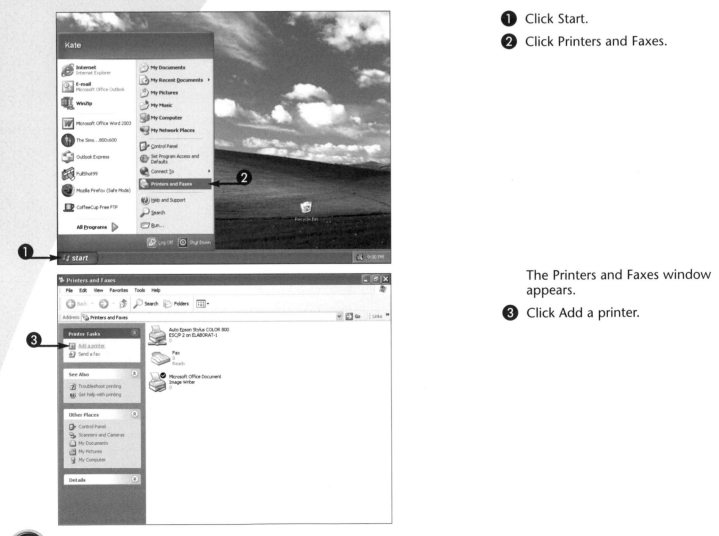

① Click Start.

② Click Printers and Faxes.

The Printers and Faxes window appears.

③ Click Add a printer.

The Add Printer Wizard opens.

4 Click Next.

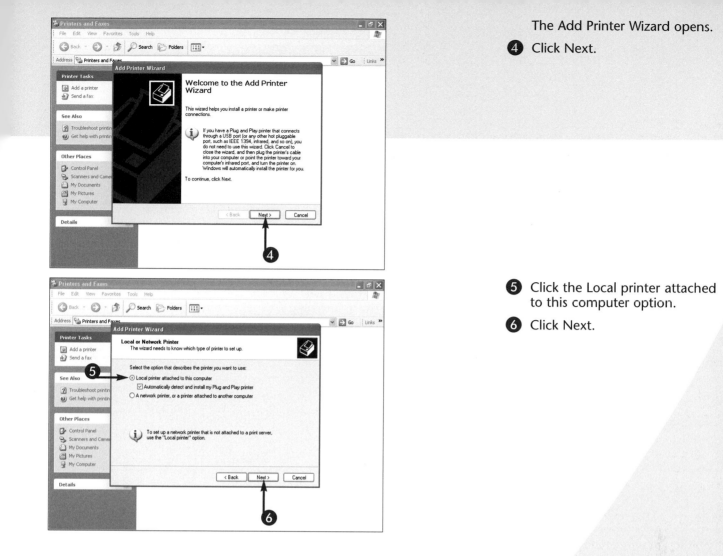

5 Click the Local printer attached to this computer option.

6 Click Next.

Attention!

Before you run the Add Printer Wizard, check the Printers and Faxes folder to ensure that the printer has not been added automatically when you installed it. To do this, click Start and then click Printers and Faxes. In the Printers and Faxes window, look for the printer that you just installed. If the printer is not listed, then launch the wizard.

Important!

You usually do not need to run the Add Printer Wizard if your printer connects through your Universal Serial Bus, or USB, port.

More Options!

If the printer that you want to add is on your network, then choose the network printer option shown in Step 5 instead. This step adds support for a network printer that is already connected to your Windows computer.

ADD PRINTER WIZARD:
Add a Printer to the Computer (Continued)

As you install a printer through the wizard, the wizard may not recognize the printer in the process. If it fails to detect the printer, then you may need to manually specify the manufacturer and the exact model.

If you need to install a fax system instead, then you can use the Fax Configuration Wizard. Faxes are grouped together with printers under Windows XP, and you can access them both using the Printers and Faxes option in the Start menu.

You may also want to add a printer that is available elsewhere on your home or small office network. When you share a printer on your network, you usually need to install it to one or more computers that are also connected to the same network.

See also>>

Add Printer Wizard

Fax Configuration Wizard

Share a Printer

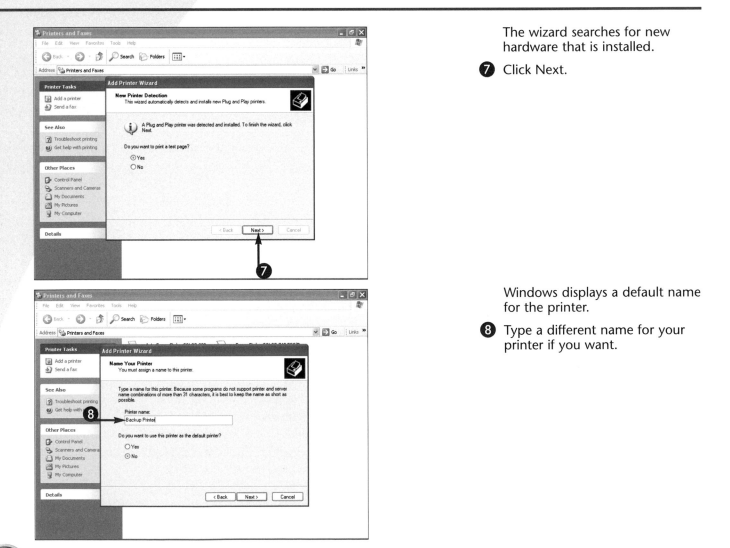

The wizard searches for new hardware that is installed.

⑦ Click Next.

Windows displays a default name for the printer.

⑧ Type a different name for your printer if you want.

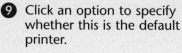

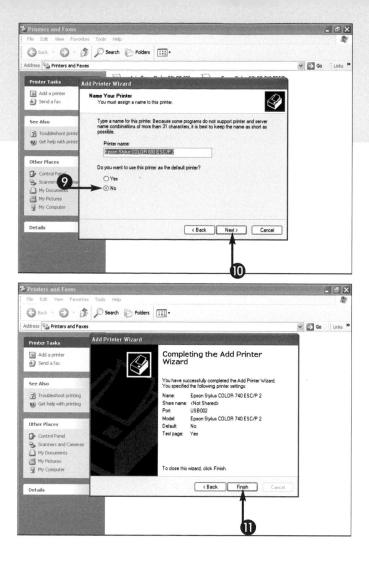

9 Click an option to specify whether this is the default printer.

10 Click Next.

11 Click Finish.

Windows adds the printer to your Printers and Faxes folder.

TIPS

More Options!

If you have additional printers that you use only rarely, such as special USB-connected printers that you often disconnect, then you should install them as shown in these steps. Support for these printers remains even when you disconnect them.

Try This!

If, after you install a printer, you find yourself unable to use the printer, then you can troubleshoot the problem. You can consult the printer documentation to ensure that you have installed it properly, and then remove and reinstall software support for the printer by re-running the wizard operation shown in these and the previous steps.

ADD OR REMOVE PROGRAMS:
Install Additional Windows Components

Windows XP usually does not install all possible features and services by default. You may not discover this until you try to use a feature that you cannot find. You can add missing components at any time in one of two ways: first, you can run Setup again from the Windows XP setup CD, or you can use the Add or Remove Programs option from the Control Panel.

Additional Windows components that are frequently not installed by default include the Microsoft Fax

Service and Internet Information Services. The Microsoft Fax Service allows you to send and receive faxes from your desktop. You can use the Internet Information Services to set up a Web server to host a Web or FTP site.

See also>>

Fax Configuration Wizard

Fax Console

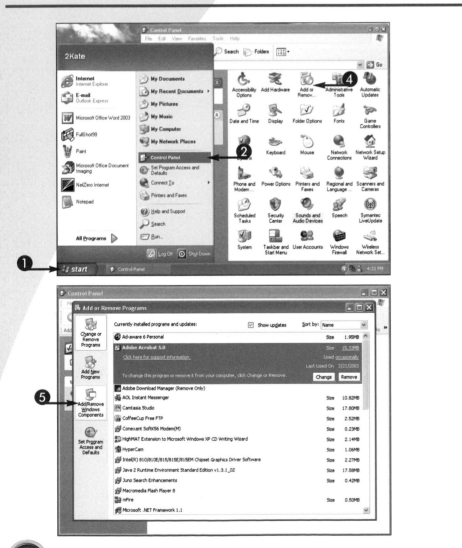

① Click Start.

② Click Control Panel.

③ In the Control Panel window, click Switch to Classic View.

④ Double-click Add or Remove Programs.

The Add or Remove Programs window opens.

⑤ Click Add/Remove Windows Components.

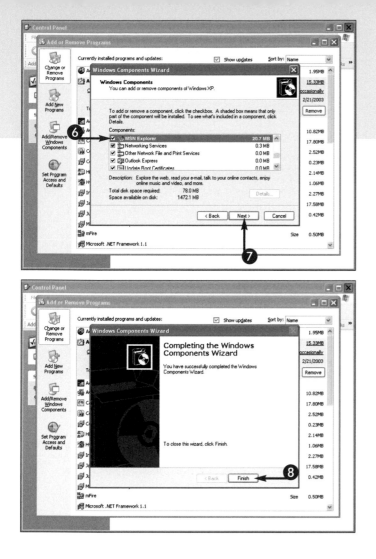

The Windows Components
Wizard opens.

6 Click to check the component
that you want to add.

7 Click Next.

A progress window appears and
then disappears automatically
when the process is complete.

8 Click Finish.

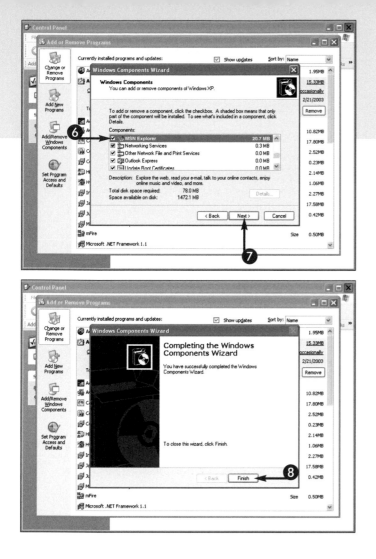

TIPS

Attention!
You may need to locate and insert your Windows
XP setup CD to install some of the additional
components. Whether you must do this depends
on how Windows was installed and whether a
copy of the setup files is in place on your hard
disk. You will be prompted during the process if
your setup CD is required.

More Options!
If you have limited hard disk space, then refer to
the information about space requirements at the
bottom-left area of the Windows Components
Wizard window. To learn more about a specific
component, click to select the component and
then click Details.

Remove It!
To remove a Windows component that is already
added, repeat the steps but click to deselect the
component that you want to delete in Step 5.

ADD OR REMOVE PROGRAMS:
Uninstall Software

When you want to delete a program that you have added to your PC, the proper way is through the Add or Remove Programs option in Control Panel. This is because most Windows programs that you install automatically launch and work with the Add or Remove Programs option. It is the safest and most thorough way to remove programs that you no longer want or need unless a program specifies that you remove it through a different method altogether.

When you remove software through Add or Remove Programs, Windows scans your system for all files

and entries that are related to the software, and deletes them. Windows tries to ensure that only those files are removed.

If you attempt to remove a program in another way, such as by manually deleting individual files, then you may inadvertently remove a file that is needed by other programs. You may also cause Windows to no longer run, or to run improperly.

See also>> **Add or Remove Programs**

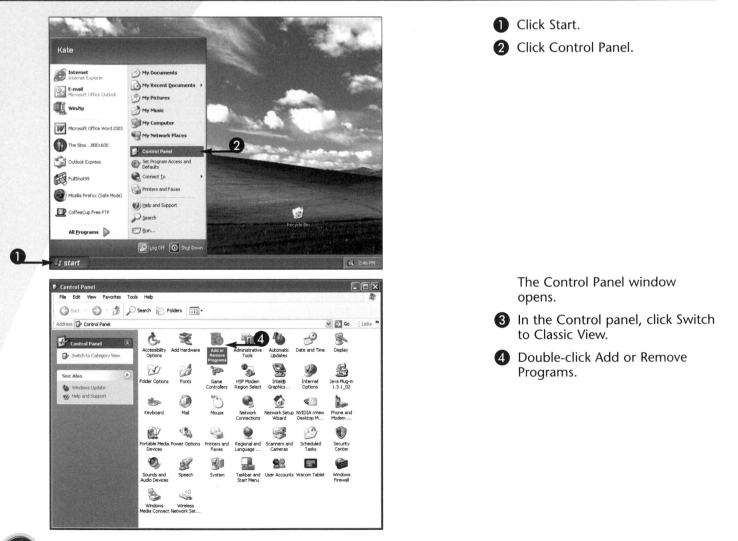

① Click Start.

② Click Control Panel.

The Control Panel window opens.

③ In the Control panel, click Switch to Classic View.

④ Double-click Add or Remove Programs.

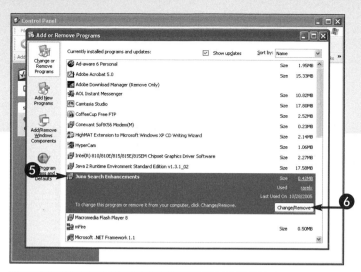

The Add or Remove Programs window appears.

5 Click the program that you want to remove.

6 Click Change/Remove.

With some software choices, you may see separate Change and Remove buttons.

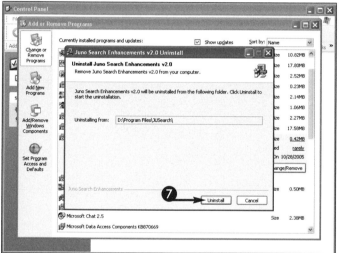

A window opens, named for the program that you want to remove.

Different programs that you remove may produce different windows. You should follow the on-screen instructions.

7 Click Uninstall.

Windows deletes the program, and it no longer appears in your Add or Remove Programs software list.

TIPS

Attention!
If you experience difficulty when you try to remove a program, then you may want to shut down and then restart your Windows computer before you try again. Restarting forces Windows to write all open files to disk before the shut down, which may eliminate a conflict that keeps you from removing the program.

Try This!
A program that you try to uninstall may refuse to be removed. In this situation, you can reinstall the software before you try to uninstall it through Add or Remove Programs. You can also check to see if the program has an uninstall tool that you can use instead.

ADDRESS BAR:
Open Local Resources

You can use the Address Bar in the Microsoft Internet Explorer Web browser to type more than your favorite Web site address. The Address Bar appears as a text dialog box where you can also type the address of a location on your network, such as a shared folder or drive found on another computer on the network. When you do this, you can work with local resources on your system without the need to open My Computer or Windows Explorer as well as your already-opened browser.

You can click within the Address Bar without typing to see a menu list of recently used Internet or network addresses. From this drop-down menu, you can click to choose a previously typed uniform resource locator, or URL, or another network resource, rather than type the address again.

When you click Favorites and then click to select a stored link, this address appears in your Address Bar, and Internet Explorer opens that Internet or network address.

Type a URL in the Address Bar

1 Click Start.

2 Click Internet Explorer.

Microsoft Internet Explorer opens.

3 Click inside the Address Bar and type the Internet or network address that you want to open.

4 Click the Go arrow or press Enter.

The selected address opens in the browser.

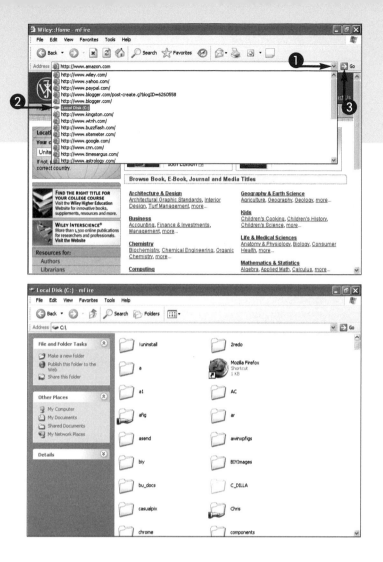

Open a Previously Typed Address

1. Click the Address Bar down arrow.

   A drop-down list box appears.

2. Click the address that you want to open.

3. Click the Go arrow.

The selected address opens in the browser.

TIPS

Attention!

If you empty your Internet Explorer history cache or use the Disk Cleanup Wizard, then previously typed or opened listings may no longer appear in the drop-down list box for you to select. However, as you use the browser, this listing will re-populate with addresses that you visit.

Did You Know?

You do not always have to type the entire address, such as the http:// preface, to open a local or Internet address. Internet Explorer makes the best guess on what to open if you type an abbreviated address.

More Options!

Instead of using the Address Bar to access a location in Internet Explorer, you can also click File and then click Open. An Open window appears in which you can type the address that you want to open on a local or network drive.

ADDRESS BOOK:
Import and Export Entries

You can import and export contact names and e-mail addresses from the Windows Address Book. The Address Book is used by Microsoft Outlook Express, the e-mail software component of Microsoft Internet Explorer. When you use the Address Book, you save time and effort that you would normally spend re-creating this information manually.

For example, you can use the Import feature to add addresses that are stored elsewhere — such as in another program or on another computer — to your Address Book. Likewise, you can export or create a copy of your Address Book listings, which you can then import into another program or transfer to another Windows computer.

When you import a file into the Address Book, you must provide the location of the Address Book file that you are importing; these files are saved with the .wab file extension. When you export a file from the Address Book, you must specify a name for the file that you want to export.

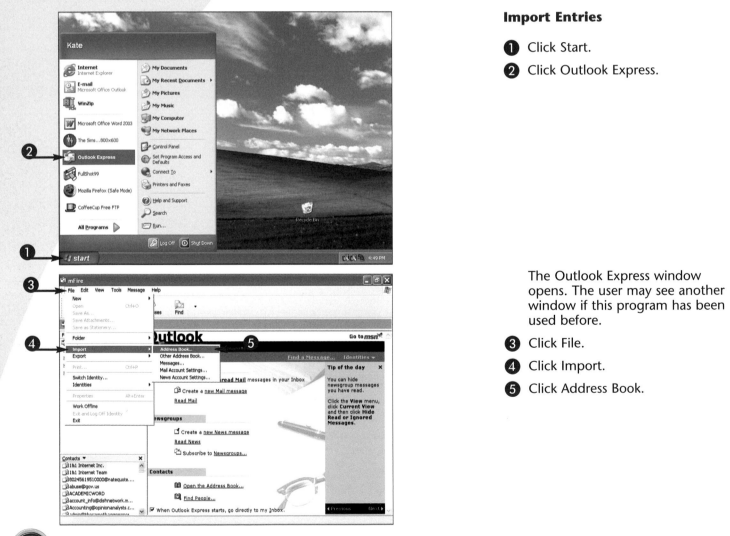

Import Entries

1 Click Start.

2 Click Outlook Express.

The Outlook Express window opens. The user may see another window if this program has been used before.

3 Click File.

4 Click Import.

5 Click Address Book.

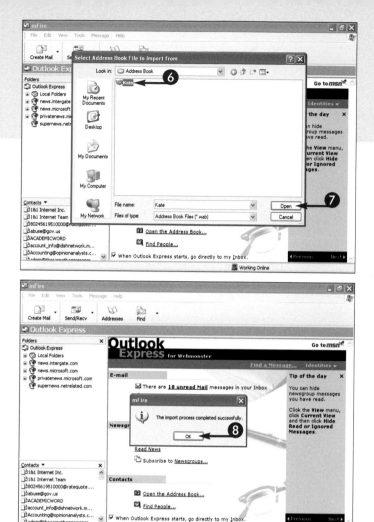

The Select Address Book File to Import from dialog box appears.

⑥ Locate and click the Address Book file that you want to import.

You can use the Search tool to help you locate the Address Book file to import. Click the Windows Start button at the bottom-left corner of the desktop and then click Search.

⑦ Click Open.

A progress window appears.

⑧ When the import process is complete, click OK.

The entries from the imported Address Book now appear in your current Address Book.

TIPS

Attention!

You can import the contents or entries from more than one Address Book into your current address list. For example, you may have multiple WAB files that you want to copy from other computer setups. Simply import each file, one at a time, by following the steps in this section.

Did You Know?

Once you import entries from another Address Book into Outlook Express, you can modify individual entries. See Address Book: Manage Contacts for more information.

Important!

If you use Microsoft Outlook instead of Outlook Express, then you can use the same basic steps to import as well as export Address Book entries. Both Outlook and Outlook Express handle Address Book entries in the same way.

ADDRESS BOOK:
Import and Export Entries (Continued)

One of the most useful things that you can do with your Address Book contact entries is to export them to a file that you can then import into another program. This feature allows you to gather your contacts from e-mail software like Outlook Express and Windows that share the same Address Book and use them to create a new file without having to retype a single field of information.

For example, you can export contact entries in the Address Book to a text file that can serve as the

basis for an Excel or other type of spreadsheet that you create. You can also use the exported file to begin an Access or other database that contains exactly the same fields — e-mail, first name, last name, and so on — as your Address Book. This saves you the time that you would otherwise spend copying them from one program to another.

See also>> **Files and Settings Transfer Wizard**

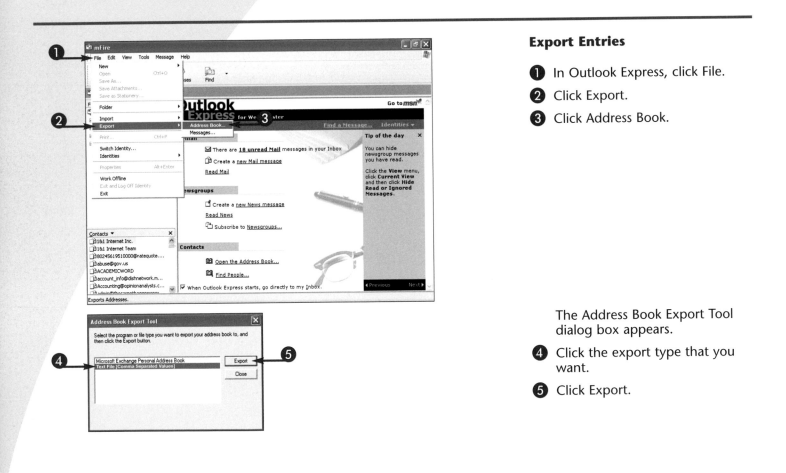

Export Entries

1 In Outlook Express, click File.

2 Click Export.

3 Click Address Book.

The Address Book Export Tool dialog box appears.

4 Click the export type that you want.

5 Click Export.

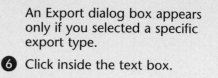

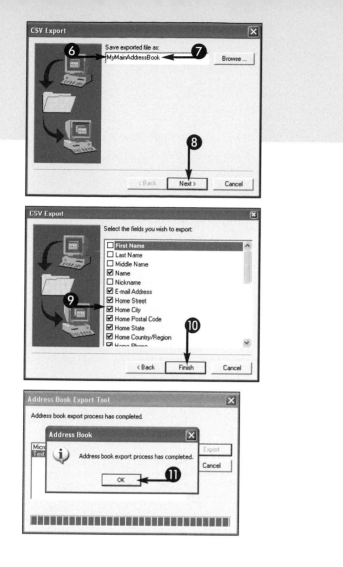

An Export dialog box appears only if you selected a specific export type.

6 Click inside the text box.

7 Type a name for the exported file.

8 Click Next.

9 Click to select the Address Book entry that you want to export.

10 Click Finish.

A progress window appears, displaying the export process.

An Address Book dialog box appears, stating that the export process is complete.

11 Click OK.

The Address Book saves your exported entries with the filename that you provided.

TIPS

Attention!

Although you can use the Search tool to locate Address Book files that you want to import, you can also find these files directly in the Documents and Settings*UserName*\\Application Data\\ Microsoft\\Address Book folder.

Caution!

When you export Address Book entries, your best option is to export them as a text file with commas between each field in each entry, as shown in Step 4. This file type is compatible with almost all other types of e-mail and other programs.

More Options!

If you need to transfer more than Address Book entries between two computers, then you can use the Files and Settings Transfer Wizard instead.

ADDRESS BOOK:
Manage Contacts

You can use tools within the Address Book to manage your contacts. The Address Book management tools become important when you have added numerous entries to your Address Book, and you find that the listing has become large and unwieldy. Unless you manage your contacts, you may discover multiple unwanted or outdated entries, or that you are missing key contact information. Your best option is to review and manage your contacts often to prevent this situation altogether.

The Address Book allows you to delete unwanted entries. You can also add or edit information to

existing entries, such as when a contact changes their e-mail address, or provides you with an additional phone number.

The more frequently that you use your Address Book to store primary contact details for people that you communicate with, the more vital it is that you manage your entries to keep them up-to-date and viable.

See also>> **Address Book**

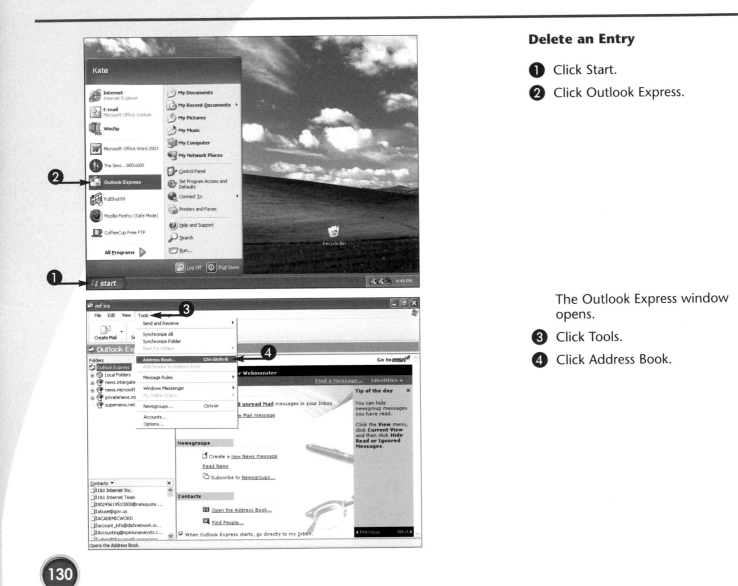

Delete an Entry

① Click Start.

② Click Outlook Express.

The Outlook Express window opens.

③ Click Tools.

④ Click Address Book.

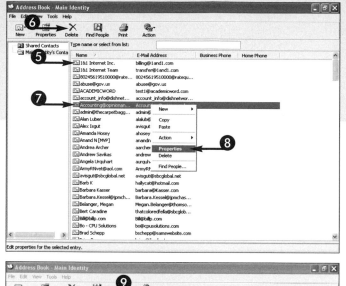

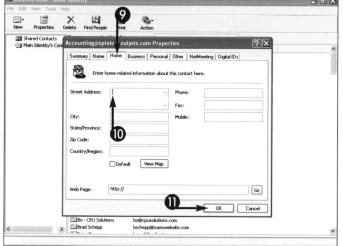

The Address Book window opens.

5 Click the entry that you want to remove.

6 Click Delete.

The entry disappears from the listing.

Modify an Entry

7 Right-click the entry that you want to change.

8 Click Properties in the submenu.

A Properties dialog box appears for the entry.

9 Click the tab that you want to change.

10 Click in the fields and type to add or edit the details.

11 Click OK.

The Address Book saves the entry changes.

TIPS

Did You Know?
Your contact list in the Address Book also shares information with other tools, such as Windows Messenger.

Important!
If you do not want to risk the loss of your contacts, then you must perform backups that include a copy of your Address book. You can do this through the Backup Wizard by selecting a backup of Documents and Settings.

Did You Know?
You can find your Address Book file in the Documents and Settings*UserName*\\Application Data\\Microsoft\\Address Book folder. The Address Book is named for your user account, with a .wab file extension. For example, if your name is John, then the name of the Address Book file is john.wab.

ALL PROGRAMS:
Locate and Launch Programs

To locate and launch a program in Windows, you can use the All Programs menu that is found in the Start menu. When you install a program in Windows, an entry for this program should automatically appear in the All Programs menu.

In some cases, the program appears directly in the All Programs menu list. In other cases, you must click a heading in the All Programs menu to display a sub-menu that contains the program name. The All Programs menu contains sub-menu categories such as Accessories and Games.

When you find the name of the program that you want, you can click it to load the application. For example, if you install Microsoft Office, then an entry appears in the All Programs menu, labeled Microsoft Office. You can click this heading to display a sub-menu where you can launch a specific program such as Microsoft Word or Excel.

See also>>   **Add or Remove Programs**

Launch a Program

1 Click Start.

2 Click All Programs.

A listing appears of all installed programs and packages.

3 Click the program that you want to launch.

Some programs may nest beneath headings. In this case, you must click an entry in the All Programs menu and then click each successive sub-menu until you reach your selection.

The program that you choose opens on your desktop.

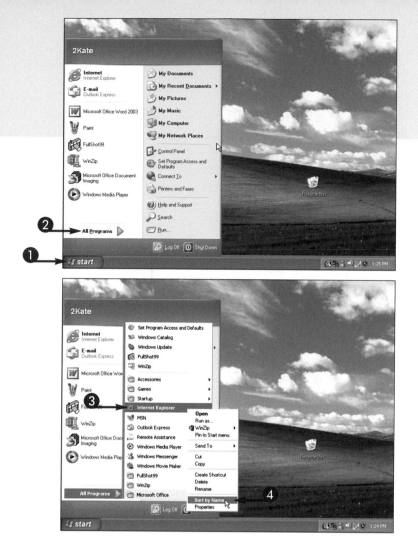

Sort All Programs Listing

1 Click Start.

2 Click All Programs.

A sub-menu appears.

3 Right-click a menu selection.

4 In the menu that appears, click Sort by Name.

The list now appears in alphabetical order by name.

TIPS

Attention!

Although the Sort feature allows you to reorder your All Programs listing alphabetically, Windows normally lists all options with sub-menus first, followed by individual program choices.

More Options!

You can rename a program listing. Right-click it, and then click Rename in the sub-menu that appears. When an outline appears around the current name, click the name, then press Delete, and then type a new name.

Did You Know?

When you sort your All Programs list by name, Windows automatically reorganizes all sub-menu listings into alphabetical order, as well.

Remove It!

If you do not want a program to appear on the All Programs list, then right-click the selection that you want to remove and click Delete in the sub-menu. Keep in mind that when you remove a selection from All Programs, it does not remove the software from your computer.

AUDIO:
Review Sound Options

You can view, configure, and refine virtually all options for playing sound through your computer in the Sounds and Audio Devices Properties dialog box, which you can access through the Control Panel. This means that you can adjust your speaker setup as well as configure for the use of an installed microphone and other devices from within Windows.

You can also set up additional speaker support, such as for a sophisticated home theatre 5:1 speaker configuration, and specify when and how sounds are played. For example, although certain events in Windows trigger specific sounds to play, you can customize this feature to play sound files that you create. This is called a sound scheme.

You can also set up and control Musical Instrument Digital Interface, or MIDI, devices through the Sounds and Audio Devices controls. You can then add a MIDI keyboard, an electronic drum pad, or other items to turn your computer into a digital recording studio.

See also>> **Volume Control**

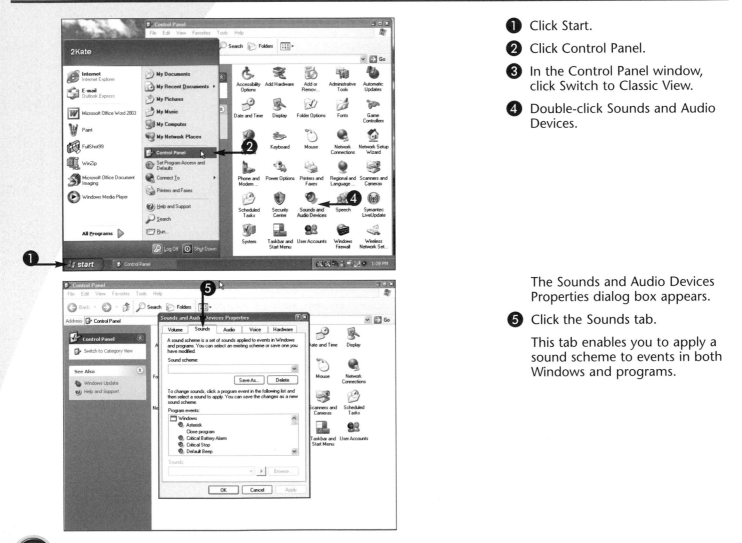

1. Click Start.
2. Click Control Panel.
3. In the Control Panel window, click Switch to Classic View.
4. Double-click Sounds and Audio Devices.

The Sounds and Audio Devices Properties dialog box appears.

5. Click the Sounds tab.

   This tab enables you to apply a sound scheme to events in both Windows and programs.

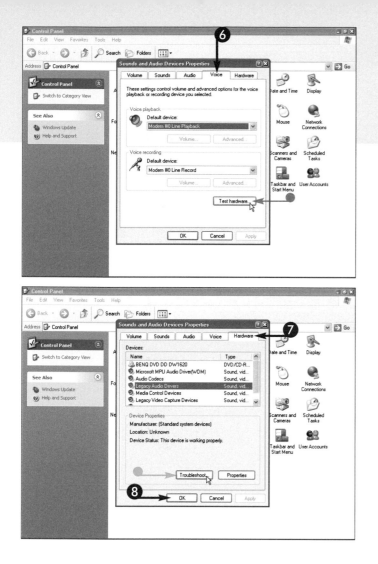

6 Click the Voice tab.

This tab enables you to control the volume for voice playback and microphone recording.

● If you set up a microphone, then click Test hardware to see if it works.

7 Click the Hardware tab.

This tab enables you to troubleshoot hardware.

● You can click a device in the list, and then click Troubleshoot to look for problems.

8 Click OK.

Your audio hardware and sounds are now configured for use.

TIPS

Did You Know?
If you experience problems with hearing sounds, then you should open the Sounds and Audio Devices Properties dialog box first. If Windows detects a sound or audio card, then this information appears on the first tab that opens. If not, the first tab reports no audio device is detected.

Try This!
The Speech feature in Control Panel is designed to help you teach Windows XP to handle voice commands and dictation, using your microphone.

Test It!
When you set up a microphone for use with Windows XP, you can open Sound Recorder to record a short sound file to test the volume and direction of the microphone. To open Sound Recorder, click Start, click All Programs, click Accessories, click Entertainment, and then click Sound Recorder. Click the red dotted button to record; click it again to stop.

AUTOMATIC UPDATES:
Configure Automatic Updates

Windows XP is a complex operating system that requires updates and patches against new security threats and viruses. Microsoft constantly develops and publishes updates for Windows to make it work better, and to be more secure and reliable.

You can manually obtain updates and patches from the Windows Update Web site, located at http://update.microsoft.com. However, manual updates do require some pre-planning and organization on your part, and your busy schedule can make it difficult for you to remember or have time to perform the updates.

Windows XP includes an Automatic Updates feature to automate the update and patch process. For example, you can schedule Automatic Updates to automatically download and install updates on a regular basis, such as every day at 2:00 A.M.

If you prefer to have more control over these updates, then you can configure Automatic Updates to download the updates but not install them until you direct it to do so. This option offers the advantage of automatic updates and notification, as well as control over when Windows applies these updates.

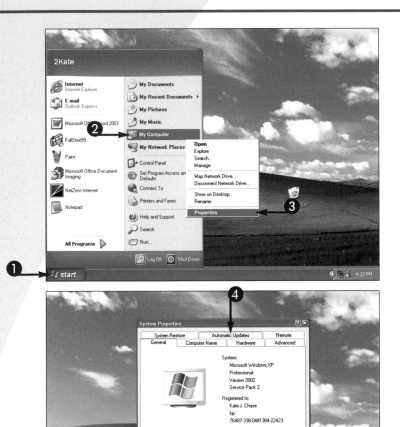

❶ Click Start.

❷ Right-click My Computer.

❸ Click Properties in the menu that appears.

The System Properties dialog box appears.

You can also open the System Properties dialog box through the System icon in the Control Panel.

❹ Click the Automatic Updates tab.

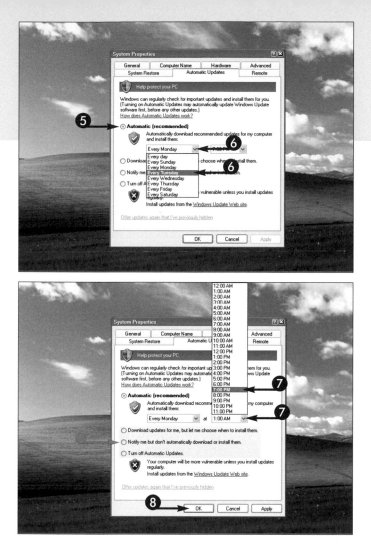
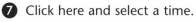

5 Click the Automatic option to turn on Automatic Updates.

6 Click here and select an update schedule.

A

7 Click here and select a time.

● Alternatively, you can select a semi-automatic update option.

8 Click OK.

You are now configured for Automatic Updates on the schedule you set.

TIPS

Attention!
Some updates may require your computer to restart in order to finish the installation procedure. If you are away from your desk when the update installs, then Windows automatically restarts.

More Options!
To review and remove an automatic update from your system, consult the list of applied updates, which is available under the Add and Remove Programs feature in the Control Panel when you click Add or Remove Windows Components.

Caution!
Occasionally, an update that is applied to your Windows XP setup may cause a problem that either prevents Windows from a normal startup or makes the system seem less stable during a session. If you suspect that a recent update does not work well with your computer, then you can review and, if necessary, remove an update.

AUTORUN:
Disable AutoRun for CD/DVD Drives

If you want to prevent other users from installing new software on your computer, then you can disable the AutoRun feature for CD and DVD drives. The AutoRun feature enables most Windows computers to instantly detect when you place a CD or DVD into the appropriate drive, and to respond accordingly.

For example, if you insert a music CD or DVD movie, then the preferred software, such as Media Player, loads and plays that disc without your help. Similarly, if the disc contains setup files for a program, then Windows launches the install routine.

You can disable AutoRun by editing the Windows Registry, which is the master information file that keeps track of all Windows settings. However, it is usually not recommended to edit the Registry unless you have a backup of your Registry files, System Restore, or a full backup of your system. You can perform a backup or create a fresh System Restore before you proceed.

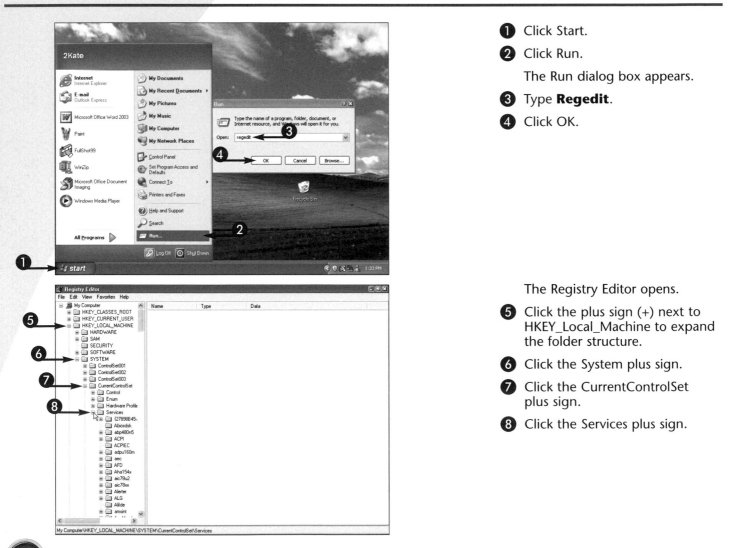

1 Click Start.

2 Click Run.

The Run dialog box appears.

3 Type **Regedit**.

4 Click OK.

The Registry Editor opens.

5 Click the plus sign (+) next to HKEY_Local_Machine to expand the folder structure.

6 Click the System plus sign.

7 Click the CurrentControlSet plus sign.

8 Click the Services plus sign.

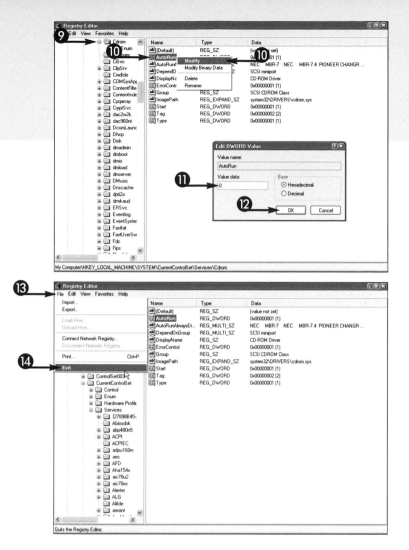

9 Click the Cdrom folder.

The registry entry, called the registry key, for this section opens in the right-hand pane.

10 Right-click AutoRun and select Modify.

The Edit DWORD Value dialog box appears.

11 Type **0** (zero) in the Value data field to replace the current value.

12 Click OK.

13 Click File.

14 Click Exit.

The editor closes with the Registry value changed to disable AutoRun.

TIPS

Attention!

In order to disable AutoRun in your Windows Registry, you must be logged in as an Administrator or a Power User. A user with Limited account status usually cannot install software. If the other users on your computer have limited accounts, then disabling the AutoRun feature is usually not necessary.

Did You Know?

AutoRun works when a specific file — one named AutoRun.inf — is located on a recorded CD or DVD. If, when you insert a disc into the drive, Windows checks and finds the AutoRun.inf file, then it immediately begins to run or load whatever program or file is on the disc. When you disable AutoRun, you stop Windows from performing this check.

BACKGROUND:
Set the Desktop Background

One of the easiest ways to customize your Windows workspace is to reset the default desktop background. You can choose one of the pre-designed backgrounds that are available through Windows, create your own background, or use a favorite Web page or photo as a background. You can create your own desktop theme or select a pre-existing Windows theme to modify your Windows environment beyond the desktop background.

If you want, you can choose from a wide range of theme choices to change your desktop every day. Your only limitation is your imagination and the

images that are available to you for your background selection. Even then, many online resources provide libraries of art that you can download and use for this purpose. You can also find themes on Microsoft's Web site.

In this section, you learn how to apply a different theme to your desktop background. If you have already customized your desktop, then you can view additional choices in the background list.

See also>> **Themes**

❶ Right-click a blank spot on your desktop.

A sub-menu appears.

❷ Click Properties.

The Display Properties dialog box appears.

❸ Click the Desktop tab.

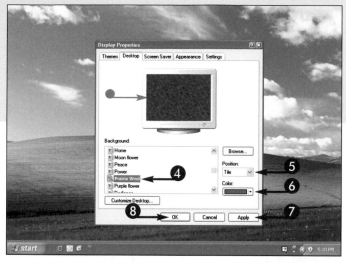

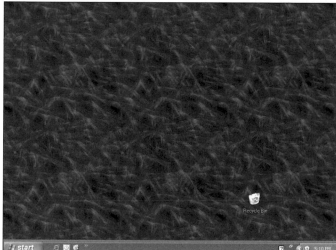

The Desktop tab appears.

4 From the Background list, select a background option.

● Your selection appears in the monitor display at the top of the window.

5 Click here and select how you want to position your background.

6 Click here and select a color to surround your background.

7 Click apply.

8 Click OK.

The new desktop background appears on the desktop.

B

TIPS

Did You Know?
Files used for background images are usually Windows bitmap files that end with the .bmp file extension. However, you can also use GIF, JPG or JPEG, DIB, or PNG files as the desktop background. You can also use an HTM or HTML file, which enables you to use your favorite Web site as the background image.

Warning!
Desktop backgrounds can be quite large, particularly those from digital cameras. The background image consumes resources, and during a very busy Windows session with many programs and files open, it may cause a low memory warning. Use an image-editing program such as Photoshop to reduce the color depth and resolution of the photo.

BACKGROUND:
Use a Digital Photo as a Desktop Background

Besides the background choices that are available to you through Display Properties in Windows, you can also use many types of images as a desktop background. For example, if you have a stunning photograph of the moon taken with your telescope, or your last vacation spot, or an adorable shot of a child or puppy, then you can also turn this image into a desktop background. The same is true of a great image that you happen to see on a Web site and that you save to your hard disk.

When you choose an image to use as a background, you may want to adjust its position on the desktop. For example, it may look better if it is centered on the desktop.

After you change your background, you can check the results on your desktop to ensure that your icons display clearly. If they do not, then you can choose a more suitable background. You can also adjust the size of your icons to make them more visible.

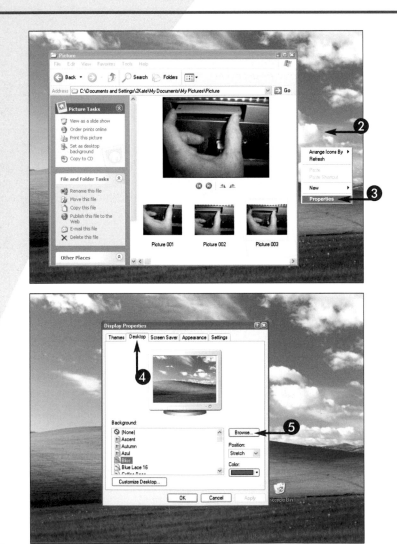

1 Locate the file that you want to use as your background image.

If necessary, convert the file into a BMP file or other compatible format.

2 Right-click a blank spot on your desktop.

A sub-menu appears.

3 Click Properties.

The Display Properties dialog box appears.

4 Click the Desktop tab.

5 Click Browse.

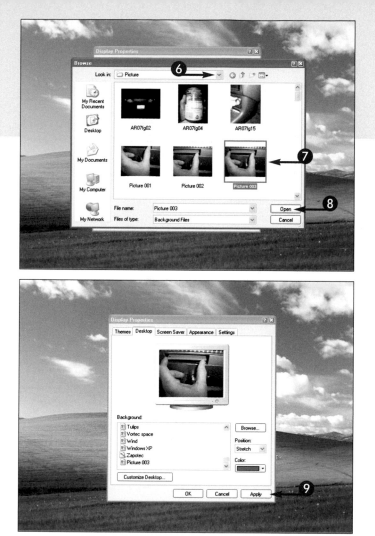

The Browse dialog box appears.

6 Locate the folder that contains your background file.

7 Select the file.

8 Click Open.

The image appears in the monitor in the Desktop tab.

9 Click Apply.

The background image you chose appears on your desktop.

TIPS

Try It!

To adjust the positioning of the background, you can click the Position drop-down list box in the Desktop tab of the Display Properties dialog box. Choose Stretch to fill the entire screen with the image, Center to place the image in the center of the screen, or Tile to display the image as tiles across the desktop.

Did You Know?

You can use an HTM or HTML file as the desktop background. This enables you to use your favorite Web page as the background. However, using an HTM or HTML file results in a static desktop. If you want a dynamic desktop that shows a live Web site on the Internet, then you must use the Windows XP Active Desktop feature. See the section, Active Desktop: Add dynamic content to the desktop.

BACKUP:
Make Backups Automatic

It is vital to make backups of the files and settings on your computer so that you can restore your system after a disaster. You can schedule backups through the Backup Wizard to run automatically, to ensure that you do not forget to perform manual backups. Also, by scheduling your backups, you can run this utility when you are away from your desktop, such as after you leave your office or home computer for the night.

It is important to have up-to-date backups because failing to do so can leave you with only a very old backup copy to depend on if you need to restore

your system due to an emergency.

Depending on the age and overall performance of your Windows XP system, the backup process can seriously affect the speed at which you can work with other programs. Scheduling backups while you are away from your desktop means that your work is not slowed down while the utility is backing up your system. Windows stores your backups with the .bkf file extension.

See also>> **Backup Tool**

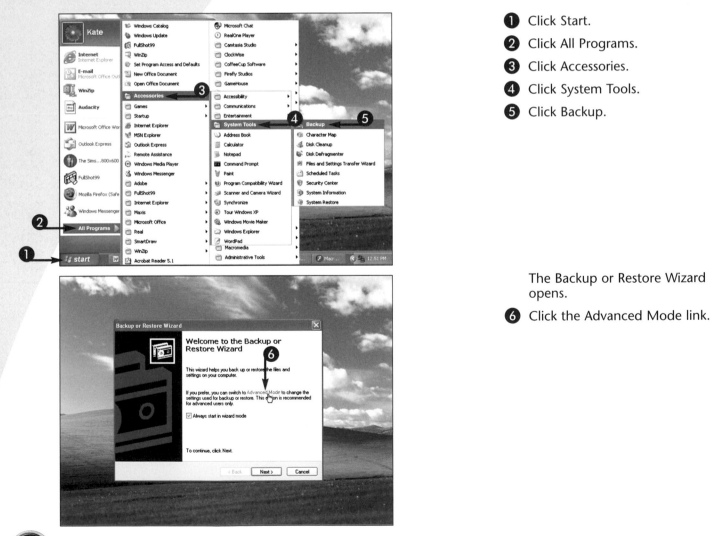

1 Click Start.

2 Click All Programs.

3 Click Accessories.

4 Click System Tools.

5 Click Backup.

The Backup or Restore Wizard opens.

6 Click the Advanced Mode link.

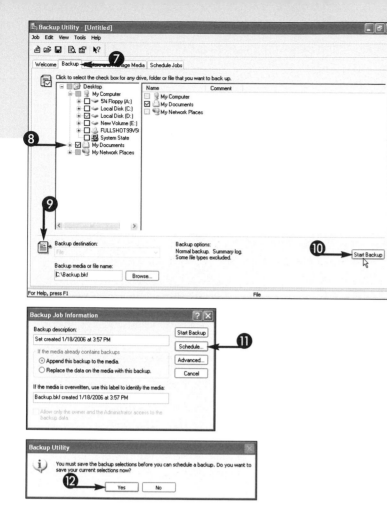

7 In the Backup Utility that opens, click the Backup tab.

8 Click to select the drive or folder that you want to back up.

9 If you need to change the storage location or filename for your backup, then click here and type a new location or filename.

If you have already performed a backup, then Windows automatically chooses the previous backup location.

10 Click Start Backup.

The Backup Job Information dialog box appears.

11 Click Schedule.

You may be prompted for your password, depending on which Windows XP Service Packs, if any, you have installed. Type the password, retype it in the Confirm Password text box, and then click OK.

The Backup Utility dialog box appears.

12 Click Yes to save your selections before you proceed.

TIPS

Attention!

Regardless of what you use your Windows computer for, it is important to back up your files on a regular basis. The best way to do this is by using automatic backups. Automatic backups can run when you are not at your computer and do not depend on you remembering to create them.

Did You Know?

When you create backups through the Backup Utility, it automatically compresses the contents of whatever drive or folder you are copying. This means that the size required for these files once they are compressed into a master backup file can be up to 50 percent less than the disk space that they require in their current drive or folder location.

BACKUP:
Make Backups Automatic (Continued)

When you select a backup drive, you must choose a drive with enough space to hold your backup file, which may require many gigabytes. You cannot back up directly to a CD drive because only smaller backups, such as Documents and Settings, can fit on a single recordable CD. Normally, a second hard disk — you do not want your backup copy stored on the same hard disk that is being backed up — is your best bet for capacity and speed.

You can schedule your backup to run every day, every week, or every month. You can also set it up to run when you are away from your desk, such as at the end of the day or during the evening. To do this, you must supply both your Windows user account name and your valid password. Without access to your account, Windows cannot run the backup as scheduled.

See also>> Scheduled Tasks Folder

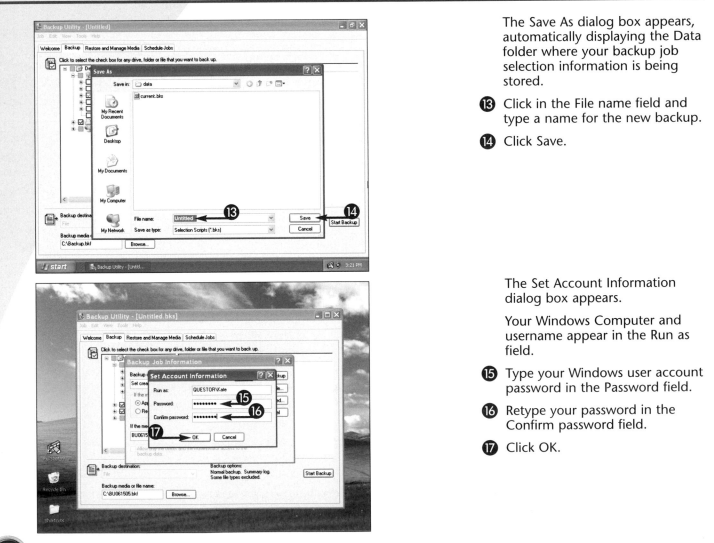

The Save As dialog box appears, automatically displaying the Data folder where your backup job selection information is being stored.

⑬ Click in the File name field and type a name for the new backup.

⑭ Click Save.

The Set Account Information dialog box appears.

Your Windows Computer and username appear in the Run as field.

⑮ Type your Windows user account password in the Password field.

⑯ Retype your password in the Confirm password field.

⑰ Click OK.

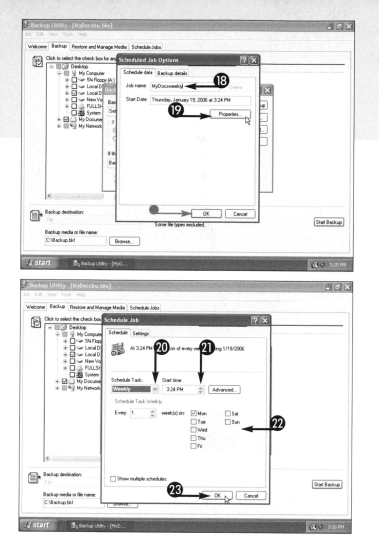

The Scheduled Job Options dialog box appears.

⑱ In the Job name field of the Schedule data tab, type a name for the new backup.

⑲ Click Properties to set a schedule for the backup.

● To start the backup immediately, you can click OK.

The Schedule Job dialog box appears.

⑳ In the Schedule tab, click here and select Weekly to make this a weekly backup.

㉑ Click here to adjust the start time.

㉒ Click here to select the start day of the week.

㉓ Click OK.

Windows sets the backup schedule according to your selections.

TIPS

Did You Know?

When you schedule a backup job, Windows adds it to your scheduled task list. When tasks are scheduled, a Scheduled Task icon appears in your Windows System Tray at the bottom-right corner of your desktop, where the time displays. Simply click this icon to display a list of scheduled operations.

Warning!

Ensure that you schedule your backup during a time that your computer will actually be on and available to perform the job. If you schedule the operation for when you are not normally at your desk, then you may want to use My Computer to browse the drive to where the backup file was stored to ensure that the backup was actually performed.

CD WRITING WIZARD:
Create CDs from Windows

Unlike earlier versions of Windows, you can create and record, or burn, CDs directly from Windows XP without special software, similar to when you copy or move files to a hard disk or floppy disk. In fact, when you insert a blank recordable CD-R or CD-RW disc into your recordable CD or DVD drive, Windows opens a window named for the CD/DVD drive letter. This window serves as a holding area into which you can copy or move your files until you are ready to create the disc.

You can use either My Computer or Windows Explorer to locate, select, and copy or move files from their current folder to the CD/DVD drive window. My Computer offers additional options in the left-hand task pane to help you as you move or copy your files. As you work, keep in mind that you cannot write more files and folders to the CD than it can handle — usually a capacity of about 650MB.

See also>> **File and Folder Management**

❶ Insert a blank recordable CD-R or CD-RW disc into your recordable CD drive.

A CD drive window opens, identifying the drive letter.

❷ Click Open writable CD folder using Windows Explorer.

Windows Explorer opens, displaying the folder window for the CD/DVD drive.

3 Click Start.

4 Click My Computer.

The My Computer window opens.

5 Click the disk or folder that contains the files or folders that you want to copy to the CD.

TIPS

Attention!

You can either permanently move files to a CD or just copy them to the CD. The difference between these operations is that a copy leaves the original versions behind on your hard disk, while moving transfers your only copy to the CD.

Try This!

If you have a very full hard disk from which you are moving files to a recordable CD, then you may need to free up some disk space before you can successfully record the CD. This is because Windows needs disk space to temporarily store these files that it is moving or copying until they are written to the CD. You can run the Disk Cleanup Wizard to free up disk space.

CD WRITING WIZARD:
Create CDs from Windows (Continued)

When you create CDs from Windows, you can perform a number of different tasks in one operation. For example, you can create a manual backup by copying important files that you do not want to lose. This enables you to retain a copy of those files, even if a disaster occurs on the hard disk or the computer where the original files are located.

You can also create a CD that contains files that you want to share with others. For example, you can

copy all of the digital photos that you took on your last vacation and send them to friends and family members.

You can create a CD of files that you need to share with a client or with other employees in your department. You can also create a CD that copies the chapters of a book or long report that you have put together, and then send the CD instead of a heavy, printed report.

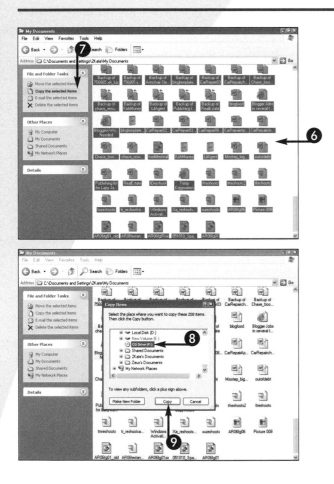

⑥ Click to select the files or folders that you want to copy.

You can press and hold the Ctrl key to select more than one file.

⑦ In the File and Folder Tasks pane, click Copy the selected items.

The Copy Items dialog box appears.

⑧ Click the CD drive in the list.

⑨ Click Copy.

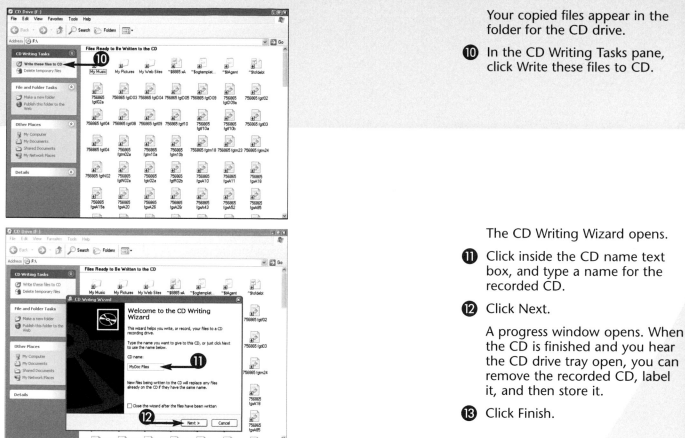

Your copied files appear in the folder for the CD drive.

⑩ In the CD Writing Tasks pane, click Write these files to CD.

The CD Writing Wizard opens.

⑪ Click inside the CD name text box, and type a name for the recorded CD.

⑫ Click Next.

A progress window opens. When the CD is finished and you hear the CD drive tray open, you can remove the recorded CD, label it, and then store it.

⑬ Click Finish.

TIPS

Attention!
A normal recordable data CD holds about 650MB. If you try to move more files than the recordable CD can hold, then Windows only warns you about this once you begin to write the files to the CD.

Did You Know?
Once you store files on a recordable CD, these files are read-only. However, if you copy them back to a hard disk, then you can once again open the files, edit them, and re-save them.

Try This!
To learn the size of a file that you want to copy to CD, right-click the file and choose Properties. The file size displays in the Properties window.

CLASSIC START MENU:
Switch to the Classic Start Menu

You can modify the appearance, and some of the functionality, of your Windows desktop and core components, such as the Start Menu, when you switch to the Classic style from the more modern Windows XP style. The effects of your change can be more than aesthetic for several reasons.

In the Windows Classic style, more options become available when you customize the Start Menu. For example, in Classic, you can *pin*, or add, a program that you frequently open to the list of available applications that appear in the Start Menu. By comparison, in the Windows XP style, Windows

determines which programs appear in the initial Start Menu.

You also gain an additional benefit when you switch styles for other core components like the Control Panel. Many Windows help articles and books convey instructions based on the Classic style. When you convert to Classic, your setup now appears the same as the setup in these instructions.

See also>>   **Start Menu**

1 Right-click an empty area on the taskbar.

A sub-menu appears.

2 Click Properties.

The Taskbar and Start Menu Properties dialog box appears.

3 Click the Start Menu tab.

④ Click to select the Classic Start menu option.

⑤ Click OK.

The Start Menu appears in the Classic style.

TIPS

Customize It!
If you want to make additional changes to the appearance of your Windows desktop, then click the Customize button in the Start Menu tab in the Taskbar and Start Menu Properties dialog box. You can choose the number of programs to show on the Start menu, or clear the current list of recently used programs.

Try This!
If you are new to Windows XP and find it hard to acclimate to the new look, then you can switch to the more familiar Classic style.

Did You Know?
When you change to the Classic style, more than your Start Menu changes. For example, shortcut icons appear along the upper-left side of your desktop for standard Windows components such as My Documents and My Network Places. You can delete these icons or leave them in place.

CLIPBOARD:
Copy Material Between Programs

If you have worked with Microsoft Office, then you know how easy it is to copy material such as text and data from one open application window to another. However, you may not know that Windows XP also offers its own Clipboard feature.

The Clipboard saves time and keystrokes and improves accuracy by allowing you to copy material between windows. For example, you may want to copy the contents of a page in your Web browser that includes both text and images. The Clipboard

allows you to do this so that you can keep a separate copy, which you can use if you want to save information that you found from a Web site in a special folder.

You can also copy text and Web page links from an open online chat room or from your instant messaging window. This technique also works when you copy from another open document, a spreadsheet, or a database record.

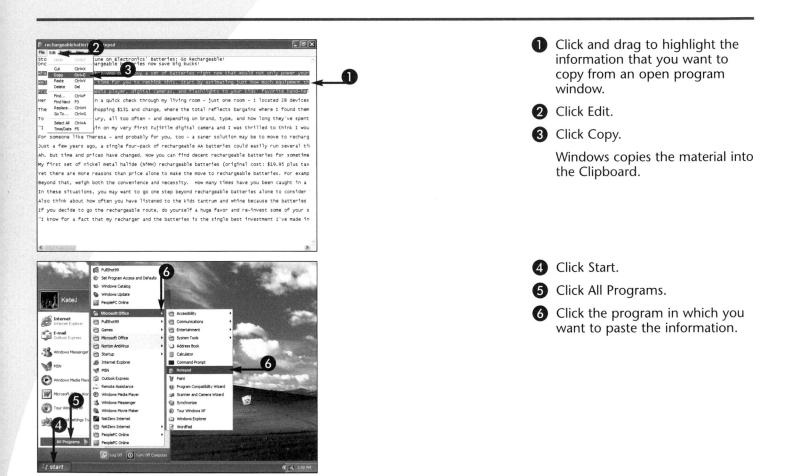

① Click and drag to highlight the information that you want to copy from an open program window.

② Click Edit.

③ Click Copy.

Windows copies the material into the Clipboard.

④ Click Start.

⑤ Click All Programs.

⑥ Click the program in which you want to paste the information.

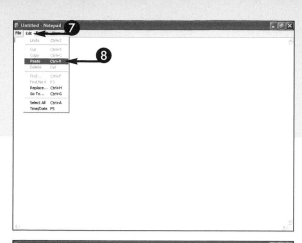

The program window opens.

⑦ Click Edit.

⑧ Click Paste.

C

The pasted material appears in the new window.

CLIPBOARD:
Take a Screenshot

If you ever want to take a picture, or screenshot, of a program window or your desktop, then Windows enables you to do this through the Clipboard. As its name implies, Clipboard is a place where you can store information as you work. Rather than download or buy and install a screen capture utility, you can use Clipboard to save your screenshot.

Once it is snapped, you can paste the screenshot into Windows WordPad, Microsoft Word, or any program that allows you to paste material from another window.

You can use the Clipboard feature in a number of different ways. For example, you can snap a copy of an entire Web page and then save it to disk. You can capture an error message window and send it to technical support when you need help with a problem. You can also take a picture of your settings in a configuration window to share with someone to show them which options should be selected.

See also>>  **Clipboard, Copy Material Between Programs**

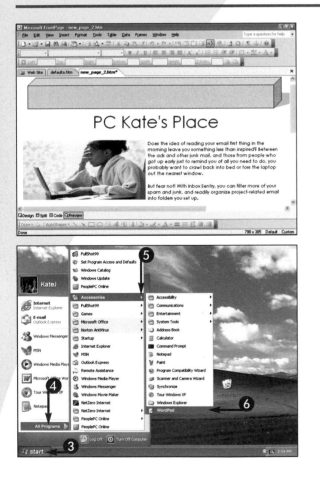

① Open or select the window or item that you want to snap.

② Press Alt+PrtScn.

Windows copies the image onto the Clipboard.

③ Click Start.

④ Click All Programs.

⑤ Click Accessories.

⑥ Click WordPad.

The WordPad window opens.

7 Click Edit.

8 Click Paste.

You can also press Shift+Insert or press Ctrl+V to paste your snapshot into the document.

Your snapshot appears in your WordPad document.

PC Kate's Place

Does the idea of reading your email first thing in the morning leave you something less than inspired? Between the ads and other junk mail, and those from people who got up early just to remind you of all you need to do, you probably want to crawl back into bed or toss the laptop out the nearest window.

But fear not! With Inbox Sentry, you can filter more of your spam and junk, and readily organize project-related email into folders you set up.

TIPS

Attention!
When you capture a snapshot in the Clipboard, you only snap the active window, which means the top-most window on your desktop. If you try to take a picture of an empty desktop, then all you usually capture is the taskbar.

More Options!
If you have difficulty when you try to capture a particular window, then click inside that window with your mouse before you copy it into the clipboard. With the mouse-click, you make that window the active window.

Try This!
You can paste your screenshots into other programs besides WordPad. For example, this technique works well with Microsoft Word or a Web page editor such as Microsoft FrontPage. Keep in mind that you must have a document open to receive your pasted screenshot.

COMMAND PROMPT:
Access Help with Commands

You may not be familiar with the commands that you need to use a tool such as the Command Prompt or Recovery Console. The Help and Support Center within Windows helps you to learn and understand these commands. It supplies a list of commands, a context for their use, and examples of how to use them.

As you work, keep in mind that when you type commands, you must type them correctly and apply *switches* where they are needed. Switches are special features that you can use with commands to specify how a command runs and what it does.

For example, when you run the disk-checking tool, CHKDSK, there are several switches available. You can check a drive and fix any errors found within that drive by entering CHKDSK /F rather than simply reporting such problems to screen. The /F is an example of a switch.

Likewise, when you type any command from the command prompt, you can add the switch /? to automatically view all information about that command. You will see this in the steps that follow.

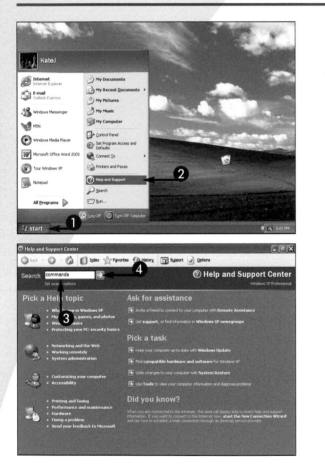

① Click Start.

② Click Help and Support.

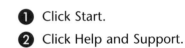

The Help and Support Center window opens.

③ In the Search text box, type **commands**.

You can also search for information about a specific tool, such as FTP, Recovery Console, or Telnet.

④ Click the Go arrow.

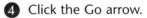

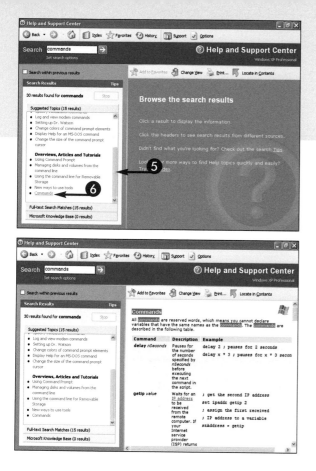

Search results display in the Search Results pane.

5 Scroll down to Overviews, Articles and Tutorials.

6 Click a command.

Information on the command appears in the right-hand pane.

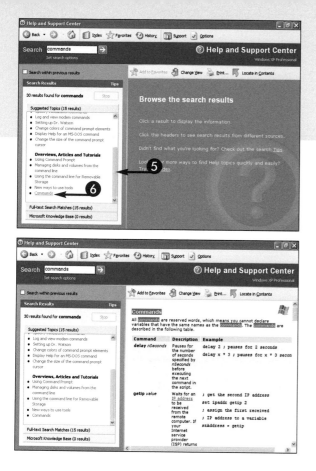

TIPS

Attention!

To access additional help with a specific command, type the command followed by **/?**, such as **ping /?**.

Did You Know?

You can also use commands when you click Start and then click Run. The Run dialog box allows you to execute both commands and their switches, usually with the result that a Command Prompt window opens on your desktop.

More Options!

You can also use the Search option in the Help and Support Center to find information on specific commands. For example, search for chkdsk, which is a disk analysis and repair tool, to learn how to use it and what switches are available for it.

COMMAND PROMPT:
Run Commands

When you need to use programs or utilities that only run from the Command Line, you can load them in one of two ways. You can either open the Command Prompt window, also called the Command console, directly, or you can use the Run option that is available from the Start Menu. You can then type your commands to execute them.

Command Prompt is known as a command line interface. A command is an executable program that usually ends with the file extensions .exe or .com — for example, ping.exe*.

Unlike Windows, where you click an icon to run a program, the commands that you use with Command Prompt are text-based. You type commands at an on-screen prompt and press Enter to run them and load different programs and tools. For example, to load the Ping utility — which you use to check whether you can connect to an Internet or network address — you type **ping** followed by the actual address.

See also>>

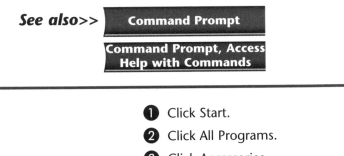

Command Prompt

Command Prompt, Access
Help with Commands

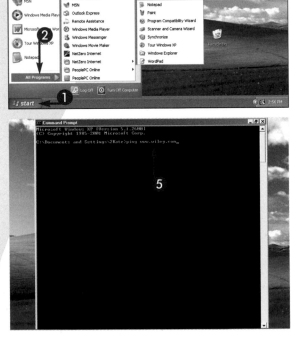

1 Click Start.

2 Click All Programs.

3 Click Accessories.

4 Click Command Prompt.

The Command Prompt console opens.

5 Type a command.

This example uses the command, ping www.wiley.com.

6 Press Enter.

- The program connected to the command or the results of the action performed by the command appear in the console.

⑦ To see what other options you have for a command, type the command name followed by **/?**.

This example uses the ping command.

⑧ Press Enter.

- Information about the command displays in the Command Prompt window.

TIPS

Did You Know?
A small number of applications in Windows can only run from the Command Prompt. For example, CHKDSK is a disk checking utility that only runs at the Command Prompt.

More Options!
The Command Prompt opens as a minimal window on your Windows desktop. Click the Maximize button — the middle button in the top-right row of three buttons — to expand the console.

Important!
You can get assistance from the Command Prompt when you type **help** at the prompt and press Enter. A list of the most frequently used commands appears in the console.

Try This!
To clear your screen in the Command Prompt, type **cls** and press Enter. Everything but the prompt disappears from the console. This command allows you to clear a cluttered screen. You can also scroll up and down within the console.

COMPUTER NAME:
Identify and Change the Computer Name

Every Windows computer has a name, either that you specify, or that Windows provides by default when you install the operating system. You can modify this name to make it unique.

This name identifies the computer, which becomes important if you add the computer to a network. On the network, the name of each computer helps to identify it as a specific workstation, even though it is the Network ID that displays when you use My Network Places and select View workgroup computers. You may also need to provide the name

of a particular computer when you copy or share files or perform other network tasks.

If two computers have very similar or even identical names, then you may want to change one or both names to differentiate them. The name that you choose can be either simple or elaborate. The only important factor is that you can easily distinguish one from another in a network environment.

See also>>

① Click Start.

② Click Control Panel.

The Control Panel opens.

③ In the Control Panel section, click Switch to Classic View.

④ Double-click System.

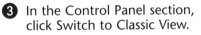

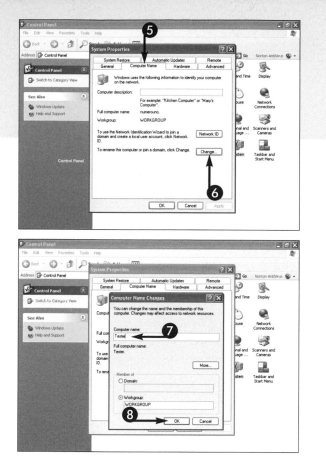

The System Properties dialog box appears.

⑤ Click the Computer Name tab.

⑥ Click Change.

The Computer Name Changes dialog box appears.

⑦ Type a new name for your computer.

⑧ Click OK twice.

Your computer name is now successfully changed.

TIPS

Attention!
You can see the names of all computers in your network through My Network Places. Click Start, click My Network Places, and then click View workgroup computers.

Important!
Keep in mind that your computer name and its network ID are not the same thing, although the terms are sometimes used interchangeably.

Did You Know?
You can also change the description of your computer, which is stored in the Windows Registry as well as appearing on the Welcome screen when you start the computer and before you log on. To do this, repeat Steps 1 to 5. Then click inside the Computer description text box. Type a new name and click OK.

CONTENT ADVISOR:
Enable Parental Controls

To restrict what types of Internet Web sites and other resources your children or anyone who shares your computer can access, you can enable Windows parental controls. Content Advisor, which is part of the Internet Explorer Web browser, serves as the configuration and management utility for these parental controls.

Through Content Advisor, you can make both general and specific selections about what you consider to be acceptable Internet content. For example, many parents want to limit the amount of sexually oriented content that their kids may see through the browser.

However, other people can use it to reduce the likelihood that they themselves will see undesirable material.

Once you enable the parental controls, no one can modify the settings without the supervisor password that you set when you activate the tool. In addition, they cannot turn off Content Advisor without the password, and anyone who tries to access the types of material that you filter out through Content Advisor cannot do so.

See also>>   **Internet Options**

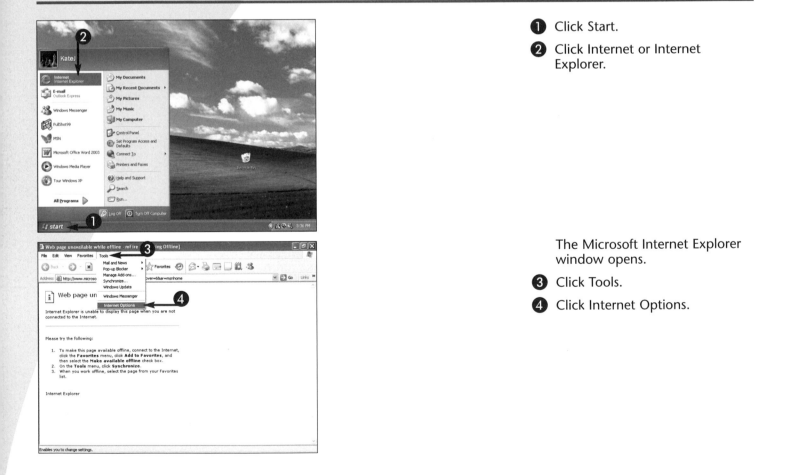

❶ Click Start.

❷ Click Internet or Internet Explorer.

The Microsoft Internet Explorer window opens.

❸ Click Tools.

❹ Click Internet Options.

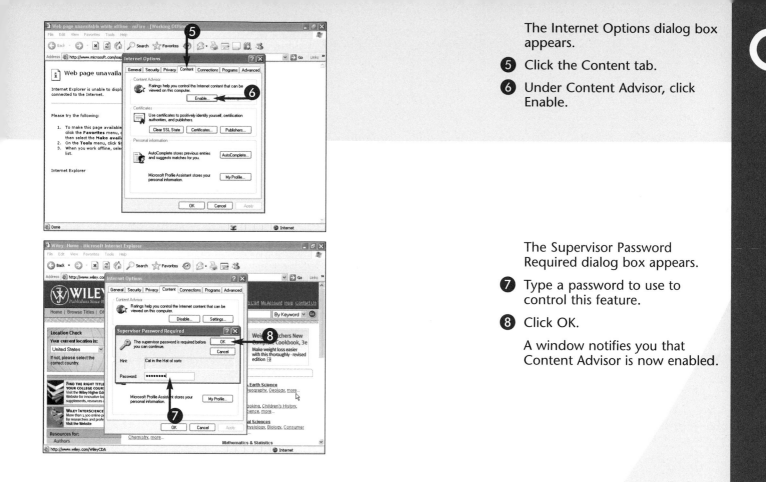

The Internet Options dialog box appears.

⑤ Click the Content tab.

⑥ Under Content Advisor, click Enable.

The Supervisor Password Required dialog box appears.

⑦ Type a password to use to control this feature.

⑧ Click OK.

A window notifies you that Content Advisor is now enabled.

C

TIPS

Attention!
Keep in mind that you should not write down your supervisor password where children can find and read it.

Important!
Use a difficult password with Content Advisor to limit the chance that a child may be able to guess what it is. Passwords of more than six characters that combine a random mix of alphanumeric characters work the best.

More Options!
You can combine the use of Content Advisor with other so-called cyber-sitting software to provide maximum coverage against unwanted material. Check the documentation for third-party software to see if it is a good match for Internet Explorer. If the other software is more comprehensive, then you can disable Content Advisor.

DATE AND TIME:
Change Your Time and Time Zone

If you relocate to another home or office, then you may need to adjust your time and time zone settings in Windows. You can quickly match the Windows date and time to your new time and time zone through the Date and Time Properties dialog box, which is available from both the time display at the bottom-right corner of your desktop and the Control Panel.

From the Time Zone tab in the Date and Time Properties dialog box, you can select any time zone around the globe. To adjust your time, you simply go

to the Date and Time tab and use the up- and down-arrows to the right of your current time display to set the minutes, hours, or AM/PM setting. Once you set it, the time should stay up to date until you reset it again. This is particularly true if you use the synchronization option that is available from the Internet Time tab.

See also>> **Date and Time, Set System Date**

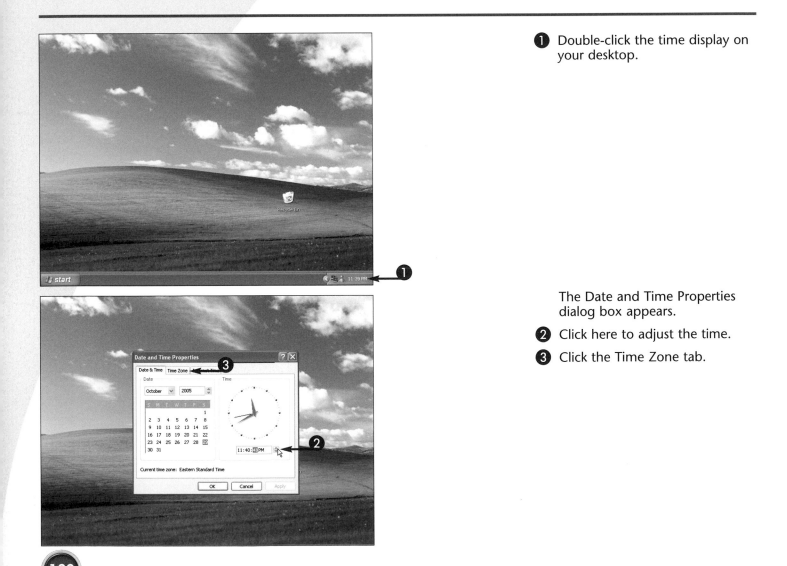

① Double-click the time display on your desktop.

The Date and Time Properties dialog box appears.

② Click here to adjust the time.

③ Click the Time Zone tab.

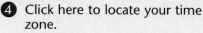

④ Click here to locate your time zone.

You may need to select the Automatically adjust clock for daylight saving changes option.

⑤ Click the time zone that you want.

⑥ Click OK.

Windows sets your time zone.

TIPS

Caution!
If you frequently adjust your date or time on the computer, then be careful which applications you open when you do this. Certain programs that base activation on current dates as Windows or log programs that monitor time you spend on a task can experience difficulty with frequent date or time changes.

Did You Know?
Windows is set up to automatically change the time to compensate for the biannual change from Standard Time to Daylight Savings Time and back again.

Test It!
If you suspect that your computer is losing time, then a good test is to reset the time and check the computer after a period when it is turned off. If the time is incorrect when you restart, then you may need to replace your CMOS battery.

DATE AND TIME:
Set System Date and Time Properties and Synchronize

Whenever you set up a new computer or move your base of operations to a new location, you can reset your system date and time to ensure that they are correct for the new location. You can also set up Windows to synchronize the time that it displays — in the System Tray at the bottom-right corner of the desktop, also called the Notification Area — with Internet-based time servers.

You can choose from two available synchronization servers — either time.windows.com or time.nist.gov. These servers help you to ensure that your Windows computer always displays the correct time.

You can use the Date and Time Properties dialog box to choose a different synchronization server, as well as adjust for time differences that may occur while you are offline. You can access the Date and Time Properties dialog box through the Control Panel, as well as through your desktop.

Keep in mind that time synchronization requires a live Internet connection, which you may not always have if you use a dial-up Web service.

See also>> **Date and Time, Change Your Time and Time Zone**

❶ Double-click the time display on your desktop.

The Date and Time Properties dialog box appears.

❷ Click here to adjust the time until it is correct.

❸ To adjust the date, click the correct day on the calendar.

❹ Click the Internet Time tab.

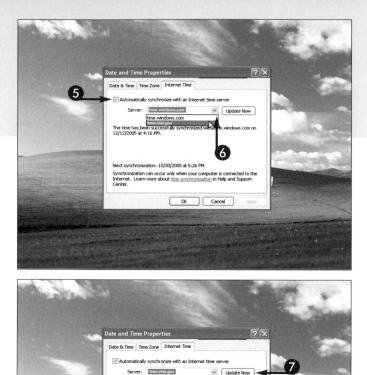

5 Click to select the Automatically synchronize with an Internet time server option.

6 Click here and select a server.

7 Click Update Now.

8 Click Apply.

9 Click OK.

Windows synchronizes and sets your time.

D

TIPS

Did You Know?
Your system date and time are also tracked in your system background, in the BIOS that serves as the programmable part of your motherboard. The CMOS battery, a special nickel-sized battery that is installed on your motherboard, keeps track of the date, time, and other settings when the computer is turned off. If this battery starts to fail, then your system date and time may display incorrectly.

Replace It!
If your CMOS battery fails, then you can replace it for about $3 to $6 from any consumer electronics store that sells batteries. Just remember to turn off the computer and disconnect it from power before you open the case. You can then remove the existing battery, and insert the new one.

DEVICE MANAGER:
Access Device Driver Information

You can use the Driver tab that is available for many hardware components in the Device Manager to check the version of your most recent driver. The driver refers to the special software that Windows uses to communicate with a piece of hardware. This driver information is useful if you are unsure whether you have the most recent driver that is listed on the manufacturer's Web site or in help articles that are related to a specific device.

When you call a technical support line, you may also be asked to provide details about the driver version

that you currently use for a particular hardware device. For example, you may see that a new driver for your display adapter has a date of May 2006. After you check your current driver information, you discover that it was updated in December 2004. This tells you that an update is available for you to download and install.

See also>>   **Device Manager**

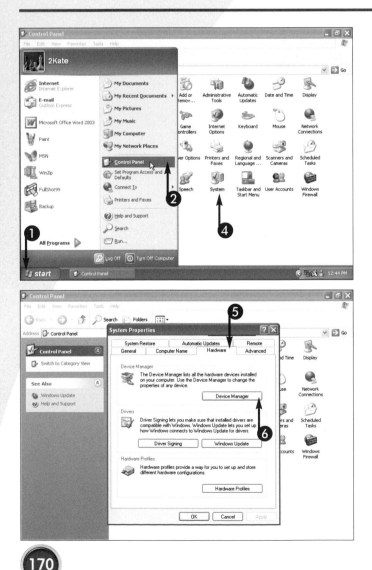

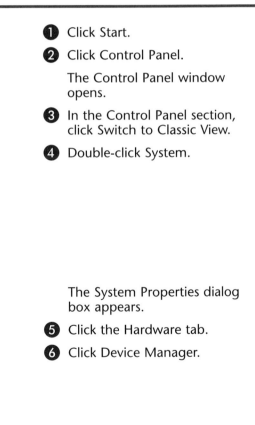

① Click Start.

② Click Control Panel.

The Control Panel window opens.

③ In the Control Panel section, click Switch to Classic View.

④ Double-click System.

The System Properties dialog box appears.

⑤ Click the Hardware tab.

⑥ Click Device Manager.

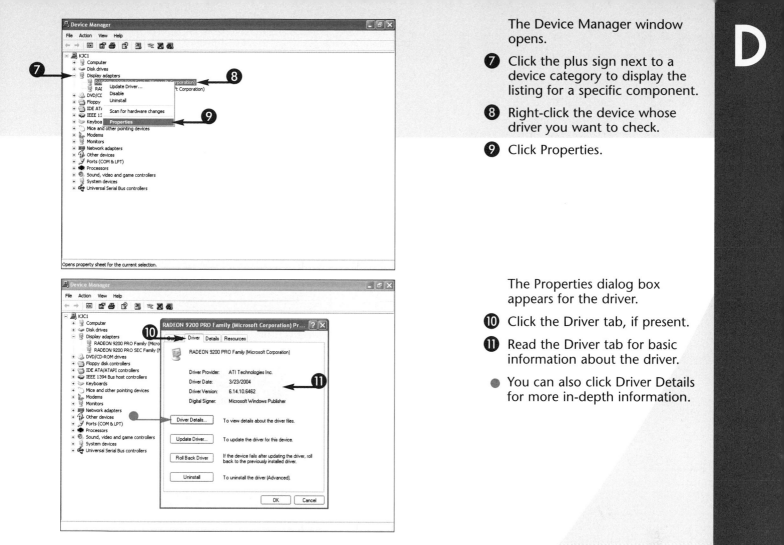

The Device Manager window opens.

⑦ Click the plus sign next to a device category to display the listing for a specific component.

⑧ Right-click the device whose driver you want to check.

⑨ Click Properties.

The Properties dialog box appears for the driver.

⑩ Click the Driver tab, if present.

⑪ Read the Driver tab for basic information about the driver.

● You can also click Driver Details for more in-depth information.

TIPS

Attention!

If you experience problems with a device or your system after you install a new driver, then you can fix this problem in the Properties dialog box for the driver. In the Details tab, click the Roll Back Driver button to return to your previous driver.

Caution!

When you visit the Web site of a manufacturer to look for new drivers, be sure to read any accompanying documentation. These notes may indicate symptoms to look for if the new driver is not fully compatible with your setup, as well as what you can do to adjust the setup.

DEVICE MANAGER:
Recognize Problems

It is a good idea to familiarize yourself with Windows Device Manager when everything works well so that you know how your system should look. Device Manager also makes it easy for you to locate and identify problems through special icons that it displays next problem devices.

When you see a red x on a device that is listed in the Device Manager, this means that support for the device is disabled. This can occur when Windows cannot work with the driver for the device, or cannot

locate the correct driver. It can also happen when you purposely choose to disable a device.

A yellow question mark usually means that Windows cannot find the driver for the device, or has a problem with the current driver. You can usually resolve this issue by reinstalling the proper driver.

See also>>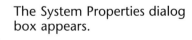

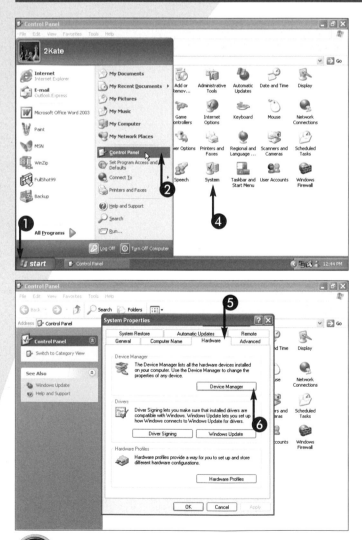

❶ Click Start.

❷ Click Control Panel.

The Control Panel window opens.

❸ In the Control Panel section, click Switch to Classic View.

❹ Double-click System.

The System Properties dialog box appears.

❺ Click the Hardware tab.

❻ Click Device Manager.

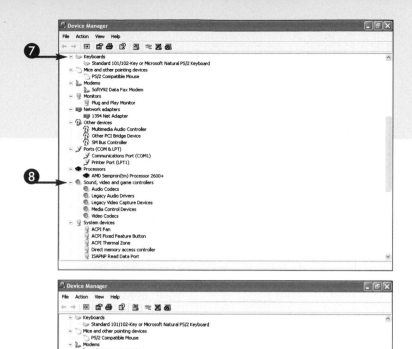

The Device Manager window opens.

7 Click the plus sign next to a device category to display the listing for a specific component.

8 Continue clicking each plus sign to expand all of the device categories.

9 Look for a yellow question mark or a red x on an entry, as well as any missing entries for hardware that you have just installed.

If you see signs of a Device Manager issue such as a red X or a yellow exclamation or question mark, then follow the on-screen instruction to troubleshoot the problem.

TIPS

Add It Automatically!

If you see a device with a red x indicating that it is disabled, then right-click the device and choose Properties. In the General tab, click in the drop-down list box below Device usage and then click Use this device (enable). Shut down and restart your system and then recheck the Device Manager to see the status of the hardware.

Did You Know?

If you disable a device — such as the video chipset on your motherboard — so that you can use an installed video or graphics adapter instead, then it is normal to see the on-motherboard video marked with a red x. This is not a problem that needs to be fixed.

DEVICE MANAGER:
Remove a Device or Driver

When you no longer use a particular device, it is a good idea to physically uninstall the hardware and to disable or remove the support for it in the Device Manager. When you do so, Windows no longer loads support for the device as it determines which hardware is connected when the operating system loads. In fact, the Device Manager does not always show the actual device, but shows the driver that helps a piece of hardware communicate with Windows.

There are other times that you may want to remove a device in the Device Manager. For example, this may

be necessary when you replace a chipset — such as video, audio, networking, or a modem — that is already integrated into your motherboard with a separate, dedicated adapter. Another situation is when you want to force Windows to re-load the driver when you are troubleshooting a problem with a device.

See also>>

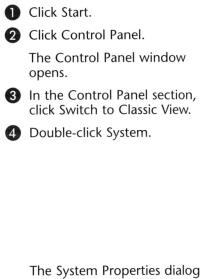

Device Manager

Windows Update

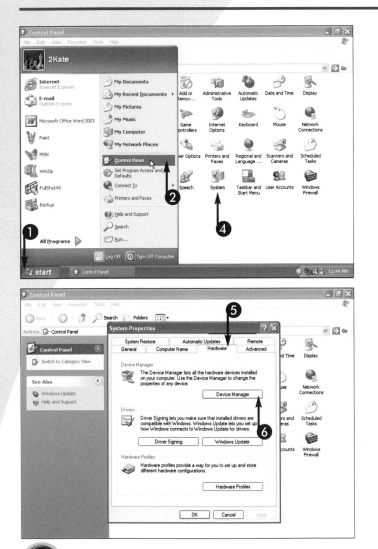

1 Click Start.

2 Click Control Panel.

The Control Panel window opens.

3 In the Control Panel section, click Switch to Classic View.

4 Double-click System.

The System Properties dialog box appears.

5 Click the Hardware tab.

6 Click Device Manager.

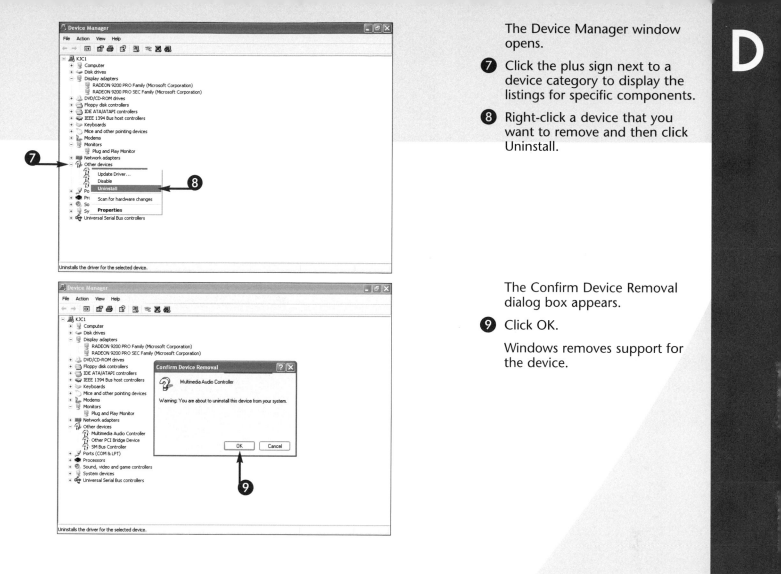

The Device Manager window opens.

⑦ Click the plus sign next to a device category to display the listings for specific components.

⑧ Right-click a device that you want to remove and then click Uninstall.

The Confirm Device Removal dialog box appears.

⑨ Click OK.

Windows removes support for the device.

TIPS

Attention!

When you uninstall a device in the Device Manager without physically removing the hardware, Windows should detect the device as brand new when it restarts, and then reload support for it. If you remove a device to enable Windows to redetect it, then you should follow the Device Manager removal by restarting your system.

Caution!

If you want to disable rather than remove all support for a piece of hardware, then perform Steps **1** to **7**, and in Step **8**, click Disable rather than Uninstall.

Did You Know?

After you make a change in the Device Manager and then restart your system, always check the Device Manager again. You should ensure that everything appears as you expect it to be.

DEVICE MANAGER:
Roll Back a Driver

Whenever you update the driver for a hardware device, you run the risk that your system may not operate properly. This can occur when the driver does not work properly with your particular Windows version or with the settings that you have specified for the device.

When this happens, your best option may be to restore the previous driver version until you can obtain a more compatible one. The Device Manager includes the Roll Back option to enable you to remove an update and restore your Windows setup to the former driver that worked properly.

Even if your system performs well after a driver update, a device may no longer work after you apply the update. These devices appear with a yellow question mark or red x in the Device Manager. Again, you should consider rolling back the driver as your best option until you can locate a better driver.

See also>>

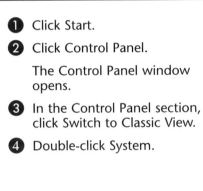

Device Manager

Windows Update

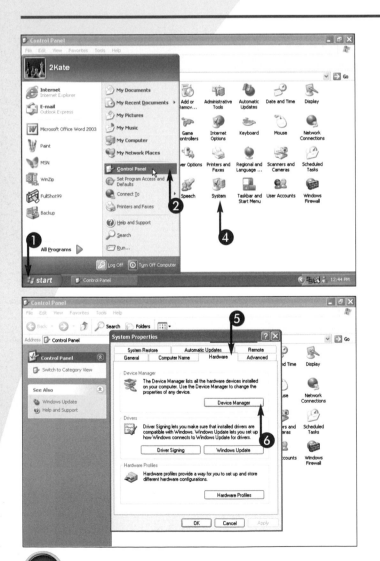

① Click Start.

② Click Control Panel.

The Control Panel window opens.

③ In the Control Panel section, click Switch to Classic View.

④ Double-click System.

The System Properties dialog box appears.

⑤ Click the Hardware tab.

⑥ Click Device Manager.

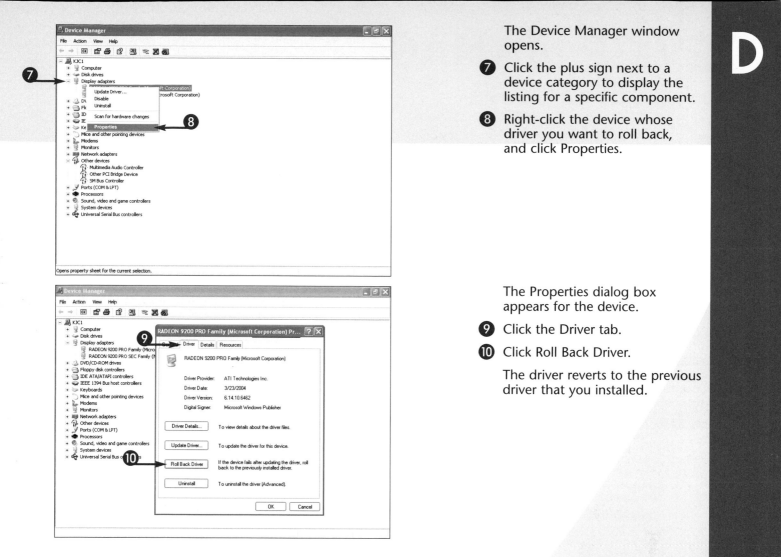

The Device Manager window opens.

7 Click the plus sign next to a device category to display the listing for a specific component.

8 Right-click the device whose driver you want to roll back, and click Properties.

The Properties dialog box appears for the device.

9 Click the Driver tab.

10 Click Roll Back Driver.

The driver reverts to the previous driver that you installed.

TIPS

Attention!

If you still experience problems with your system after you roll back a driver to the previous version, click Start, click Log off, and then click Restart. After the system reloads, see if the problem remains. If it does, then run Windows Update to see if any additional drivers, patches, or other software are available for your computer that may resolve the issue.

Try This!

Always check the date that the driver was updated under Driver Details in the Driver tab for a device before you install a replacement driver. This tells you the date of the previous driver so that you can distinguish the two drivers after you install the newer one.

DEVICE MANAGER:
Update Device Drivers

You can help to maintain your Windows XP system at peak performance by ensuring that your hardware drivers — the software that allows Windows to communicate with and control computer devices — are up to date.

As you make changes to Windows and add other hardware, an existing device driver may no longer work as well. Although Windows Update provides essential patches for the operating system and for specifically supported hardware, this service does not necessarily watch for updates for all of your system components. This is your responsibility, and you can manage it through the Device Manager.

All hardware that is listed in the Device Manager displays a Properties dialog box, often with an option to update the driver. You can usually find this option in the Driver tab if one is available. You can often obtain the updated driver by downloading it from the Web site of the device manufacturer.

See also>>   **Device Manager**

Windows Update

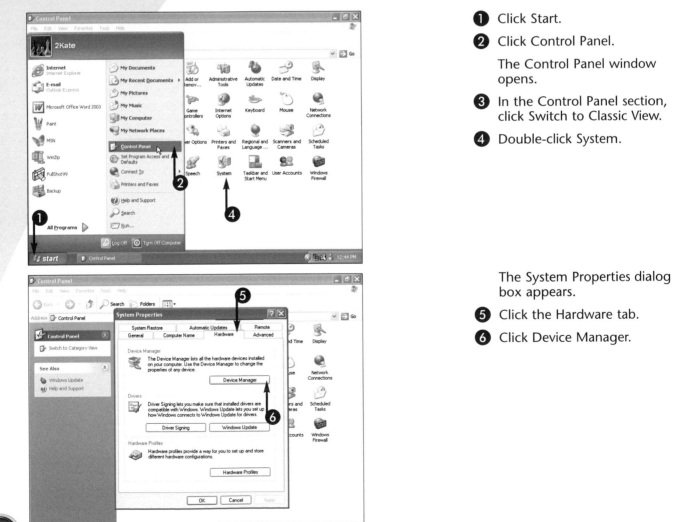

① Click Start.

② Click Control Panel.

The Control Panel window opens.

③ In the Control Panel section, click Switch to Classic View.

④ Double-click System.

The System Properties dialog box appears.

⑤ Click the Hardware tab.

⑥ Click Device Manager.

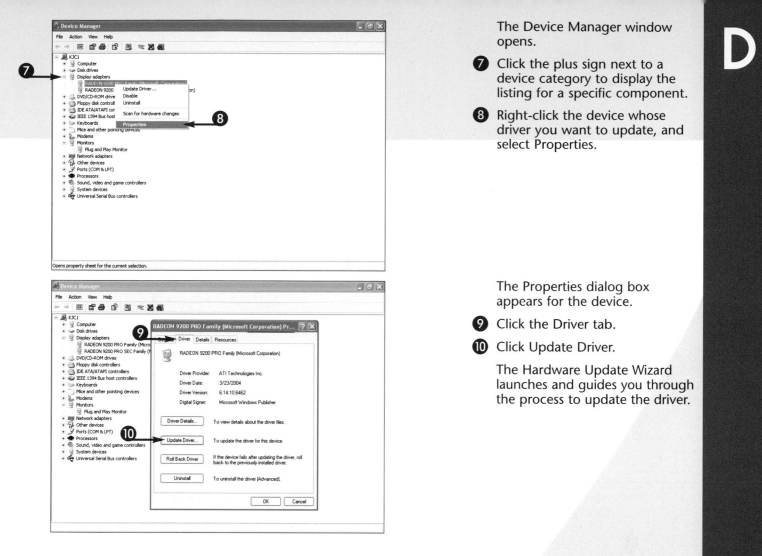

The Device Manager window opens.

⑦ Click the plus sign next to a device category to display the listing for a specific component.

⑧ Right-click the device whose driver you want to update, and select Properties.

The Properties dialog box appears for the device.

⑨ Click the Driver tab.

⑩ Click Update Driver.

The Hardware Update Wizard launches and guides you through the process to update the driver.

TIPS

Attention!
Always thoroughly read the documentation that accompanies a new driver. This documentation may include specific steps that differ from the standard procedure for updating device drivers.

Caution!
Do not assume that anything that you download from a manufacturer's Web site is safe. Always scan downloaded software for viruses, regardless of the source.

Important!
When you replace one piece of hardware with another, carefully examine the accompanying documentation for warnings. For example, when you install certain types of video adapters to replace a motherboard-integrated video chipset, you may achieve better results when you disable the onboard video in the Device Manager and then restart your system in Safe Mode to prepare to install the new driver.

DISK CLEANUP:
Manage Hard Disk Space

In addition to the files that you actively create or save as you work on your computer, there are many more files that are created, changed, and saved automatically by Windows. Many of these are temporary files that you may never use directly, but that reside on your disk until you clean them up. Over time, you can end up with a gigabyte or more of unneeded files that take up valuable space on your hard drive. You can use the Disk Cleanup tool to find and remove them.

You can run the Disk Cleanup tool regularly as part of standard disk management, along with tools such as Disk Defragmenter. The tool first asks you to specify the drive that you want to clean up and then identifies and reports the total amount of disk space that is currently in use by various file categories. These categories include temporary Internet files and the files that are left over by open applications, as well as Office Setup files.

See also>> **Disk Defragmenter**

① Click Start.

② Click All Programs.

③ Click Accessories.

④ Click System Tools.

⑤ Click Disk Cleanup.

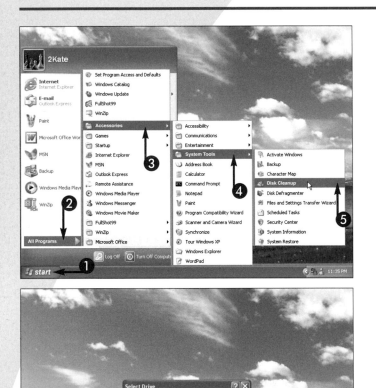

The Select Drive dialog box appears.

⑥ Click here and select the drive that you want to clean up.

⑦ Click OK.

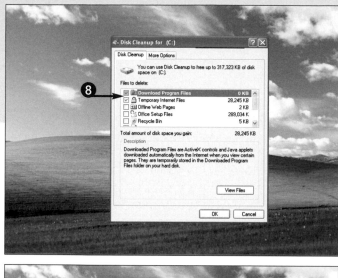

The Disk Cleanup dialog box appears.

⑧ Click to select any file categories that you want to clean up or to deselect those files that you do not want to clean up.

⑨ Click OK.

The Disk Cleanup tool runs and automatically removes all files for the categories that you selected.

TIPS

Did You Know?
Similar to the temporary files that are left over from Web browsing, many applications create temporary working files that store the contents of open files before they are saved to disk. These files may be stored with various filename extensions, such as .bak and .tmp. They can also be found in a number of different folders that are scattered throughout your hard disk.

Important!
When you remove Office Setup files as part of the disk cleanup process, you eliminate files that were left behind to allow you to change Office without needing to insert the Office setup master disk. As long as you have this disk, you can remove these files without any problems.

DISK DEFRAGMENTER:
Defragment a Drive

You can use the Disk Defragmenter system tool to reorganize and reorder the contents of your hard drive. When your drive is severely fragmented, it is difficult for Windows to find and load both files and applications, which can slow your system down.

Fragmentation can occur on your hard drive whenever a program fails to close properly or when you shut down your computer without going through the normal shutdown procedure, which writes the files appropriately to disk. Over time, fragmentation can make the system sluggish as it takes longer and

longer to open files and applications. Defragmentation reorders the disk so that files are stored properly.

Before you run Disk Defragmenter, you need to close all open programs on your desktop that may interfere with the process. You may also want to perform a Disk Cleanup to remove unnecessary files. You should also remove any applications that you no longer use through the Add or Remove Programs option in the Control Panel.

See also>>

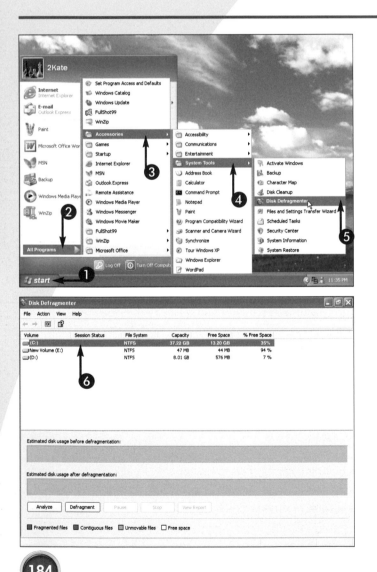

1 Click Start.

2 Click All Programs.

3 Click Accessories.

4 Click System Tools.

5 Click Disk Defragmenter.

The Disk Defragmenter window opens.

6 Click to select the drive that you want to defragment.

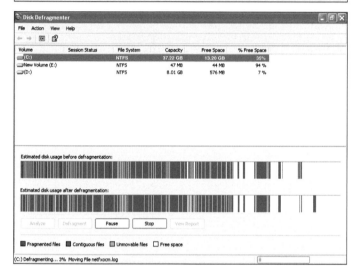

⑦ Click Defragment.

Disk Defragmenter first analyzes the disk.

If a certain percentage of the drive appears fragmented, then it proceeds with the defragmentation process.

If less than the minimum amount appears fragmented, the tool presents a dilog box that asks you if you want to proceed. If you do, then click Yes.

TIPS

Attention!
When you run Disk Defragmenter, you should first close all other programs on the desktop. If you try to run applications at the same time, then Disk Defragmenter may continuously restart because open programs write to the disk that it is trying to reorder. You should run the tool only when you are about to leave the computer for a few hours.

Did You Know?
If you use Norton Utilities, then you can use an option called SPEEDISK, which is very similar to Disk Defragmenter. You can use one or the other tool, but there is no need to run both disk utilities.

Try This!
You can add Disk Defragmenter as a regular job task to the Scheduled Tasks folder.

DISPLAY PROPERTIES:
Configure Display Properties

You can modify your display properties to change the appearance of your desktop as well as how applications look when you open them. This feature allows you to improve the appearance of your desktop, as well as specify how many windows you can have open at one time.

The most common change that users make to their desktop is the screen resolution, or the overall size of the Windows desktop in relation to its content. The higher the screen resolution, the smaller the windows appear. For example, the windows in a screen with a resolution of 640x480 are much larger than in a screen with a resolution of 800x600 or higher. A larger monitor often requires a higher screen resolution.

You can also change the number of colors that can appear in Windows. While some monitors and video adapters — also called graphics cards — can distinguish between many thousands of colors, others can draw millions of colors. The number of colors that can display depends on your monitor and video adapter, as well as their drivers.

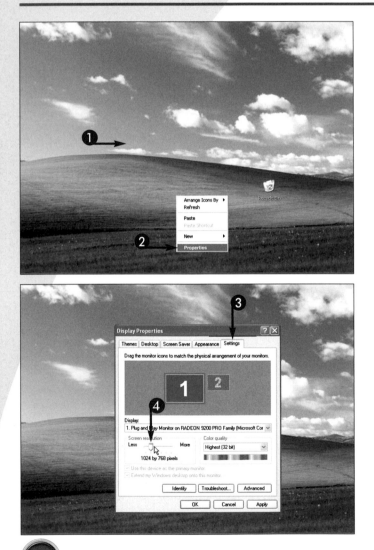

1 Right-click a blank area of your desktop.

A sub-menu appears.

2 Click Properties.

The Display Properties dialog box appears.

3 Click the Settings tab.

4 Under Screen resolution, click and drag the slider to increase or decrease the resolution.

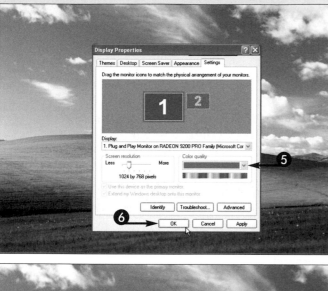

5 Under Color quality, click here and select the color level that you want.

6 Click OK.

Windows automatically changes the resolution, and a dialog box appears, asking if you want to keep these settings.

7 Click Yes to keep the settings or No to revert back to the previous settings.

If you keep your settings, then the monitor changes to the new screen resolution.

TIPS

Did You Know?

You may be very limited in terms of screen resolution and color settings if your display is provided by a video chipset that is integrated directly into the motherboard. In order to make custom changes, you may need to install a separate video adapter.

More Options!

If you were able to make changes to your display settings in the past, but you now cannot, then this could mean that you have a corrupted video driver. You can update the driver either through the Device Manager or through Windows Update.

Try This!

If you cannot change settings immediately after you update a driver, then you may want to use the Roll Back Driver option in the Device Manager to revert to the previous settings

DRIVE LETTERS:
View and Change Drive Letter Assignments

Although Windows automatically assigns drive letters to all drives that are installed on your system, you may not like the letters that have been assigned. For example, you may not like the fact that your CD drive appears in the middle of the selection of hard disk letters. You can change these drive letters to suit your needs.

One of the primary reasons why you may want to change drive letter assignments is that Windows works in alphabetical order as it scans to locate and open files and programs. This order usually starts

with the C drive, which is the drive where Windows is typically installed and from which your computer boots up. If a drive that you install receives a letter assignment later in the alphabet than drives that you use less often, then it takes longer for Windows to recognize the drive that you want.

You can also change drive letters to assign CD and DVD drives contiguous letter assignments if you have both types. This helps to prevent confusion.

See also>> **My Computer Folder**

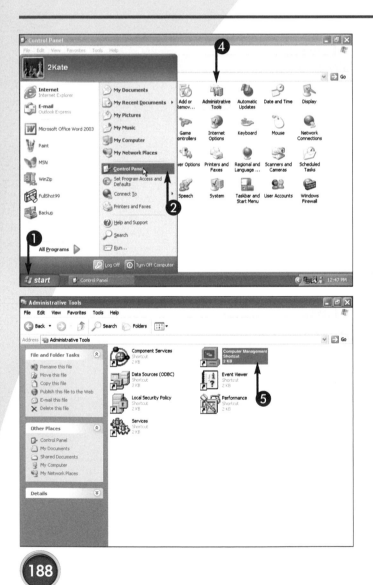

1 Click Start.

2 Click Control Panel.

The Control Panel window opens.

3 In the Control Panel section, click Switch to Classic View.

4 Double-click Administrative Tools.

The Administrative Tools window opens.

5 Double-click Computer Management.

Alternatively, you can click Start, right-click My Computer, and the select Manage to open the Computer Management console window

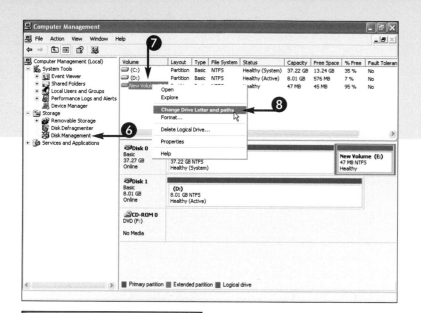

The Computer Management console opens.

6 Click Disk Management in the left-side task pane.

A list of drives opens in the right pane.

7 Right-click the drive whose letter you want to modify.

8 Click Change Drive Letter and Paths.

The Change Drive Letter and Paths dialog box appears.

9 With the current drive letter highlighted, click Change.

The Change Drive Letter or Path dialog box appears.

10 Click here and select the letter that you want to use for the drive.

11 Click OK twice to close your dialog boxes.

Windows changes the drive letter. You can view the letter change in the Computer Management right-side pane with Disk Management selected at left, or when you open My Computer.

TIPS

Attention!

You are not limited to the 26 letters in the alphabet to assign drive letters. For example, you can assign drive letters AA or AB.

Did You Know?

The reason why drive letters begin as C is that the letters A and B were traditionally assigned to floppy or other removable disk drives. The letters A and B are not always present today, because some PGs do not have floppy drives..

Important!

Windows assigns drive letters to individual drives installed on your computer, as well as to large-capacity hard drives that have been partitioned or divided into two or more logical drives or disk volumes. Through a feature called Map Network Drives, you can also create a shortcut to a drive that is located on another computer on your network with its own drive letter.

EDIT:
Cut, Copy, and Paste

You can perform the same basic text-editing functions in virtually every Windows application that you use. The editing tools, found in the Edit menu in most programs, include Cut, Copy, and Paste. Cut allows you to select and remove material — such as text — from one place to move it to another. Copy allows you to select and copy material without removing it. Paste allows you to paste into place the material that you have copied or cut.

Windows allows you to cut and paste, as well as copy and paste, from one open window to another. For

example, you can copy and paste sentences from a Web page into a Notepad or WordPad document. You can use the same technique to copy or cut and paste between two open Microsoft Office files, as well as two instant-messaging chat windows.

See also>>

Notepad

WordPad

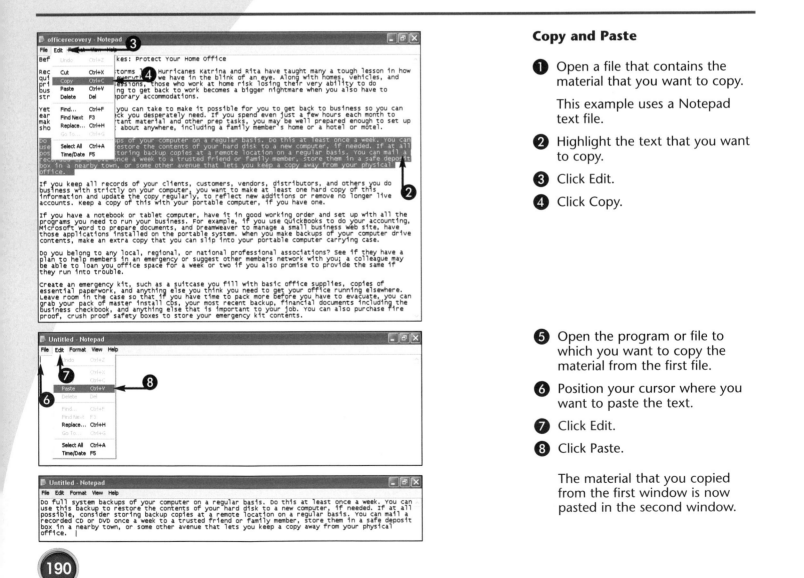

Copy and Paste

➊ Open a file that contains the material that you want to copy.

This example uses a Notepad text file.

➋ Highlight the text that you want to copy.

➌ Click Edit.

➍ Click Copy.

➎ Open the program or file to which you want to copy the material from the first file.

➏ Position your cursor where you want to paste the text.

➐ Click Edit.

➑ Click Paste.

The material that you copied from the first window is now pasted in the second window.

Cut and Paste

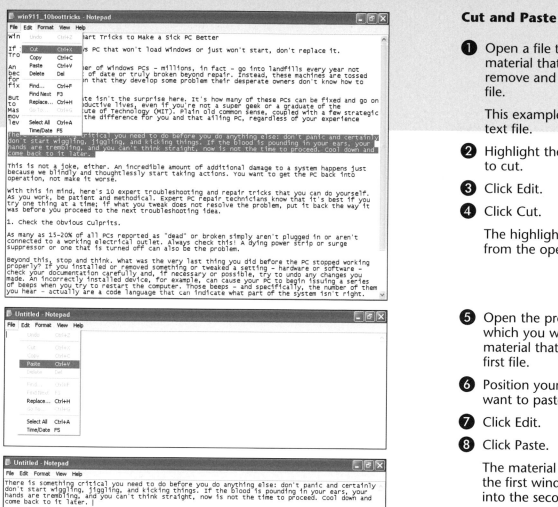

① Open a file that contains the material that you want to remove and paste into another file.

This example uses a Notepad text file.

② Highlight the text that you want to cut.

③ Click Edit.

④ Click Cut.

The highlighted text disappears from the open file window.

⑤ Open the program or file into which you want to insert the material that you cut from the first file.

⑥ Position your cursor where you want to paste the text.

⑦ Click Edit.

⑧ Click Paste.

The material that you cut from the first window is now pasted into the second window.

TIPS

Did You Know?

If you use Microsoft Office, then every bit of text that you cut or copy and paste is copied into the Office Clipboard, which is a cut-and-paste buffer. You can then retrieve the text to use elsewhere in the same Windows session. When you log off, shut down, or close Microsoft Office, the contents of the Clipboard are cleared.

More Options

The Copy, Cut, and Paste functions are all available using keyboard shortcuts that are usually the same between different Windows programs. You can copy when you use Ctrl+C or Ctrl+Insert, cut when you use Ctrl+X, or paste when you use Ctrl+V or Shft+Insert.

EMERGENCY BOOT DISK:
Boot Your Computer with a Boot Disk

You can use an emergency boot disk — a special floppy disk that contains the files that you need to start a system — to boot a computer when a hard drive or Windows problem prevents normal startup. When you boot a computer from a boot disk, you force the computer to start from the files on that floppy disk, rather than from the files on your computer hard drive.

When you use the emergency disk to boot your system, a very basic version of the operating system loads a Command Prompt, where you can type commands, copy files, or run non-Windows diagnostic tools.

Commands that you type can also have switches, or special letter combinations, that you can use to directly affect the results of the command. For example, you can type chkdsk d: to check your D: drive. To both check and fix problems with your D drive, you would add the /f switch, as follows: chkdsk d: /f.

See also>> **Emergency Boot Disk**

Recovery Console

① Insert the boot disk into the floppy disk drive.

② Start or restart your computer.

The system continues the boot process and loads the Command Prompt.

If your computer does not recognize that a boot disk has been inserted into the floppy disk, first check to ensure that the disk is fully inserted and then restart the computer.

If the computer still does not recognize the disk, then restart the computer again. Follow the on-screen instructions to access Setup. From Setup, locate the option that sets boot disk order, and add the floppy disk drive to the boot sequence list.

TIPS

Caution!
When you work from the Command Prompt, especially if you do not regularly use commands, you are far more likely to make a critical error. For example, you may accidentally delete a file or erase the contents of an entire hard disk. You should use this feature with care.

More Options!
You may also want to try other options, such as the Recovery Console or loading Windows through Safe Mode.

Try This!
If you have not used commands before, then you may want to review what types of commands are available and what they do. To do this, click Start and then click Help and Support. From the Search window, type commands and then click the white arrow.

EMERGENCY BOOT DISK:
Create an Emergency Boot Disk

One of the tools that you can use when you have trouble with your computer is an emergency boot disk, also called a Windows startup disk. This is a disk that you can use to start your system if the computer does not start normally and load Windows.

You can use an emergency boot disk when you need to troubleshoot your system or run an application that only runs from the command line.

In order to create a boot disk, you need a blank floppy disk. Also, both the computer where you make

the boot disk, and on which you use it, must have a working floppy disk drive. You format this floppy disk so that you can use it to start a computer that refuses to load Windows normally.

See also>>

Command Prompt

Recovery Console

① Insert the blank floppy diskette into your computer's floppy drive.

② Click Start.

③ Click My Computer.

The My Computer window opens.

④ Click the floppy drive icon.

⑤ Click File.

⑥ Click Format.

194

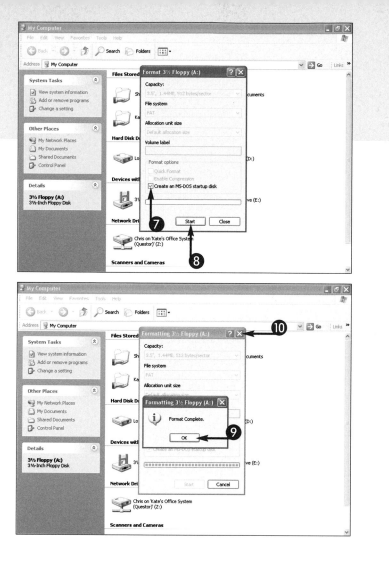

The Format dialog box appears.

7 Click the Create an MS-DOS startup disk option.

8 Click Start.

A bar indicates the disk formatting progress.

When the formatting is complete, a dialog box appears.

9 Click OK.

10 Click Close in the Formatting dialog box.

11 Remove the floppy disk from the disk drive.

12 Label the disk as a boot disk, with the date and your Windows version.

TIPS

Caution!

Even if you already have an emergency boot disk that you created through a different Windows version, you should create and use a boot disk specifically for Windows XP. This is because possible incompatibilities with older versions could damage your system.

Did You Know?

Although a boot disk is also called a Windows startup disk, you cannot use it to start and work in a normal Windows session. The disk only allows you access to your drives and their contents, as well as disk-based commands.

More Options!

If you have certain diagnostic or system software such as Norton SystemWorks, Norton Ghost, or an antivirus package, then you may have other special boot disks to help you use these utilities from the Command Prompt.

ENCRYPTING FILE SYSTEM:
Enable Encrypted Files and Folders

A great way to protect your confidential files is to enable file and folder encryption, which encodes and scrambles your data. When you encrypt your files, you make it difficult for someone else to spy on your system when they try to read data that is contained in your files and folders.

You can use the Encrypting File System, or EFS, in Windows to secure and manage any files or folders that you store on an NTFS drive. When you open an encrypted file, Windows prompts you for a virtual decoding key to unlock the code to open and view the file.

When you enable encryption for files and folders, you add a security layer that goes beyond *file permissions*, or the rules that govern user access to files. You can set file permissions and other options through security policies like the Group or Local Security Policy. Professional network setups concerned about data security use both file encryption and file permissions.

See also>>   **Group Policy Snap-In**

Local Security Policy

① Click Start.

② Click My Computer.

The My Computer window opens.

③ Double-click the drive that you want.

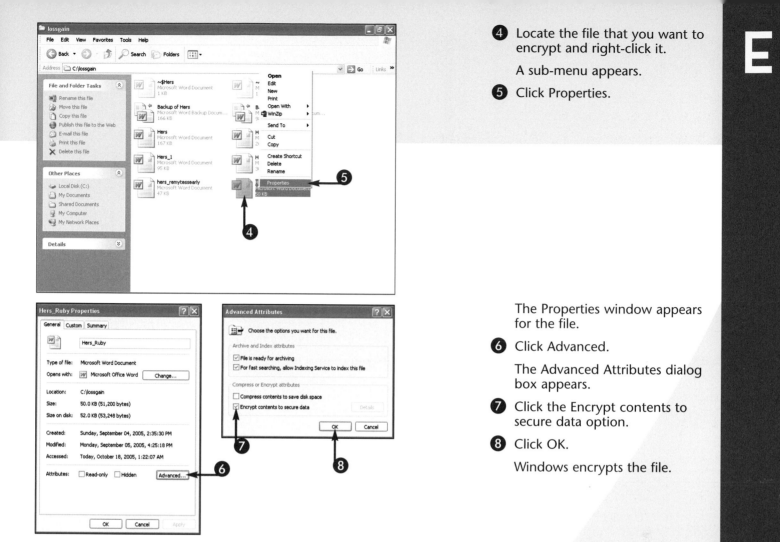

④ Locate the file that you want to encrypt and right-click it.

A sub-menu appears.

⑤ Click Properties.

The Properties window appears for the file.

⑥ Click Advanced.

The Advanced Attributes dialog box appears.

⑦ Click the Encrypt contents to secure data option.

⑧ Click OK.

Windows encrypts the file.

TIPS

Did You Know?

When you encrypt an entire folder, you automatically encrypt all of the files and sub-folders within it.

Remove It!

You can decrypt, or remove encryption, from any file or folder that you encode. To do this, you repeat Steps 1 to 8, but in Step 7, you click to deselect the Encrypt contents to secure data option.

Did You Know?

You cannot encrypt all files and folders. If a file or folder is not stored on an NTFS drive, the native file system of Microsoft Windows NT, then you cannot encrypt it. You are also unable to encrypt compressed files and folders, and Windows does not allow you to encrypt certain other types of files, such as System files that support your operating system.

EVENTS:
Review Events in Event Manager

When you need to troubleshoot your Windows XP system, it is vital that you review the notable system occurrences, or *events*, that occur in the background of your system. You can use Event Manager in Windows XP to view a list of these events, see what types of events have occurred, and view more details about these events.

Event Manager organizes all of these events into three major types: information, errors, and warnings. When you use Event Manager regularly to better understand both what events occur and which events

routinely produce errors, you are more likely to be able to determine what is going wrong on your system.

Events occur normally in the course of computer operation. Windows initiates some events, while you schedule others, such as when you add a maintenance job like Backup to the Scheduled Tasks folder. However, some events may indicate a serious problem or failure when they produce chronic error entries in Event Manager.

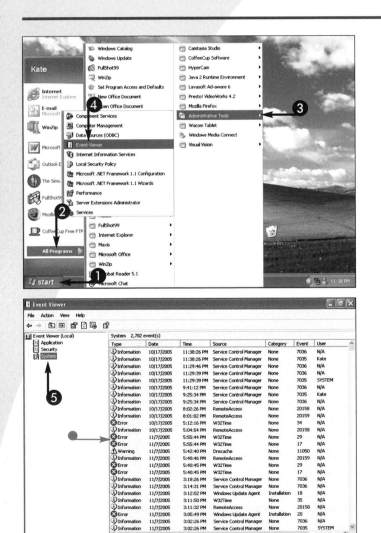

① Click Start.

② Click All Programs.

③ Click Administrative Tools.

④ Click Event Viewer.

If the Administrative Tools folder does not appear in the Start menu, then click Start, click Control Panel, click Performance and Maintenance, double-click Administrative Tools, and then double-click Event Viewer.

The Event Viewer window opens.

⑤ Click System.

● The System event logs appears in the right pane.

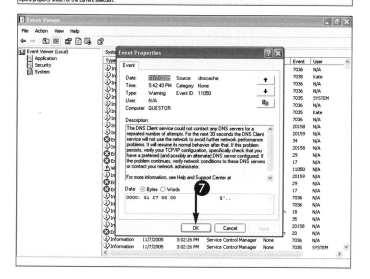

6 Right-click an event log in the right pane and select Properties.

The Event Properties dialog box appears for the log.

This dialog box often includes a link to a help article that discusses the issue.

7 Click OK.

TIPS

Desktop Trick!

You can easily add the Administrative Tools folder to the Start menu to make it easy to access tools like the Event Viewer. Right-click the taskbar and choose Properties. Click Start Menu, click Customize, and then click Advanced. Scroll through the Start Menu items list to locate System Administrative Tools, and then specify how you want the item to display in the Start Menu.

Did You Know?

The Event Viewer can show other event logs, depending on the services and applications that are installed on your computer. Typically, a Windows XP workstation only includes the three default logs — System, Application, and Security. Although additional logs are more common on Windows Server platforms, they are still available on some Windows XP workstations.

FAST USER SWITCHING:
Enable Fast User Switching

If you share your computer and want to be able to access your own user account quickly when someone else is already logged on, then you can use Fast User Switching.

Windows XP usually enables Fast User Switching by default. This allows other users who have their own account on the computer to log onto their account at roughly half the time that it normally takes for the first user to log off and the new user to log on.

This feature saves time because the first user is not completely logged off when the new user logs on. As a result, any programs or files that the first user has open remain open, even while the second user is working on the desktop.

Although Fast User Switching is normally enabled, you need to be sure that it is in place before you try to use it. If it is not turned on, then you must turn it on.

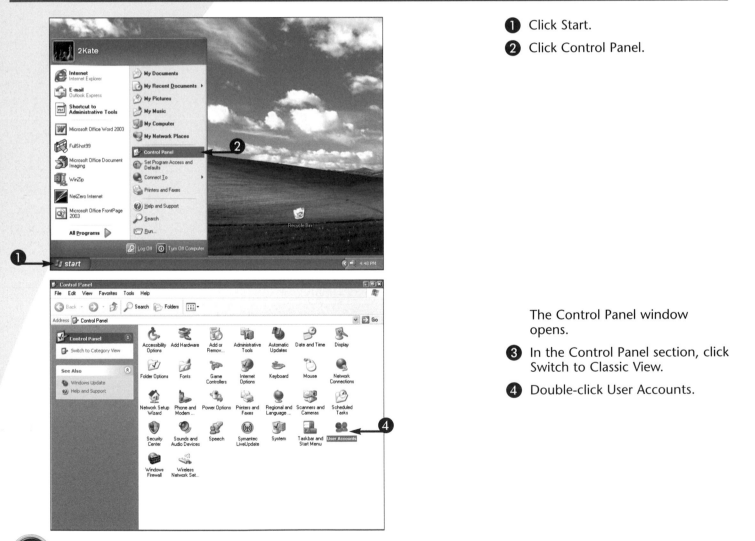

1 Click Start.

2 Click Control Panel.

The Control Panel window opens.

3 In the Control Panel section, click Switch to Classic View.

4 Double-click User Accounts.

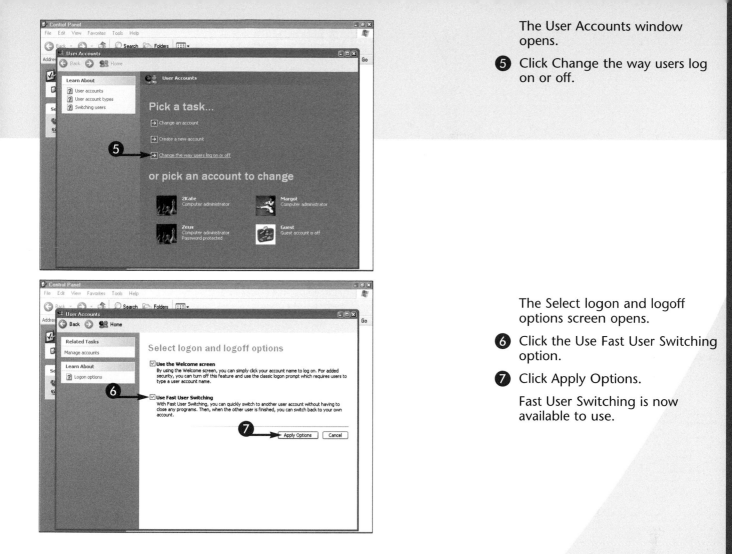

The User Accounts window opens.

5 Click Change the way users log on or off.

The Select logon and logoff options screen opens.

6 Click the Use Fast User Switching option.

7 Click Apply Options.

Fast User Switching is now available to use.

TIPS

Did You Know?

If you have the Offline Files feature enabled, then you are prompted to turn it off before you can turn on Fast User Switching. Windows transports you to a dialog box where you click to deselect it, and then click OK. You can then turn on Fast User Switching.

Important!

Use Fast User Switching with care if you have limited resources. Fast User Switching keeps two or more accounts open in Windows simultaneously, along with all the programs each has launched. For example, if you have just 128 MB of memory installed, you could run out of desktop resources and see Windows Virtual Memory Low warnings along with a slow desktop.

FAST USER SWITCHING:
Use Fast User Switching

After you enable Fast User Switching, if you have multiple users logged on, then you can quickly shift from one user to another. You do not need to log the first user off before the other user logs on, and so both user accounts can remain open.

An advantage of Fast User Switching is the speed with which you can switch user accounts, while keeping the first user logged on. However, this feature also presents certain security challenges. For example, by keeping the first user account open, it is possible for another user to access that account after switching back from his or her account.

To use Fast User Switching, you can simply select the icon in the Welcome screen that represents your account. If you require a password to access your account, then you are prompted to supply this password.

See also>>

Security

Security Zones

① When another user is logged onto the computer, click Start.

② Click Log Off.

The Log Off Windows dialog box appears.

③ Click Switch User.

The Welcome screen appears.

④ Click your user account name.

Windows logs you onto your account.

⑤ When you finish, click Start.

⑥ Click Log Off.

Windows returns the desktop to the session for the first user.

TIPS

Did You Know?

If you have the Offline Files feature enabled, then you are prompted to turn it off before you can turn on Fast User Switching. Windows displays a dialog box where you click to deselect it, and then click OK. You can then turn on Fast User Switching.

Remove it!

To turn off Fast User Switching, click Start and then click Control Panel. In the Control Panel window, double-click User Accounts. In the User Accounts window, click Change the way users log on and off. Click to deselect the Use Fast User Switching option, and then click Apply Options.

Caution!

There are two situations in which you should not use Fast User Switching. The first is when you are concerned about computer security, because with multiple accounts open, there is potential for abuse or damage. The second is when your computer has limited available disk space or memory.

FAX:
Send a Fax

When you want to send a document, spreadsheet, photograph, or Web page as a fax, you can do this in Windows with Microsoft Fax Services. To use this service, you must first have it installed, and your computer must have a fax-compatible modem installed, as well. If you do not have a modem, then you can choose a Fax Services provider when you set up the fax service, which allows you to send a fax as e-mail through the Internet, usually for a fee.

You can send any text or image file that you would normally send as a fax. This includes word-processing files, invoices, receipts, and newspaper clippings.

Several programs, including Microsoft Word, include a SendTo option from the File menu through which you can send a file as a fax to a recipient that you specify. You can also quickly set up and send a one-page fax, such as a cover letter.

See also>>

Fax Configuration Wizard

Fax Console

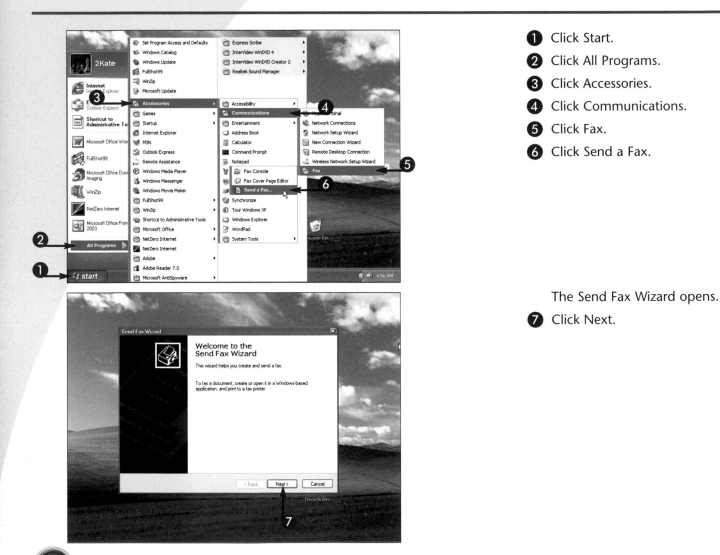

❶ Click Start.

❷ Click All Programs.

❸ Click Accessories.

❹ Click Communications.

❺ Click Fax.

❻ Click Send a Fax.

The Send Fax Wizard opens.

❼ Click Next.

The Recipient Information screen opens.

8 Type the name of the recipient.

9 Type the fax number.

10 Click here and select a style for the cover page template.

11 To add text to the cover page, click inside the Subject line field and type a topic name for the fax.

12 Click inside the Note field and type the information that you want to appear on the cover sheet.

13 Click Next.

14 Click to select options for when to send the fax and fax priority.

You can also accept the default settings, which transmit the fax almost immediately.

15 Click Next.

16 In the final screen, review the summary of your fax settings. If everything appears correct, click Finish.

The Send Fax Wizard sends the document to the Fax Console, which begins to dial the number that you specified.

TIPS

Attention!

You cannot edit a fax once you have scheduled it to be sent. You need to delete the current fax from the Fax Console before it is sent, and then create a new one.

Did You Know?

When you have a fax waiting to be sent or when you load the Fax Console to monitor for incoming fax transmissions, a new icon appears in the shape of a fax machine in the System Tray, located in the lower-right corner of the desktop. If you click this icon, the Fax Monitor opens, and displays a current status window. If a fax is in progress, the Fax Monitor displays the details.

FILE AND FOLDER MANAGEMENT:
Find Default Folders

Certain files are stored in specific locations on your hard drive because Windows XP has designated various default folders as the storage place for these file types.

When you install Windows XP, it sets up a number of default folders, including the My Documents folder, which holds many of the files that you create through applications such as Microsoft Word and Microsoft Excel. The My Pictures folder is your default storage space for images. The My Music folder stores your audio-related files. The My Webs folder stores any

Web sites or Web pages that you set up on the Internet, while the My Downloads folder is the default location for files that you download while you are online.

Although these are the default folders, you can also browse to a different location when you save a file or folder to the hard drive, including when you install a new application.

In many applications, you can select Options from the Tools menu to locate the default folder for storing files that you create in that application.

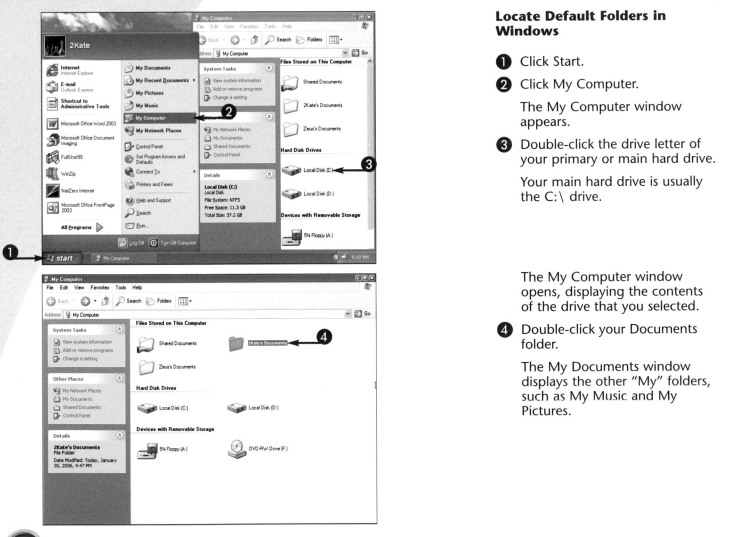

Locate Default Folders in Windows

① Click Start.

② Click My Computer.

The My Computer window appears.

③ Double-click the drive letter of your primary or main hard drive.

Your main hard drive is usually the C:\ drive.

The My Computer window opens, displaying the contents of the drive that you selected.

④ Double-click your Documents folder.

The My Documents window displays the other "My" folders, such as My Music and My Pictures.

Locate Default Folders in Applications

① Click Start.

② Click All Programs.

③ Click the application whose default folder you want to check for saving files.

The program launches on your desktop.

④ In the program window, select the command that displays the program's configuration options.

In Microsoft Word, you can click Tools, and then click Options.

A dialog box should display information about your file default save folder for that application.

Customize It!

To add a new folder, right-click anywhere in the drive or folder that you want to use in My Computer. Click New and then click Folder.

Try This!

If you cannot locate the default folder that is used to save files, then you can click File and click Save. In the Save window, check to see which folder is selected — this is the default folder used by that application. Click Cancel to stop from saving a file to disk.

Customize It!

If the default location for saving files is in a folder used by many different programs, then this folder may become very crowded, making it difficult to locate individual files. To prevent this, you can select new default save folders for your programs.

FILE AND FOLDER MANAGEMENT:
Modify Default Folders

If you find that certain folders on your computer — such as My Documents in the Documents and Settings main folder — become very cluttered with files from a number of different applications, then you can fix this problem. You can change the default folder location for some of your applications to reduce the clutter.

It is not unusual to see the My Documents folder of a typical computer user containing several hundred files of all different types, including documents,

spreadsheets, Web pages, and digital photos. By managing your files and folders, you can avoid having to page through many screens, trying to locate a particular file that you need.

Using a folder such as My Documents as your default storage folder for many programs can also cause an additional problem: applications may leave behind temporary, or working, files in this folder. These files use a *.tmp or *.bak file extension.

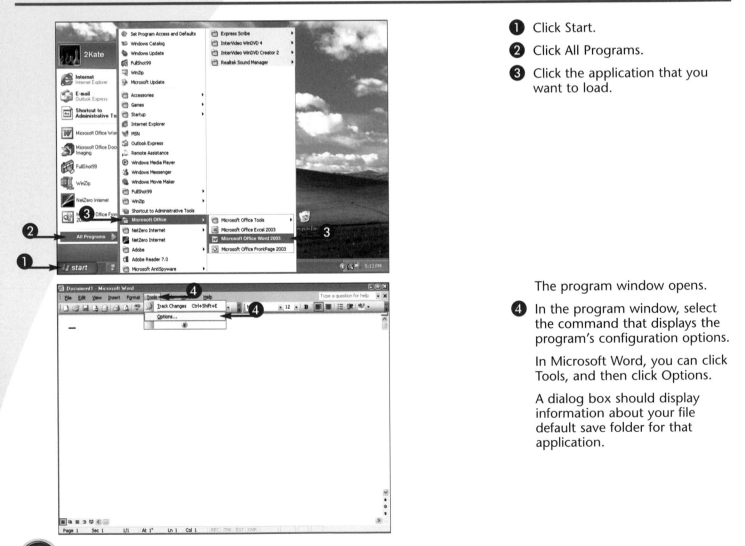

① Click Start.

② Click All Programs.

③ Click the application that you want to load.

The program window opens.

④ In the program window, select the command that displays the program's configuration options.

In Microsoft Word, you can click Tools, and then click Options.

A dialog box should display information about your file default save folder for that application.

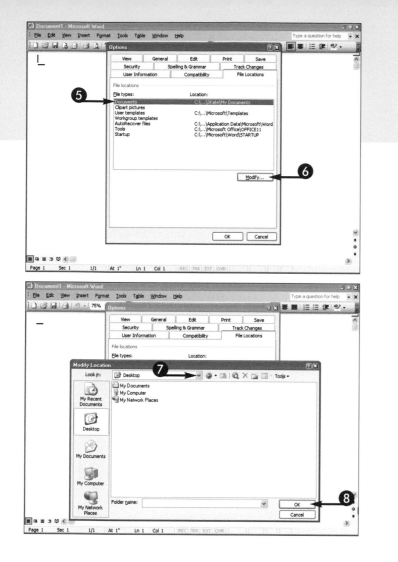

The Options dialog box appears.

5 Confirm your current default folder.

6 Select the command to modify the default folder.

In Microsoft Word, you can click Modify.

7 Click here and select a default location where you want to save files in this program, or type the drive and folder where you want to save your files.

8 Click OK.

The program changes your default file save location to the new location.

F

FILE AND FOLDER MANAGEMENT:
Move Files and Folders in My Computer

When you want to move files and folders around on your computer, an easy way to do this is through the My Computer window. This window displays your system from the perspective of the drives on your computer. The fuller the drives become, the easier it is to view and manage the drive contents by using My Computer because its interface becomes less crowded by comparison.

In the My Computer window, you can view all of the drives connected to your system, including the floppy drive, hard drive, and CD/DVD drive. You can also locate files and folders on each of these drives and move them between drives, such as when you want to burn a CD or DVD, or move or store files from your hard drive.

The difference between copying and moving files is that copying makes a duplicate copy so that there are two versions of the file, while moving removes the file from the original location and moves it to the new location.

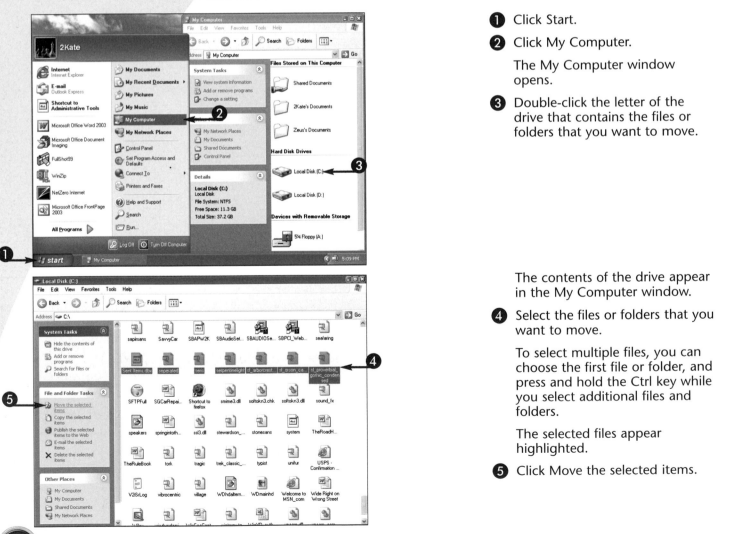

❶ Click Start.

❷ Click My Computer.

The My Computer window opens.

❸ Double-click the letter of the drive that contains the files or folders that you want to move.

The contents of the drive appear in the My Computer window.

❹ Select the files or folders that you want to move.

To select multiple files, you can choose the first file or folder, and press and hold the Ctrl key while you select additional files and folders.

The selected files appear highlighted.

❺ Click Move the selected items.

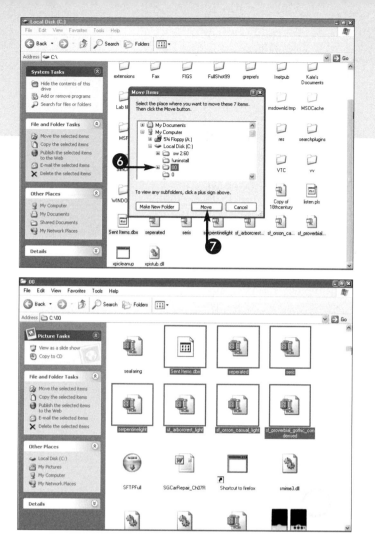

6 When the Move Items window opens, select the location where you want to move these files, such as your CD or DVD drive.

You can also click the plus sign next to a drive letter to choose a location on that drive.

7 Click Move.

Windows moves the files and folders to the location that you specified.

TIPS

Did You Know?
If you want to set up a new folder in which to store the moved files and folders, then click the Create New Folder option from the Move Items window in Step 5. Provide a name for the folder before you select the folder from the drive contents listing.

Important!
If you need to make a copy of files and folders rather than just store them in a new location, then use the Copy the selected items option from the left-hand menu in Step 5 rather than the Move option.

FILE AND FOLDER MANAGEMENT:
Move Files and Folders in Windows Explorer

When you need to move files and folders to a new location on one of your drives, then you have one of two choices: you can move them through My Computer or through Windows Explorer. Both of these windows allow you to perform similar operations; Windows Explorer is best for users who are comfortable with a classic Windows interface, and My Computer offers a more updated interface, similar to the Web page-like appearance that newer users often prefer.

You can move files in one of two ways: you can drag-and-drop files and folders from one location to another, or you can right-click the files, choose Cut, use the left-handed navigation menu to open the drive or folder where you want to move these items, right-click again, and choose Paste.

If you want to cut the files from their current location, then you can press Ctrl+X and then press Ctrl+V to paste them in the new location.

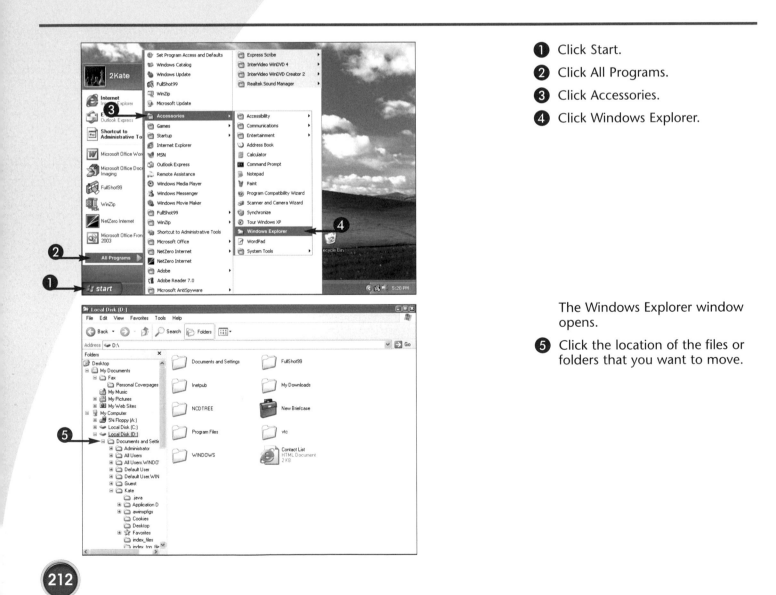

① Click Start.

② Click All Programs.

③ Click Accessories.

④ Click Windows Explorer.

The Windows Explorer window opens.

⑤ Click the location of the files or folders that you want to move.

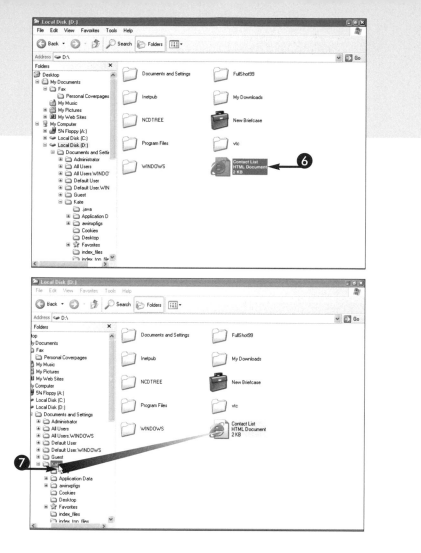

6 Click the folder or file you want.

To choose multiple files or folders, click the first file or folder and then press and hold the Ctrl key as you click additional items.

7 Drag the file or folder to a drive or folder located in the left navigation pane.

8 Release the mouse.

The file or folder drops into place in the selected location.

If you have used previous versions of Windows Explorer, then this version looks different, similar to the My Computer window. Also, the name of the utility does not appear on the title bar at the top of the window; instead it displays the drive or folder that you have chosen to view.

TIPS

Caution!
Always be careful when you are performing any type of file management. You do not want to delete files accidentally, and you want to remember where you have moved important files and folders.

Did You Know?
If Windows Explorer seems cumbersome, then you can try using My Computer to perform the same tasks.

Try This!
Windows default save folders can become very cluttered over time, and so you should use different storage locations to reduce this problem. Some of these default folders include the My Documents folder, the My Pictures folder, and the root C: or D: folder on your hard drive, which often store unneeded files.

FILE AND FOLDER MANAGEMENT:
View and Set File and Folder Properties

Each file and folder in Windows includes a selection of properties that determine specific characteristics for the file or folder. You can customize the way a file or folder appears and works through its properties.

The properties for a folder include the folder name and path, the file size, the number of folders and files that it contains, and the date that it was created. Some properties can only be read, while you can modify others. For example, you can configure the folder as a music album to simplify listening to the contents of the folder in Windows Media Player. Other properties control the icon that is used for the folder

and the picture that is used to identify a thumbnail folder for pictures.

In addition, the folder's sharing properties allow you to share the folder with others on the network, set permissions to determine the actions that others can perform with the shared folder, and apply other restrictions.

You can also change the Summary properties for some types of files. These properties enable you to add information that the document may not otherwise support.

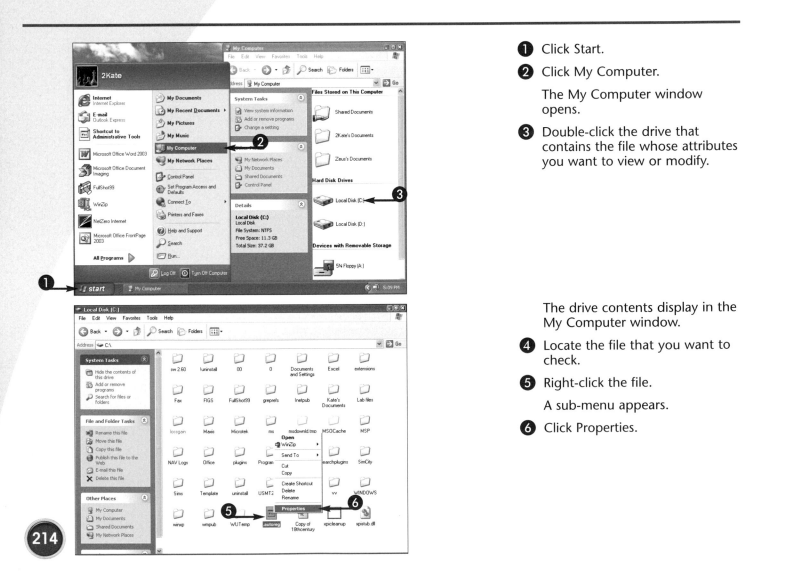

① Click Start.

② Click My Computer.

The My Computer window opens.

③ Double-click the drive that contains the file whose attributes you want to view or modify.

The drive contents display in the My Computer window.

④ Locate the file that you want to check.

⑤ Right-click the file.

A sub-menu appears.

⑥ Click Properties.

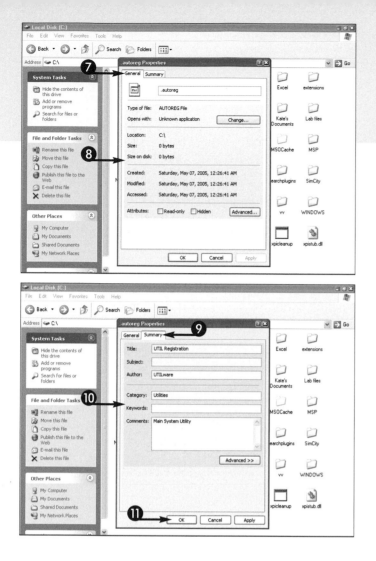

The Properties window appears for the file that you selected.

7 Click the General tab.

8 View the path, name, creation date and time, and other read-only information.

9 Click the Summary tab.

10 View extended information about the file.

11 Click OK to close the Properties dialog box.

TIPS

Try This!

You can change the properties for a music folder to make it easier to play music in Windows Media Player. Open the My Music folder, right-click any artist folder, and then click Properties. The folder should be set to the Music Artist folder type. If not, then select Music Artist from the drop-down list, and click OK.

Customize It!

If you do not like the icon for a folder, then you can change it. Right-click the folder and click Properties. Click the Customize tab and then click the Change Icon button. Select an icon from the list and click OK. Click OK again to apply the change.

FILE AND FOLDER SHARING:
Set Sharing Properties and Share a Folder

If your computer is part of a home or small-office network, then you can share files and folders on your hard drive so that your system files are accessible from other computers on the network. This allows you to share documents, images, movies, and audio files around the network so that copies do not need to exist on each hard disk in the network. This not only saves hard disk space but also offers convenience, especially when you work in another room and want to open a file that is located elsewhere.

When you set up a file or folder share, you can specify whether anyone on the network can access the file with or without a password. A password can help you to limit which people are able to open, read, modify, and delete files on your system.

You normally share only certain folders. When you share a folder, you also share the files that the folder contains.

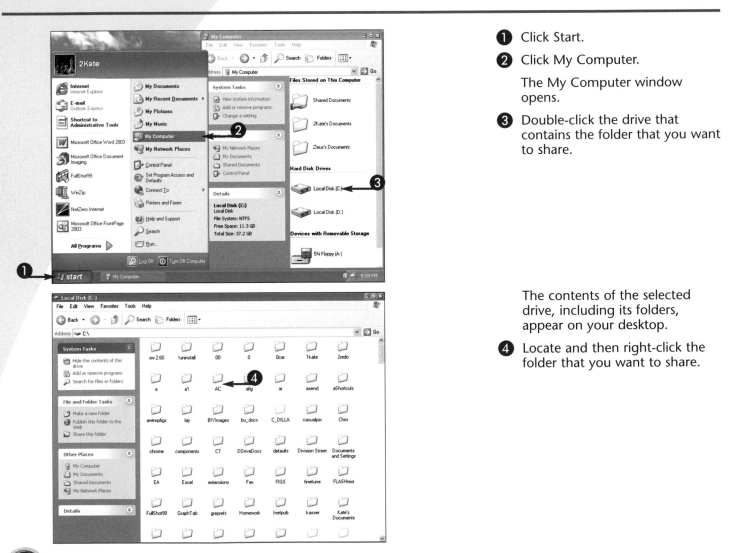

① Click Start.

② Click My Computer.

The My Computer window opens.

③ Double-click the drive that contains the folder that you want to share.

The contents of the selected drive, including its folders, appear on your desktop.

④ Locate and then right-click the folder that you want to share.

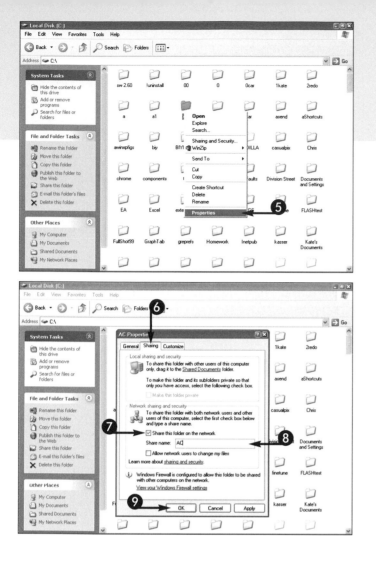

A sub-menu appears.

5 Click Properties.

6 In the Properties dialog box that appears, click the Sharing tab.

7 Under Network sharing and security, click to select the Share this folder on the network option.

8 In the Share name text box, type a name for this folder.

You can also use the default name provided.

9 Click OK.

Your folder is now shared with, and available to, others on the network.

TIPS

Attention!

On the Sharing tab, under Network sharing and security, the option to allow others to change files on your computer is deselected by default. This prevents other users from making unauthorized changes. However, if you want to allow access to change files from elsewhere on the network, then click to select this option.

Caution!

Although you can share entire hard drives, such as your C: or D: drives, it is usually better to share only selected files and folders on your computer. When you share your entire drive, you are making your computer more vulnerable to certain types of spyware and computer viruses. You also make it more likely that others on the network could modify your files in a negative way.

FILE EXTENSIONS AND TYPES:
Set File Associates

In many cases, files are associated with a particular program through their file extensions. For example, if you install Microsoft Office, then files with a .doc file extension are associated with Microsoft Word. Another example is the .txt file extension, which is associated with Notepad. File associations enable you to open documents simply by double-clicking the document — you do not have to first open the program and then open the document.

You may find it useful to view and modify these file associations. For example, with Microsoft Office

installed, the Microsoft Office Document Imaging program becomes the default for viewing files with a .tif or .tiff file extension. However, the Windows Picture and Fax Viewer is generally more useful for browsing a selection of TIF files.

Although you can change file associations to have a different program open a specific file type, you should be careful when you do this. An incorrect change could make it difficult for you to open that type of document until the association is restored to its original setting.

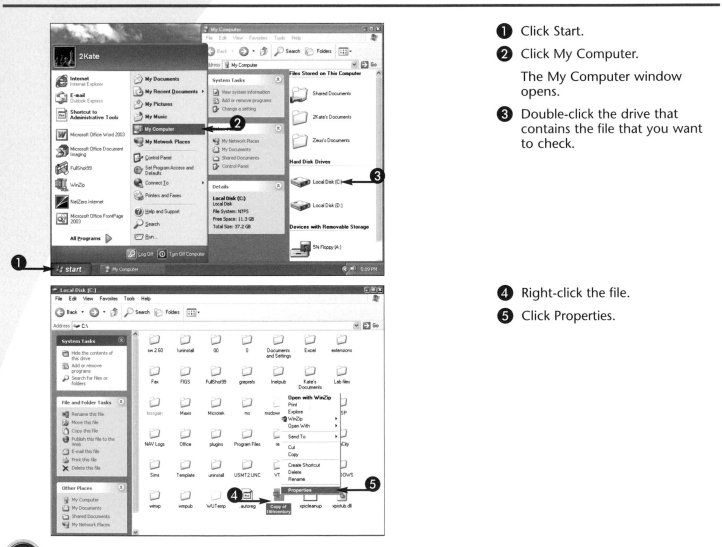

❶ Click Start.

❷ Click My Computer.

  The My Computer window opens.

❸ Double-click the drive that contains the file that you want to check.

❹ Right-click the file.

❺ Click Properties.

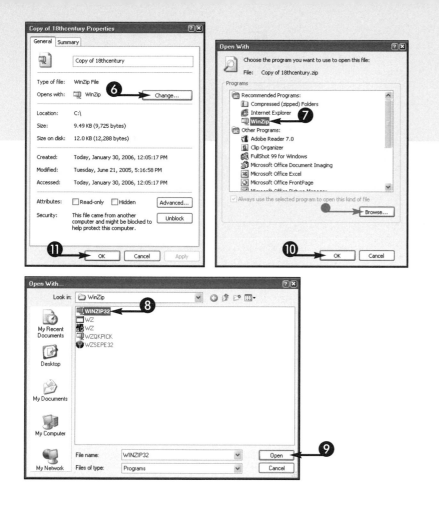

The Properties dialog box appears for the file.

6 Click Change.

The Open With dialog box appears.

7 In the Programs list, locate the program that you want to use to open the file.

● If the program does not appear in the list, you can click Browse to locate it.

A second Open With dialog box appears.

8 Locate the program that you want to associate with the specified file type, and click the program's main executable file, which typically has an .exe file extension.

9 Click Open.

10 Click OK to close the Open With window.

11 Click OK to close the Properties window.

The window closes.

The program that you chose will now open the selected file type when you double-click it.

TIPS

Did You Know?

You can change the Summary properties for some types of files. For example, you can specify the Title, Subject, and Author for Microsoft Office documents. These properties enable you to add information that the document may not otherwise support.

Did You Know?

If you cannot find a file of the type that you want to change, then you can change file associations through the Folder Options dialog box. In any folder, click Tools and then click Folder Options. In the Folder Options dialog box that appears, click the File Types tab. Locate the file extension in the Registered file types list, and then click Change. Then follow the steps on this page.

FILE PROPERTIES:
View and Set File and Folder Attributes

Each file includes a selection of *attributes* that determine specific characteristics for the file. These file attributes serve two purposes: some attributes identify the type of file, while others determine what actions you can take with the file.

You should always know the attributes of a particular file that you use because it may affect what you can do with the file. For example, a read-only attribute prevents the file from being modified, a hidden attribute marks the file as a hidden file, and a system attribute marks the file as belonging to the operating system.

In some situations, it is useful or even necessary to view and modify file attributes. For example, you can turn off a file's read-only attribute if you need to modify the file. You can also turn off the hidden attribute of a file to make it visible in Windows Explorer.

You can view and modify file attributes in one of two ways: through the Windows Explorer interface or from a command console.

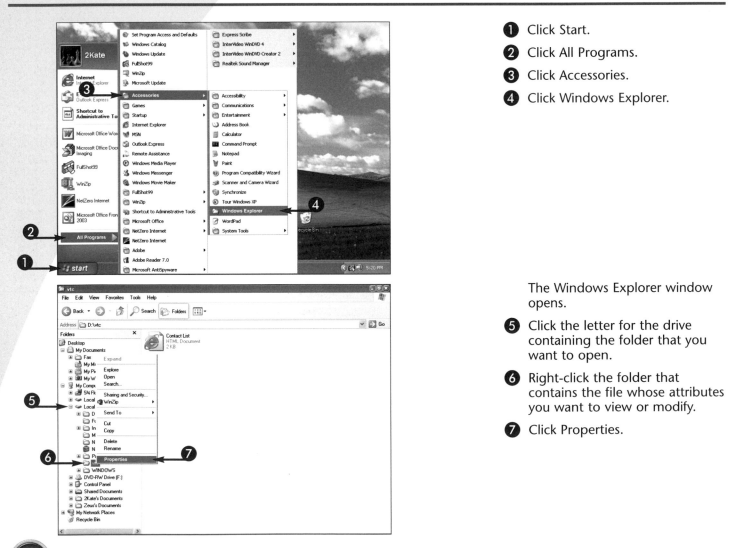

① Click Start.

② Click All Programs.

③ Click Accessories.

④ Click Windows Explorer.

The Windows Explorer window opens.

⑤ Click the letter for the drive containing the folder that you want to open.

⑥ Right-click the folder that contains the file whose attributes you want to view or modify.

⑦ Click Properties.

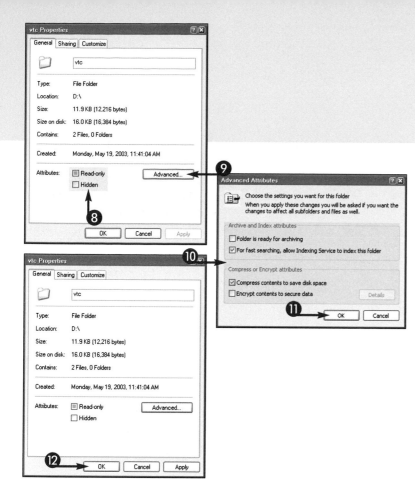

The Properties window appears for the file.

8 To change the Read-only or Hidden attributes, click to select or deselect the option for the attribute.

9 To set other file attributes, click Advanced.

The Advanced Attributes dialog box appears.

10 Select or deselect the options for the attributes that you want to change.

11 Click OK.

The Properties dialog box reappears.

12 Click OK.

The Properties dialog box closes.

Windows applies your changes to the file attributes.

TIPS

Did You Know?
Because files on CD and DVD are read-only, you cannot change any attributes for these media types. In some situations, the read-only attribute is also applied to files that you copy to your computer's hard drive. If you are having trouble modifying a file on your hard drive, then check the status of the read-only attribute.

Did You Know?
Encryption and compression are mutually exclusive. You can apply one or the other to a folder or file, but not both. In addition, encryption and compression both require NTFS and are not supported for the FAT32 file system. Talk to your system Administrator before encrypting any folders or files, because recovering those files may be difficult if you lose your encryption key.

FOLDER OPTIONS:
Set General Folder Options

You can modify the way folders and their contents display. For example, you can specify whether a folder uses the Windows Classic appearance or the more modern appearance of Windows XP.

You can also select whether you want to single-click or double-click a file to open it. This depends on whether you are accustomed to using a single-click or the more common double-click method.

When you make changes, you should watch the effects of these changes to determine whether you

are comfortable with the settings. If not, then you can revert back to the original settings. You can make these changes in the General tab of the Folder Options dialog box.

If your computer crashes after you make these changes, then it is very likely that your new settings will be lost when you restart your computer. You may need to repeat these steps to restore the new folder settings.

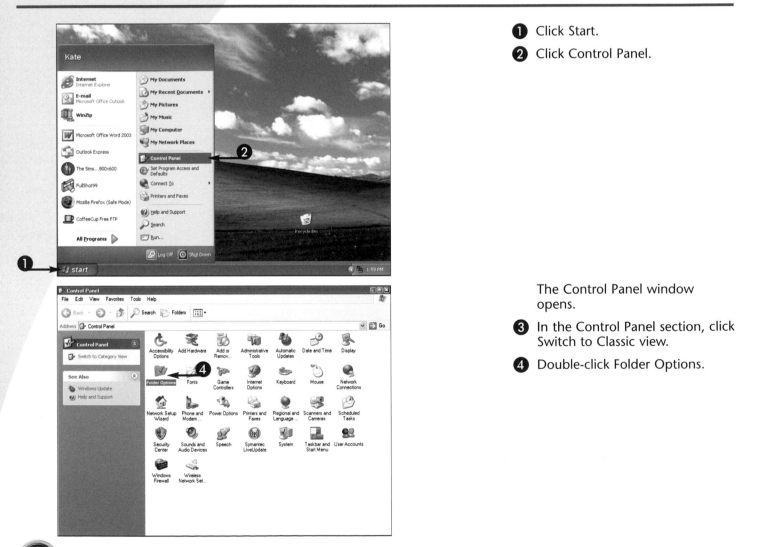

① Click Start.

② Click Control Panel.

The Control Panel window opens.

③ In the Control Panel section, click Switch to Classic view.

④ Double-click Folder Options.

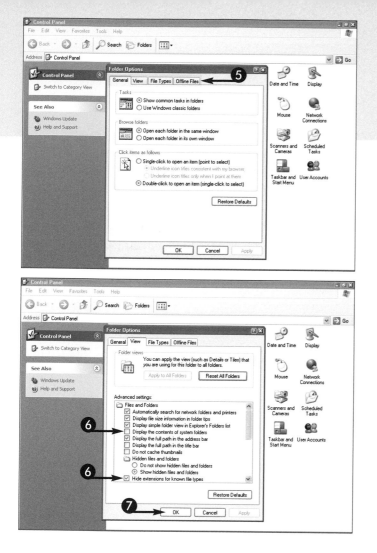

The Folder Options dialog box appears.

5 Click each tab to review the available options.

6 Click to select or deselect the options that you want.

7 Click OK.

Windows applies your changes.

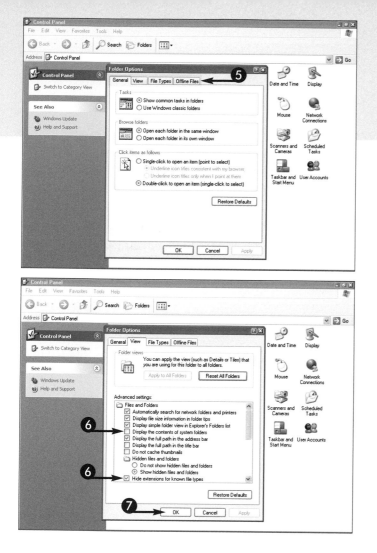

TIPS

Attention!
If you change your folders to Classic view, then you remove some of the Windows XP options that are available. These include the Copy these items and Move these items options that normally appear in the menu in My Computer.

Important!
When you change folder settings on a computer where there are multiple users, you only modify those settings for the current user. Your changes do not affect how other users see their desktop and folders.

Did You Know?
If your computer crashes after you make these changes, then it is very likely that your new settings will be lost when you restart your computer. You may need to repeat these steps to restore the new folder settings.

FOLDERS:
Copy a Folder

You can copy a folder to place it in a second location, such as on another drive, in addition to its original location. This is a useful technique when you want to write a folder to a recordable CD or DVD, to a secondary hard drive, or to some other location.

When you copy a folder, you ensure that your data will not be lost in an emergency where you cannot access the original files. This can happen because of a malfunctioning hard drive or the corruption of individual files. You should always make the copy of the folder on a different location than the original hard drive where it resides.

If you want to permanently remove a folder from one location and move it to another, then you can use the Move feature instead of the Copy feature.

See also>> File and Folder Management

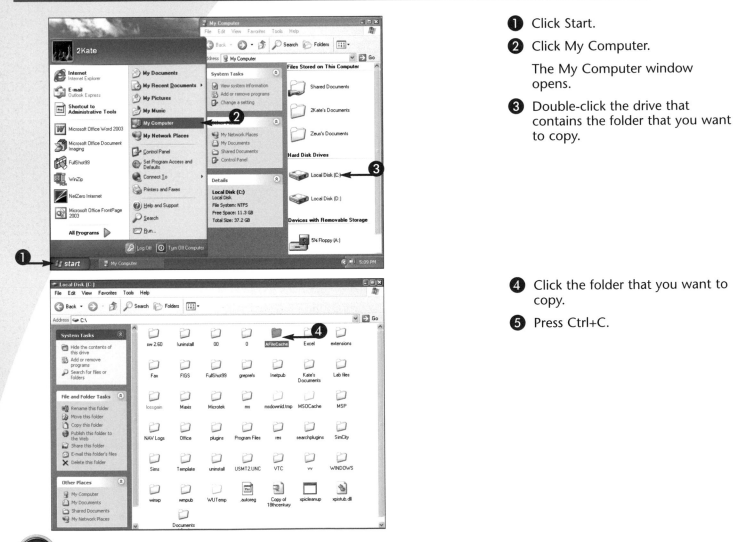

① Click Start.

② Click My Computer.

The My Computer window opens.

③ Double-click the drive that contains the folder that you want to copy.

④ Click the folder that you want to copy.

⑤ Press Ctrl+C.

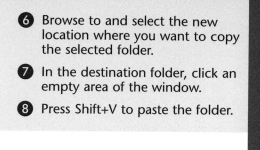

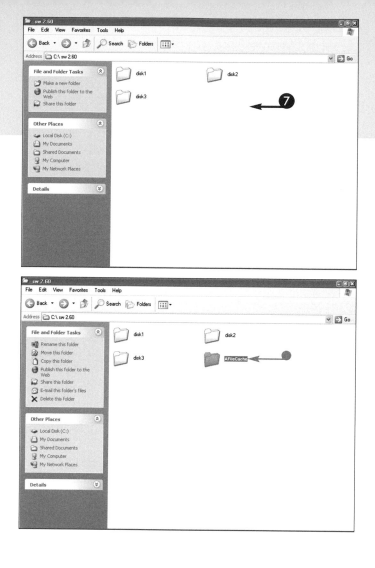

⑥ Browse to and select the new location where you want to copy the selected folder.

⑦ In the destination folder, click an empty area of the window.

⑧ Press Shift+V to paste the folder.

● The folder appears in the new location.

TIPS

Attention!
Once you create your new folder, you can move and copy files as well as other folders into it. You can do this in the My Computer window.

Important!
You should not attempt to copy a folder into the same folder where it is currently located. If you do, then Windows creates a folder called "Copy of [this folder]".

More Options!
You can also drag and drop a new or copied folder from one location to another using My Computer.

Remove It!
To delete a new folder that you have created, simply click the folder and press Delete, or right-click the folder and select Delete.

FOLDERS:
Create a Folder

When you are managing your files and folders, you may need to create new folders, as well as copy existing folders to a different location. Windows allows you to perform this task easily.

When you create a new folder, you can rename it from the default name, New Folder, to a more descriptive title. Your new name should help you to identify what the folder contains. You can create a new folder anywhere on your hard drive, whether in the main or root folder, or within a sub-folder.

You can copy folders either to another folder on the same hard drive or to another drive. You can also copy folders to burn them to a recordable or rewritable CD or DVD in order to store a copy away from your main hard drive for safe-keeping.

Unlike when you move folders, copying folders does not remove them from their original location; instead, it creates a duplicate of the folder in another location.

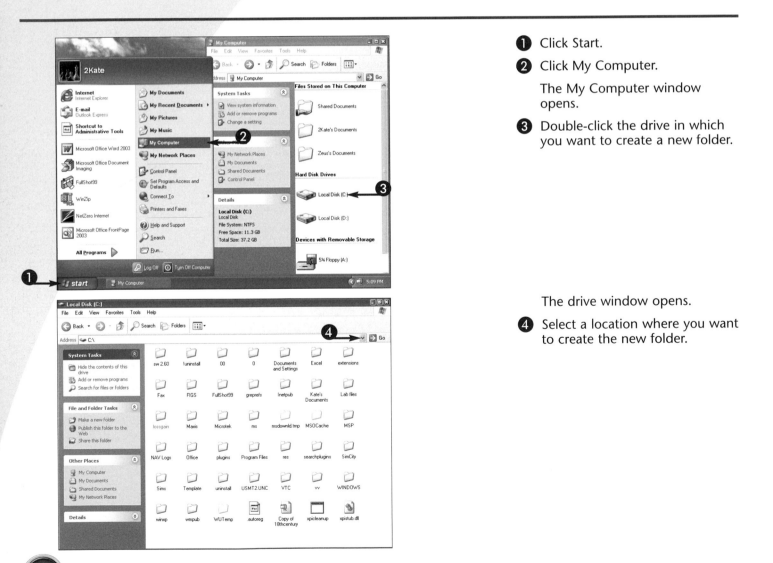

1 Click Start.

2 Click My Computer.

The My Computer window opens.

3 Double-click the drive in which you want to create a new folder.

The drive window opens.

4 Select a location where you want to create the new folder.

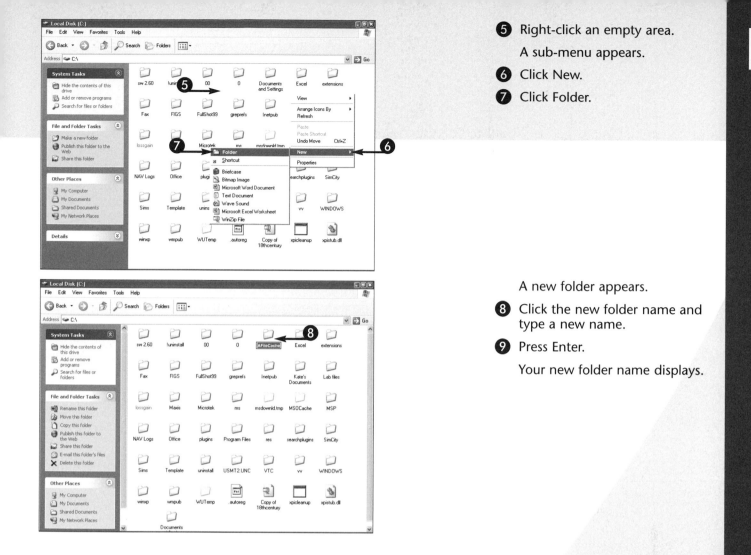

5 Right-click an empty area.

A sub-menu appears.

6 Click New.

7 Click Folder.

A new folder appears.

8 Click the new folder name and type a new name.

9 Press Enter.

Your new folder name displays.

TIPS

Did You Know?

When you create new folders within existing folders, you can organize material and keep track of different versions of files that you revise frequently.

Try This!

You can always rename a folder to better reflect what it contains. Simply double-click the folder name, and then type a new name.

Important!

Two sub-folders within the same folder cannot have the same name. If you try to use the same name for a second folder, then an error message appears. In some cases, Windows may simply add a -1 or a -2 to the name without displaying the error message.

FONTS:
Manage Installed Fonts

If you often install new fonts on your computer, then you probably have dozens if not hundreds of additional fonts that require some management.

Every font that you install takes up a certain amount of hard disk space, and it can also affect available desktop resources when you open documents and other files that use this font. Although Windows does not limit the number of fonts that you can add to your computer, most people only use a few fonts on a regular basis.

If you rarely use some fonts, then you may want to remove them from your system. This saves disk space and shortens the list of possible fonts that appear in the font lists of word processors and other programs that use them. You can manage your fonts through the Fonts option in the Control Panel.

See also>> | **TrueType Fonts**

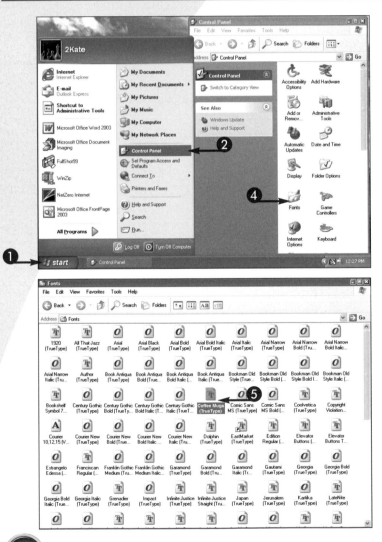

① Click Start.

② Click Control Panel.

The Control Panel window opens.

③ In the Control Panel section, click Switch to Classic View.

④ Double-click Fonts.

The Fonts window opens, displaying all of the fonts that are installed on your system.

⑤ Locate and right-click the font or fonts that you want to remove.

To select multiple fonts, you can click the first font, and then press and hold your Ctrl key while you click the additional fonts.

A sub-menu appears.

6 Click Delete.

A dialog box appears, asking you to confirm the deletion.

7 Click Yes.

Windows deletes the selected fonts from the Fonts folder.

TIPS

Attention!

Once you delete fonts from the Fonts window, you no longer see them in the fonts menu in your word processor or other programs.

Caution!

You should not delete fonts that were originally installed on your computer through Windows or through programs such as Microsoft Word.

Try This!

If you want to have a large number of fonts available but you do not want to have them all installed at the same time, then you can store them in a separate folder or burn them to a recordable CD. You can access and install these fonts at anytime you need them, and then remove them when you are done.

FORMAT:
Format a Disk

When you install a new hard drive, you need to partition and then format the drive, so you can start receiving files you want to store on your operating system. This is a necessary step in the preparation of a new hard drive; otherwise, you will be unable to use it.

If you also buy floppy disks that are not pre-formatted to use with the drive, then you need to format these disks before you can write files to them.

Although the Windows XP Setup disk allows you to automatically partition and format a newly added

hard drive, there may be other times when you want to format a drive. For example, although you may not be installing an operating system, you may want to add a secondary hard disk for storage, or to format a floppy diskette. In these situations, you can use the Format command in the My Computer window.

See also>> **Disk Cleanup Wizard**

Disk Defragmenter

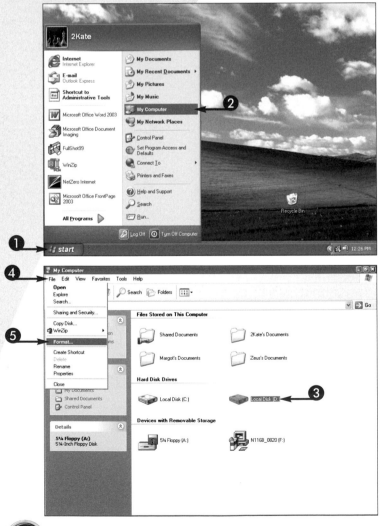
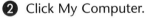

Note: *If you need to format a floppy disk, then you must insert a blank disk into your floppy drive; if the drive is a hard disk, then you must physically install this disk and partition it first.*

① Click Start.

② Click My Computer.

The My Computer window opens.

③ Click the letter of the disk that you want to format.

④ Click File.

⑤ Click Format.

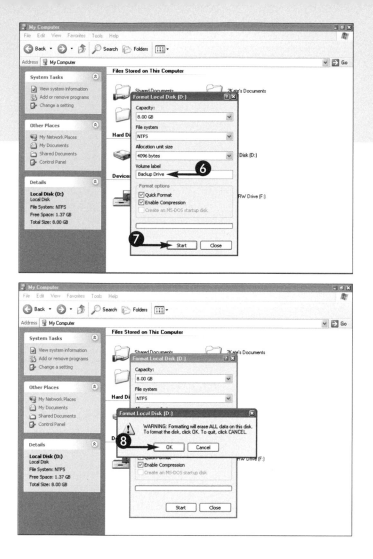

The Format Disk dialog box appears for the disk that you selected.

6 Type a Volume label, or name, for the disk.

7 Click Start.

A warning dialog box appears, notifying you that formatting will erase all data from the disk.

8 Click OK.

Windows begins the formatting process.

TIPS

Attention!
You can completely reformat a hard drive that you are already using. However, you should first back up your important files because they will be deleted during formatting.

Caution!
Be sure to select the correct disk in the My Computer window that you want to format. If you choose a hard drive when you actually want to format a floppy disk, then you will lose all of the data on the hard drive.

Did You Know?
You may think that reformatting a disk completely erases its contents. However, trained specialists can usually recover these contents. Keep in mind that if you sell, donate, or throw out a computer with a hard disk, it is possible for someone to recover your confidential information.

FTP:
Use FTP from the Command Console for File Transfer

When you need to transfer files over the Internet using File Transfer Protocol, or FTP, you usually have three choices: you can use special FTP software, your Internet Explorer Web browser, or the FTP program that comes with Windows XP.

The Windows XP FTP program is not designed to run like other Windows programs. Instead, you must run it from the Command Console, which opens as a black screen on your Windows desktop. This

means that the FTP program does not have the point-and-click graphical interface that you usually find in Windows. It requires either a basic knowledge of DOS — an earlier command-line operating system — or the ability to follow a few on-screen prompts to proceed.

If you find the FTP program too difficult to use, then you may want to use your Internet Explorer Web browser, instead.

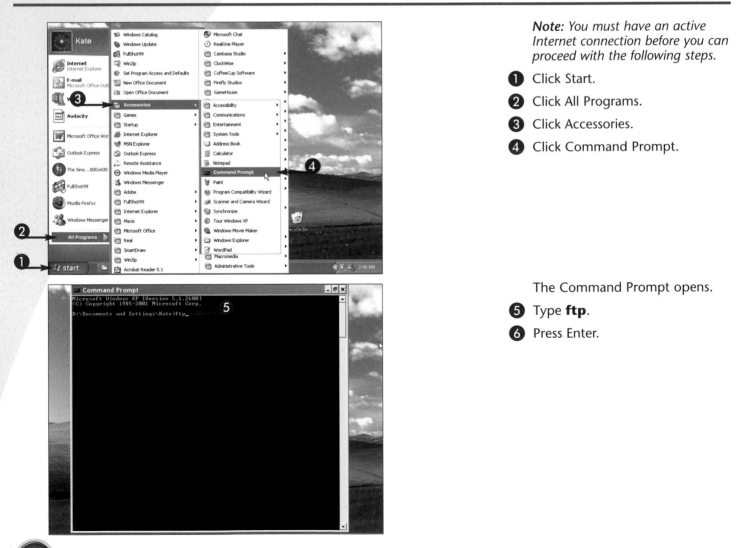

Note: *You must have an active Internet connection before you can proceed with the following steps.*

❶ Click Start.

❷ Click All Programs.

❸ Click Accessories.

❹ Click Command Prompt.

The Command Prompt opens.

❺ Type **ftp**.

❻ Press Enter.

The command console displays an ftp Command Prompt.

7 Type **ftp.ftpname.com** where ftpname.com is the actual name of the FTP server that you want to access.

8 Press Enter.

9 Type your FTP username.

10 Type your FTP password.

After you log in, you can transfer files using the Send command, or download files using the Get command.

F

TIPS

Try This!
To upload a file, type **send filename**. To download a file, type **get filename**. To disconnect from the FTP server and end your current session, type **quit**.

Try This!
If you want extra features with your FTP sessions, such as uploads or downloads that can automatically resume, or the ability to send multiple files at once, then you can download an FTP client such as CuteFTP, CoffeeCup FTP, or WSFTP.

Caution!
Always be careful when downloading files from any source, including FTP sites. Once you download your files, check them using a virus scanner to ensure that they are safe to use. It is also a good idea to scan files that you intend to upload before you transmit them.

FTP:
Use FTP in Internet Explorer

You may sometimes need to visit a File Transfer Protocol, or FTP, site to upload and download files. However, if you do not have FTP software installed, then you can access most FTP sites directly through your Microsoft Internet Explorer Web browser.

Using FTP through your Web browser does not require any special software or browser add-ons. You simply need the address of the FTP server. If the server requires a username and password to access the site, then you need this information as well. Otherwise, you can log in as an anonymous user.

Keep in mind that FTP sites tend to have very simple interfaces. They display folders and files, similar to what you see when using Windows Explorer to perform file management. To upload a file, you can click a link on the page, and to download a file, you can simply double-click the file. When you download a file, you must also specify where on your disk the file should be transferred.

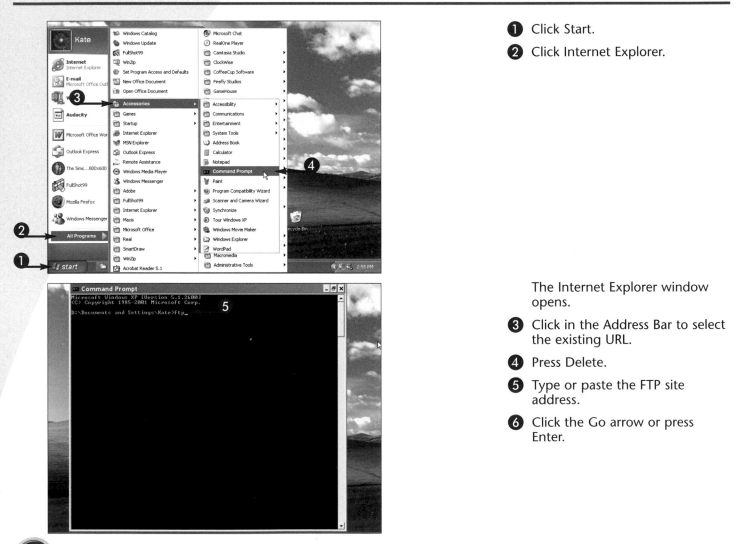

❶ Click Start.

❷ Click Internet Explorer.

The Internet Explorer window opens.

❸ Click in the Address Bar to select the existing URL.

❹ Press Delete.

❺ Type or paste the FTP site address.

❻ Click the Go arrow or press Enter.

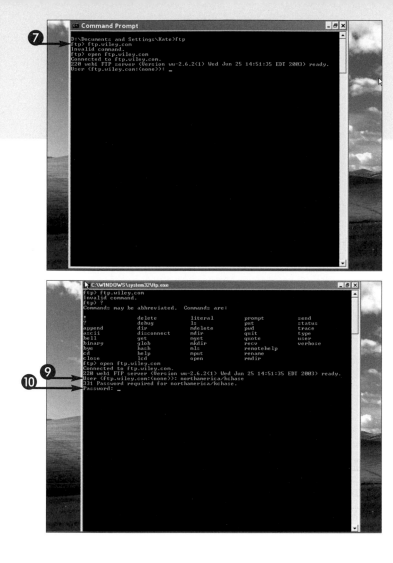

The FTP site displays in the Internet Explorer window.

7 If the FTP site requires that you log in, then click File.

8 Click Login As.

The Log On As dialog box appears.

9 Type your username.

10 Type your password.

11 Click Log On.

12 Locate the file or folder that you want to download.

13 Right-click the file or folder.

14 Click Copy or Copy To Folder.

To upload a file, or copy it from another location or from the FTP site, you can right-click an empty area and choose Paste.

Windows copies the selected file to your computer, or uploads it to the FTP server.

TIPS

Attention!
If you cannot access an FTP site, then it may require a username or password. Contact the Administrator of the FTP site to obtain this access information and then try again.

Attention!
After you copy the file in Step 14, you may be prompted for the location on your drive where you want to transfer the file. Click Browse to select this location.

Caution!
Even if the FTP site from which you download or copy files is a trusted site, you should still use caution when opening any files from an outside source. If you have a virus scanner, then use it to scan this file before you open it.

GENERAL PROPERTIES:
View General Properties for the Computer

If you want to know which version of Windows you are using or what type of central processor unit, or CPU, you have on your computer, then you can find this out in the General System Properties tab. You can also find out whether or not a service pack has been installed to the system, and how much memory, or RAM, you have installed. You can view your Windows product key here, which is helpful if you need to call Microsoft Windows technical support, as they often want some evidence that your copy of Windows is legitimate and registered with them.

This general information is vital in determining whether you have the necessary system requirements for adding a particular piece of hardware or software, as well as how powerful and up-to-date your system is. If you have a busy desktop, then you can view the General tab to see how much memory is installed; if you have less than 256MB installed, then you may want to add more memory.

① Click Start.

② Click Control Panel.

③ In the Control Panel section, click Switch to Classic View.

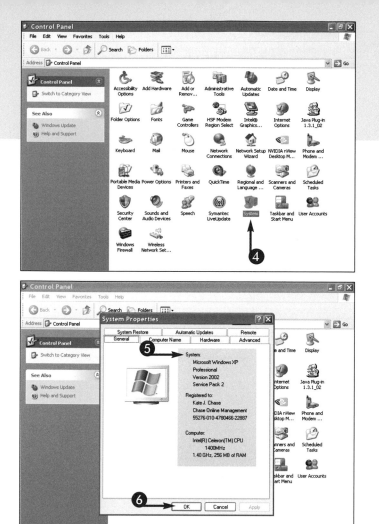

④ Double-click System.

The System Properties dialog box appears, displaying the General tab by default.

⑤ Read the information under the General tab.

⑥ When finished, click OK.

The System Properties dialog box closes.

TIPS

Caution!

In some cases, the information in the General tab may be different from what you expect. If it is, then ensure that you are not using a different computer than you normally do. Also, if your computer appears to have less memory than you thought, then the memory may not be correctly installed, or one or more memory modules may be failing.

Did You Know?

Although a product key appears in the General tab, it does NOT match the product key that you typed in when you first installed the package. Instead, it is a *final* key that was generated from that initial product key.

GROUPS:
Create Groups

Windows XP offers two types of security objects: accounts and groups. Both of these object types enable you to control access to local resources such as shared folders and printers. In addition, you can use groups to simplify the application of permissions on these resources.

You may have two sets of users on a network, where the first set of users needs to read files in a specific folder on your computer, and the second set of users also needs to modify files. The simple solution is to create two user groups, grant one Read permission

and the other Read and Write permission, and then place into each group those users who need the level of access offered by that group.

You can use the Local Users and Groups console in Windows XP to create local groups. After you create a group, you can add individual user accounts to the group. You can also add groups to a group, which is called *nesting groups*. All of the members of the nested group receive the permissions that are assigned to the higher-level group.

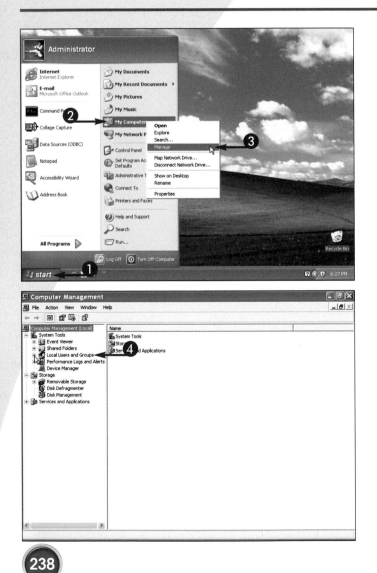

① Click Start.

② Right-click My Computer.

③ Click Manage.

The Computer Management console opens.

④ Click the plus sign next to Local Users and Groups.

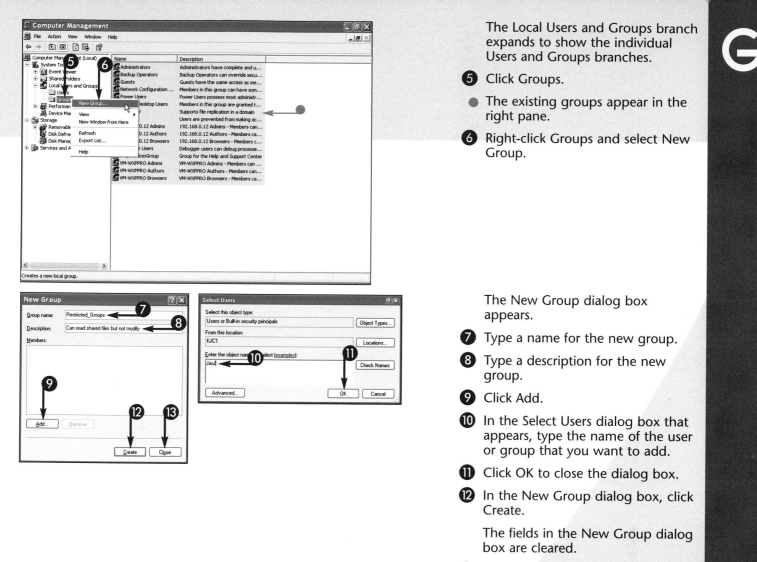

The Local Users and Groups branch expands to show the individual Users and Groups branches.

5 Click Groups.

● The existing groups appear in the right pane.

6 Right-click Groups and select New Group.

The New Group dialog box appears.

7 Type a name for the new group.

8 Type a description for the new group.

9 Click Add.

10 In the Select Users dialog box that appears, type the name of the user or group that you want to add.

11 Click OK to close the dialog box.

12 In the New Group dialog box, click Create.

The fields in the New Group dialog box are cleared.

13 Click Close.

TIPS

Did You Know?

Windows XP creates several groups by default, and some of these groups are used by the system. For example, the all restricted user accounts are members of the built-in Users group. Accounts that you create with administrative rights are members of the Administrators group. In addition, adding certain applications results in new groups being added automatically.

Delete It!

It is just as easy to delete a group as it is to create one. Simply open the Computer Management console, open the Groups branch under Local Users and Groups, click the group, and press the Delete key on the keyboard. Click Yes when prompted to confirm the deletion.

HELP AND SUPPORT CENTER:
Access Help and Other Information for Windows

From your desktop, you can use the Help and Support Center in Windows XP to find help articles, step-by-step instructions, special tools, and additional resources. This feature helps you solve problems and learn about additional options in Windows XP when questions surface. When you use the center along with your available Internet connection, you can find assistance both from help files on your system as well as the huge online library of Windows content that is available from Microsoft.

To start, you can click one of the many categories that appear in the Help and Support Center, such as Remote Assistance. You can also type a word or phrase into the Search text box at the top-left corner of the window, and then look it up both online and off. Another method is to click other listed items to navigate deeper into the help information that is available so that you can learn at your own pace.

See also>>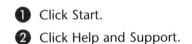

① Click Start.

② Click Help and Support.

The Help and Support Center window opens.

③ Type a word or phrase into the Search text box.

This example uses Configure IP Address.

④ Click the Go arrow to search.

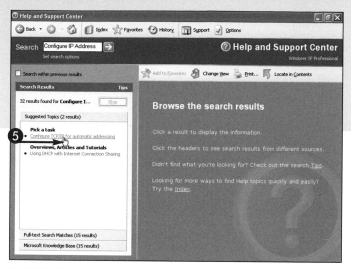

Search results appear in the left-hand pane.

5 Click the closest matching entry.

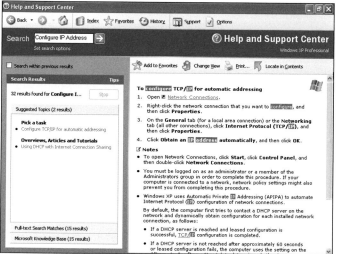

The article opens in the right-hand pane.

TIPS

Did You Know?
You access the best results in the Help and Support Center when you use it with a live Internet connection. If you have a dialup connection, then click to connect before you open the center so that you have access to the online library as well as the offline library.

More Options!
At the bottom of many articles and help pieces, you will see the Related Topics link. Click this link to see a list of articles that relate to what you just read, or click a specific link to open the corresponding article in the right-hand pane.

Try This!
You can click many of the blue underlined links that appear in help articles and other content in the Help and Support Center to either view a definition of a term or launch the listed tool or option.

ICONS:
Set Icon Size and Spacing

If you want your icons to appear larger or smaller, then you can set their size as well as their horizontal and vertical spacing. Using this option, you can control the appearance of your desktop to customize the layout and to make the icons more visible to you. You can also customize icon size and spacing to better match your screen resolution or the size of the windows on your desktop.

In addition to icon size and spacing, there are other changes that you can make, including the size and type of the font that you use to label an icon.

You may want to experiment until you achieve the right combination of maximum icon visibility and an uncluttered desktop. Also, each person who shares a computer can set their own custom desktop configuration with a separate user account, so that they are not constrained by the customizations of another user.

See also>> **Desktop Cleanup Wizard**

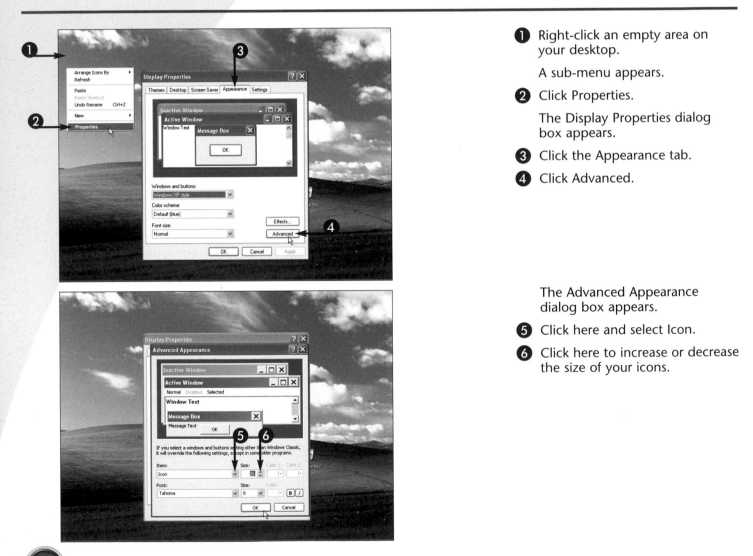

❶ Right-click an empty area on your desktop.

A sub-menu appears.

❷ Click Properties.

The Display Properties dialog box appears.

❸ Click the Appearance tab.

❹ Click Advanced.

The Advanced Appearance dialog box appears.

❺ Click here and select Icon.

❻ Click here to increase or decrease the size of your icons.

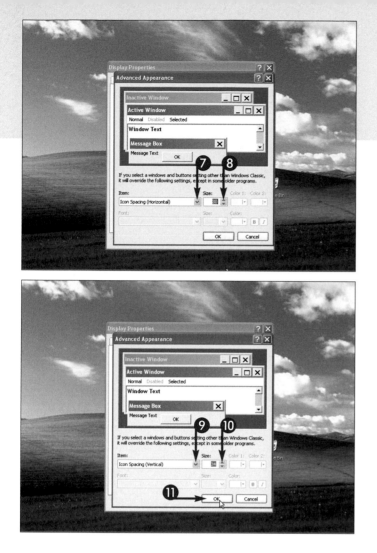

⑦ Click here and select Icon Spacing (Horizontal).

⑧ Click here to increase or decrease the horizontal spacing.

⑨ Click here and select Icon Spacing (Vertical).

⑩ Click here to increase or decrease the vertical spacing.

⑪ Click OK.

⑫ Click OK to close the Display Properties dialog box.

Windows applies your changes to the desktop icons.

TIPS

Attention!

You may want to note default settings with icon size and spacing before you begin to adjust specific options here. When you take this extra step, you ensure that you can revert to your previous desktop appearance if you do not like the changes you made. You can then go back and try different size and spacing choices.

Important!

If you work in a corporate environment or on a system under the control of an administrator, it is possible you will not be able to adjust desktop settings such as icon size and spacing. Contact your system or network administrator if you have questions. He or she may be able to change options for you or permit you access to do so.

IMPORT/EXPORT:
Import and Export Favorites in Internet Explorer

When you set up a new computer or hard drive, you may want to copy your Microsoft Internet Explorer Favorites list from your old setup to your new one. When you do so, you create consistency between two or more computers in your home or small office. You also save time spent to recreate or send these links individually in email or an instant messaging system such as Windows Messenger. The Favorites list contains links to Web sites or network resources that you choose to save; these are sometimes called

bookmarks. You can use the Import/Export tool in the Web browser on your new Windows setup to import a copy of these links from the original setup.

You run the Import/Export Wizard on both computers, starting with the original computer, to guide you through the necessary steps to complete the two-part process. The Import process takes just moments to successfully finish, far less time than it would take you to recreate these links manually.

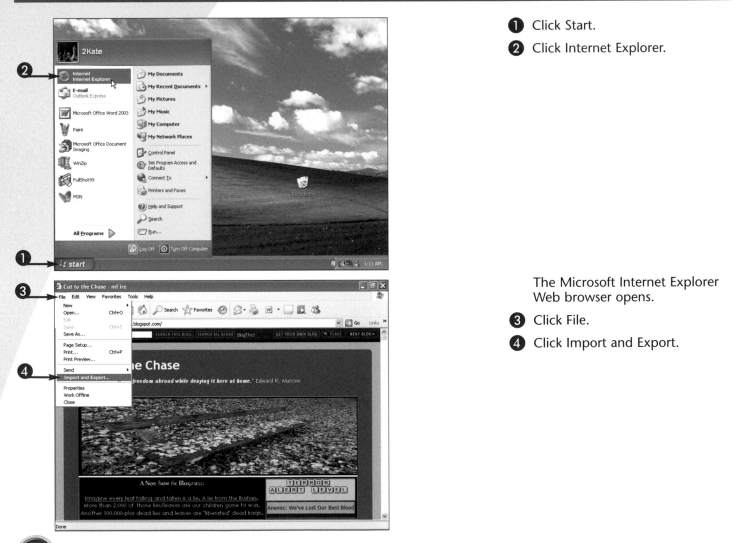

① Click Start.

② Click Internet Explorer.

The Microsoft Internet Explorer Web browser opens.

③ Click File.

④ Click Import and Export.

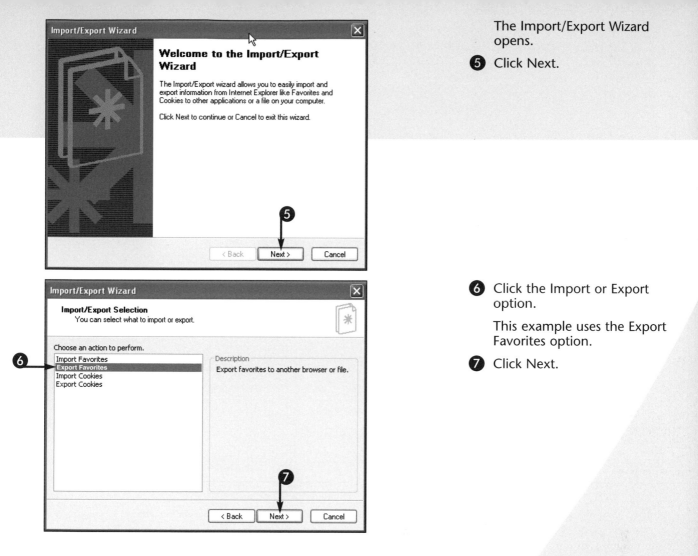

The Import/Export Wizard opens.

5 Click Next.

6 Click the Import or Export option.

This example uses the Export Favorites option.

7 Click Next.

TIPS

Did You Know?

Is your Favorites list long and filled with entries that you do not necessarily want to export to a new setup? If so, then you can organize your links and delete the unwanted ones before you export the final list. To do this, click Favorites, and then click Organize Favorites. When the Organize Favorites window opens, you can click a link and then click Delete to remove it.

Try This!

You can also share a copy of your Favorites with friends, family, and co-workers by sending them a copy of the file that you create when you export your favorite links. The export file is small enough to send as an e-mail attachment or through instant messaging software.

IMPORT/EXPORT:
Import and Export Favorites in Internet Explorer (Continued)

You can quickly prepare a new computer with options and settings from another computer by importing them. When you want to copy your favorite Web page links from an existing Windows setup to another one, you first must export the Favorites list from the current setup. You can then import the exported Favorites list file into the newly installed Internet Explorer application so that you can use the links on the new system. These imported Favorites are available through the Favorites menu in the Web browser.

Once you import the Favorites list into the new setup, you can then maintain separate Favorites lists on each computer. This means that you can organize and customize each list and delete copied links that you do not want.

Even when you do not need to copy Favorites between different setups, you can create a copy of your Favorites list by using the Export tool so that you can keep this list as part of your file backup. To recover the links, all you need to do is import them again.

⑧ Click to select an import or export option.

This example uses the Export to a File or Address option.

⑨ Click Browse to locate the file or address.

The Select Bookmark File dialog box appears.

⑩ Click here to find the location where you want to save the file.

You should choose a storage location that you can access from the new computer. In this example, the export file can fit easily on a floppy disk if you choose to store it on one.

⑪ Type a filename.

⑫ Click Save.

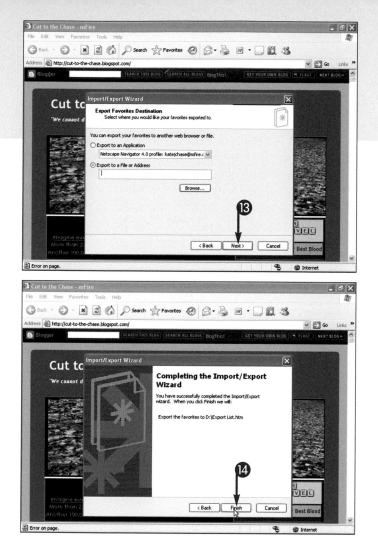

The Select Bookmark File dialog box closes, returning you to the Import/Export Wizard.

13 Click Next.

The wizard completion page appears.

14 Click Finish.

The Import/Export Wizard closes.

You have successfully imported or exported your Favorites list.

TIPS

Desktop Trick!

Your Favorites list appears in the new setup exactly as it did in the old setup from which you exported it. If the link list is out of alphabetical order, then click Favorites to open the list, right-click the listing, and then click Sort by Name to re-order it.

More Options!

If the Favorites list that you export is unwieldy and poorly organized, then you can manage your links to make individual entries easier to locate. Click Favorites and then click Organize Favorites. When the Organize Folder window appears, click Create a Folder to add a folder, and then name the folder. You can then click a Favorites link to delete it or to move it to the new folder.

INTERNET OPTIONS:
Configure Options in Internet Explorer

You can configure various aspects of the Microsoft Internet Explorer Web browser. For example, you can activate or deactivate Content Advisor, the parental controls feature that restricts access to adult content by a child. In addition, you can configure these controls to limit what a child or other person who uses your computer can access on the Web. You can also custom-configure security zones that the browser uses to determine whether to accept cookies. Cookies are small files that are passed by many Web sites to help to identify you and what you read while you are there.

You can access these features through the Internet Options selection under the Tools menu. This option opens a multi-tabbed window where you can configure specific settings that are related to privacy and communications, as well as advanced options that control how the browser functions. For example, you can specify how the browser handles your Internet connection.

See also>>   **Content Advisor**

Content Advisor

① Click Start.

② Click Internet Explorer.

The Microsoft Internet Explorer window opens.

③ Click Tools.

④ Click Internet Options.

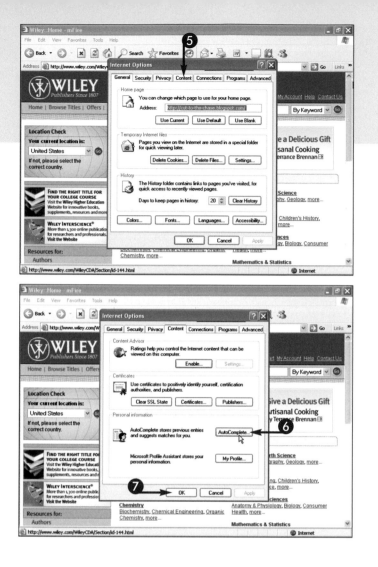

The Internet Options dialog box appears.

5 Click the tab for the option that you want to modify.

6 Click to make the change that you want.

7 Click OK when you have completed your selections.

Windows applies your changes.

INTERNET PRINTING PROTOCOL:
Use the IPP to Print to a Remote Printer

When you configure the Internet Printing Protocol, or IPP, you can print a document or Web page to your home computer as you browse the Web from work, or vice versa. For example, if you need an application for personal use that you can only access from your high-speed network connection at the office, then you can direct this document to print on your home inkjet printer so that it awaits you at the end of the day. You simply need to know the address where the printer is located.

Unlike a standard print process where you click File and then click Print, or press Ctrl+P, the IPP allows you to start to print once you type the address of the printer in the Address Bar, just as you would any other Internet address. This printer location can be at work, at home, or at any other address.

You can use this feature to broadcast information to people in a community group, your team at the office, or any other organization with whom you need to share printed details or reports.

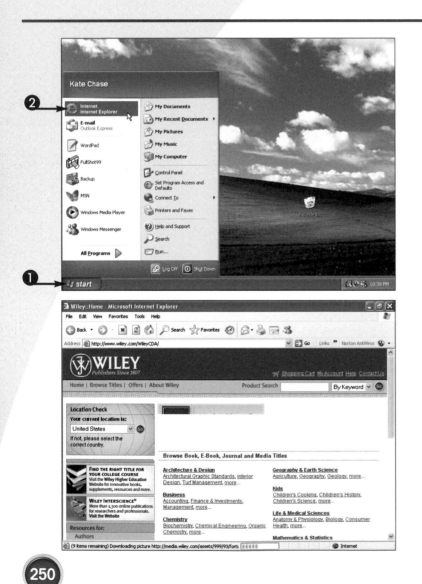

① Click Start.

② Click Internet Explorer.

The Microsoft Internet Explorer window opens.

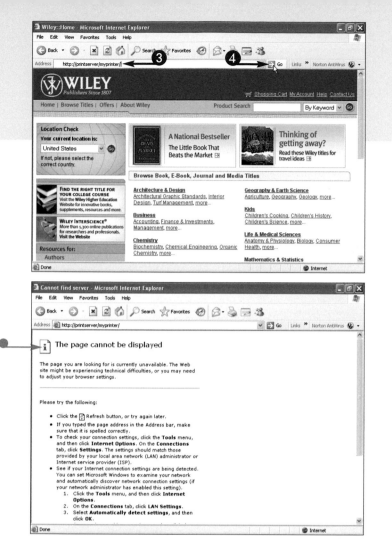

3 Type the Internet address of the printer into the Address Bar.

This example uses the address http://printserver/myprinter/.

4 Click the Go arrow.

If there is a problem, then the Web browser displays a warning message.

● In this example, the warning message is *This page cannot be displayed.*

If no error message displays, then you can assume that the document printed.

When the printing finishes, you can close the browser or continue to surf the Web.

Caution!

When you enable the Internet Printing Protocol, you also make it possible for someone else to abuse that capability, even if you use a firewall to protect your setup. For example, another user can send you files that you do not want by sending them to your printer to output as hard copy.

Important!

If you plan to use this feature on a regular basis, then you must ensure that your printer is ready. You should have adequate toner or print cartridges in place, along with the paper that you need to print whatever you may be sending over the Internet. If you do not prepare your printer properly, then this can result in a print failure.

IP ADDRESSES:
Configure a Computer IP Address

When you set up a new Internet access service account through an Internet Service Provider, or ISP, you may need to configure your Internet Protocol, or IP, address to set up the service. You may also need to do this when you set up a new computer on a network where one computer serves as the gateway to access the Internet while other computers share that Internet connection.

You must first determine what the ISP requires for your Internet configuration before you can configure the IP address on your computer. You also need to find out whether the service expects you to supply a

specific address or allows Windows to automatically assign one. The latter option is much easier for you to set up, while the former option requires that you provide specific settings for different aspects of the service configuration.

Your decision usually depends on the information that is provided by your ISP or your network Administrator when you set up your connection.

See also>> **IPconfig**

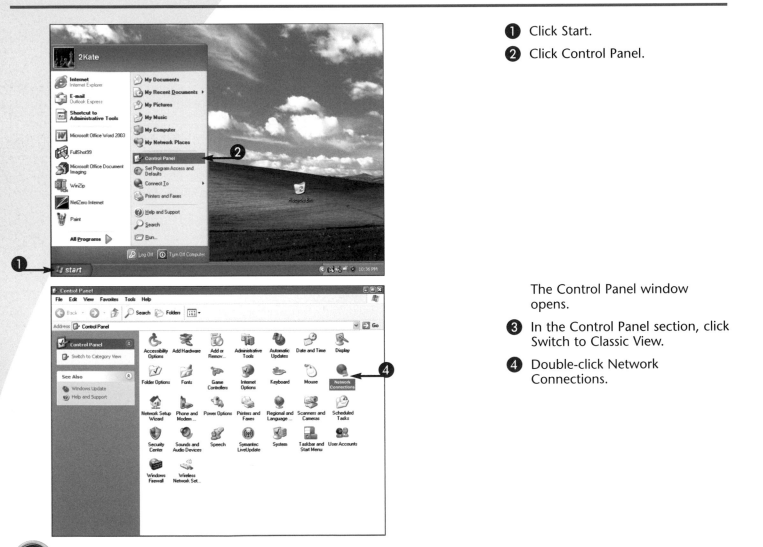

① Click Start.

② Click Control Panel.

The Control Panel window opens.

③ In the Control Panel section, click Switch to Classic View.

④ Double-click Network Connections.

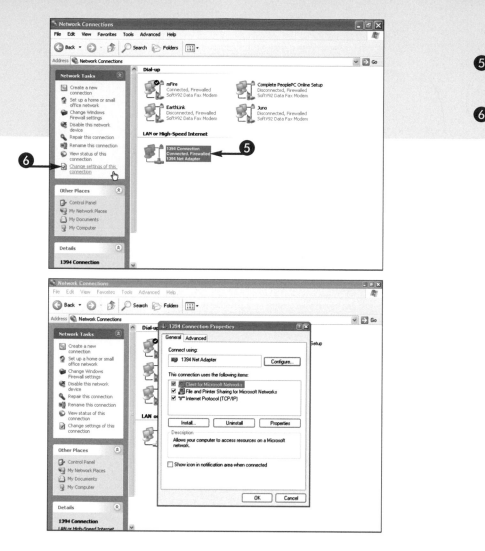

The Network Connections window opens.

⑤ Click a listed connection that you want to configure for an IP address.

⑥ Click Change settings of this connection.

The Properties dialog box appears for the connection that you chose.

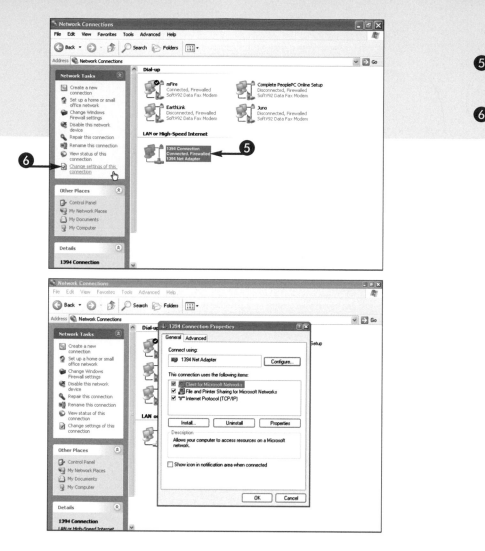

TIPS

Attention!
No two computers that access the Internet can have identical IP addresses because an IP address is used to identify each connection.

Important!
IP addresses come in two types: static, which means that the IP address is fixed and never changes; and dynamic, which means that a new IP address is used each time you access the Internet. Most broadband Internet access services issue static IP addresses, while dial-up and other types of connection services use dynamic IP addresses.

More Options!
If you have more than one network adapter installed or you use more than one Internet service — such as a laptop computer that uses both home and work Internet access — then you may have multiple IP addresses.

IP ADDRESSES:
Configure a Computer IP Address (Continued)

When you configure the IP address for a computer, you must be careful when you select options and type addresses. One small typographic error or wrong choice can prevent you from being able to connect successfully with the Internet.

Normally, if your ISP or network Administrator has not specified whether to allow the server to assign an IP address automatically or for you to provide exact IP addresses, then it is best to try automatic assignment first. If you cannot connect to the Internet through the automatic settings, then you can use the same steps outlined here to specify

exact IP addresses, based on information provided by your ISP or Administrator.

When you configure your IP address, you may also need to configure a domain name server, or DNS, address. This refers to a server that is set up to translate a numbered IP address into a name, and vice versa. For example, the DNS server can translate the IP address 208.215.179.146 into www.wiley.com.

See also>>

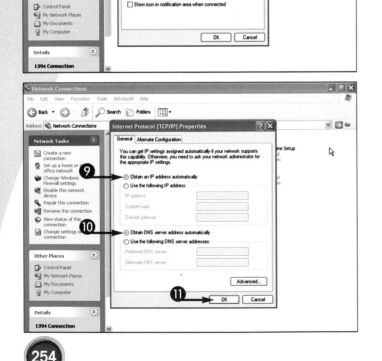

7 In the Properties dialog box, click Internet Protocol (TCP/IP).

8 Click Properties.

The Internet Protocol (TCP/IP) Properties dialog box appears.

9 To use an automatic configuration, click to select the Obtain an IP address automatically option.

10 Click the Obtain DNS server address automatically option.

11 Click OK.

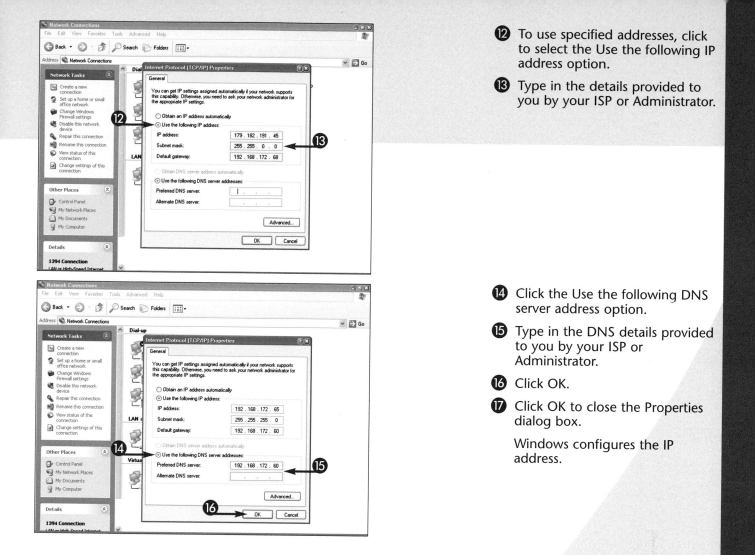

⑫ To use specified addresses, click to select the Use the following IP address option.

⑬ Type in the details provided to you by your ISP or Administrator.

⑭ Click the Use the following DNS server address option.

⑮ Type in the DNS details provided to you by your ISP or Administrator.

⑯ Click OK.

⑰ Click OK to close the Properties dialog box.

Windows configures the IP address.

TIPS

Attention!
Once you configure your IP address, you should be able to connect with the Internet. If you cannot, then you should recheck your IP configuration details, as well as any specific instructions from your ISP or Administrator.

More Options!
If you sometimes use an alternate IP address, then you can configure an alternate address that Windows uses if your main IP configuration does not work. To do this, click the Alternate Configuration tab in the Internet Protocol (TCP/IP) Properties dialog box and provide the alternate configuration addresses. These addresses are available from your ISP or network Administrator.

IPCONFIG:
View and Manage TCP/IP Settings from the Command Console

To learn your current Internet Protocol, or IP, address and other details about your current Internet and network settings, you can use the IPconfig command. IPconfig is a utility that runs exclusively from the Command Console, or MS-DOS Command Prompt. This means that you cannot click options as you do in normal Windows utilities. However, you can use this tool without advanced knowledge of the Command Console.

Through IPconfig, you can also manage TCP/IP, or network protocol, settings. You can renew or release

certain network settings such as the identity, or class ID, for a specific adapter that is used with domain-based networks. To do this, you need to add switches to the command that allow you to modify exactly what the IPconfig tool does. For example, if you type ipconfig by itself, then you see only a display of information about your current settings. However, if you type ipconfig /renew, then you renew the lease that is used with a domain name service client.

See also>> **IP Addresses**

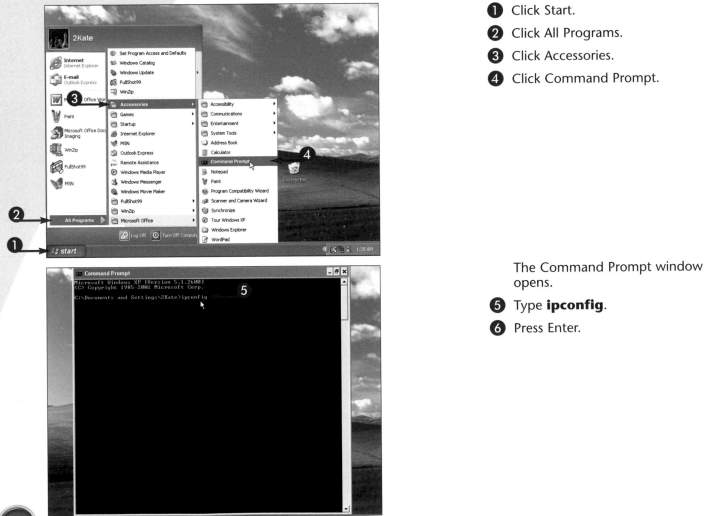

1 Click Start.

2 Click All Programs.

3 Click Accessories.

4 Click Command Prompt.

The Command Prompt window opens.

5 Type **ipconfig**.

6 Press Enter.

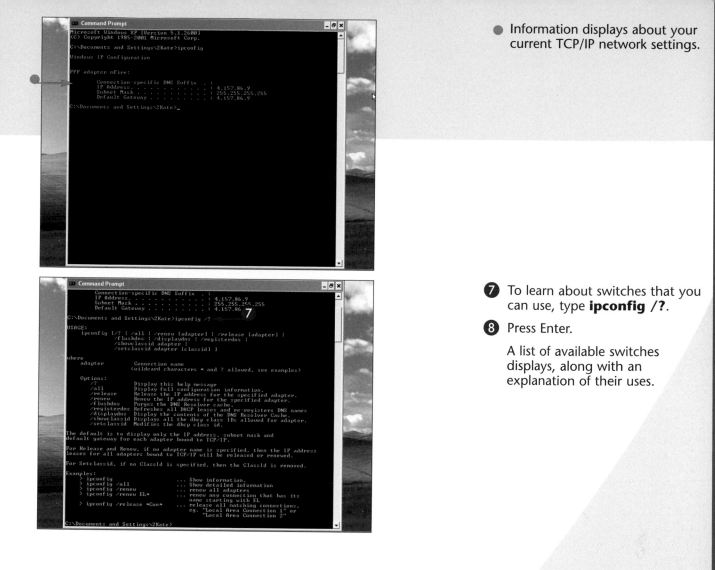

● Information displays about your current TCP/IP network settings.

7 To learn about switches that you can use, type **ipconfig /?**.

8 Press Enter.

A list of available switches displays, along with an explanation of their uses.

TIPS

Attention!

Unlike some other Command Console tools that you can easily launch from the Start Menu, IPconfig only opens very briefly. In fact, the window simply flashes on your screen, with too little time to see the information that it provides. Use the steps in this section to launch the Command Console so that you can use IPconfig.

Important!

Unless your Windows XP computer is on a network that uses Domain Host Control Protocol, or DHCP, settings, some switches, such as /renew and /release, may only return an error. This happens because you do not have network hardware configured for this purpose.

KEYBOARD:
Configure Keyboard Settings

The Keyboard options in the Control Panel allow you to adjust your keyboard settings. For example, if you are uncomfortable with the speed and responsiveness of your keyboard, then you can configure your keyboard settings to match the way you type.

The Keyboard Properties dialog box allows you to adjust settings that change the input signal to the computer. For example, by adjusting the Character repeat sliders, you can set the speed rate of a key when it is pressed, as well as the rate of a key when you press it multiple times. You can then test these

settings until you find one with which you are comfortable. You can also adjust the cursor blink rate that displays on your screen.

Some high-performance keyboards have special programmable settings beyond what you can adjust through Windows. You should refer to your keyboard documentation and any accompanying software to make these adjustments.

See also>> **Regional and Language Options**

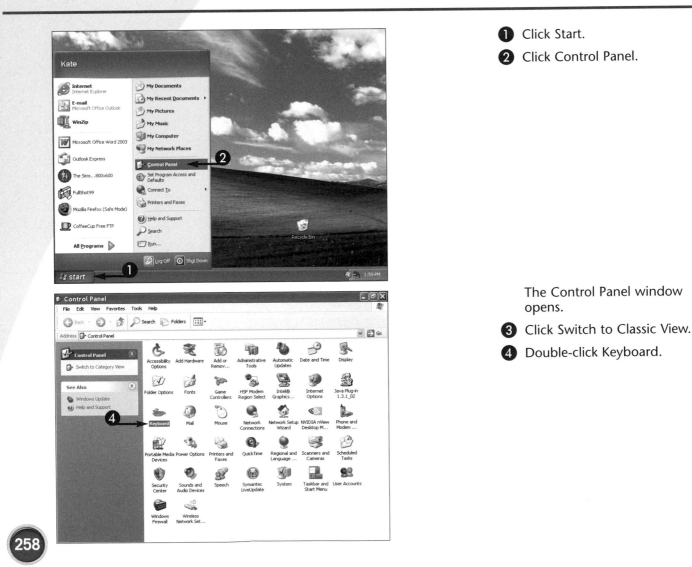

① Click Start.

② Click Control Panel.

The Control Panel window opens.

③ Click Switch to Classic View.

④ Double-click Keyboard.

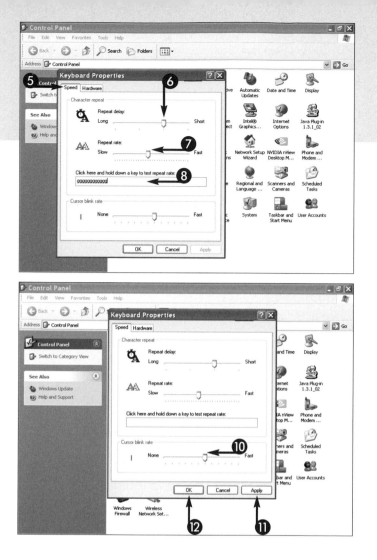

The Keyboard Properties dialog box appears.

5 Click the Speed Tab.

6 In the Character repeat section, click and drag the Repeat delay slider to adjust the setting.

7 Click and drag the Repeat rate slider to adjust the setting.

8 Click here and then press and hold a key to test the repeat rate.

9 Repeat Steps 6 to 8 to make additional adjustments, if necessary.

10 Click and drag the slider to adjust the cursor blink rate.

11 Click Apply.

12 Click OK.

Your keyboard properties change to reflect the modifications you made.

TIPS

Did You Know?
If you purchase an advanced keyboard, such a device may come with software specifically designed to make changes such as the ones in Keyboard Properties. Yet such keyboard utilities may also provide you with other changes you can make to customize the use of the keyboard. For example, you can assign specific functions to various keys as well as remap the keyboard for your personal use.

Try This!
If you find it difficult to make the right adjustments to the keyboard settings on a new Windows XP setup, but you are happy with your old system, then try this. On the computer where your keyboard settings are satisfactory, open the Keyboard properties dialog box, and note the settings. Then return to the new Windows XP setup and adjust the settings to match the older ones.

LOCAL AREA CONNECTIONS:
Change Connection Settings

After you create and configure settings for a network connection, you may need to edit these settings on one or more computers. For example, your Internet service provider, or ISP, may give you new configuration settings to use with your high-speed Internet connection, or you may need to adjust a network address to enable all of the computers to be detected on the network.

Before you begin, there are two things that you need to do. First, you must find out whether your ISP or network Administrator supplies software that allows you to run a program to configure the connection.

Software options are simpler to perform and usually configure properly the first time. Second, you must check the configuration details to ensure that they are clear. Specific information such as the unique Internet Protocol, or IP, address for each computer must be typed accurately; a simple typo can cause problems. If you have complete directions for changing the settings for the service, then you need to follow them precisely.

See also>>  **Local Area Connections**

1 Click Start.

2 Click Control Panel.

The Control Panel window opens.

3 In the Control Panel section, click Switch to Classic View.

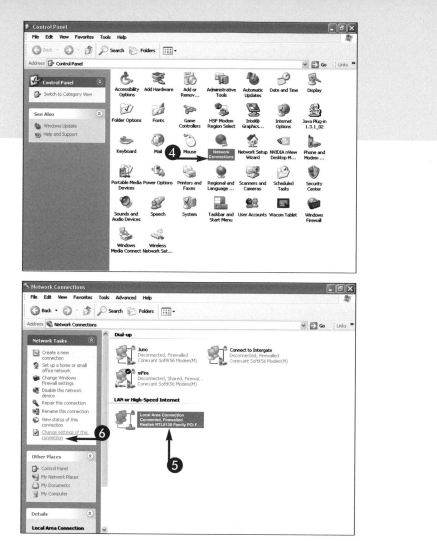

4 Double-click Network Connections.

The Network Connections window opens.

5 Click the Local Area Connection that you want to adjust.

6 Click Change settings of this connection.

TIPS

Did You Know?

To preserve your existing network connection settings until you are sure that the new settings work, you can use a different technique. Instead of changing the current connection properties, you can create a new connection to which you add all of the new settings. Once you verify that the new connection works, you can delete the old connection by right-clicking it and pressing Delete.

Test It!

Whenever you need to reconfigure the settings for a network connection, you should verify all connections again. Check each computer on the network to ensure that it connects to the network and the other computers display through My Network Places. This helps to ensure that you did not make changes to one computer that disabled another one.

LOCAL AREA CONNECTIONS:
Change Connection Settings (Continued)

When you edit your network connection settings, the first decision you make is whether to allow Windows to automatically detect settings or to add these settings manually. You can find out from your Internet service provider, or ISP, or the network Administrator at your workplace, if you need to reconfigure for your work connection. They should also be able to supply you with the connection settings that you need to access the Internet or your office network.

If you do need to reconfigure connection settings manually, then you can choose between two options.

First, you can try using automatic detection to see if the computer is configured properly for the connection. If this is successful, then you are done once you verify the network connection.

However, if the computer does not detect or is not detected by the network, then you can manually configure the individual settings. As you work, double-check each Internet Protocol, or IP, address — such as 209.92.155.4 — that you type for accuracy, because improperly typed IP addresses are a common source of errors.

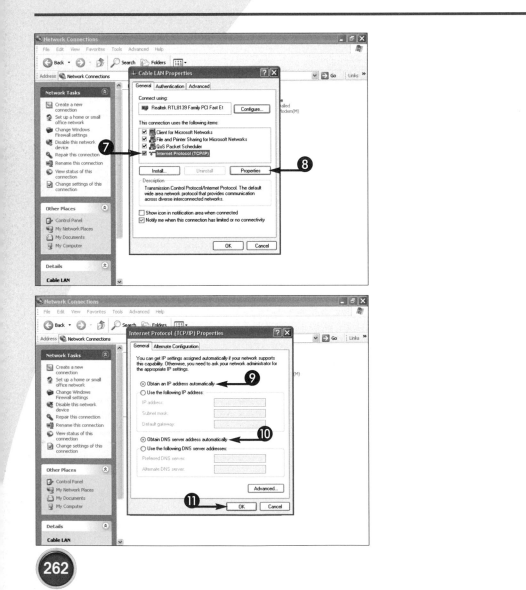

The Properties dialog box appears for the local area connection that you selected.

7 Click the Internet Protocol (TCP/IP) option.

8 Click Properties.

The Internet Protocol (TCP/IP) Properties dialog box appears.

9 Click the Obtain an IP address automatically option.

10 Click the Obtain DNS server address automatically option.

11 Click OK.

You may be prompted to restart your computer. If so, click Yes to proceed.

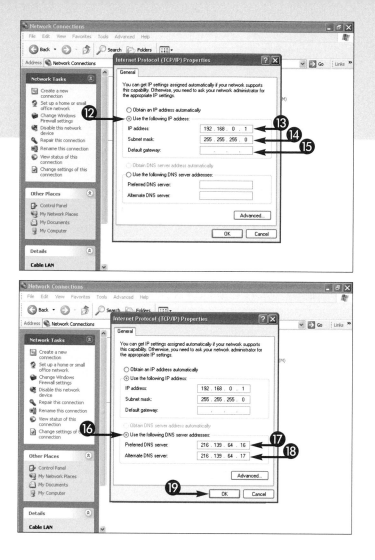

The Internet Protocol (TCP/IP) dialog box appears.

⓬ Click the Use the following IP address option.

⓭ Type the IP address.

⓮ Type the Subnet mask, if provided.

⓯ Type the default gateway, if provided.

⓰ Click the Use the following DNS server addresses option.

⓱ Type the preferred DNS server address.

⓲ Type the alternate DNS server address.

⓳ Click OK.

Windows applies your connection settings.

TIPS

Important!
When you return to change settings for a network connection that you previously set up, you should first carefully review the existing settings to ensure that there are no errors. This is particularly important if you need to troubleshoot your network when it does not detect a newly connected computer.

Try This!
When you check existing network connections, you may want to write down the current settings before you change them. If you discover that the new settings that you add do not allow you to connect to the network, then you can edit the settings again to revert them to the original configuration.

LOCAL AREA CONNECTIONS:
Check and Repair Network Connections

You can view and repair any network connection that you have set up under Network Connections in Windows. When you check the connection, you can determine whether any active network communications are currently in progress. If you do not see any network activity — the number of bytes being sent or received do not change — then you may want to restart or repair the connection. You may also determine that the network connection is not working because you cannot open files on another computer.

When you double-click a local area connection, a status window appears, displaying basic information

such as how long it has been since the network connection was made, as well as maximum connection speed.

When you use the repair option, it only works to clear the network communications channel. It does not detect or report serious problems to you. You can and should investigate other issues, such as proper network connection configuration and the hardware that is used, if the repair tool does not help.

See also>> **Local Area Connections**

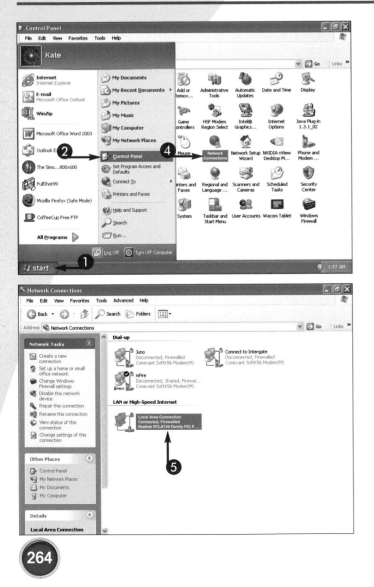

① Click Start.

② Click Control Panel.

The Control Panel window opens.

③ In the Control Panel section, click Switch to Classic View.

④ Double-click Network Connections.

The Network Connections window opens.

⑤ Double-click the local area connection that you want to check.

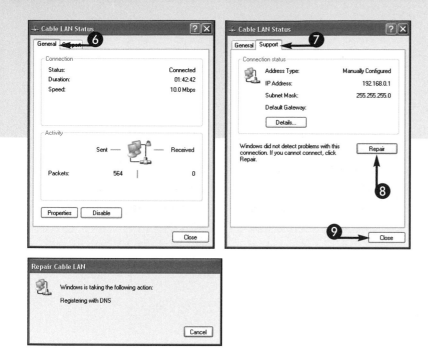

The Status dialog box appears for the local area connection that you selected.

6 Review the information on the General tab.

7 If necessary, click the Support tab.

8 Click Repair.

A Repair dialog box appears and reports the status of the repair.

9 Click Close to close the Status dialog box.

L

265

TIPS

Did You Know?

You can have multiple Local Area Connection listings in Network Connections. For example, you may use one to connect to a standard home network and another for a wireless network in your home or small office. To help identify a connection, right-click it, click Rename, and then type a descriptive name for the connection.

Try This!

You can right-click a Local Area Connection listing and then click an option in the resulting sub-menu to perform many actions, such as Repair. You can also select Properties to open the Properties window.

LOCAL AREA CONNECTIONS:
Configure Network Connections

Windows XP offers you two ways to configure network connections for a computer. First, you can allow Windows to do this automatically when you run the Network Setup Wizard or the New Connection Wizard. Second, you can add information such as the Internet Protocol, or IP, address manually when you edit the connection properties.

An IP address is an entity with four sets of numbers separated by periods. For example, an IP address may look like this: 192.168.114.68.

You can allow Windows to automatically detect and assign IP addresses for the computer and the network services that it uses, or you can manually type the required network addresses. You usually need the IP address for the computer that you configure. You also need its subnet mask, which is a special filter applied to the IP address, and you may also need the IP address for the gateway. A gateway refers to the network computer that is directly connected to the Internet.

① Click Start.

② Click Control Panel.

The Control Panel window opens.

③ In the Control Panel section, click Switch to Classic View.

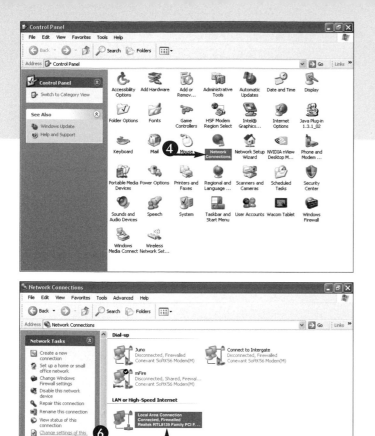

4 Double-click Network Connections.

The Network Connections window opens.

5 Click the local area connection that you want to adjust.

6 Click Change settings of this connection.

TIPS

Important!

Before you run configuration software that is supplied by your network Administrator or Internet service provider, check the documentation to ensure that the software is compatible with Windows XP. Different versions of Windows use various protocols or settings packages, not all of which are compatible with one another. You can inadvertently break or disable all network communications if you run incompatible configuration software.

Did You Know?

If you receive automatic configuration software from your Internet service provider or network Administrator, then you can run the software that usually installs and configures your network connection settings for you. Documentation for this software also usually lists the manual configuration details.

LOCAL AREA CONNECTIONS:
Configure Network Connections (Continued)

When you configure settings for a network connection of any type, you are providing a series of Internet Protocol, or IP, addresses for the computer to use to establish and support two-way communications. The IP addresses function similar to phone numbers, but instead of one computer calling another by standard telephone, they address communications through the unique Internet address that is assigned to each of them.

An IP address is a set of four numbers, each separated by periods, such as 192.168.78.12. To some degree, these numbers are used to help identify from where in the country or world a connection originates.

When you adjust settings, wherever you do not have Windows automatically obtain an IP or other network address, you must use the specific IP address that is assigned to the service that you use. Although your local network addresses are assigned as you proceed, IP addresses for Internet services through which you connect are registered through recognized Internet authorities.

See also>> Network Setup Wizard

Network Connections

The Local Area Connection Properties dialog box appears.

7 Click the Internet Protocol (TCP/IP) option.

8 Click Properties to display the Internet Protocol (TCP/IP) Properties dialog box.

The Properties dialog box appears.

9 Click the Obtain an IP address automatically option.

10 Click the Obtain DNS Server address automatically option.

11 Click OK.

You may be prompted to restart your computer. If so, click Yes to proceed.

The Internet Protocol (TCP/IP) Properties dialog box closes.

268

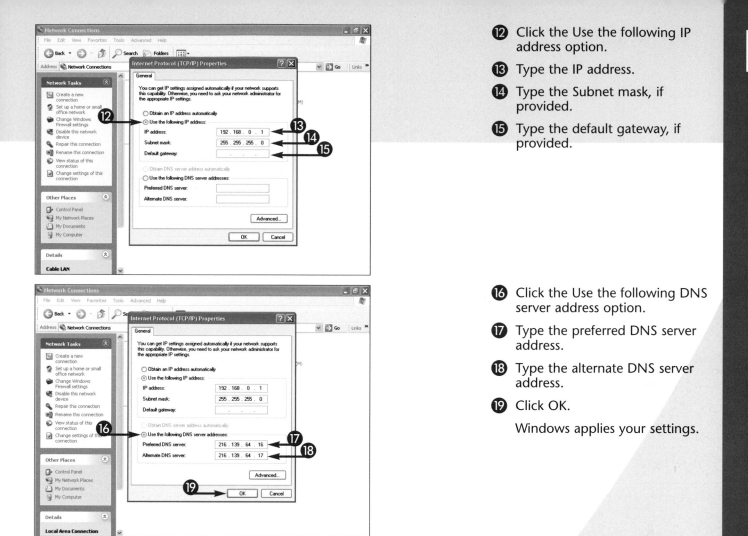

L

⑫ Click the Use the following IP address option.

⑬ Type the IP address.

⑭ Type the Subnet mask, if provided.

⑮ Type the default gateway, if provided.

⑯ Click the Use the following DNS server address option.

⑰ Type the preferred DNS server address.

⑱ Type the alternate DNS server address.

⑲ Click OK.

Windows applies your settings.

TIPS

Did You Know?

When a network connection becomes corrupted, its settings are damaged and can no longer be read. If you find that you cannot open, view, or edit a network connection, then you may need to delete it and create a new connection with new settings. You can delete a network connection by clicking its listing in the Network Connections window and pressing Delete.

Try This!

If the computer that you configure does not have its own Internet connection but shares a DSL or cable modem that is installed on another computer on the network, that other computer is known as the gateway. To determine the IP address of a gateway computer, consult the Network Connection Properties dialog box on the computer with the modem.

LOGON:
Change the Way Users Log On or Log Off

The easiest way to control how users who share your computer log on or log off the system is to set your options within User Accounts. The options that you choose can either increase or decrease computer security. Security and convenience are often mutually exclusive; to make it easy to access your computer, you must reduce security, and vice versa. For example, you can enable or disable the Welcome screen, where users click icons to log on automatically. You can also turn on or off Fast User Switching, where a second user can log on without the first user logging off.

You can apply either or both of these options simultaneously. Without the Welcome screen enabled, the standard logon window appears, prompting you for your username and password when you start or restart Windows or return to your computer desktop. If you do not enable Fast User Switching, then each user must log off before another user can log on.

See also>>

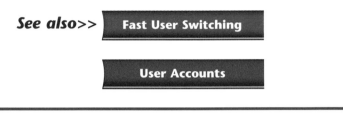

Fast User Switching

User Accounts

① Click Start.

② Click Control Panel.

The Control Panel window opens.

③ In the Control Panel section, click Switch to Classic View.

④ Double-click User Accounts.

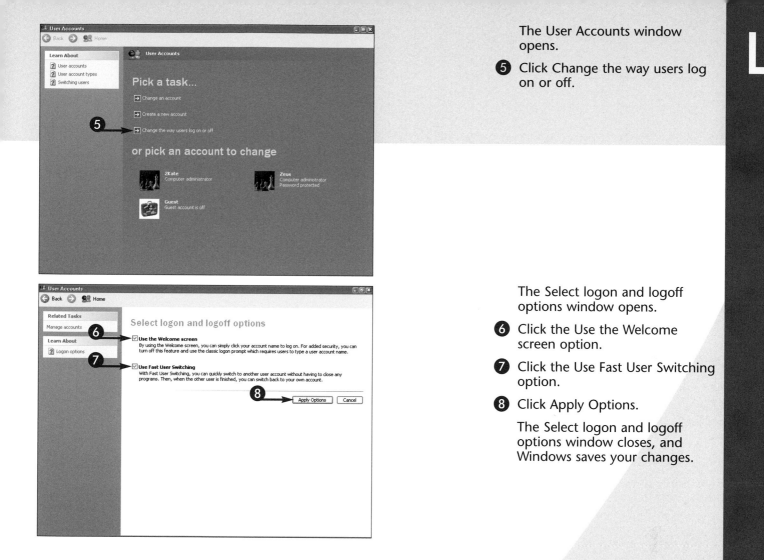

The User Accounts window opens.

5 Click Change the way users log on or off.

The Select logon and logoff options window opens.

6 Click the Use the Welcome screen option.

7 Click the Use Fast User Switching option.

8 Click Apply Options.

The Select logon and logoff options window closes, and Windows saves your changes.

TIPS

Did You Know?
Certain options that you turn on in Windows can affect whether the Welcome screen or Fast User Switching features are available. For example, if you enable and use Offline Files, then Fast User Switching is automatically disabled in User Accounts. You are prompted to ask whether you want to change the status of Offline Folders in order to enable Fast User Switching.

Customize It!
To further customize how Windows allows users to log on, you can set Local Security Policy, which are a group of settings that give you control over how users access a Windows computer.

Did You Know?
You can visit the Windows Security window by pressing Ctrl+Alt+Del. However, if you have the Welcome screen enabled, then this keystroke combination opens Task Manager, instead.

MAP NETWORK DRIVE:
Identify Network Drives

When you map your network drives, you help your system to identify the network storage resources that are available. Windows stores a copy of these drives on your system, just as if they were on your computer hard drive, where you can easily access them. As a result, it is easier to locate resources that you need, when you need to use them.

From these mapped drive folders, you can easily open or move files back and forth between your computer and a network location to which you have access. This saves you time and effort.

In large-scale network environments, Administrators use scripts — that they usually write themselves — to specify network-mapping options. However, Windows XP makes it easy for you to specify options through the Tools menu in My Computer or Windows Explorer.

See also>>

My Network Places Folder

Network Setup Wizard

① Click Start.

② Click My Computer.

The My Computer window opens.

③ Click Tools.

④ Click Map Network Drive.

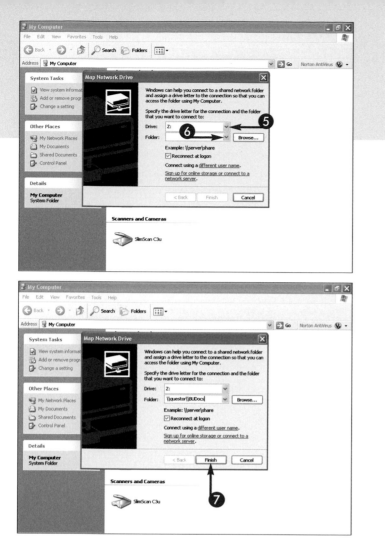

The Map Network Drive dialog box appears.

5 Click here and select a drive letter.

6 Click here and select the name of the network folder with which you want to connect the drive.

You can select Browse to search for your folder location.

7 Click Finish.

The Map Network Drive command runs and identifies the specified drive and folder.

TIPS

More Options!

When you open the Tools menu from My Computer or Windows Explorer, the Synchronize command displays along with Map Network Drive. You can use the Synchronize command with mapped network drives, but you must enable and configure Offline Files to do this.

Remove It!

If you no longer want nor need a network drive that you have mapped, then you can disconnect it. When you do this, you do not physically disable that network drive. Instead, you break the connection that you have established between that network drive and your computer through the Map Network Drive command. To disconnect a network drive, repeat Steps 1 to 3 and then click Disconnect Network Drive in the drop-down menu.

MEDIA PLAYER:
Record a Music CD

Although there are a number of programs available to help you burn audio CDs, you can use Windows Media Player, which is already installed in Windows, to do this. Media Player requires no registration or additional cost. You can burn a CD from files in your existing Media Library, or add new files to the library before you record.

Media Player requires more than software and a list of song files to record your CD. You also need a blank recordable CD, as well as a CD or DVD drive that is capable of recording audio CDs.

If you are connected to the Internet when you record an audio CD, then Windows Media Player automatically retrieves specific details about each song from the online Compact Disk Database, which is a repository of music data. Windows Media Player also supports DVDs if you have a DVD drive.

Although Media Player makes it easy for you to copy a pre-recorded CD, you are responsible to take care in not violating copyright infringement laws. See your CD package for details of proper use.

See also>> **Media Player**

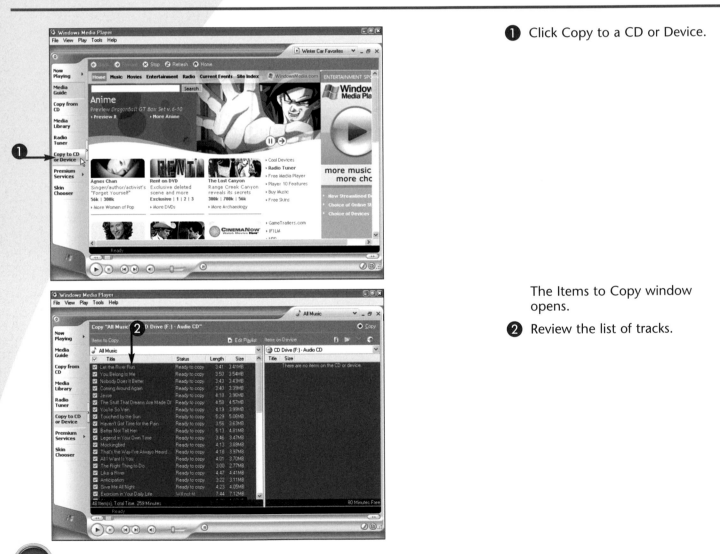

① Click Copy to a CD or Device.

The Items to Copy window opens.

② Review the list of tracks.

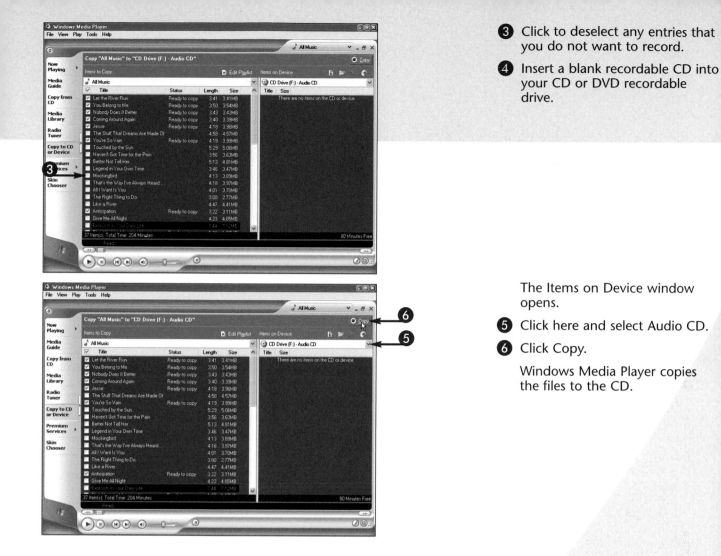

③ Click to deselect any entries that you do not want to record.

④ Insert a blank recordable CD into your CD or DVD recordable drive.

The Items on Device window opens.

⑤ Click here and select Audio CD.

⑥ Click Copy.

Windows Media Player copies the files to the CD.

TIPS

More Options!

You can also use Media Player to rip, or copy, a previously recorded CD to a new, blank CD to create your own copy. To do this, insert the CD that you want to copy into your CD or DVD drive and then click the Rip Music icon in the Media Player toolbar. After copied, you can then record these songs to a new CD. Always look for copyright information before copying.

Caution!

Do not try to play an audio CD while you copy or record a new CD. This can affect playback, especially on systems with limited memory. In fact, Microsoft recommends that you perform no other actions while you record a CD for optimal results.

MEDIA PLAYER:
Set Up Your Media Library

If you regularly use Windows Media Player to watch and listen to media files such as videos and MP3s, then you may want to set up your own custom media library. In this library, you can store your entire collection of multimedia files.

After you set up your library, you no longer have to search for files that you want to play; you can just call them up from your media library. Having a library also makes it easier for you to create playlists

or burn media CDs. You can also consult your library to see what selections you are missing so that you can add them from another source.

As you set up the library, Media Player searches your drives to locate compatible files that it can add to the library roster. Once the library is set up, you can return to edit or delete entries, or create playlists.

See also>> **Media Player**

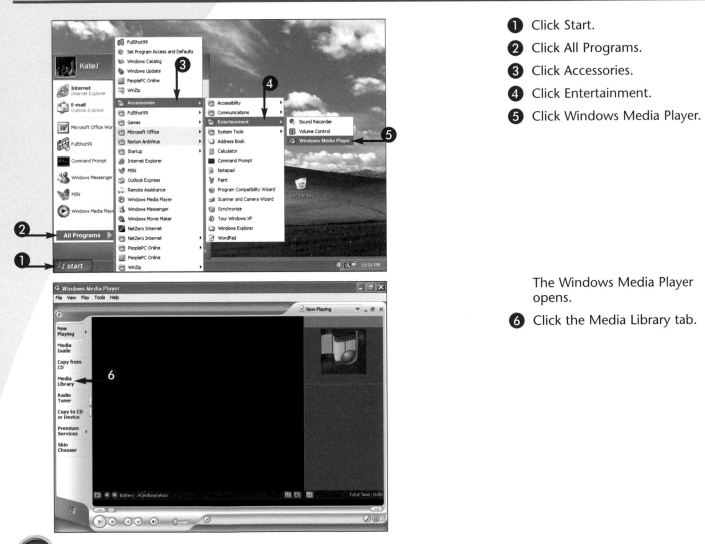

1 Click Start.

2 Click All Programs.

3 Click Accessories.

4 Click Entertainment.

5 Click Windows Media Player.

The Windows Media Player opens.

6 Click the Media Library tab.

7 Click File.

8 Click Add to Media Library.

9 Click By Searching Computer.

The Media Player searches through the files on your hard drive, and adds the media files that it finds to your Media Library.

![TIPS]

More Options!

You can sort and re-sort your Media Library, based on ascending or descending order, for each column of information, such as Title, Album, or Artist. Click a column heading to sort the entries, based on the column data.

Remove It!

To remove a media entry from your library, right-click it and then click Delete.

Customize It!

If the columns in the Media Library are too narrow to read all of the necessary information, then you can resize them one at a time. To do this, click and drag the border at the right side of a column heading. You can also specify which columns appear in the Library list. Right-click any column heading and then click to deselect any columns that you want to hide.

MOVIE MAKER:
Start a Simple Movie

When you want to create a movie from your digital photos and other images, you can use the Movie Maker feature to do this. Movie Maker is a tool that allows you to use images that are already stored on your computer to create a moving slideshow. You can also import live video through your digital camera or through another device that you connect to a video capture card that is installed in your system.

You can use Movie Maker to create family slideshows and movies, to share personal productions with friends and co-workers, and to produce professional-looking

video tutorials or promotional movies. Although you can produce a simple movie in just minutes, the latest version of Movie Maker offers enough extra tools to produce relatively sophisticated movies, as well. The final results can depend on your hardware as well as your production skills.

The Movie Tasks pane guides you through the movie creation process. You can then add more options to your movie, such as audio.

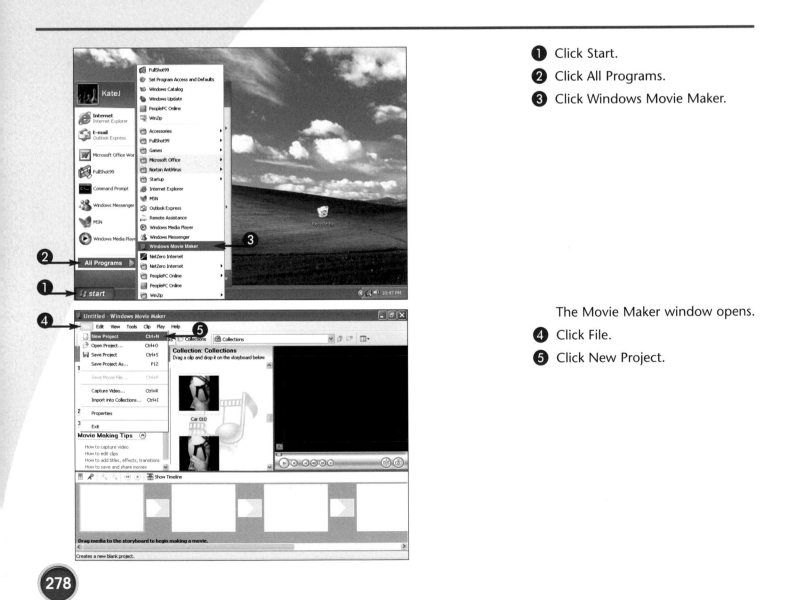

1 Click Start.

2 Click All Programs.

3 Click Windows Movie Maker.

The Movie Maker window opens.

4 Click File.

5 Click New Project.

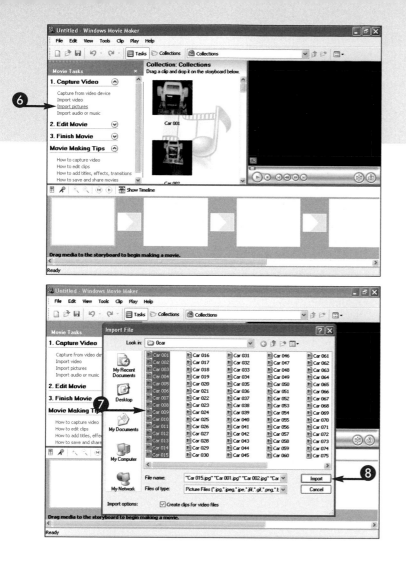

6 In the Movie Tasks pane, click a Capture Video preference.

7 Click to select your video, movie, or audio clips.

8 Click Import.

The video, pictures, or audio that you chose now appear in the Movie Maker window, ready for you to edit and finish.

TIPS

Attention!
Although Movie Maker recognizes many types of media files, it only allows you to save your movies in the WMV format, which requires Windows Media Player to view.

Caution!
For best results, create your movies on a Windows XP computer with 256MB or more of memory, and at least 2GB of free disk space. You should also have a robust video card, also called a display or graphics adapter.

Did You Know?
A new version of Movie Maker is available in the Windows Service Pack 2 collection. If you have downloaded or installed the disc to upgrade to Service Pack 2, then you should have this updated feature.

More Options!
Additional options in Movie Maker allow you to create titles and record audio narration.

MY RECENT DOCUMENTS:
Configure and Clear My Recent Documents List

My Recent Documents is a list of your most recently opened documents that you can access through the Start Menu. Normally, the My Recent Documents entries change dynamically. As you open new files, older files rotate off the list, with the last ten opened documents displaying on the list.

You can specify different settings for this feature. For example, while many people use the My Recent Documents list to access a file quickly that they worked with yesterday or the day before, you may

not want this list to display for the sake of privacy. In this case, you can clear the list.

The list repopulates when you open more files, and so you need to clear the list regularly if you do not want other users to see it. You can also disable the listing altogether.

See also>> **My Recent Documents**

Start Menu

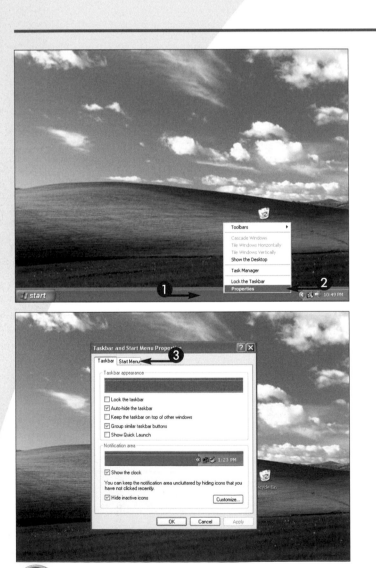

① Right-click a blank area of your taskbar.

A sub-menu appears.

② Click Properties.

The Taskbar and Start Menu Properties dialog box appears.

③ Click the Start Menu tab.

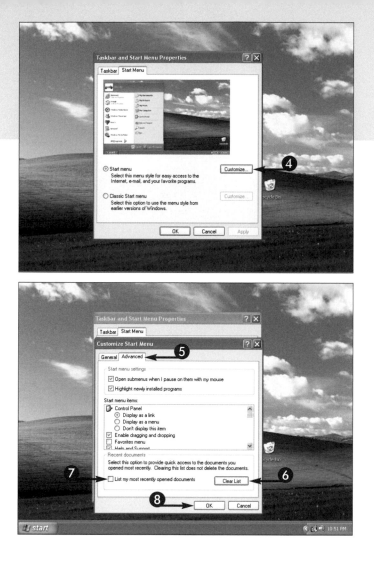

④ Click Customize.

The Customize Start Menu dialog box appears.

⑤ Click the Advanced tab.

⑥ In the Recent documents section, click Clear List.

⑦ To disable the list, click to deselect the List my most recently opened documents option.

⑧ Click OK.

Windows disables the list.

TIPS

Did You Know?
More than word processor and text files appear in the My Recent Documents list. Your entries include images, spreadsheets, PowerPoint presentations, and other document types.

More Options!
The My Recent Documents list allows you to perform actions on items in the list. Click Start and then click My Recent Documents. Right-click an entry and then click an option, such as Delete or Rename.

Customize It!
If multiple people share your computer, then each different user has his or her own list of most recently accessed documents. This is true only if each person has his or her own user account. For more privacy, establish separate accounts for each computer user.

NETWORK CONNECTIONS:
Manage Network Connections

You can manage your network connections in the Network Connections window, which is available through the Control Panel. You can also open the Network Connections window from the left-hand task pane in My Network Places through the Start Menu.

In the Network Connections window, you can perform all management tasks that are related to various types of network connections. For example, you can add, remove, view, check the status of, and troubleshoot connections, including those that you create for dial-up or broadband Internet service accounts, for your home or business network, and for wireless networks. You can also reconfigure or repair a connection from this window.

Each connection that you set up has an icon in the Network Connections window. You can double-click or right-click a connection icon to display its Properties dialog box. You can also use the Network Tasks pane in the left side of the window to perform specific actions.

See also>>

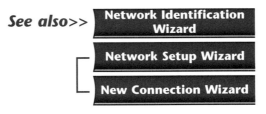

Network Identification Wizard

Network Setup Wizard

New Connection Wizard

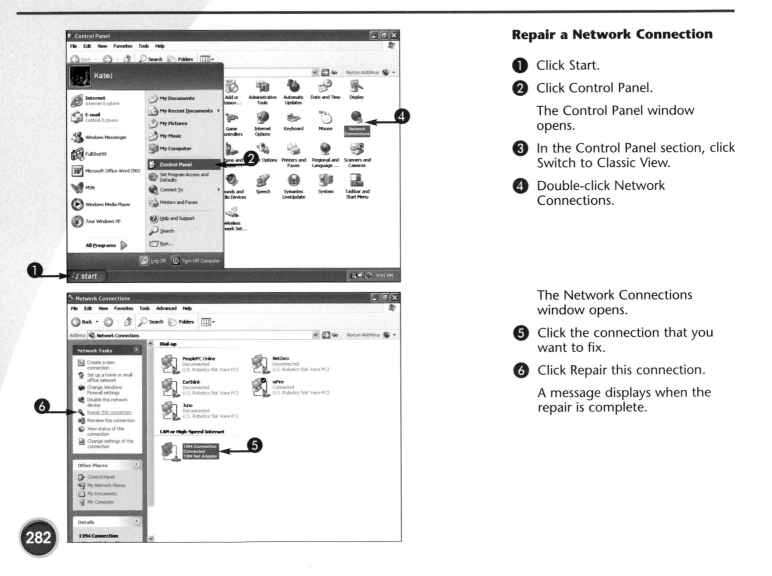

Repair a Network Connection

① Click Start.

② Click Control Panel.

The Control Panel window opens.

③ In the Control Panel section, click Switch to Classic View.

④ Double-click Network Connections.

The Network Connections window opens.

⑤ Click the connection that you want to fix.

⑥ Click Repair this connection.

A message displays when the repair is complete.

282

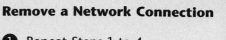

Remove a Network Connection

① Repeat Steps 1 to 4.

② In the Network Connections window, click the connection that you want to delete.

③ Click Delete this connection.

The connection disappears from the Network Connections window.

TIPS

Caution!

Before you change your connection settings, be sure to review the current settings as well as any notes you have on recommended changes. This helps you to avoid making a simple typing error that could disable a connection rather than establish one.

Remove It!

Occasionally, a network connection can become corrupt, which means that some aspect of the connection, such as the settings, no longer allows Windows to establish a connection. If this happens, then delete the connection and create a new one.

Important!

Different error messages may appear when you try to repair or perform other jobs on your network connections. For example, a message often reports than no TCP/IP has been configured. Follow the instructions in the message window to resolve the problem.

NETWORK IDENTIFICATION WIZARD:
Add a Computer to a Network Domain

When you want to add a new or existing computer to a domain-based network — which is often used in a larger office setting — you can run the Network Identification Wizard to help you. Using the wizard, you can connect the computer to the domain and create a user account for that domain, if necessary.

A domain-based network differs from a home or small office network. This is because a home or small office uses a peer-to-peer network, where all computers communicate together, whereas a domain network generally uses a central computer system to manage

all of the individual computer workstations. If you only use a home or small office network, then you may not need to create or join a domain.

When you run the Network Identification Wizard, it helps you to evaluate whether you need to join a network domain in the first place. If not, then you are prompted to close the wizard.

See also>>
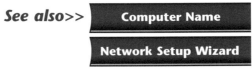

Computer Name

Network Setup Wizard

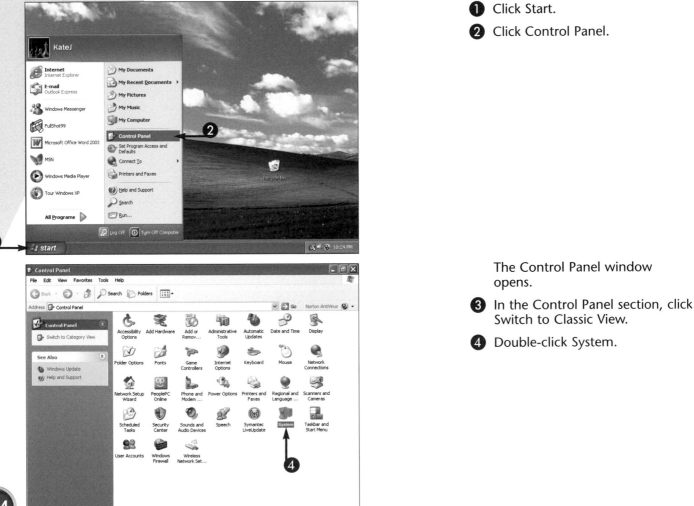

① Click Start.

② Click Control Panel.

The Control Panel window opens.

③ In the Control Panel section, click Switch to Classic View.

④ Double-click System.

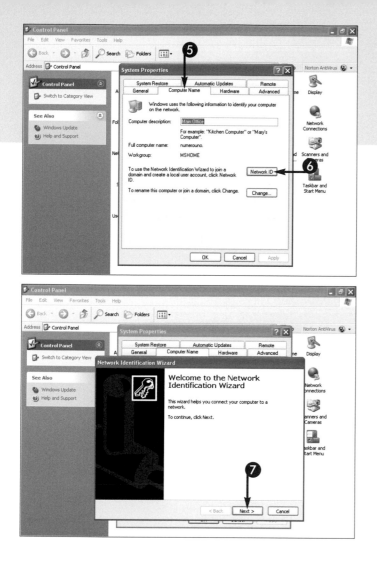

The System Properties dialog box appears.

5 Click the Computer Name tab.

6 Click Network ID.

The Network Identification Wizard opens.

7 Click Next.

8 Follow the steps provided to specify options and relevant information.

9 Click Finish.

The wizard closes, and your computer connects to the domain-based network.

TIPS

Attention!

If you run a home or small office network, then you probably do not operate as part of a domain. In this case, you can use the Network Setup Wizard to prepare your network.

More Options!

If you are an advanced user, then you can connect to a domain directly, rather than through the wizard. Perform Steps 1 to 5 and then click the Change button in the Computer Name tab to provide your details.

Important!

If someone else manages your domain-based network, then ask them for specific configuration information, such as the domain name and your user account details, before you run the wizard to connect your computer to the domain.

NETWORK SETUP WIZARD:
Configure a Small Network

After you set up the necessary hardware to create a network between two or more computers, you can run the Network Setup Wizard. This wizard guides you through the setup of a new home or small office network. Using the wizard saves you time and frustration, and helps to ensure that you set up your network correctly the first time.

The Network Setup Wizard initially displays a checklist of equipment that you need to connect your network. The wizard then asks you for information about the type of network that you have physically

connected. For example, it asks you to specify whether the current computer has its own direct connection to the Internet or shares its online access with another computer on the network.

When the wizard is finished, it displays the name of the new connection that you have just created in the steps. You can double-click that connection to view its status and additional details.

See also>> **New Connection Wizard**

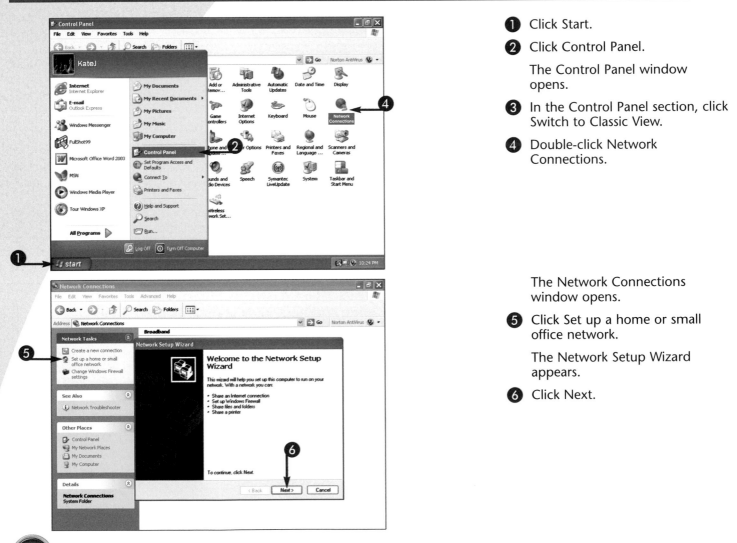

① Click Start.

② Click Control Panel.

The Control Panel window opens.

③ In the Control Panel section, click Switch to Classic View.

④ Double-click Network Connections.

The Network Connections window opens.

⑤ Click Set up a home or small office network.

The Network Setup Wizard appears.

⑥ Click Next.

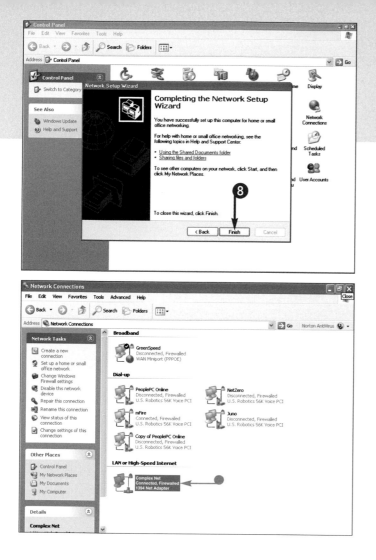

⑦ Consult the network checklist, which displays the common types of networks that you can set up, and follow the on-screen directions, clicking Next to continue.

A completion screens appears.

⑧ Click Finish.

● A new connection appears under the LAN or High-Speed Internet heading in the Network Connections window.

TIPS

Attention!

If an error message appears at the end of the wizard, stating that the network could not be set up, then there may be a problem with your network hardware. Review the hardware manuals before you relaunch the wizard.

Did You Know?

If you set up a network that shares a single high-speed Internet connection, then only one connection appears under the LAN or High-Speed Connection category.

More Options!

If you do not detect any activity or active connection after you set up a new network, then click the connection icon and click Repair this connection in the Network Tasks section.

Remove It!

If you want to remove an existing connection after you set up a new home or small office network, then click the icon for the connection that you do not want, and press Delete.

NEW PARTITION WIZARD:
Create a New Disk Partition

When you buy a hard disk, you must first prepare it for use after you physically install it. This preparation involves partitioning, which creates the structure for file storage, and formatting, which sets up the disk to install an operating system.

Your Windows setup CD allows you to partition and format a new drive. You can also partition an unused part of a hard disk at any time using the Windows New Partition Wizard. Whenever you partition and format a drive, you remove all existing files and programs from the drive.

The New Partition Wizard takes the guesswork out of the process and guides you through every step. As you proceed, keep in mind that you want a partition that is large enough to provide adequate storage but not so big that it takes forever to search for files or perform maintenance such as defragmenting. For example, you may want to partition an 80GB hard disk into two 40GB partitions.

See also>>   NTFS File System

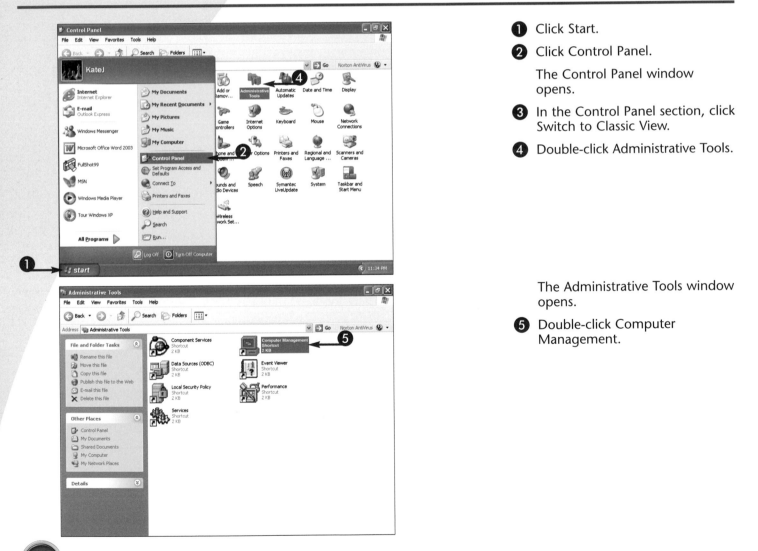

① Click Start.

② Click Control Panel.

The Control Panel window opens.

③ In the Control Panel section, click Switch to Classic View.

④ Double-click Administrative Tools.

The Administrative Tools window opens.

⑤ Double-click Computer Management.

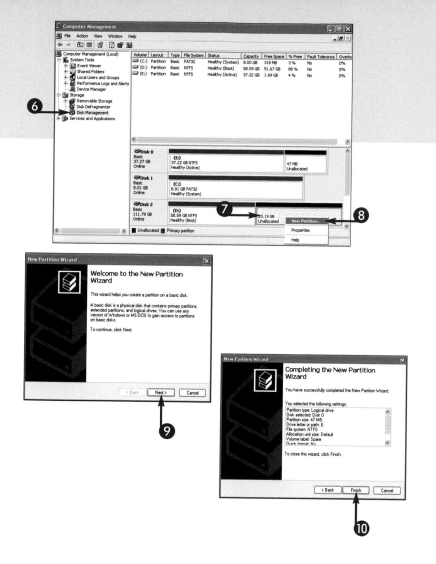

The Computer Management Console opens.

6 Click Disk Management.

7 Right-click a free, unallocated space on a drive.

A sub-menu appears.

8 Click New Partition.

The New Partition Wizard opens.

9 Click Next and proceed through the wizard until you are finished.

10 Click Finish.

The wizard creates the partition and then closes.

TIPS

Did You Know?

Some help articles may still suggest that you use FDISK, the old command line-based partition tool, to prepare a drive. Not only is this tool difficult to use, but it is also no longer available with Windows installations. FDISK has been replaced by a new tool called DiskPart. Regardless, you should find the New Partition Wizard, or the partition and format options in the Windows setup CD, more appropriate to use.

Important!

How you partition a drive often depends on how you will use it. Avoid very large partitions because they require a lot of time to search and maintain. One type of partition is the boot drive does not need to be very large because it only needs to store the operating system.

.NET PASSPORT WIZARD:
Add a Passport to an Account

Microsoft offers a service called Microsoft Passport that enables you to identify and authenticate yourself at specific sites on the Internet. Many Microsoft tools, such as MSN Messenger, MSN Hotmail, and MSN Music, as well as other Internet sites, use Microsoft Passport to log in. You can add your Microsoft Passport to your Windows XP account to simplify using Passport-enabled sites and applications.

To set up a .NET Passport, you need access to the Internet and an e-mail account and password of your choice. These become your username and password in the .NET Passport service.

Windows XP includes a tool called the .NET Passport Wizard that guides you through the process of adding a Passport to your Windows account. This simplifies using Passport-enabled sites because Windows and any Passport-enabled applications can use your Passport automatically, thus eliminating the need for you to enter the information each time. Instead, you can simply log in to Windows and start using these applications.

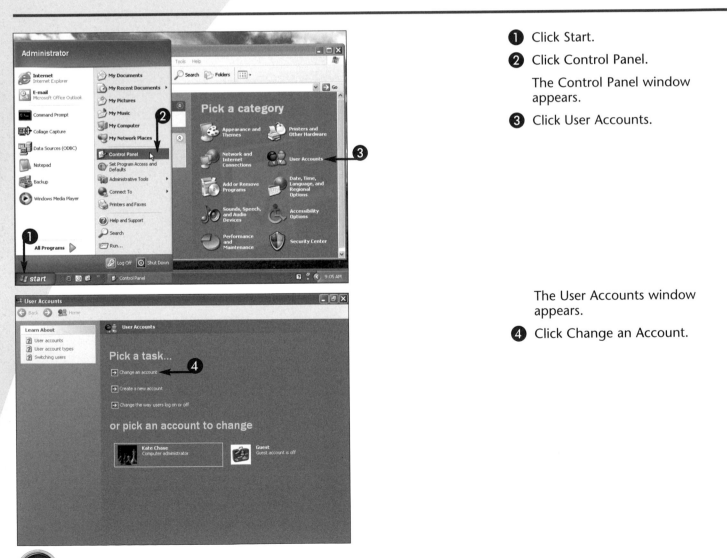

❶ Click Start.

❷ Click Control Panel.

The Control Panel window appears.

❸ Click User Accounts.

The User Accounts window appears.

❹ Click Change an Account.

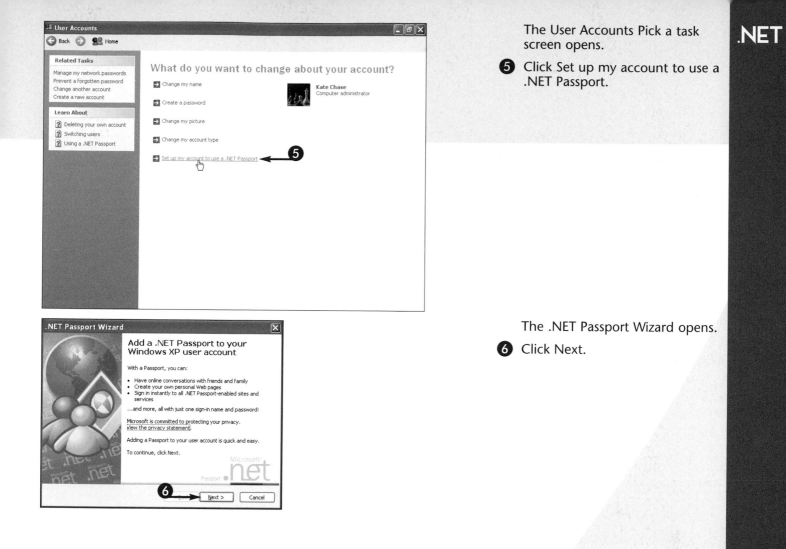

The User Accounts Pick a task screen opens.

⑤ Click Set up my account to use a .NET Passport.

The .NET Passport Wizard opens.

⑥ Click Next.

TIPS

Attention!

After you add the Passport to your account, you will find a Change my .Net Passport link in the properties for your account in the User Accounts page, which you access through the Control Panel. This link allows you to modify your password. When you change your password regularly, such as every month, you increase security and decrease the chance that someone else can access your .Net Passport account.

Did You Know?

You can set up a free MSN Hotmail account to use as the e-mail account for your .NET Passport. When the .NET Passport Wizard starts, select your existing e-mail address and in the next window, click the option to set up a free Hotmail account to use with this Passport.

.NET PASSPORT WIZARD:
Add a Passport to an Account (Continued)

If you already have a Microsoft Passport, then you can simply use the wizard to associate the Passport with your Windows account. You can enter the e-mail address associated with the Passport, along with the password for your Passport account.

These steps assume that you already have an e-mail address and a Passport. If you do not have a Passport, then you can use the wizard to obtain one. If you do this, the wizard opens the Microsoft Passport site in your Web browser, which then guides you through the process of setting up the Passport.

You must provide a valid e-mail address, password, and password-recovery question and answer.

Near the completion of the wizard, you have the option of associating the Passport with your user account. If you prefer, you can simply create the Passport but not associate it with your account. For example, you may want to do this when you are working with an account that you use infrequently. After creating the Passport, you can run the wizard at a later time to associate the Passport with the appropriate account.

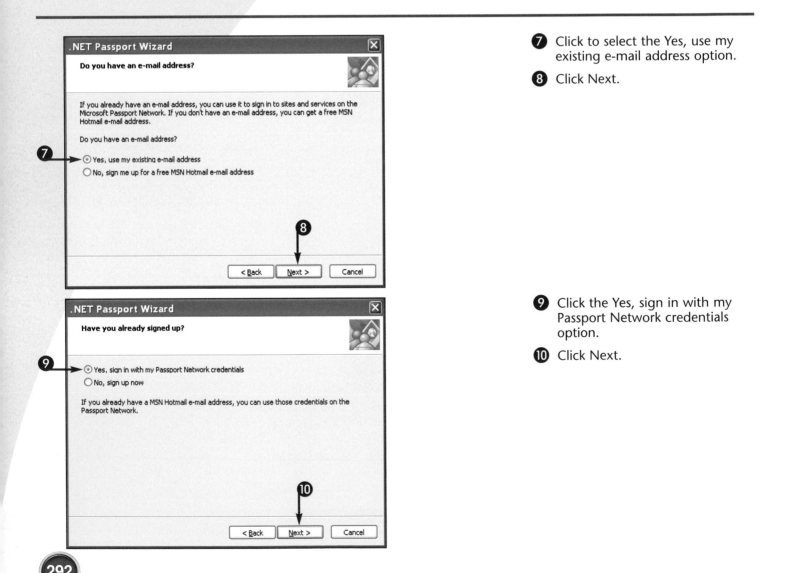

⑦ Click to select the Yes, use my existing e-mail address option.

⑧ Click Next.

⑨ Click the Yes, sign in with my Passport Network credentials option.

⑩ Click Next.

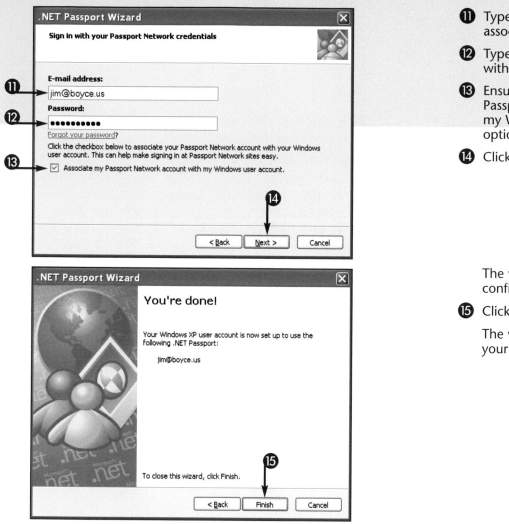

⑪ Type the e-mail address associated with your Passport.

⑫ Type the password associated with your Passport.

⑬ Ensure that the Associate my Passport Network account with my Windows user account option is selected.

⑭ Click Next.

The wizard displays a confirmation page.

⑮ Click Finish.

The wizard adds the Passport to your Windows account.

TIPS

Did You Know?

If your computer is a member of a domain, then you must use a slightly different method to add a Passport to your account. Click User Accounts in the Control Panel. When the User Accounts dialog box appears, click the Advanced tab. Then click .NET Passport Wizard to start the wizard.

Attention!

You should change your Microsoft Passport password on a regular basis, just as you should change your Windows password on a regular basis. For example, you should change both of these passwords at least once a month for better security.

OFFLINE FILES:
Configure Offline Files

You can work on network or server files when you are not connected to the network by selecting the Offline Files option. This option enables you to work on files offline on a portable computer or another computer that is part of the network sharing system.

With the Offline Files feature, you can copy files from shared folders or drives on your network to your computer hard drive. After moving the files to your hard drive, you can work on them, even if you are

not connected to the network. When you reconnect to the network, Windows XP synchronizes the files on your hard drive with the files on the network.

Synchronizing is a process by which your computer file system checks the versions of all files on your hard drive against the network files, and then updates the archived zipped or compressed files, to make the file contents identical.

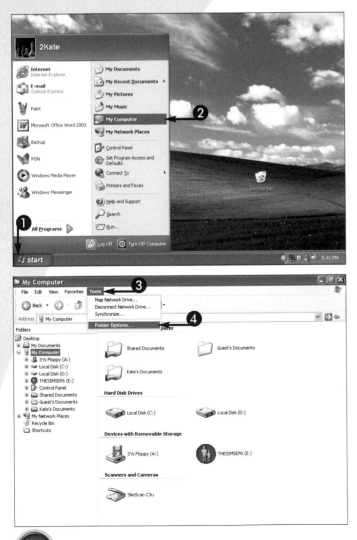

Enable Offline Files

① Click Start.

② Click My Computer.

The My Computer window opens.

③ Click Tools.

④ Click Folder Options.

The Folder Options dialog box appears.

⑤ Click the Offline Files tab.

⑥ Click to select the Enable Offline Files option.

⑦ Click Apply.

⑧ Click OK.

The Offline folder options are now available to you.

TIPS

Attention!

If you do not see the Enable Offline Files check box in Step 6, then you must turn off Fast User Switching. To do this, click Start, click Control Panel, and then double-click User Accounts. From the User Accounts window, click the Change the way users log on or off option. Deselect the Use Fast User Switching option and then click Apply Options. You can now enable offline files.

Did You Know?

The Offline Files option is better equipped for working over a network than the Briefcase feature. Briefcase is an older tool that was designed to help transfer files between a computer and a removable drive when moving files to and from the office.

OFFLINE FILES:
Synchronize Offline Files

When you work with shared files offline, there are three steps that you need to follow. First, you must enable Offline Files. Then you must select and share specific files that you want to use offline. Finally, as you begin to work on files that you transfer from the network, you need to synchronize your copy of these files with the versions that reside on the network.

The synchronization process transfers updated copies of the files back to the original folders to reflect the changes that you made offline. If the file on the network changes but the offline version does not, then a copy of the changed network file is transferred to the offline file folder.

You can only synchronize files while you are connected to the network. You can adjust synchronization settings to specify how frequently Windows XP checks for differences between file version, as well as view and delete offline file copies.

1 With your computer connected to the network, click Start.

2 Click My Computer.

The My Computer Window opens.

3 Click Tools.

4 Click Synchronize.

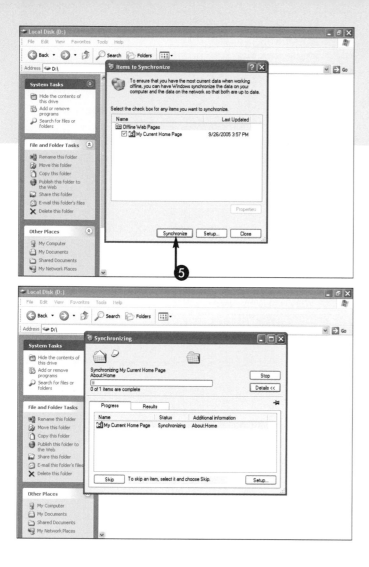

The Items to Synchronize dialog box appears.

5 Click Synchronize.

The Synchronizing dialog box appears.

Windows compares and updates your network and offline file copies.

TIPS

Important!
You cannot use Fast User Switching with Offline Folders enabled, or vice versa. If you want to turn on Fast User Switching later, then you are prompted to disable Offline Folders.

More Options!
To view your list of offline files, repeat Steps 1 and 2. Click Tools and then click Folder Options. In the Folder Options dialog box, click the Offline Files tab and then click the View Files button. Your Offline Files Folder opens to display your files.

Customize It!
To specify how frequently Windows XP performs the synchronizing process, repeat Steps 1 to 4. In the Items to Synchronize dialog box, click the Setup button. The Synchronization Settings dialog box appears. Select your synchronizing options. Click Apply to accept the changes.

OPEN WITH COMMAND:
Open a File in a Different Program

When you open a particular file, Windows automatically recognizes and loads the appropriate program for the file. However, you can also open a document or file by using a program other than the default one. For example, you may normally open a Web page — a file that is saved with the .htm or .html file extension — through your Web browser. To edit the HTML code on the page, you can open the file by using a different program, such as Windows Notepad, WordPad, or Microsoft FrontPage 2003.

There are two reasons why you may want to open a file with an alternate program. First, a different program may enable you to edit or view the file in a way that the default program does not. Second, when you have trouble opening the file with the default program, you can open the file with an alternate program, and then resave it so that you can open the file with the default program.

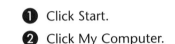

1 Click Start.

2 Click My Computer.

The My Computer window opens.

3 Double-click the drive letter that contains the file that you want to open with an alternate program.

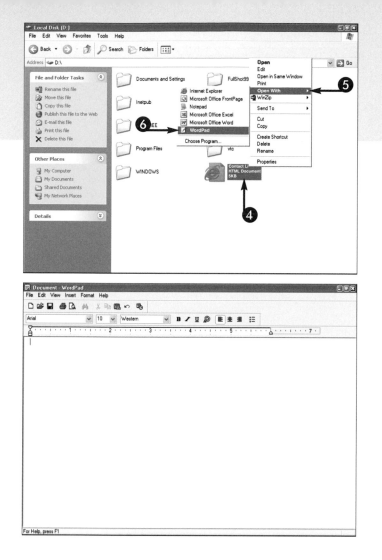

The contents of the drive appear in the My Computer window.

④ Right-click the file that you want to open with the alternate program.

⑤ In the sub-menu, click Open With.

⑥ Click the program that you want from the list of compatible choices.

The file opens in the program that you selected.

TIPS

Attention!
Try to match the file type you want to open with an alternate program that can open your file. For example, an image file ending with a .tif, .jpg, or .gif file extension requires a graphics program to open it, such as Microsoft Paint.

Caution!
If you see an error message that the program cannot open the file, or if the file displays strangely, then close the file without saving it and try to open it in another program.

Try This!
If you are worried about making incompatible changes from one program to another in a file, then you can make a copy of the original file, make the changes that you want to the copy, and save your changes with a new filename.

PASSWORDS:
Change a User Password

If you use passwords to increase security on your Windows XP computer or network, then you should make these passwords difficult to guess, and change them frequently. Typically, you should change your password every 30 to 90 days. When you select a new password, you can make it secure by combining both letters and numbers in a random mix. The more secure you make your password, the less chance of someone randomly guessing it and accessing your account.

If you log on to Windows with an Administrator account, then you can change more than your own

password. You can also reset the passwords of every other user, and add a password to an account that another user has not yet configured. This can force a user to become more serious about computer security, especially when they cannot log on.

See also>>

> **Forgotten Password Wizard**
>
> **User Accounts**
>
> **User Accounts**

① Click Start.

② Click Control Panel.

The Control Panel window opens.

③ Double-click User Accounts.

The User Accounts window opens.

④ Click Change an account.

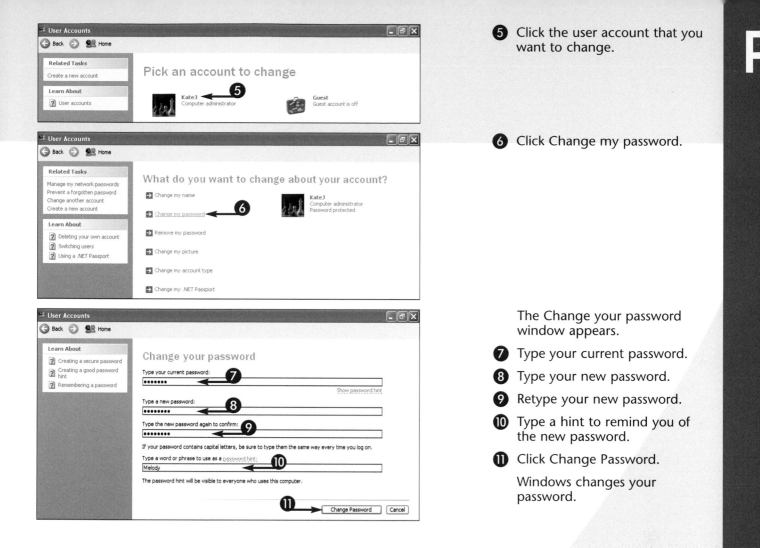

5 Click the user account that you want to change.

6 Click Change my password.

The Change your password window appears.

7 Type your current password.

8 Type your new password.

9 Retype your new password.

10 Type a hint to remind you of the new password.

11 Click Change Password.

Windows changes your password.

TIPS

Attention!
If you have created a recovery disk through the Forgotten Password Wizard, then you must re-run the wizard and create a new disk each time you change your password. Remember to label the new disk and discard or erase the old disk.

Did You Know?
The most frequently used password is the word *password*. Pet names and birth dates are also common. These are not good examples because they can be easily guessed by anyone who knows you.

Caution!
Because you may forget a new password, you can use the Forgotten Password Wizard to create a recovery disk. This disk helps you to access Windows if you cannot remember your current password, and takes you directly to User Accounts where you can change the password again.

PATH:
Set the System Path

You can set or edit your system path to add folders that you want to be part of a quick access list. A system path is a list of the primary folders that Windows checks as it loads. You can think of a system path as a road map to the key areas on your drives. Your programs first check any folder that is present on the path, so that any files located in those designated areas can be found quickly.

Your drive root directory — such as C:\ or D:\ — is almost always found within the system path. Your Windows folder appears there, too.

Although you can add other key folders to the path, you should use only those folders that contain important executable files. You should limit the number of folders that you include in the path; if you add too many, you may slow down the load-and-search process.

An example of a system path statement looks like this: path=c:\windows;c:\keydocs;d:\diagnostics; e:\pending.

① Click Start.

② Click All Programs.

③ Click Accessories.

④ Click Command Prompt.

The Command Prompt window opens.

⑤ Type **set path**.

⑥ Press Enter.

The current path displays in the Command Prompt console.

⑦ To create a new path, type a path to your key folders, for example, Path=C:\;C:\Windows\;D:\;D:\BUDOCS;E:\WINDOWS.

⑧ Press Enter.

⑨ To verify your path, type **set path**.

⑩ Press Enter.

The Command Prompt displays your newly changed system path.

TIPS

More Options!
You can set the path to include sub-folders within a master folder such as Windows. For example, one entry in your path statement may be C:\Windows\System32.

Try This!
If you make a mistake when you create your system path, then simply repeat the steps in this section.

Caution!
Choose the folders that you add to your path wisely and use only those that are important to avoid littering your path with folders.

Important!
Always verify the system path when you change it. Even a small typographic error, such as the omission of a semi-colon, can leave your path statement incomplete.

POWER:
Save Energy through Power Settings

Because Windows users often leave their computers on all the time, Windows XP now offers some features that compensate for the extra energy that these computers consume. You can enable special power settings in Windows to switch idle devices such as your monitor or hard disk into low power mode.

Although power-saving settings were difficult to use in the past, both Windows XP and newer hardware are able to handle these energy settings more gracefully and easily.

Depending on the options that you set and the hardware that you use, your computer may become so quiet in low power mode that it appears to be off. This is because some of the noisier components, such as the power supply fan, may be in sleep mode.

When you press a key on the keyboard or move the mouse, the system returns to its normal operating state within a few seconds.

See also>>  **Device Drivers**

1 Click Start.

2 Click Control Panel.

The Control Panel window opens.

3 In the Control Panel section, click Switch to Classic View.

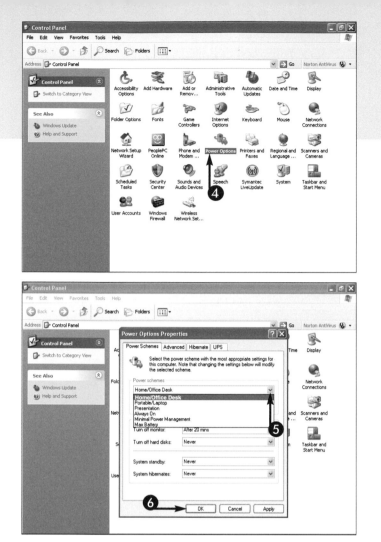

④ Double-click Power Options.

The Power Options Properties dialog box appears.

⑤ Click here and select the power-saving features that you want.

You can select features such as computer type, and whether to turn off the monitor or hard disk after a specified period of time.

⑥ Click OK.

Windows applies your power-savings options by turning off devices after the specified period of inactivity.

TIPS

Caution!
You may want to experiment with power settings to see how your system responds to low energy modes. For example, you should not specify short idle periods, such as 15 minutes or less.

Important!
If you experience difficulty when setting your energy-savings options, then you should consult your computer, motherboard, monitor, and hard disk documentation.

Attention!
Although most computer hardware today is fully compatible with the advanced power-management settings used in Windows, you may sometimes have difficulty in making certain devices behave properly. For example, if your computer does not recognize a key press or mouse motion, then you may need to update the hardware device drivers.

P

PROGRAM COMPATIBILITY WIZARD:
Enable Older Programs to Run

When programs that were designed to work in older versions of Windows cannot run properly in Windows XP, you can use the Program Compatibility Wizard to try to enable the older software to operate. You can use this wizard with programs that do not install, as well as with programs that no longer run.

The Program Compatibility Wizard creates a special, custom-configured environment for each program, that attempts to enable the older software to run. For example, the wizard may trick the software into

thinking that it is running in an earlier version than Windows XP. When you run the wizard, you can select options that you think may work best with a particular piece of software.

Your success with the Program Compatibility Wizard can vary from program to program. However, it is worth the effort if it allows you the opportunity to play a favorite game or access important data from an older database that otherwise would not load.

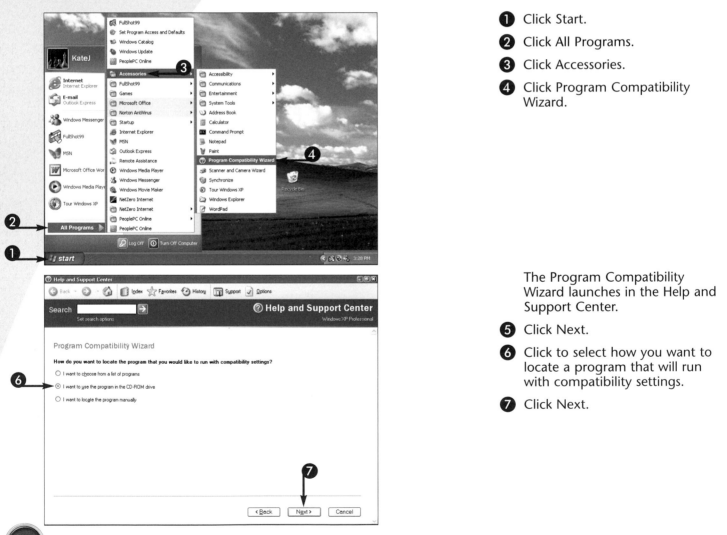

① Click Start.

② Click All Programs.

③ Click Accessories.

④ Click Program Compatibility Wizard.

The Program Compatibility Wizard launches in the Help and Support Center.

⑤ Click Next.

⑥ Click to select how you want to locate a program that will run with compatibility settings.

⑦ Click Next.

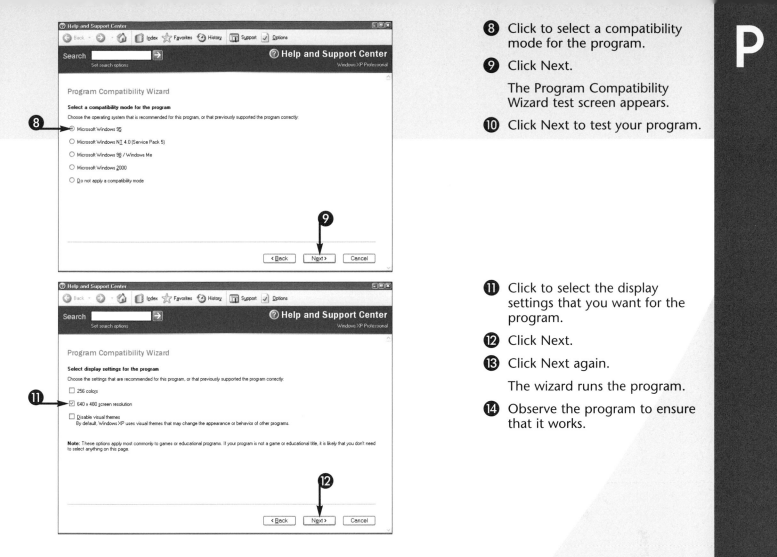

⑧ Click to select a compatibility mode for the program.

⑨ Click Next.

The Program Compatibility Wizard test screen appears.

⑩ Click Next to test your program.

⑪ Click to select the display settings that you want for the program.

⑫ Click Next.

⑬ Click Next again.

The wizard runs the program.

⑭ Observe the program to ensure that it works.

Attention!
After you run the Program Compatibility Wizard and load the older program, watch carefully for signs of system instability. If Windows misbehaves while the software is open, then you can relaunch the wizard, or consider using a different program.

Caution!
Do not try to use the Program Compatibility Wizard to run older utilities that only support earlier versions of the Windows file system. You risk damaging the contents of your Windows XP disk.

More Options!
You can run the Program Compatibility Wizard more than once to test different settings. If the wizard does not work, then ensure that your drivers are up to date, and run Windows Update before you relaunch the wizard or the program.

P

QUICK LAUNCH BAR:
Add and Remove Programs on the Quick Launch Bar

The Quick Launch Bar contains icons for some of the most popular programs in Windows, such as Microsoft Internet Explorer, QuickTime Player for playing movies and Show Desktop. When you add a program to the Quick Launch Bar, you are essentially creating a shortcut to that program, without cluttering up your desktop with shortcut icons.

You can add and remove programs and documents easily to and from the Quick Launch Bar. However, before you add icons, you should consider which programs you run the most frequently or that are

the most difficult for you to locate in the Start sub-menus. For example, some good candidates for the Quick Launch Bar are your favorite word processor, a document or file that you often need to access, or a utility.

Over time, you can remove Quick Launch icons that you no longer want or use, and replace them with icons for other more useful programs.

See also>> **Quick Launch Bar**

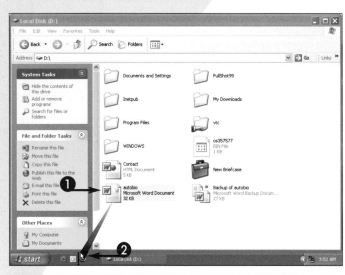

Add a Program

1 Use your desktop, My Computer, or Windows Explorer to locate the icon for the program or file that you want to add to the Quick Launch Bar.

2 Click and drag the icon to the Quick Launch Bar.

As you drag the icon, an outline appears around your cursor on the desktop.

3 Release your mouse button to drop the icon into place.

The icon for the program or file appears on your Quick Launch Bar.

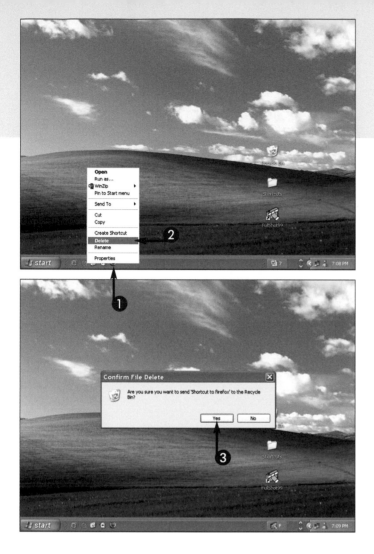

Remove an Icon

① Right-click the item on the Quick Launch Bar that you want to remove.

② Click Delete.

A Confirm File Delete dialog box appears.

③ Click Yes.

The icon for the program or file disappears from the Quick Launch Bar.

Q

TIPS

Attention!
Because the Quick Launch Bar has limited space, use the bar only for those programs that you need to access quickly.

Did You Know?
When you move an item to the Quick Launch Bar, this action does not remove the program from its original location. Similarly, when you delete an icon from the bar, you do not remove the program from your system.

Important!
The Quick Launch Bar operates differently from the programs that you add to your Windows Start Menu. The programs in the Start Menu run in the background throughout your Windows sessions, and each program consumes a lot of desktop resources. The Quick Launch Bar programs do not require as many desktop resources.

QUICK LAUNCH BAR:
Customize and Use the Quick Launch Bar

You can use the Quick Launch Bar to launch your most frequently used programs more quickly in Windows. The Quick Launch Bar is a special toolbar that contains icons for programs, utilities, and even documents so that you can open them quickly and easily.

Unlike the Start Menu, which displays the most recently or frequently used programs by default, the Quick Launch Bar allows you to decide which items appear on the bar. You can also change the programs

and documents that display on the bar whenever you want. Keep in mind that the Quick Launch Bar does not display by default, and so you need to turn it on to use it.

Another useful feature of the Quick Launch Bar is the Show Desktop icon. When you click this icon, Windows minimizes all applications so that you can see the Windows desktop. You can then quickly access any of the shortcuts on the desktop to launch programs or open documents.

① Right-click the taskbar.

② Click Properties.

The Taskbar and Start Menu Properties dialog box appears.

③ Under the Taskbar tab, click to select the Show Quick Launch option (☐ changes to ☑).

④ Click OK.

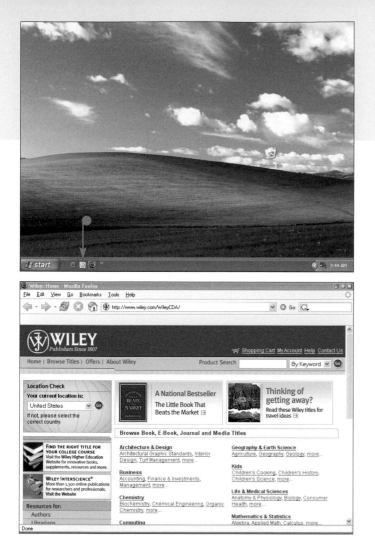

● The Quick Launch Bar appears between the Start button and the entries for any applications that are open on your desktop.

5 Click an icon in the Quick Launch Bar to open the selected item.

The program or file that you click in the Quick Launch Bar opens on your desktop.

TIPS

Customize It!

You can customize the Quick Launch Bar to add additional programs or documents that you want to access quickly. The Quick Launch Bar can hold several items.

More Options!

You can use a variety of shareware and commercial utilities to add a launch bar to your desktop, similar to the Quick Launch Bar. However, you should only use one of these utilities at a time.

Attention!

When other programs are open, with their entries appearing in the taskbar, the Quick Launch Bar may be condensed. If this happens, then click the right-pointing double arrows at the right of the Quick Launch Bar to expand it to its full size.

QUICK LAUNCH BAR:
Remove the Quick Launch Bar

You can position your Quick Launch Bar somewhere else on the taskbar other than between the Start button and the entries for other programs that reside in the taskbar. For example, you can easily move the Quick Launch Bar to the other end of your taskbar, next to the System Tray if you prefer it to appear there. You can even remove the Quick Launch Bar completely from the taskbar; this is a good choice if you do not use this feature or would prefer your taskbar be free of additions.

You can quickly and easily turn the Quick Launch Bar on and off to suit your needs. Each user can also specify in his or her user profile if he or she wants to use the Quick Launch Bar. When you do this, you configure the toolbar for your use while allowing other users the option to choose to hide it when they log on.

See also>> **Quick Launch Bar**

Move the Quick Launch Bar

❶ Position your mouse over the seven vertical dots that display between the Start button and the taskbar.

The pointer turns into a two-way horizontal arrow.

❷ Click and drag the Quick Launch Bar to where you want it, and drop it into place.

The Quick Launch Bar now displays where you moved it.

Remove the Quick Launch Bar

1️⃣ Right-click the taskbar.

2️⃣ Click Properties.

The Taskbar and Start Menu Properties dialog box appears.

3️⃣ Click to deselect the Show Quick Launch option.

4️⃣ Click OK.

The Quick Launch Bar disappears from your taskbar.

TIPS

Attention!
When several programs are running, the icons that represent these programs in the taskbar may crowd the opposite end of the taskbar from the Quick Launch Bar. The presence of the Quick Launch Bar may also require that your taskbar extends to two rows. You can use the arrows at the far right of the taskbar, next to the System Tray, to scroll between the top and bottom lines of the taskbar.

Try This!
If your computer crashes in the same session where you set up the Quick Launch Bar, then you may not see it when you restart the computer. You need to turn the bar on again because your changes were not saved.

RECOVERY CONSOLE:
Use Recovery Console

When your computer no longer loads Windows properly, you can use a powerful tool called Recovery Console to troubleshoot your system. Through this command-line utility, you can run commands to analyze system details, copy files, and turn services on and off. You can also format or reformat a hard disk or repair a damaged boot sector, which is the part of a hard disk from which the computer boot process launches.

You can only use Recovery Console if you already have an Administrator account on that system. You must also have some knowledge of Windows

commands and organization because this utility can be difficult to use.

Even if you are not familiar with commands, you may still be able to repair your system if you follow specific instructions. You can use the Help and Support Center to locate and run the commands that you need.

Keep in mind that you must be very careful when typing commands in Recovery Console. You can follow instructions from help articles or other sources when you use this utility.

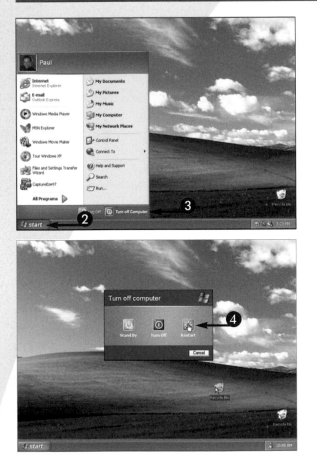

❶ Insert your Windows XP setup CD into your CD or DVD drive.

❷ Click Start.

❸ Click Turn Off Computer.

❹ In the dialog box that appears, click Restart.

Windows displays a message telling you to press any key to boot from the CD.

❺ Press a key.

❻ When the Setup screen appears, type **r** to repair.

❼ Type the number that corresponds to the listed Windows installation on which you want to work.

❽ When prompted, type the Administrator password.

❾ In the Recovery Console after your work is complete, type **exit**.

Your computer restarts.

RECYCLE BIN:
Empty the Recycle Bin

When you delete files in Windows, they do not completely disappear. Instead, they transfer into the Recycle Bin, where they stay until you empty it. Only then does the Recycle Bin purge these files from your system. In this way, the Recycle Bin allows you one last chance to restore these files before they are permanently lost.

The Recycle Bin is similar to the Trash icon in the Macintosh operating system, as well as to the Trash icon that displays in many programs such as photo-editing software. Its sole purpose is to act as a holding area for deleted files.

The Recycle Bin also provides a Restore feature so that you can recover accidentally erased files. You can choose to recover either a single file or every item in the bin.

You should empty the Recycle Bin on a regular basis to keep your hard disk from becoming cluttered with orphaned and unwanted files. Before you purge, determine if there are any files you need to restore.

① Double-click the Recycle Bin.

The Recycle Bin window opens.

② Review the list of files.

③ Click Empty the Recycle Bin.

The files disappear from the Recycle Bin window.

You can now close the window.

RECYCLE BIN:
Restore an Accidentally Deleted File from the Recycle Bin

If you think that you have deleted a file by accident, then you should first check the Recycle Bin. If you see the file listed there, then you can use the Restore option to pull the file from the Recycle Bin window and restore it to its former location. You can access the Restore option in the left-hand task pane or by right-clicking a file.

If you think that a file is missing from your system, then you can use one of three ways to locate it. First, you can use Search Companion to look through your drives to find the file. Second, you can go directly to the Recycle Bin, to see if the file is there so that you can restore it. Third, you can recover the missing file from your most recent backup.

Although you can move the Recycle Bin icon around your desktop, you cannot delete this icon unless you first make changes to your system to enable you to delete the Recycle Bin.

See also>>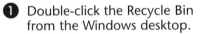

Restore a Single File

❶ Double-click the Recycle Bin from the Windows desktop.

The Recycle Bin window opens, displaying its contents.

❷ Click to select a file that you want to recover.

❸ Click File.

❹ Click Restore.

The file disappears from the Recycle Bin and returns to its original location on your hard drive.

Restore All Recycle Bin Files

R

1 Double-click the Recycle Bin from the Windows desktop.

The Recycle Bin window opens, displaying its contents.

2 Click Restore all items.

All files disappear from the Recycle Bin and return to their original locations on your hard drive.

TIPS

Caution!
You should review the list of files in the Recycle Bin before you empty it. This allows you one last chance to restore a file if you want.

Important!
Not every file that you delete may be found in the Recycle Bin. For example, extremely large files are too big to move to the Recycle Bin; as a result, you are prompted to delete these files directly. If you click Yes, then Windows erases the files without sending them to the Recycle Bin.

Caution!
You should never delete files using the Command Prompt unless you want to remove them permanently. These files do not go into the Recycle Bin but are directly deleted.

REGIONAL AND LANGUAGE OPTIONS:
Add a Language to Windows XP

When you create, view, or receive files in another language than the default language in Windows, you need to add support for that other language. You can do this through the Regional and Language Options dialog box, which you access through the Control Panel. Until you add another language, you are limited to working only in the default language that you selected when you installed Windows.

When you install additional languages, Windows supplies direct support for these languages as well as any necessary changes to the virtual keyboard

layout. Each language that you add comes with a custom keyboard layout.

If you normally work in a corporate environment that uses a Windows network server, then you may already have many additional languages available to you. You can see which languages are installed in the Regional and Language Options dialog box. However, if you use applications that support many languages, then you may also want to check the options that are set in each program.

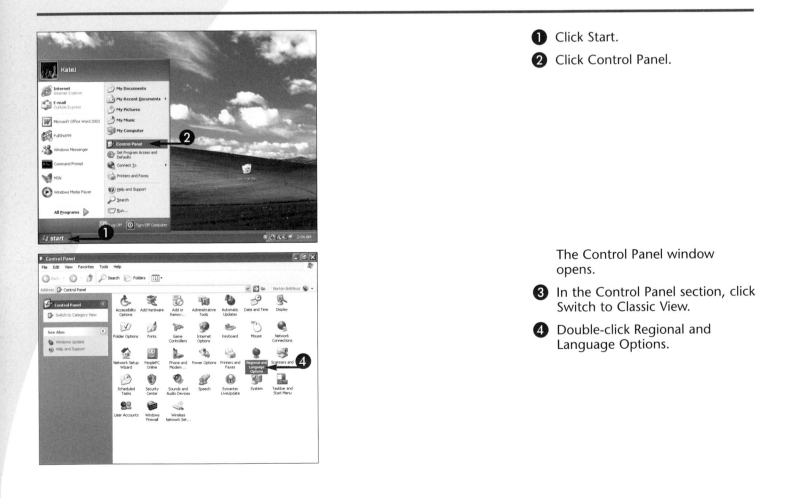

❶ Click Start.

❷ Click Control Panel.

The Control Panel window opens.

❸ In the Control Panel section, click Switch to Classic View.

❹ Double-click Regional and Language Options.

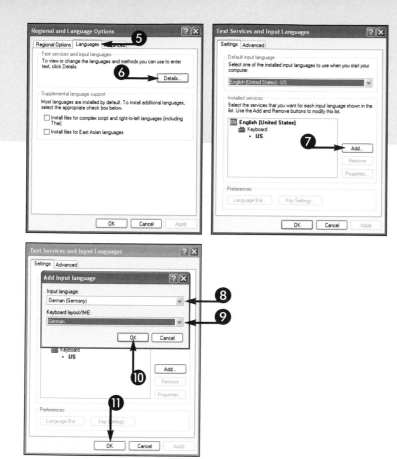

The Regional and Language Options dialog box appears.

5 Click the Languages tab.

6 Click Details.

The Text Services and Input Languages dialog box appears.

7 Click Add.

The Add Input language dialog box appears.

8 Click here and select the input language that you want to add.

9 Click here and select the keyboard layout that you want to use.

10 Click OK.

11 Click OK.

Windows adds support for the language that you chose.

TIPS

Attention!

You can quickly add support for most languages. However, for some languages, you may be prompted to insert your Windows XP setup CD. This is necessary because less-common language support files do not copy to your computer during Windows installation.

Important!

You may need a live Internet connection to add certain languages or support for different keyboard languages through Regional and Language Options. This is necessary whenever the files you want to add are not already available on your PC or through your Windows XP setup CD.

More Options!

You can also add language and keyboard support for complex languages, such as Arabic, which is written from right to left, and East Asian languages. You can click to select these options in the Languages tab shown in Step 5.

REGIONAL AND LANGUAGE OPTIONS:
Change Data Format

You can adjust how Windows displays and formats certain types of data in the Regional and Language Options dialog box, which you can access from the Control Panel. This is often necessary because many languages display certain types of data differently.

You can use the Regional and Language Options dialog box to adjust how specific data formats and appears. This allows you to make all information that you type or view in an application compatible with the language of your choice. This is a useful feature in a global environment where you trade files with people in offices around the world.

For example, when you use a European language in addition to English, you may want your data to display in a European-compatible format. Through the Options dialog box, you can choose a language and automatically configure Windows to format money, dates, and other types of data to match the region and language. This means that currency displays in the Euro format to match that currency type, rather than in American dollars.

See also>> **Regional and Language Options**

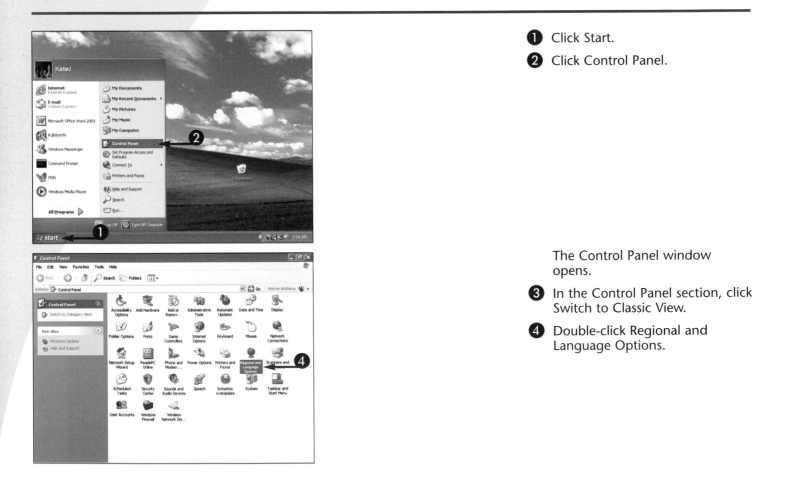

❶ Click Start.

❷ Click Control Panel.

The Control Panel window opens.

❸ In the Control Panel section, click Switch to Classic View.

❹ Double-click Regional and Language Options.

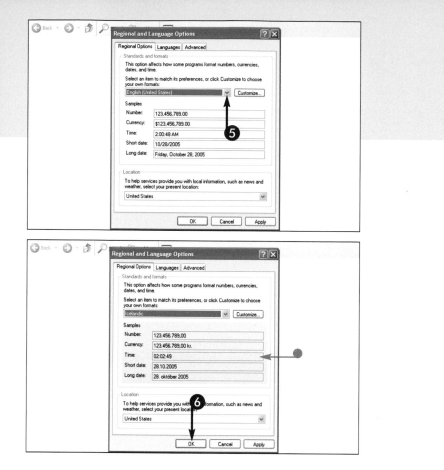

The Regional and Language Options dialog box appears, displaying the Regional Options tab.

5 Click here and select a language.

● The Samples section displays the appropriate formats for the language that you selected.

6 Click OK.

Your changes are reflected when you work with files in the selected language.

R

TIPS

Attention!
You can only modify the data format for one language at a time through the Settings tab in the Text Services and Input Languages dialog box. If you need to adjust for a different language, then complete Steps 1 to 6 again.

Customize It!
If you share your computer, then be sure to set up a user account for each person so that they can specify their own language and regional options.

Try This!
If you need to install additional language support and you are prompted to supply your Windows XP setup CD but do not have it, then you may have an alternative. You can visit the Microsoft Windows site or use Windows Update to download special packs that add language support.

RENAME FILES:
Change the Name of a Closed File

You may sometimes want to change the name of a file to be more descriptive. Windows XP offers you several different ways to do this. A few of these techniques do not even require that you open the file first or re-save it with the new name, although you can do this as well.

Two easy ways that you can rename a file without first opening it are available through My Computer and Windows Explorer. In almost every window where you can open or save files, you can click an

existing filename, and either delete the old name and replace it with a new one or edit the existing filename.

You can also rename a file through the Open or Save dialog boxes that appear when you open or save a file in most Windows applications. To access the Open dialog box, you can press Ctrl + O in Word.

See also>> **File and Folder Management**

1 Click Start.

2 Click My Computer.

The My Computer window opens.

3 Double-click the drive letter where the file that you want to rename is stored.

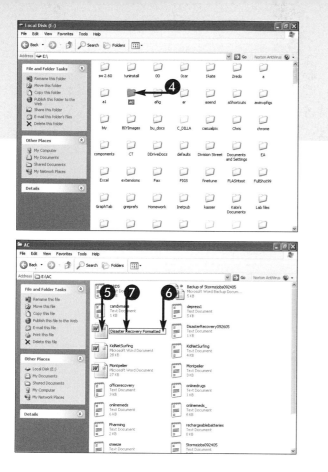

My Computer displays the contents of the drive.

④ Double-click the folder that contains the file.

The contents of the folder appear.

⑤ Click the file icon once.

⑥ Click the filename.

An outline appears around the filename.

⑦ Click inside the outline and type the new name for the file.

⑧ Press Enter.

The file appears with its new name.

TIPS

Attention!
If you try to rename a file to the same name as another file in the same folder, an error message appears. Type a different filename.

More Options!
If you want to keep a copy of the file with its original name but also store a copy with a new name, then first right-click the file, and then click Copy. Right-click in the My Computer window and click Paste. You can now rename the file copy with a new name.

Try This!
You cannot rename a file that is stored only on a recordable disc such as a CD-R, CD-RW, DVD-R, or DVD-RW. You must first copy the file to a hard disk and then rename the file.

REMOTE DESKTOP CONNECTION:
Configure Remote Desktop Connection

When you configure your computer to use a Remote Desktop Connection, you can manage that computer from the keyboard and monitor of another computer. The other computer can be located on your network in another room, or in a remote location across the Web. You can also manage your home computer from work or vice versa just as if you were seated at the other computer. The major advantage is you do not need to go to another location physically to work with the desktop or files found there; you can accomplish all this from the Remote Desktop Connection.

But unless you specifically configure the Remote Desktop Connection option, you will not be able to use this feature. In addition, if you use Windows Firewall, you may need to adjust Firewall settings so you can work with Remote Desktop Connection. For example, you may need to manage exceptions that appear when you try to access another computer remotely with the firewall engaged.

See also>>   **Remote Desktop Connection**

① Start up the computer on which you want to configure the Remote Desktop Connection feature.

② Click Start.

③ Click Control Panel.

The Control Panel window opens.

④ In the Control Panel section, click Switch to Classic View.

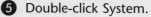

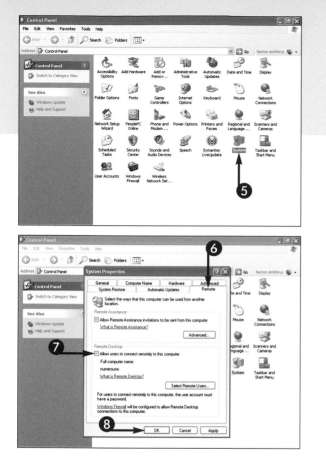

5 Double-click System.

The System Properties dialog box appears.

6 Click the Remote tab.

7 Click the Allow users to connect remotely to this computer option.

8 Click OK.

The computer is now configured to receive remote connections.

TIPS

Attention!
The Remote Desktop Connection feature works best when used between two Windows XP systems.

Caution!
Even with the use of the Windows Firewall, there is always the possibility that an unwanted party may be able to access a remote computer and do damage with the Remote Desktop Connection turned on. For this reason, you may want to disable the feature whenever you are not using it. You can always re-enable the connection later.

Try This!
If you want to experiment with a remote connection but do not want to pay for a third-party software package, such as PC Anywhere, that allows you to do this, then Remote Desktop Connection is a good alternative.

SAFE MODE:
Boot the Computer in Safe Mode

Whenever you experience a problem that prevents Windows XP from starting up properly, you can start up again in Safe Mode to troubleshoot Windows.

Safe Mode is not designed for normal Windows operation. It is a special limited-access, diagnostic mode only. Only secured drivers for devices can load, and you cannot launch and use many of the programs and tools that you normally can. Sometimes when your system experiences a serious error or problem in booting up, it launches automatically in Safe Mode without your intervention.

While in Safe Mode, you can check devices that are loaded, revert to a safe version of a driver for a misbehaving device such as a graphics card, make specific changes to your system, and even run System Restore to restore your setup to a previous state. Sometimes, simply running Safe Mode, exiting, and restarting Windows normally is enough to restart your system successfully.

See also>>  **System Restore**

① Click Start.

② Click Turn Off Computer.

The Turn off computer dialog box appears.

③ Click Restart.

Windows XP shuts down, and your computer restarts through the boot process.

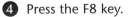

If you have multiple operating systems installed, then you need to select your Windows setup as well.

● A message appears, asking you to select the operating system that you want to start.

④ Press the F8 key.

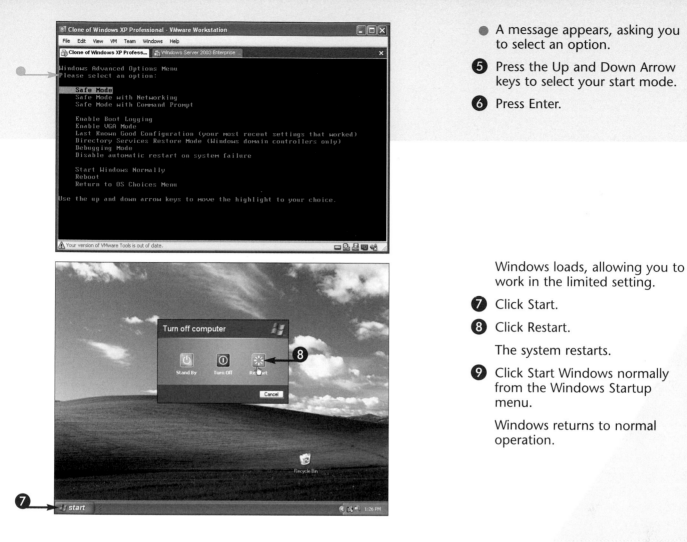

- A message appears, asking you to select an option.

5 Press the Up and Down Arrow keys to select your start mode.

6 Press Enter.

Windows loads, allowing you to work in the limited setting.

7 Click Start.

8 Click Restart.

The system restarts.

9 Click Start Windows normally from the Windows Startup menu.

Windows returns to normal operation.

TIPS

Attention!
Safe Mode is often used as a testing mode to ensure that basic drivers and settings work properly. A seriously disabled Windows installation may not allow you to boot in Safe Mode.

Important!
You cannot work normally in Safe Mode. For example, you cannot launch many applications, listen to music, or perform other regular operations.

Caution!
Although you can review and troubleshoot various options in Safe Mode, you should avoid making drastic changes unless you know what you are doing. When troubleshooting, it is a good idea to make a small change, see how the system performs, and then, if it does not help, return the setting to its original status before you try something else.

SAFE MODE:
Recover a Previous System Restore Point

You can use System Restore in Windows XP to record Restore Points that save all of your files and settings at a specific point in time. Then, when you find that you cannot load Windows normally, you can use Safe Mode to load System Restore and recover your system to a recorded Restore Point. This should allow you to restart the system as you normally would and return to work fairly quickly.

To use the System Restore feature, it must already be enabled, and at least one Restore Point must already have been recorded. When you load Windows in Safe

Mode, you can only restore a Restore Point; you cannot record a new one. This ensures that you cannot create a recording that copies problems with your system — and the limited settings of Safe Mode — into a Restore Point that you may accidentally use later. You also avoid taking up disk space with a faulty Restore Point.

See also>>

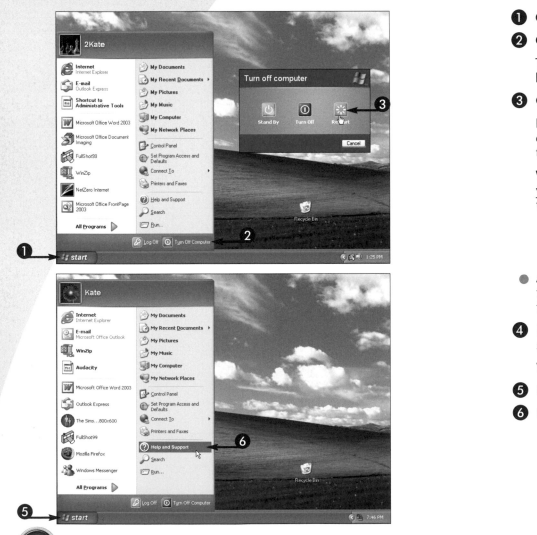

① Click Start.

② Click Turn Off Computer.

The Turn off computer dialog box appears.

③ Click Restart.

If the computer is not currently on, then press the power button to start it.

Windows XP shuts down, and your computer restarts through the boot process.

● A message appears, asking you to select the operating system that you want to start.

④ Press the F8 key to reboot the system in Safe Mode.

Windows loads in Safe Mode.

⑤ Click Start.

⑥ Click Help and Support.

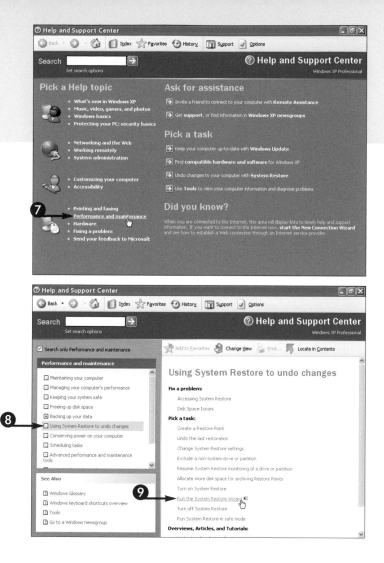

The Help and Support Center window opens.

7 Click Performance and maintenance.

8 Click Using System Restore to undo changes.

9 Click Run the System Restore Wizard.

10 Follow on-screen instructions to select a Restore Point to recover your system.

When finished, Windows should prompt you to restart your system.

After the system restarts, choose to load Windows in Normal mode.

Windows returns to Normal mode.

TIPS

Attention!

It is usually best to choose the most recently recorded Restore Point that was created before the current problems began. If you choose a very old Restore Point, then it may not reflect the more recent changes that you have made.

Did You Know?

If you do not like the results of the Restore Point that you have applied, then you can repeat the process to use a different Restore Point.

Important!

To ensure that System Restore is enabled before you follow these steps, click Start, click Control Panel, and then click System. Select the System Restore tab and ensure that the Turn off System Restore on all drives option is not selected.

SCHEDULED TASKS WIZARD:
Automate Your Tasks

When you have certain jobs that you need to run regularly on your system, such as once a day or twice a week, you can automate these tasks using the Scheduled Tasks Wizard. The wizard allows you to create a timetable that runs these chores automatically at the time, day, and frequency that you want.

One advantage of this feature is that once you automate these jobs, you do not have to be at your desktop when they run. This is beneficial because some maintenance routines work best when they do not have to compete with you for desktop resources.

You can add system maintenance tools — such as Disk Cleanup Wizard, Disk Defragmenter, and your Backup — to your Scheduled Task list through the wizard to automate these tools. This ensures that these chores run when they should. You can also set up your virus scanner and other tools to operate through the Scheduled Tasks Wizard.

See also>>

| Backup |
| Disk Cleanup Wizard |

1 Click Start.

2 Click Control Panel.

The Control Panel window opens.

3 In the Control Panel section, click Switch to Classic View.

4 Double-click Scheduled Tasks.

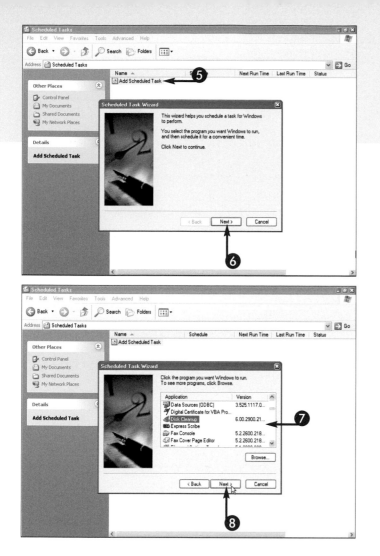

The Scheduled Tasks window opens.

5 Click Add Scheduled Task.

The Scheduled Task Wizard opens.

6 Click Next.

7 Follow the on-screen instructions to add the task that you want.

8 Click Next to continue.

9 When you are done, click Finish.

Windows adds the task to the Schedule.

TIPS

Important!

Some utilities that you install may automatically set up scheduled tasks for you, such as Norton Antivirus. Some of these tasks may appear in your Scheduled Tasks folder. However, others may simply run from the third-party software that you install and configure. These tasks may not show up in Scheduled Tasks at all and must be managed from the third-party software.

Attention!

When you create an automated Backup job using the Backup Wizard, a scheduled task is automatically created for you. You do not need to set up a second Backup job through the Scheduled Task Wizard. You can also manage Backup jobs directly from the Backup tool in Windows.

SCREENSAVER:
Set Up a Screensaver

You can set up a screensaver in Windows XP to prevent others from seeing your work on your desktop while you are away from your computer. You can also use a screensaver to add fun or personalized images to your desktop.

Windows XP offers a number of default screensavers from which you can choose. You can also configure options such as how long your computer should be inactive before the screensaver appears. In addition, you can configure Windows to require a password in order to return to the active desktop. This ensures that unauthorized users cannot simply click your

mouse to deactivate the screensaver and work at your keyboard.

You can download and install other screensavers from the Internet. You may also create your own screensavers through a number of third-party utilities, which you can download from the Internet, sometimes for free.

See also>>   **Background**

**Display Properties,
Configure Display Properties**

1 Right-click an empty area on your desktop.

A sub-menu appears.

2 Click Properties.

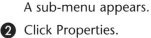

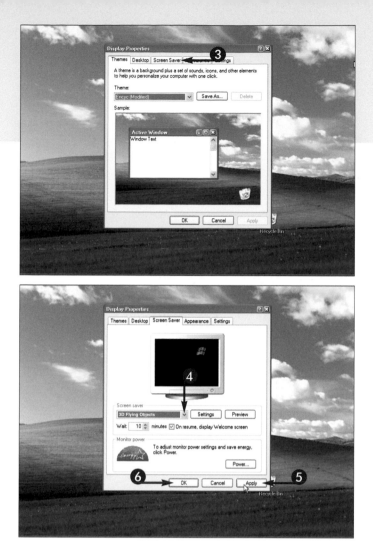

The Display Properties dialog box appears.

3 Click the Screen Saver tab.

4 Click here and select a screensaver.

5 Click Apply.

6 Click OK.

The Display Properties dialog box closes, and Windows enables the screensaver.

TIPS

Attention!
If the screensaver is enabled, and you want to return to your desktop, then move your mouse or press a key on your keyboard. The screensaver should disappear and return you to your desktop.

Try This!
If you have trouble with a custom screensaver that you download, then you can return to Display Properties and choose a standard Windows screensaver, instead.

Important!
You may not be able to deactivate the screensaver when you try to return to the computer desktop with the screensaver on. If this happens, then keep trying. If all else fails, then press and hold your computer power button for approximately ten seconds to shut down Windows. You can now press the power button again to restart the computer.

SEARCH COMPANION:
Locate Files with Search Companion

You can use Search Companion to locate files on your computer. Through Search Companion, you can configure your searches to make them as broad or as focused as you want.

Search Companion allows you to search by filename or type of file — such as by all documents or all images — or by the last time that you accessed or modified a particular file. The latter type of file search is useful when you want to find all of the files that you created or modified within a certain period of time, such as in the past week. You can also

search by only part of a filename, such as *.doc, to find all documents with this file extension, or search for a phrase that appears in the file.

As your search runs in the Search Companion, the results appear in the right-hand pane. From this pane, you can right-click any file and choose Properties to learn more about the file, including where it is located on your computer. You can also double-click a listed file to open it directly.

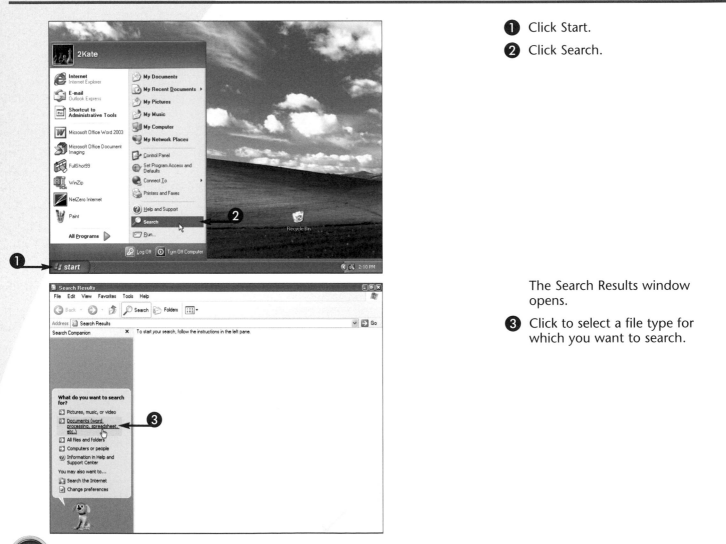

1 Click Start.

2 Click Search.

The Search Results window opens.

3 Click to select a file type for which you want to search.

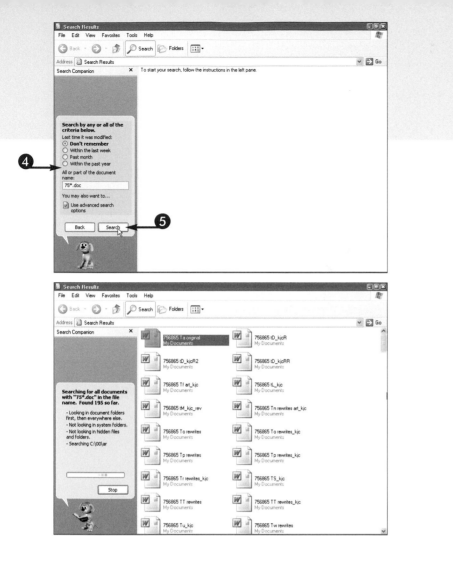

④ Follow the instructions to finish selecting your variables.

⑤ Click Search.

The matches for your search appear in the right-hand pane.

TIPS

More Options!

You can also use the Search Companion to look for people in your Address Book or for other computers on your home or office network. You can also perform an Internet search directly from the Search Companion if you have a live Internet connection. To do this, use the Computers or people option from the main search window.

Attention!

If your search fails to return any files that meet your search criteria, then you can perform a new search with different criteria. For example, if you initially chose to search for a specific file by its full name, then you can now search by all files with the same file extension, such as *.txt, to see all text files.

SECURITY:
Secure Accounts

You can secure your system from others who want to access your confidential programs and files. To do this, you can start by securing your user accounts to log in to Windows. This is the most basic level of security that you can add to your system.

The simplest and most direct way to secure a Windows system is to add a different password to the account name of each user who shares the computer. People who log in to their account must then correctly enter the password before they can log in to Windows.

Passwords should be as difficult as possible — for example, they should be hard to simply guess by others who know the user — and changed regularly to reduce the chance that someone who obtains your password can use it for long.

To further improve account security, you should also disable the Guest account in Windows and turn off the Welcome screen and Fast User Switching.

See also>>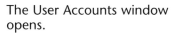

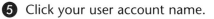

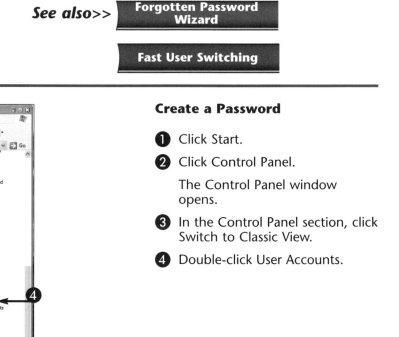

Create a Password

1 Click Start.

2 Click Control Panel.

The Control Panel window opens.

3 In the Control Panel section, click Switch to Classic View.

4 Double-click User Accounts.

The User Accounts window opens.

5 Click your user account name.

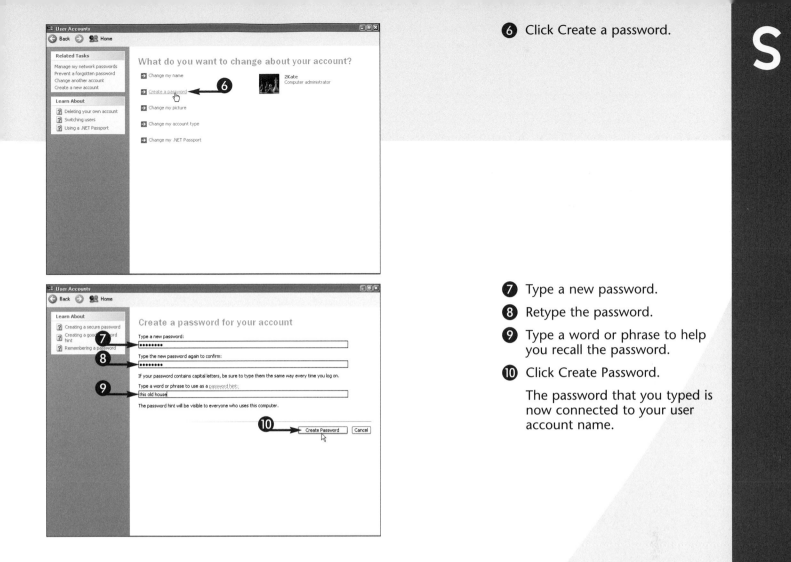

6 Click Create a password.

7 Type a new password.

8 Retype the password.

9 Type a word or phrase to help you recall the password.

10 Click Create Password.

The password that you typed is now connected to your user account name.

TIPS

Attention!
Once you add a password, you are prompted at login to type in the password after you select your user account.

Try This!
For the best security, passwords should be random, at least six characters — but preferably at least eight — and a combination of alphanumeric characters, such as 88dh47ph9 or ra38ts77o.

Caution!
Once you add a password to your account, there is always the possibility that you will forget your password, especially if you change your password every 30 to 90 days. For this reason, you should use the Forgotten Password Wizard to create a password reset disk to help you if you forget your password and cannot access your account.

SECURITY:
Secure Accounts (Continued)

In addition to adding a password to an account to make it secure, there are many other measures that you can take to increase the security of individual accounts, as well as the entire system.

If you choose a password and then use it month after month, year after year, then you may want to rethink this practice, as it is an example of poor account security. Good user account security involves regularly — at least every 30 to 60 days — changing your password and using longer passwords.

You can turn off the Guest account that provides access to the computer for users who do not have their own user account. You should also turn off the Windows Welcome Screen because it allows a user to merely click an icon to access the computer.

You can also combine all three solutions. This means that you create longer and frequently changed passwords, and turn off the Guest account and the Windows Welcome screen. This combination allows you to more effectively block some of the ways through which problems can occur.

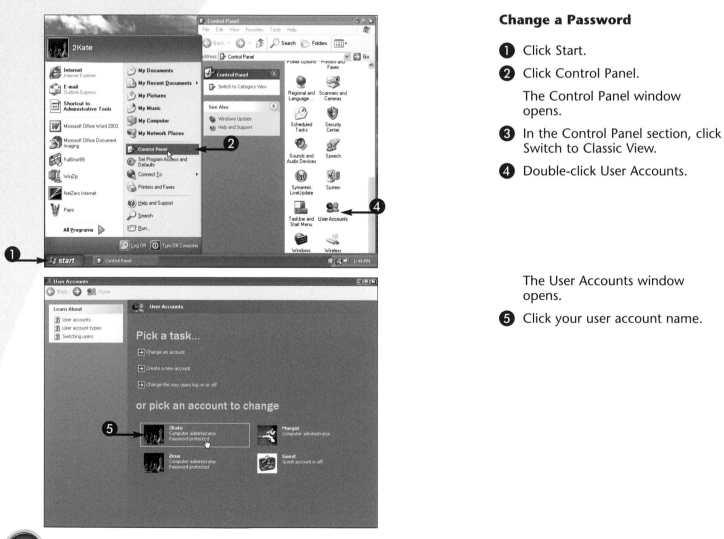

Change a Password

❶ Click Start.

❷ Click Control Panel.

The Control Panel window opens.

❸ In the Control Panel section, click Switch to Classic View.

❹ Double-click User Accounts.

The User Accounts window opens.

❺ Click your user account name.

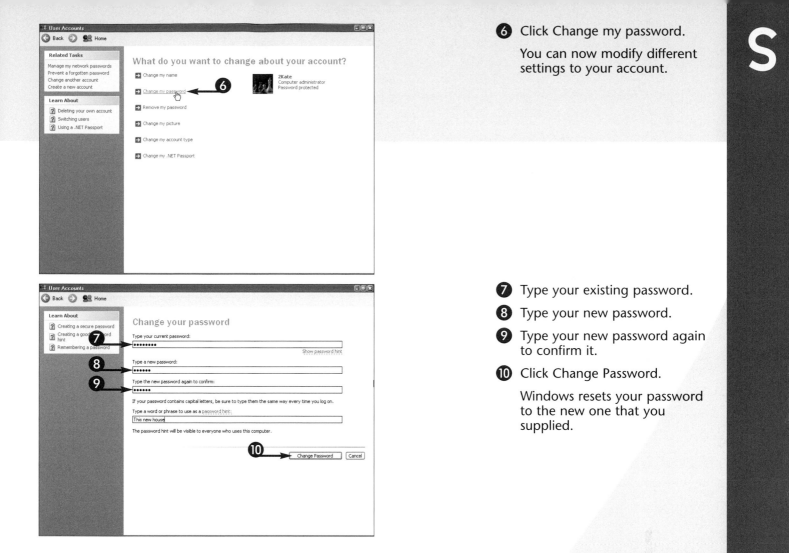

6 Click Change my password.

You can now modify different settings to your account.

7 Type your existing password.

8 Type your new password.

9 Type your new password again to confirm it.

10 Click Change Password.

Windows resets your password to the new one that you supplied.

S

TIPS

Important!
You must log in with an Administrator account before you can change the passwords for any other users.

Try This!
If you cannot remember your current password to access Windows or the Change password feature, then try this: If you previously created a Forgotten Password Wizard disk, then you can use it to access Windows and then go directly into User Accounts to modify your password.

Attention!
Windows may display an error message in the last window in the steps for changing your password if the first new password that you supply does not match the password that you type again to confirm it. Be sure to type the exact password in both the new password and confirm text boxes to avoid this problem.

SECURITY:
Secure Accounts (Continued)

When you first install Windows XP or buy a new computer with Windows XP installed, you will notice two major features: a Welcome screen and a Guest account. The Welcome screen makes it very easy for you to log on to Windows by simply clicking your user account icon.

The Guest account is a limited-option account that is available from the Welcome screen. For example, you can permit an overnight guest to work on the computer or surf the Web without having to create a separate account, or allowing him or her to use your account.

However, the Welcome screen can be too easy to access, especially if you do not assign a password to your user account. A user simply clicks once to access Windows. The Guest Account, even though limited, presents certain security challenges. For example, a very knowledgeable person can bypass basic security measures to access your account or your confidential files. Even worse, they can make changes to your system that you do not want.

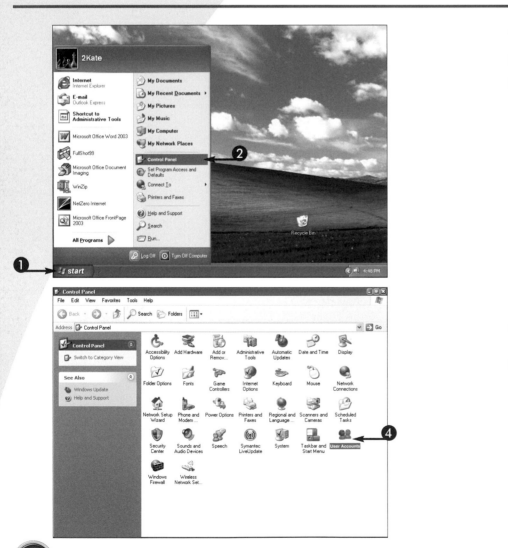

Apply Options

❶ Click Start.

❷ Click Control Panel.

The Control Panel window opens.

❸ In the Control Panel section, click Switch to Classic View.

❹ Double-click User Accounts.

340

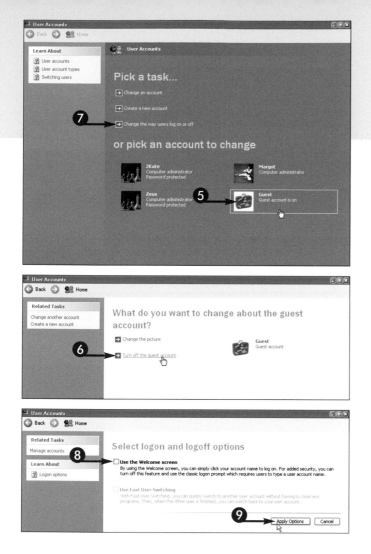

The User Accounts window opens.

5 Click the Guest account.

Information for the Guest Account appears.

6 Click Turn off the guest account.

The Guest account is no longer available.

7 In the User Accounts window, click Change the way users log on and off.

8 Click to deselect the Use the Welcome screen option.

9 Click Apply Options.

The icon-based Welcome screen no longer appears during logon.

TIPS

Important!
When you turn off the Windows Welcome screen, you automatically disable the Fast User Switching option.

Try This!
If you think that you may forget your new password, then you can type in a word or phrase to use as a hint on the same screen where you change your password by supplying a new one.

Caution!
If you use a password reset disk and you change your password, then you must create a new password reset disk for use in emergencies. The Forgotten Password Wizard available through the User Accounts window helps you to do this.

SECURITY:
Secure Your System

You do not need to be familiar with elaborate and sophisticated security measures to protect your Windows XP system. There are a number of simple but powerful changes that you can make to increase the overall security of your Windows system and network, as well as your Internet connection.

The best way to protect your Internet connection, as well as your Windows files and setup, is by using a firewall. This acts as a shield between your online connection and your computer. Windows XP, as well as some earlier versions, offers the Internet

Connection Sharing Firewall, which you can configure and enable to provide the protection that you need.

If you have not already done so, then you should obtain and install the Windows XP Service Pack 2. This is a major update to Windows XP that provides greater security with a more secure browser, firewall enhancements, and other features.

See also>>   **Windows Firewall**

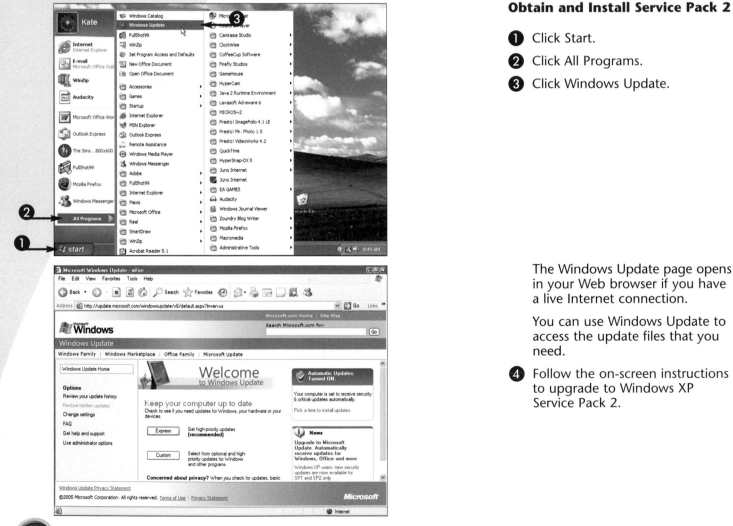

Obtain and Install Service Pack 2

① Click Start.

② Click All Programs.

③ Click Windows Update.

The Windows Update page opens in your Web browser if you have a live Internet connection.

You can use Windows Update to access the update files that you need.

④ Follow the on-screen instructions to upgrade to Windows XP Service Pack 2.

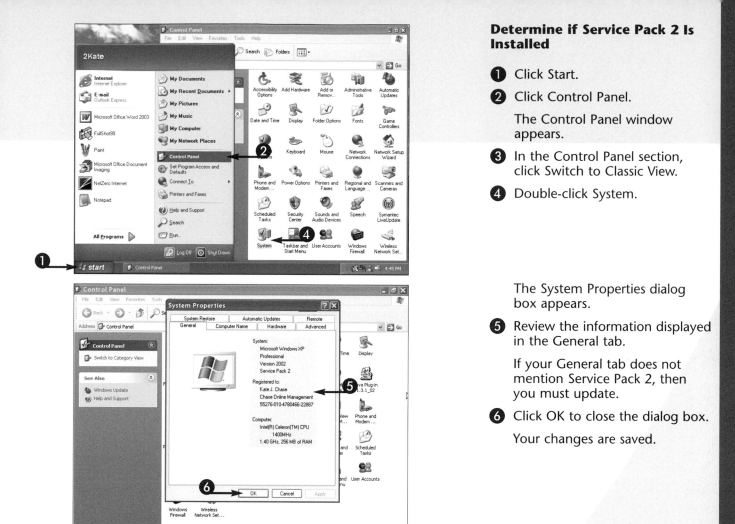

Determine if Service Pack 2 Is Installed

1 Click Start.

2 Click Control Panel.

The Control Panel window appears.

3 In the Control Panel section, click Switch to Classic View.

4 Double-click System.

The System Properties dialog box appears.

5 Review the information displayed in the General tab.

If your General tab does not mention Service Pack 2, then you must update.

6 Click OK to close the dialog box.

Your changes are saved.

TIPS

Attention!

It is extremely important that you update your Windows XP system with the Service Packs available, especially Service Pack 2. This is because, if you use Windows Updates, you will find that Microsoft now only provides updates to those who use Windows XP with either Service Pack 1 and/or Service Pack 2 installed. Obtain and install these packs as soon as possible.

More Options!

If you have a very slow, non-broadband Internet connection or have a Windows XP system without a modem attached, you can obtain Service Pack 2 on CD for a small shipping charge directly from Microsoft. See the Windows Update site for details on how to order this disk.

SECURITY ZONES:
Customize Privacy Settings for All Web Sites in Internet Explorer

If you are concerned about privacy and the use of Web cookies, then you may want to customize the privacy settings to greater levels than the basic Internet Explorer settings. Cookies are the tiny files that are transmitted to your browser and hard drive from Web sites that you visit. These cookies help to identify you, as well as what you have viewed at a site.

One technique that you can use to manage Web security is to customize privacy settings for all Web sites that you visit and specify how cookies from these sites are handled.

However, before you adjust these settings, it is important that you understand that some Web sites expressly insist that a cookie be delivered to your browser in order for you to use their site. For example, if you have an account at a site, the username and password for your account is often stored in a cookie. If you do not accept the cookie, then you may not be able to use the site, or at least not use it to its full capacity.

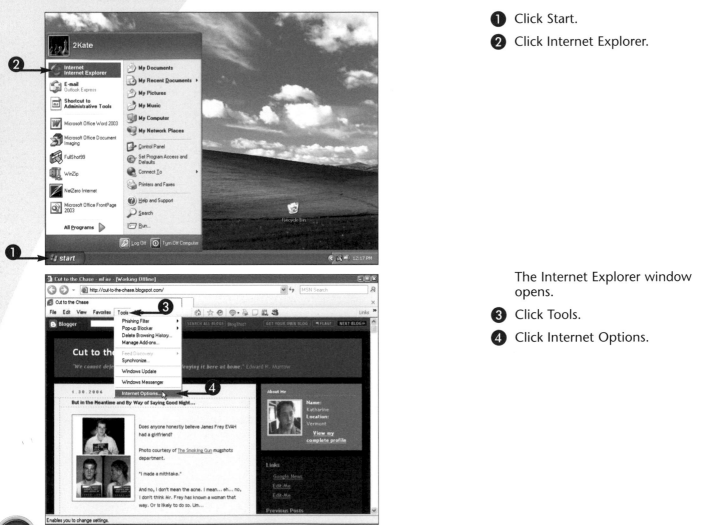

① Click Start.

② Click Internet Explorer.

The Internet Explorer window opens.

③ Click Tools.

④ Click Internet Options.

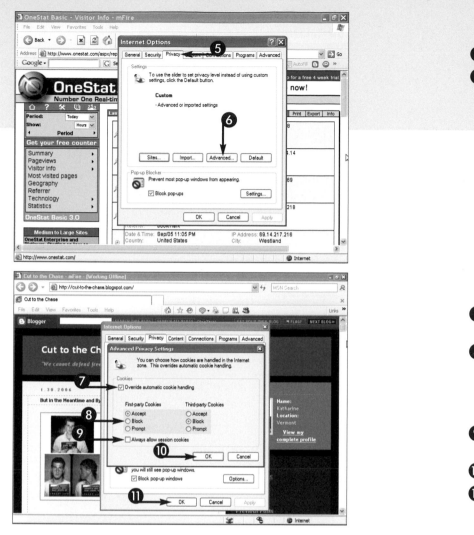

The Internet Options dialog box appears.

5 Click the Privacy tab.

6 Click Advanced.

The Advanced Privacy Settings dialog box appears.

7 Select the Override automatic cookie handling option.

8 Select your first-party and third-party cookies options to determine whether to always accept or block cookies, or to prompt you.

9 Select the Always allow session cookies option.

10 Click OK.

11 Click OK.

The Internet Options window closes.

TIPS

Caution!
Watch your ability to open and operate within Web sites after you make these changes. For example, some sites require you to accept a cookie simply to open the site, while others permit you to visit but require a cookie to use a specific feature. You may need to adjust your settings again — for example, by changing Block to Prompt or Accept — to browse normally.

Attention!
You can always reset your privacy settings at any time by returning to the Privacy tab.

Did You Know?
First-party cookies are received from the Web site that you are currently visiting. Third-party cookies refer to all other sites than the current one, such as to a site that the current Web site redirects you to visit.

SECURITY ZONES:
Manage Security Settings for Zones in Internet Explorer

With security zones built into the Microsoft Internet Explorer Web browser, you can manage how your browser responds when it moves from one type of zone to another. For example, this feature can limit the information that is transferred through the browser or that displays within the browser.

Internet Explorer comes with four preset zones — Local Intranet, Internet, Trusted Sites, and Restricted Sites — each with its own level of security. You can customize and adjust the level of security for each of these zones, except for the Local Intranet zone.

Although the Microsoft Internet Explorer Web browser has security zones pre-configured to the recommended level of security, you can modify the security level and details for each zone to either increase or reduce the level of protection needed. For example, if you experience problems loading a particular page, then you may need to reduce the security level, at least temporarily, to view the page normally.

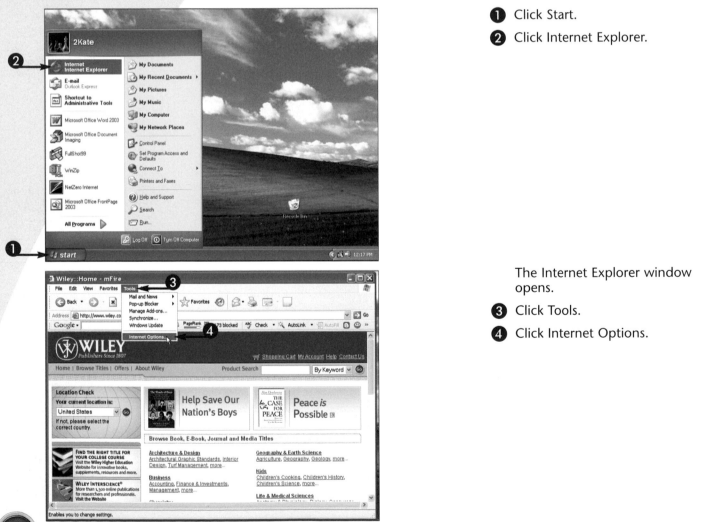

1 Click Start.

2 Click Internet Explorer.

The Internet Explorer window opens.

3 Click Tools.

4 Click Internet Options.

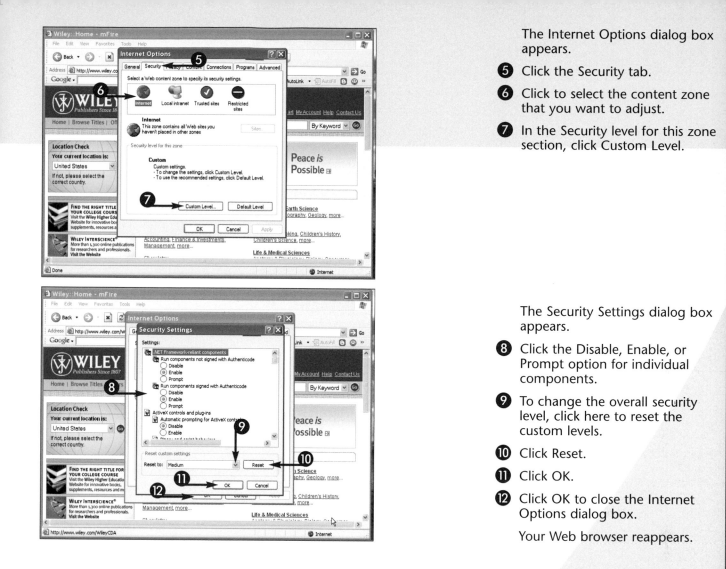

The Internet Options dialog box appears.

⑤ Click the Security tab.

⑥ Click to select the content zone that you want to adjust.

⑦ In the Security level for this zone section, click Custom Level.

The Security Settings dialog box appears.

⑧ Click the Disable, Enable, or Prompt option for individual components.

⑨ To change the overall security level, click here to reset the custom levels.

⑩ Click Reset.

⑪ Click OK.

⑫ Click OK to close the Internet Options dialog box.

Your Web browser reappears.

Did You Know?

Default Level refers to the security level that Microsoft recommends for a particular zone.

Remove It!

If you find that you do not like your custom settings, then you can remove them at any time by resetting the security zone to its default level. To do this, repeat Steps 1 to 3. Then, under Security level for the zone, click Default Level. Then click Apply.

Attention!

You can tell which zone you are in by checking the bottom-right corner of your Internet Explorer Web browser window, in the status bar.

Did You Know?

An intranet is a private network with some of the same properties as the Internet, but it is local to your home, small-office, or company network.

S

SEND TO:
Simplify Common Tasks for Files and Printing

If you use very popular Windows and Office applications such as Microsoft Word, then you can use the Send To feature. You can perform common tasks such as preparing your files to send through e-mail or fax, as well as to print. This allows you to begin processing a fax or e-mail from a document that you are currently working on without having to leave the application to do so.

Once you select the Send To option that you want, Windows loads the appropriate task. For example, it may load the Microsoft Fax Service or an e-mail

client such as Microsoft Outlook or Outlook Express to perform the job for you automatically, once you provide the recipient's e-mail address. With a Microsoft Word document open on your desktop, you can also send it as a fax.

In addition to Microsoft Office, you can also use this feature in some other Windows applications.

See also>>   Fax, Send a Fax

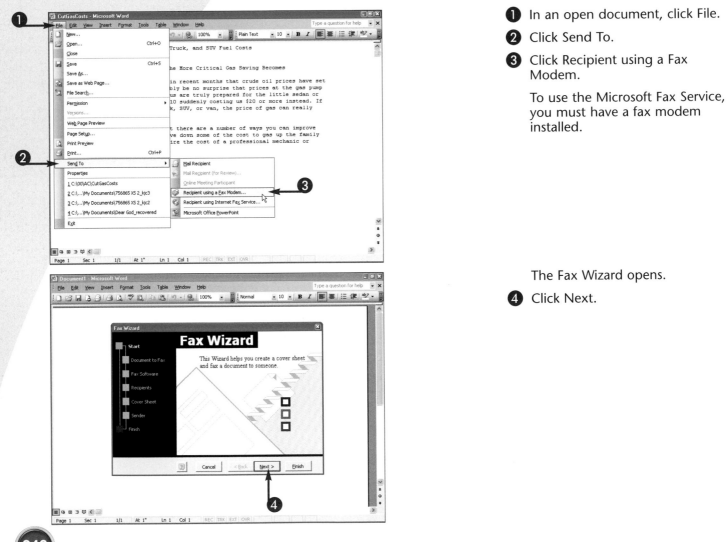

① In an open document, click File.

② Click Send To.

③ Click Recipient using a Fax Modem.

To use the Microsoft Fax Service, you must have a fax modem installed.

The Fax Wizard opens.

④ Click Next.

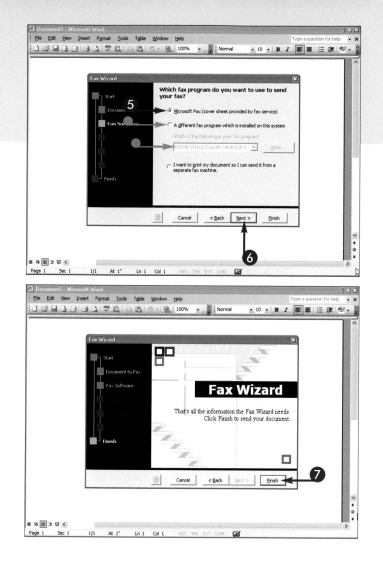

5 Click to select a fax option.

● To choose a different program, you can click here and select it.

6 Click Next.

7 Click Finish.

The Send Fax Wizard opens.

After you run the Send Fax Wizard, the document is then sent as a fax to the Fax Console, which delivers it according to the settings that you specified.

TIPS

Attention!

You can stop a fax from being sent by deleting it through the Fax Console.

Important!

If you want to change a document and re-send it, then you must repeat the entire process. You can also use the Send Fax Wizard in the Fax Console to specify the documents or files that you want to send without using Microsoft Word or another program.

Try This!

If you only need to send a one-page fax such as a cover page, then you can use the Send a Fax Wizard. To attach a file to the fax, you can use the Send To feature. After selecting the file, the Send To command launches the Send a Fax Wizard, where you can select and add a cover page.

SHARE A PRINTER:
Share a Printer on the Network

If your home or small office has a network that connects two or more computers, then you can share a printer that is installed on one computer among the other network-connected computers.

To share a printer, you first need to add the printer as a shared resource on your network. Then, from the other computers where you want to share the printer, you can add the printer as an available device. Once you do this, a printer that is directly installed to one computer becomes available for printing to the other computers on the same network.

You can also share more than one printer at any given time. For example, if you have five computers on a network and one has a standard inkjet printer while another has a laser printer, then you can share both printers out, and configure each computer to make these printers available to them. This saves the cost of purchasing a separate printer for each computer.

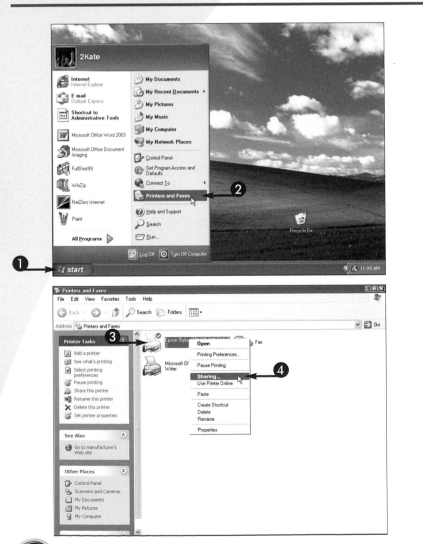

Share the Printer

1 Click Start.

2 Click Printers and Faxes.

The Printer and Faxes window opens.

3 Right-click the printer that you want to share on the network.

4 Click Sharing.

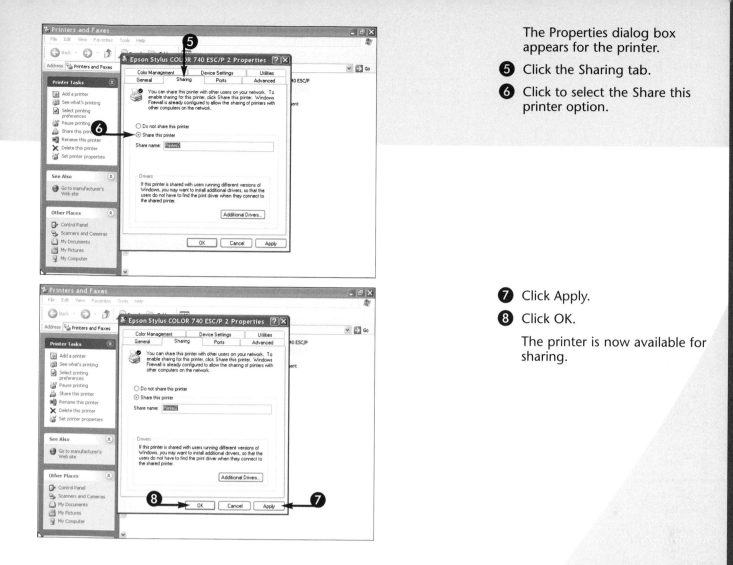

The Properties dialog box appears for the printer.

5 Click the Sharing tab.

6 Click to select the Share this printer option.

7 Click Apply.

8 Click OK.

The printer is now available for sharing.

TIPS

Did You Know?
With a printer added as a resource on a network, the printer acts as if it is directly installed to each individual computer on the network.

Important!
Remember to use the Add a Printer feature on each computer that does not have its own printer on the network; these computers can then use one or more printers installed elsewhere on the network.

Attention!
If you want to use a printer that is connected to a different computer on your network, then first ensure that the printer is shared on the network. You need to add this shared printer to your Windows setup so that your computer recognizes it as being available to use.

SHORTCUTS:
Create and Manage Shortcuts (Continued)

There are additional steps that you can take to manage your shortcuts, such as renaming a shortcut or moving it from one location to another.

You can rename a shortcut to make it easier to distinguish from other shortcuts. Keep in mind that renaming the shortcut does not change the name of the file or program to which it links.

You can also move a shortcut from one location, such as an overcrowded Windows desktop, to another location. This can be done either through the cut-and-paste method or by selecting, dragging, and then dropping the shortcut from one drive location to another.

Some users prefer to set up a special Shortcuts folder to store shortcuts. You can create a folder on your desktop, name it, and then place all new and existing shortcuts into it. It is a good idea to keep your shortcuts in one place to avoid desktop clutter.

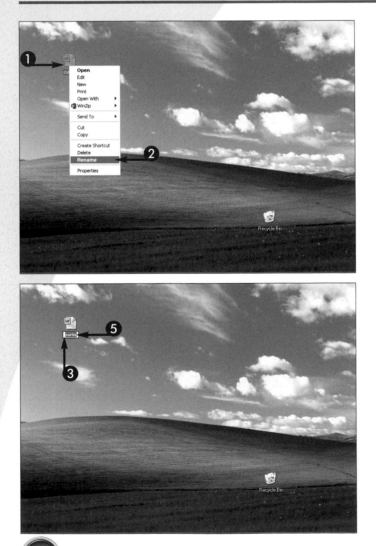

Rename a Shortcut

① Right-click the shortcut that you want to rename.

② Click Rename.

A highlight and an outline appear around the shortcut name.

③ Click within the outline.

④ Click Delete.

⑤ Type a new shortcut name.

⑥ Press Enter to save the new shortcut name.

Your shortcut now appears with the new name.

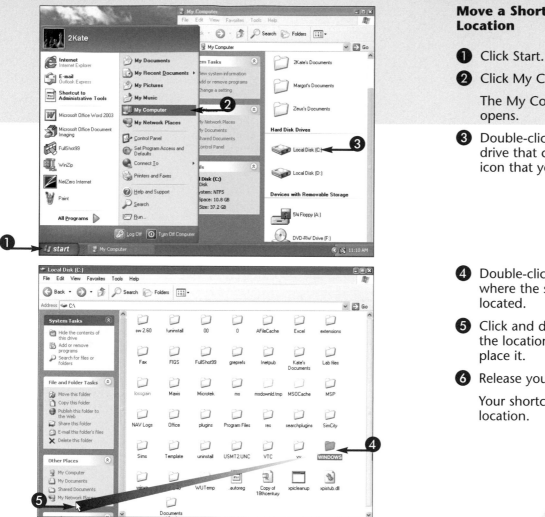

Move a Shortcut to a New Location

1 Click Start.

2 Click My Computer.

The My Computer window opens.

3 Double-click the letter of the drive that contains the desktop icon that you want to move.

4 Double-click to open the folder where the shortcut is currently located.

5 Click and drag the shortcut to the location where you want to place it.

6 Release your mouse button.

Your shortcut appears in the new location.

TIPS

Attention!

If you try to rename a shortcut with the name of an existing shortcut, then an error message appears. Follow the steps again, providing a slightly different name.

More Options!

If you create a Shortcuts folder on your desktop to store these links, then you can click and hold your mouse button on the shortcut icon and then drag and drop the icon on the Shortcuts folder. The shortcut moves into the folder.

Try This!

Rather than dragging and dropping the shortcut, you can right-click the shortcut, and then select Cut. Browse through My Computer to the new location where you want to place the shortcut, right-click again, and click Paste.

STANDBY:
Suspend and Restore the System to Save Power

If you leave your computer on for long periods of time even when you are not working at the computer, then you may want to consider how to reduce the overall power consumption of the system. One option is to use power management features such as Standby.

Standby is a low power mode that your computer enters once the system determines that no one is working on it. This is similar to the feature that laptops use when they are left on but not in use.

A screensaver appears on the screen while it waits for input. It eventually goes dark, the hard drive slows down, and the CPU rests in Standby mode. You can configure the idle time and the delay time before your computer goes into Standby mode.

When you either type a key or move your mouse while the system is in Standby mode, the computer wakes up, the monitor turns on, and the hard disk starts to spin. You can also set up a password that is required to access the system.

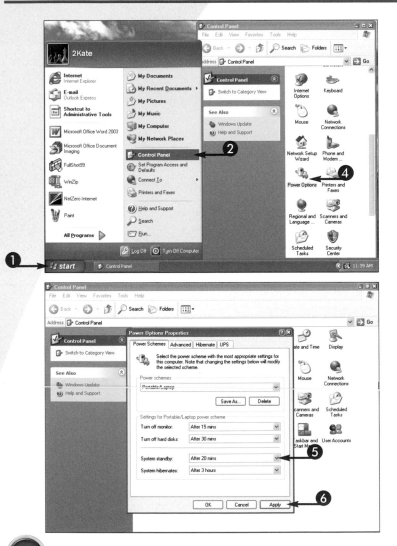

Configure Standby Mode

1 Click Start.

2 Click Control Panel.

   The Control Panel window opens.

3 In the Control Panel section, click Switch to Classic View.

4 Double-click Power Options.

   The Power Options Properties dialog box appears.

5 Under System standby, click here and select a time for the computer to wait until Standby mode begins after the first indication of idle status.

6 Click Apply.

   Windows activates the power saving options on your system.

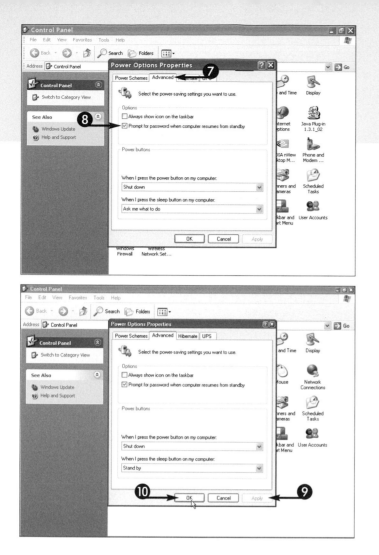

⑦ Click the Advanced tab.

⑧ Click to select the Prompt for password when computer resumes from standby option.

⑨ Click Apply.

⑩ Click OK.

The next time your computer goes into Standby mode, you are prompted for your user account password to access the system.

TIPS

Caution!

If you experience problems bringing your computer back from Standby mode, then you should run Windows Update to see if there are any driver updates for your computer, such as your graphics card or video adapter.

Important!

While a password for exiting Standby mode is not required, it improves your overall system security. A password makes it difficult for someone to access your confidential files or send e-mail through your computer in your absence.

More Options!

You can experiment with different power management settings to match the way in which you work. For example, if you do not usually touch the keyboard while you work, then you can set Standby mode to begin later than the default setting.

START MENU:
Customize the Start Menu

Your Windows XP Start Menu serves as your center for many things. For example, you can locate and launch programs, open frequently used applications, start tools such as the Search tool, open My Computer, find and open recently created or used files, and load your Web browser and e-mail client.

The Start Menu also dynamically changes. When you open the Start Menu, the last several entries in the lower-left column display a list of the programs that you have used the most frequently or recently. Once

you begin to use a program less often than another program, you will see that the other program replaces the first program in your Start Menu.

You can customize the Start Menu in several different ways. For example, you can add or remove an item from the Start Menu as well as automatically extend the All Programs sub-menus. You can also clear the Recent Documents list or expand or contract its listing to show more or less documents.

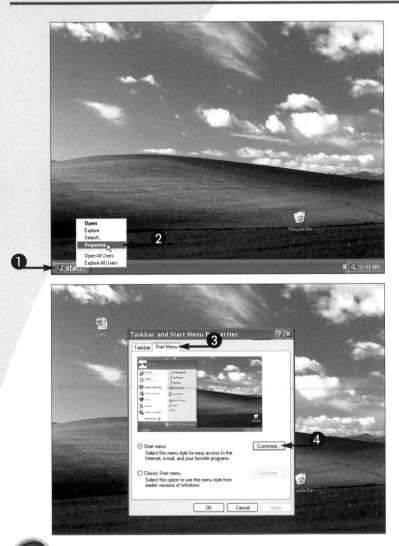

Add or Remove an Item

1 Right-click Start.

2 Click Properties.

The Taskbar and Start Menu Properties dialog box appears.

3 Click to select the Start menu option.

4 Click Customize.

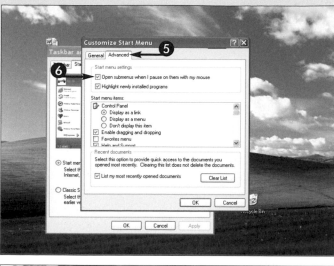

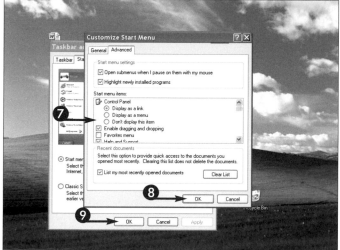

The Customize Start Menu dialog box appears.

⑤ Click the Advanced tab.

⑥ To automatically open sub-menus, click to select the Open submenus when I pause on them with my mouse option.

⑦ Click to select the options that you want.

⑧ Click OK to close the dialog box.

⑨ Click OK to close the Taskbar and Start Menu Properties dialog box.

Your changes are reflected in the Start Menu.

When you open the Start Menu, any item with a sub-menu opens as you place your mouse over it.

TIPS

Try This!
You can increase or decrease the number of the most frequently used programs in the Start Menu. In the General tab of the Customize Start Menu dialog box, click the up arrow to increase program listings or the down arrow to reduce the number shown.

More Options!
The Recent documents option in the Advanced tab allows you to clear the most recently opened and modified documents that are available in the Recent Documents entry in the Start Menu.

Windows allows you to choose from two Start Menu styles, the more modern Windows XP Start Menu, or the Classic Windows Start Menu that was used in older versions of Windows.

If you are using the Windows Classic Start Menu, then you may want to change to the standard Windows XP Start Menu to take advantage of its special customization options. For example, the pin and un-pin tools allow you to display special programs on the menu.

However, the Classic version also has a few advantages. For example, it is more familiar to many Windows users and it allows you to add or remove programs more easily than the Windows XP Start Menu.

If you would like a program to appear at the top left of your Start Menu so that it is available each time you click Start, then you can add it manually. You can select any file or program that is available from your desktop, My Computer, Windows Explorer, or even from the list of recently used programs that already displays in the Start Menu.

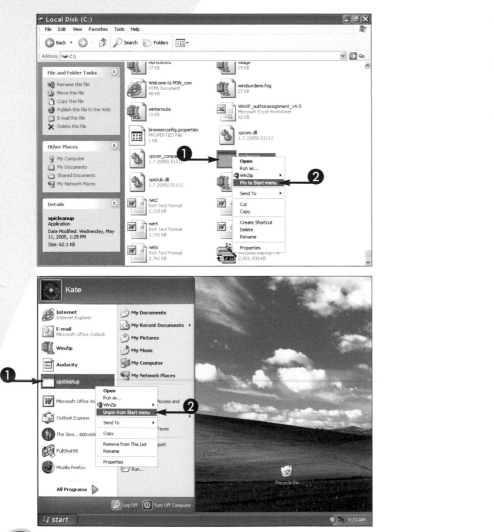

Add a Program to the Start Menu

❶ Locate the program that you want to add and then right-click it.

❷ Click Pin to Start menu.

Windows adds the selected program or file to the top of the Start Menu.

Remove a Program from the Start Menu

❶ Right-click the program that you want to delete from the Start Menu.

❷ Click Unpin from Start menu.

Windows removes the program from the Start Menu.

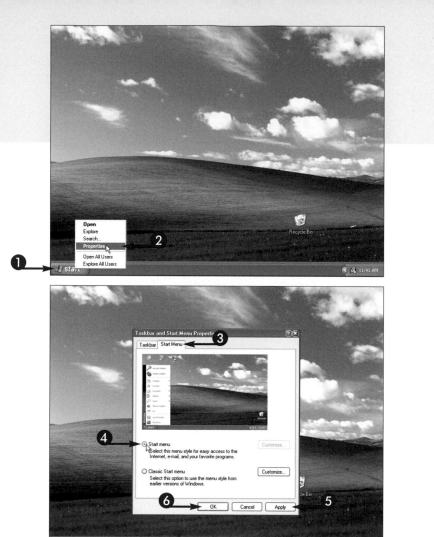

Change Start Menu Styles

1 Right-click Start.

2 Click Properties.

S

The Taskbar and Start Menu Properties dialog box appears.

3 Click the Start Menu tab.

4 To change from Classic to standard Windows XP mode, click the Start menu option.

5 Click Apply.

6 Click OK.

The menu style changes to the standard Windows XP style.

TIPS

Attention!
If you want to change to Windows Classic mode from the standard Windows XP mode, then select the Windows Classic Start menu option in the Start Menu tab of the Taskbar and Start Menu Properties dialog box.

Customize It!
To change the order of the items that are listed at the top left of the Start Menu, click an item, and then drag and drop it to a different position.

Important!
You can only pin and unpin items from the standard Windows XP Start Menu, and not the Windows Classic Start Menu.

Try This!
You can also access the Taskbar and Start Menu Properties dialog box by right-clicking the desktop, and choosing Properties.

STARTUP FOLDER:
Control which Programs Start Automatically

When you add a shortcut to a program or tool to your Windows Startup Folder, Windows automatically loads that executable file each time it boots or restarts. Programs that run in the Startup Folder are usually displayed in the Windows System Tray at the bottom-right corner of your desktop, where the time and date display. As you add files to startup, you must be careful that you do not add too many. To do so can cause problems for your system and prevent other necessary programs from running properly. This provides you with an excellent way to make programs available immediately after your PC starts and Windows loads.

Before you add programs to the Startup Folder from the Start menu, keep in mind that every additional program that you add loads and runs each time you launch a session, and this consumes desktop resources. On a computer with 256MB or less of system memory, this may lead to low virtual memory warnings after you have worked for a few hours with many programs open on your desktop, in addition to those programs that you loaded at Startup. As a result, you want to choose only the programs that you will really need for every session.

❶ Right-click Start.

❷ Click Properties.

The Taskbar and Start Menu Properties dialog box appears.

❸ Click the Start Menu tab.

❹ Click the Classic Start menu option.

❺ Click Customize.

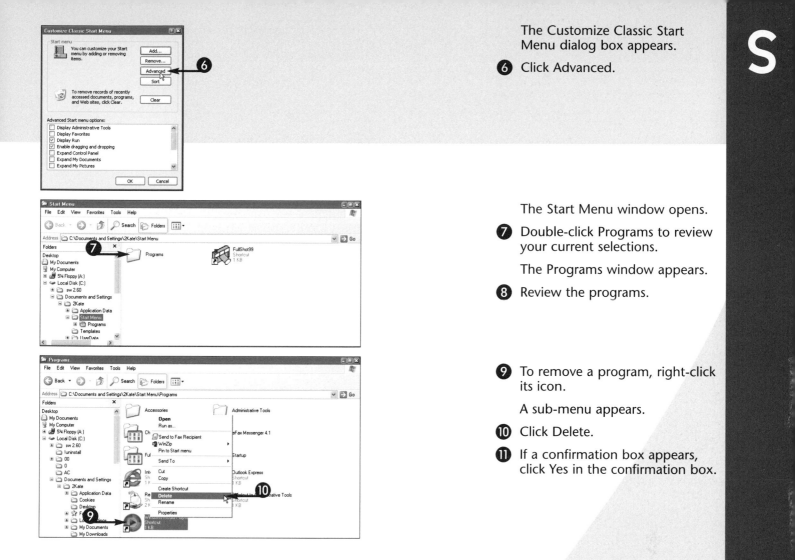

The Customize Classic Start Menu dialog box appears.

6 Click Advanced.

The Start Menu window opens.

7 Double-click Programs to review your current selections.

The Programs window appears.

8 Review the programs.

9 To remove a program, right-click its icon.

A sub-menu appears.

10 Click Delete.

11 If a confirmation box appears, click Yes in the confirmation box.

S

TIPS

Attention!
If you change to the Classic Start Menu display, then you have fewer customization options available, for example you will no longer be able to add programs to the Start menu.

Remove It!
You can remove programs that are currently displayed in the Start Menu through the Advanced Start menu options listing in the Advanced tab. You can also clear recently used programs and options here.

Caution!
You should avoid adding far more programs to the Startup Folder than you need. This also prevents you from overextending your desktop resources. At least once a month, if not once a week, you should review the items in your Startup Folder and remove any of those items that are not absolutely necessary.

STICKYKEYS:
Configure StickyKeys for Accessibility

You can configure and use the StickyKeys Accessibility option when you have difficulty holding down two or more keys simultaneously. StickyKeys is useful when you need to press keystroke combinations, such as Ctrl+Alt+Del to access Task Manager. These combinations are commonly referred to as keyboard shortcuts.

If you find using keyboard shortcuts to be a challenge, then StickyKeys helps you by allowing you to press a key once and have it stay engaged until you press another key. When you activate StickyKeys and then press a modifier key, such as Ctrl or Shift or the

Windows logo key from a Windows-compatible keyboard, that key remains engaged until you turn it off.

Although StickyKeys is designed to help users with physical limitations, some users without these limitations can also use the tool to help them perform multiple, simultaneous keystrokes. If you use a lot of keystroke combinations in your work, then you can try using StickyKeys to see if it is helpful to you.

See also>>   **Accessibility Wizard**

① Click Start.

② Click Control Panel.

The Control Panel window opens.

③ In the Control Panel section, click Switch to Classic View.

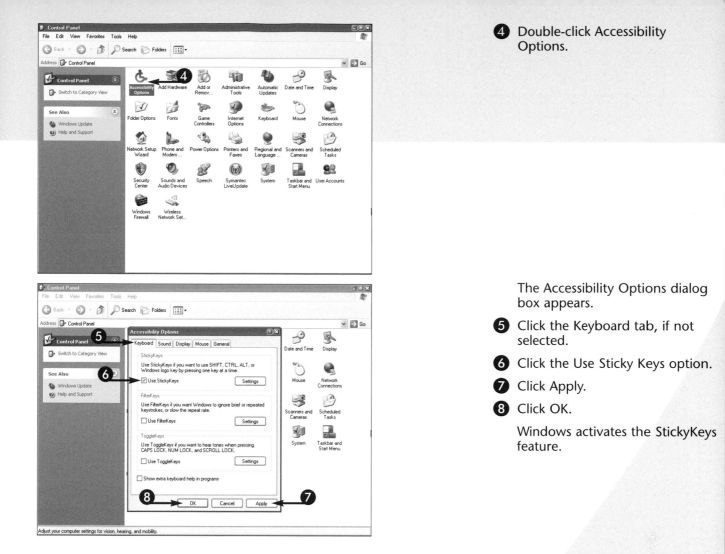

④ Double-click Accessibility Options.

The Accessibility Options dialog box appears.

⑤ Click the Keyboard tab, if not selected.

⑥ Click the Use Sticky Keys option.

⑦ Click Apply.

⑧ Click OK.

Windows activates the StickyKeys feature.

TIPS

Attention!

The very first time you use StickyKeys — or any other of the Accessibility Options for that matter — you may discover it does not work quite as you want. Typically, you may need to adjust settings. Infrequently, you may find it harder to work with the tool than if you work without it. See which works best for you after you make any configuration changes.

More Options!

You can return to Accessibility Options at any time to make changes to the way StickyKeys or any other of the Accessibility Options tools configures for your use. This is usually smart to do.

Try This!

To turn off StickyKeys, repeat the steps above and click to uncheck StickyKeys.

SYSTEM FILES:
Locate and View System Files

If you want to locate and view the system initialization files — such as BOOT.INI, SYSTEM.INI, and WIN.INI — that help to configure your Windows system, then you can do this through the MSCONFIG System Configuration utility.

When you start up your computer, Windows accesses all of these files to check for notations that are stored within them. The BOOT.INI file details anything that loads as part of the computer boot process before Windows launches and displays the graphical interface on-screen. The SYSTEM.INI file lists those system

options that run in the background when Windows loads or immediately afterwards. TheWIN.INI file loads those options that are configured to run with Windows open on your desktop.

The INI files are actually carefully created text files, with INI being short for initialization. You can open and even modify them in any text editor, such as Windows Notepad.

You can also scan system files for problems directly through Windows by using the System File Checker, or SFC, tool.

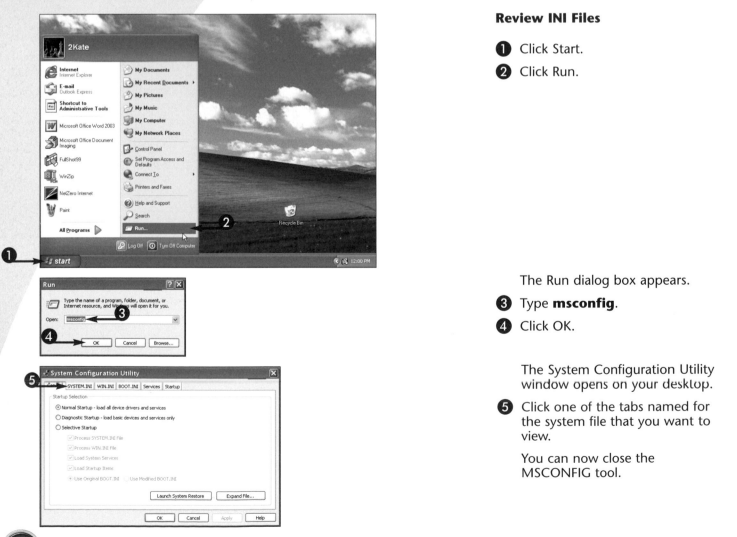

Review INI Files

1 Click Start.

2 Click Run.

The Run dialog box appears.

3 Type **msconfig**.

4 Click OK.

The System Configuration Utility window opens on your desktop.

5 Click one of the tabs named for the system file that you want to view.

You can now close the MSCONFIG tool.

❶ Click Start.

❷ Click Run.

The Run dialog box appears.

❸ Type **sfc /scannow**.

❹ Click OK.

The Windows File Protection scanning window opens and displays the progress of the scan.

Note: If serious problems are found, then the SFC tool reports them to you. If no problem is found, then the scan finishes and closes automatically.

TIPS

Caution!
You should not make changes to these files or disable features in them. Doing so may result in problems with a device or feature, or it could potentially affect the ability of Windows to load.

Important!
If you want to learn more about the SFC tool, then from the Command Console, type **sfc /?;** to list all possible switches that you can use with the tool, as well as what they do.

Did You Know?
The SFC tool runs from the Command Prompt because it has to run below Windows, which is using those system files to operate. Keep in mind that this tool may require some time to run and can make it difficult to perform other duties on your computer while it scans.

SYSTEM RESTORE:
Create a System Restore Point

Windows System Restore allows you to record, or take a virtual snapshot of, all of the details about your setup and files as they exist at a particular point in time. Later on, you can revert your computer setup to this previously recorded Restore Point. For example, you can restore your setup to the time before a driver upgrade or an application installation causes a serious problem that affects Windows and your computer.

To use System Restore, you must first enable the tool and record a Restore Point. Windows stores these

Restore Points on your hard drive as you create them. System Restore records these points automatically as well as creating a backup.

Restore Points record information such as your custom user settings, the contents of folders and e-mail messages in your Outlook Express mailbox, and your Web browser history. Anything that you add to the system after you record a Restore Point and before you apply the Restore Point is usually not retained.

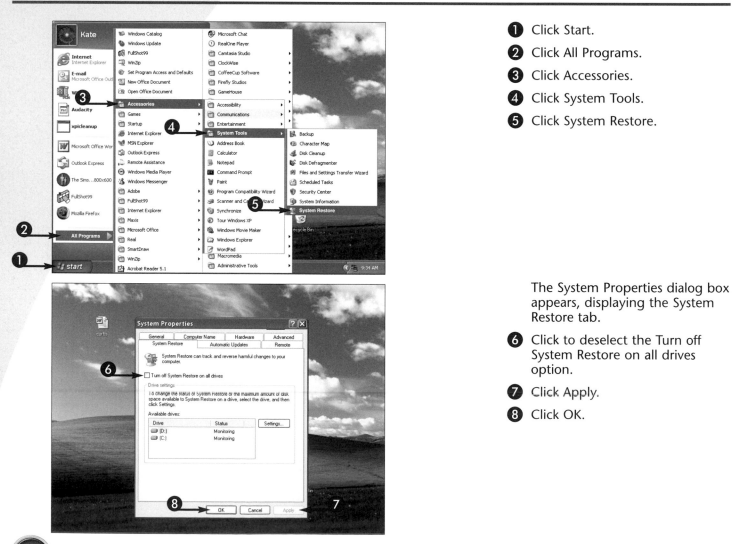

1 Click Start.

2 Click All Programs.

3 Click Accessories.

4 Click System Tools.

5 Click System Restore.

The System Properties dialog box appears, displaying the System Restore tab.

6 Click to deselect the Turn off System Restore on all drives option.

7 Click Apply.

8 Click OK.

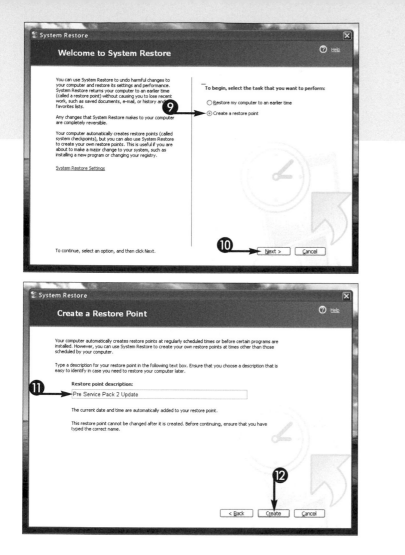

The System Restore window opens.

9 Click to select the Create a restore point option.

10 Click Next.

11 Type a short descriptive title for the Restore Point to help you identify it later.

12 Click Create.

13 Click Close when you see the confirmation window.

System Restore is now enabled, and a Restore Point is created.

If you must access System Restore again, then you can open it from the Start Menu.

Important!

To view and modify more details about System Restore, click Start, click Control Panel, double-click the System icon, and then click the System Restore tab. As long as the Turn Off System Restore on all drives option is deselected, you can see a Settings button. Click this button to access more settings that you can review and modify, such as how much space is set aside on your drives for Restore Points.

Try This!

To view your System Restore settings, click the System Restore Settings link in the System Restore window.

Caution!

If you have previously enabled System Restore — many new computers ship with System Restore operational — then a window appears, asking if you want to turn it back on. Click Yes.

SYSTEM RESTORE:
Roll Back/Recover with a System Restore Point

You may sometimes experience problems, such as when a Windows update causes chaos or when a newly installed application or piece of hardware prevents Windows from loading properly. In these situations, you can try to recover your computer to the way it was before the problem occurred. System Restore is a tool that allows you to do this by applying a previously recorded Restore Point to your system. The way in which this works is to revert your system to an earlier point in time.

When System Restore creates a Restore Point, it makes copies of everything, from your personalized settings to the files that you have on your system, as well as any other customizations and additions that you have made. By selecting and applying a saved copy, or Restore Point, you can quickly return to work with few negative effects to your system. It is also much faster to restore your system using this technique than it is to restore from a backup file that you have made.

Keep in mind that you can only recover your system using System Restore if this feature is already on and you already have recorded a Restore Point.

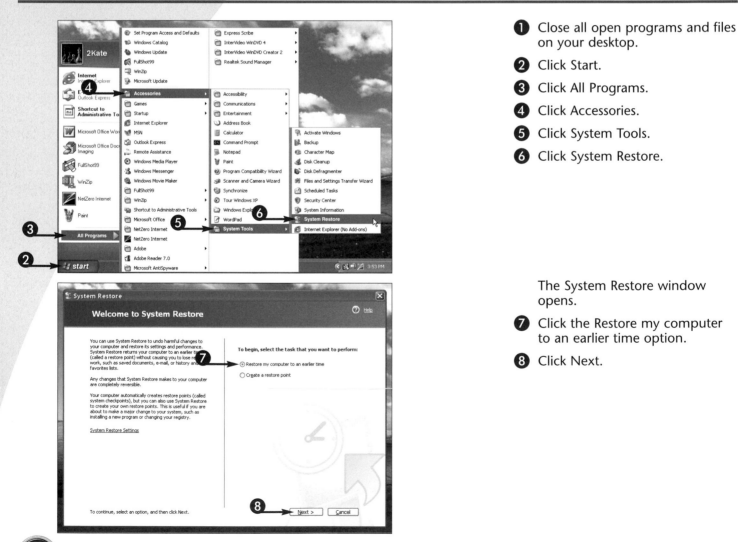

① Close all open programs and files on your desktop.

② Click Start.

③ Click All Programs.

④ Click Accessories.

⑤ Click System Tools.

⑥ Click System Restore.

The System Restore window opens.

⑦ Click the Restore my computer to an earlier time option.

⑧ Click Next.

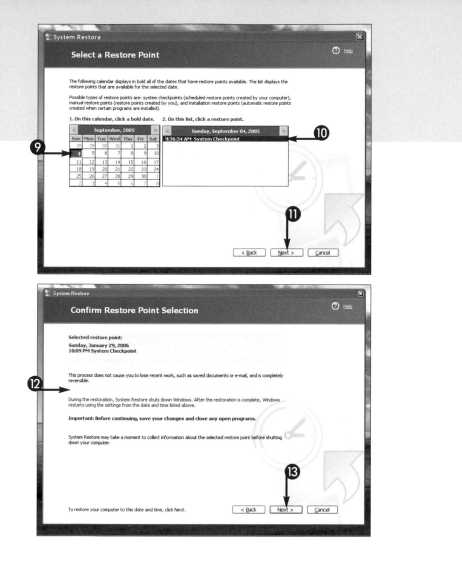

9 Click the date for an available Restore Point.

You can use the arrows at the top of the left-hand calendar to move backward or forward to a different month.

10 Click to select a specific Restore Point from the list.

11 Click Next.

12 Review the on-screen information.

13 Click Next.

Note: After Windows shuts down and restarts, you may be prompted to choose whether to keep the changes made through the Restore Point.

Windows restores your system to the way it was at the time of the selected Restore Point.

TIPS

Important!

When you restore from a previous Restore Point, you may possibly lose all changes that you made since you recorded it. These changes may include new e-mail messages, updated documents, and other files that you stored on your drive since you recorded the Restore Point. At the end of the restore process, you can revert back to the way the system was before you applied the Restore Point.

Attention!

It is a good idea to record Restore Points when your system is operating well. Appropriate times include after you perform drive and system maintenance, when you add or remove a system component and Windows and the computer are both running well, and prior to any major system changes.

SYSTEM STATE DATA:
Back Up Your System State Data

When a computer crisis affects your Windows system, it is vital that you recover your System State data. This data is the highly specialized information that is contained within the Windows Registry and other core components. By having a backup of this critical data, you ensure that your system recovery will be relatively quick, easy, and free of anxiety.

Within Windows XP, System State data specifically refers to core files that are needed to successfully boot the system, as well as the Registry, customized

database information, and files that are monitored and kept under the Windows File Protection service.

Most users do not know exactly which files are necessary to back up to recover the System State data. Without this technical knowledge, you may transfer the wrong files, or transfer more or less files than you actually need. Fortunately, a feature of Windows Backup allows you to create a special backup of the System State data that you can later use to restore your system.

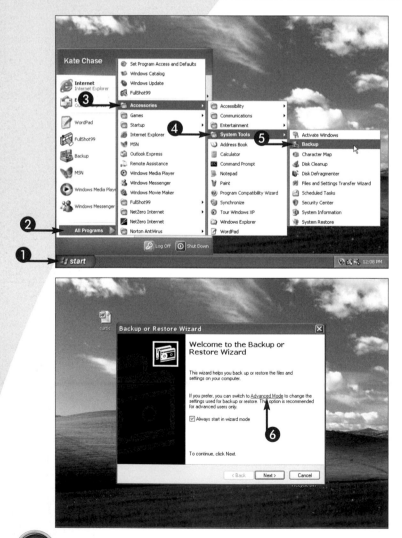

❶ Click Start.

❷ Click All Programs.

❸ Click Accessories.

❹ Click System Tools.

❺ Click Backup.

The Backup or Restore Wizard opens.

❻ Click the Advanced Mode link.

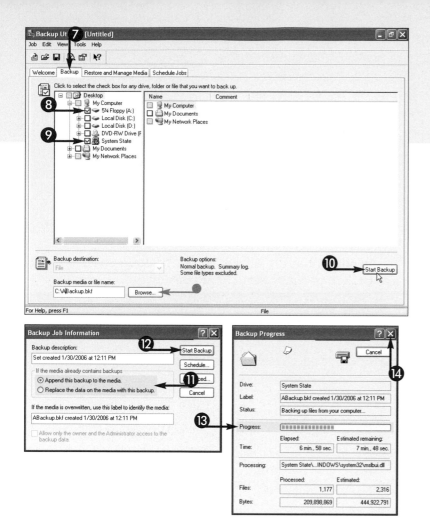

The Backup Utility window opens.

7 Click the Backup tab.

8 Click to select the drive that you want to back up.

9 Click to select the System State option.

● To change the location where the backup file is stored, you can click Browse and then select the drive you want.

10 Click Start Backup.

The Backup Job Information dialog box appears.

11 Select the option to append the new backup onto the end of a previous backup or to replace an existing backup with the new files.

12 Click Start Backup.

The Backup Progress dialog box appears, displaying details of the process.

13 After the backup is done, follow the on-screen prompts to finish.

14 Click Close to close the dialog box.

Windows backs up your files.

You may be prompted to restart your computer after the restoration is complete. If so, then click Yes.

TIPS

Attention!
You must be logged into your Windows XP computer as an Administrator in order to create this backup, as well as to restore from this backup once it is created.

Caution!
Store your backed-up System State data to a safe location, preferably not on the same drive where your System State data is stored within your main Windows installation — usually a primary hard disk or C: drive.

Try This!
If you suspect that your system files are corrupt, then you may want to either restore your backed-up System State data or, if necessary, a system Restore Point. This can save you from doing extensive system troubleshooting or making hit-or-miss changes to your system, where you could create more problems than you solve.

SYSTEM STATE DATA:
Restore from Your System State Data Backup

If you encounter serious problems when starting or operating Windows, then you can try to restore your system using the System State data backup that you have created. If you have not already backed up your System State data, then you should do so immediately. However, if you cannot back up this data, then you may be able to use a tool such as System Restore to boot the computer into either regular or Safe Mode, and then restore from a previous Restore Point.

The best and easiest way to restore a System State data backup is with Windows up and running. If you

cannot load Windows normally, then you may be able to use Safe Mode to access Windows and then either load a Restore Point from System Restore or use the Backup restoration feature to try to apply the saved System State data.

See also>>

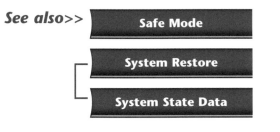

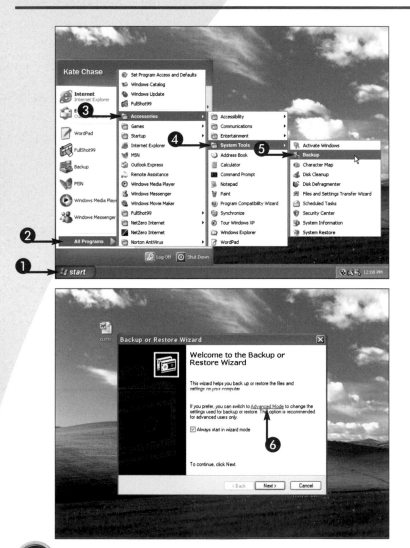

① Click Start.

② Click All Programs.

③ Click Accessories.

④ Click System Tools.

⑤ Click Backup.

The Backup or Restore Wizard opens.

⑥ Click the Advanced Mode link.

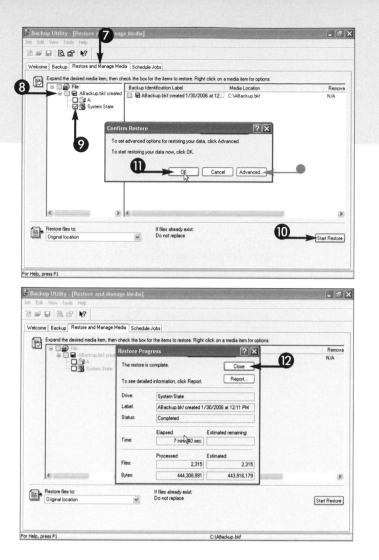

The Backup Utility window opens.

7 Click the Restore and Manage Media tab.

8 Double-click the backup copy that contains your System State data.

9 Click to select System State.

10 Click Start Restore.

Note: If a warning dialog box notifies you that proceeding will overwrite your current System State data, then click OK.

● In the Confirm Restore dialog box, you can click Advanced to specify more options for restoring your System State data.

11 Click OK to begin.

A Restore Progress dialog box shows you the status of the restoration.

12 When the restoration is complete, click Close.

You may be prompted to restart your computer. If so, then click Yes to restart.

TIPS

Attention!
You should make at least two copies of your System State data. If you store them on a Zip drive, or a recordable CD or DVD disc, then be sure to properly label and date them.

Caution!
If you have trouble running either the Backup or the Restore feature, then ensure that you are logged in as a computer Administrator. Guests and users with limited options cannot use these tools.

Important!
You can only restore the System State data to the computer that you are currently using, and not to another network computer.

Try This!
You should make a new copy of the System State data backup on a regular basis, especially after you perform an update to your system using Windows Update.

TASK MANAGER:
Work with Task Manager

You can use Windows Task Manager to see what tasks are running on your computer at any given moment, as well as to obtain other useful information. This is helpful when you need to troubleshoot or test your system performance.

Through Task Manager, you can view all of your open applications as well as processes and services that run in the background. By familiarizing yourself with the contents of the Processes tab during normal operation, you can identify any problems that appear when your system is not operating properly. You can

also use Task Manager to view current system performance, as well as network activity.

When an application fails to respond and you need to force it to close, you can do this through Task Manager. This allows you to avoid restarting your computer if you only need to shut down a single misbehaving program. After you shut down the program through Task Manager, you can usually reopen the program again through the Start Menu.

See also>> **Task Manager**

View Your System with Task Manager

❶ On your computer desktop, press Ctrl+Alt+Del.

❷ In the Windows Security dialog box that appears, click Task Manager.

The Windows Task Manager window opens.

If you do not use the Welcome screen to log on, then you will see an intermediate Windows Security screen. Click Task Manager.

❸ Click the Applications tab to view its contents.

❹ Click each of the remaining tabs to view the information.

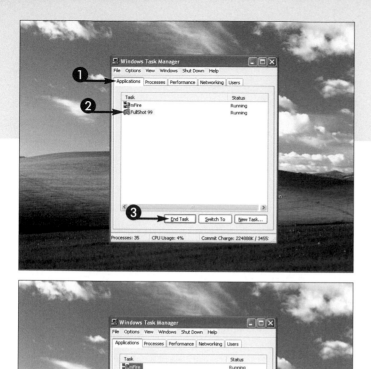

Force-quit an Application

① Open the Windows Task Manager window.

② Click the Applications tab.

③ Click the program that you want to end.

This is often a program that is not responding.

④ Click End Task.

If the program does not quit immediately, under the Application tab, Click the unresponsive program in the Task list and then click End Now.

The program closes and disappears from the Windows Task Manager window.

TIPS

Attention!
Always try to close a non-responding program normally before you resort to using Task Manager. This is because you can render Windows unstable if you force certain applications or processes to end prematurely.

More Options!
If you do not recognize some of the services and processes that are listed in the Processes tab, then you can use the Help and Support Center to search for the process name to see what it does.

Try This!
If you have difficulty when you try to shut down or restart your computer, then open Windows Task Manager, click the Shut Down menu, and then select the option you want. This will make Windows respond to your request.

TASKBAR:
Customize the Taskbar

Because you use the Windows Taskbar constantly, you can modify it to match the way you work to create a more comfortable desktop experience. For example, you can drag the Taskbar to a different position on your desktop. You can also add options such as the Quick Launch Bar for fast access to frequently used programs.

You can expand the Taskbar to show open applications in two or more tiers. You can also hide the Taskbar when you do not need it, in order to maximize available desktop space. You can configure

the Taskbar to always sit on top of other open windows so that it does not disappear when your desktop is very crowded.

By customizing the Taskbar, you can make it easier to re-open minimized windows and access the tools that you use most often.

See also>>

Taskbar

Quick Launch Bar

Hide the Taskbar

❶ Right-click a blank area on the Taskbar.

A sub-menu appears.

❷ Click Properties.

The Taskbar and Start Menu Properties dialog box appears.

❸ Click to select the Auto-hide the taskbar option.

❹ Click OK.

Your Taskbar disappears whenever it is not in use.

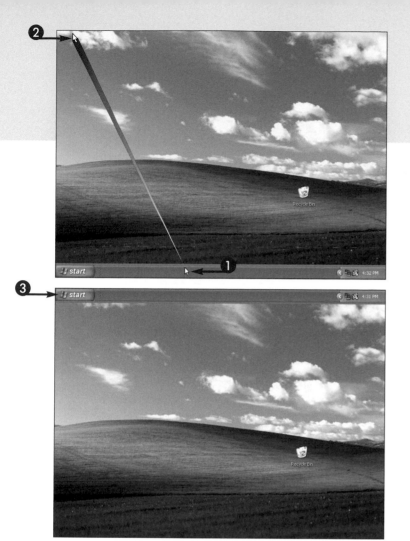

Move the Taskbar

① Click and hold the mouse cursor on the Taskbar.

② Drag the Taskbar to a different location, such as the top, left, or right side of your desktop.

③ Release the mouse button.

The Taskbar drops into place in the new location.

TIPS

Did You Know?
You can close a program or program group by right-clicking the program on the Taskbar and then clicking Close or Close Group.

More Options!
If you want the Taskbar to always appear on top of other windows, then open the Taskbar and Start Menu Properties dialog box. Click to select the Keep the taskbar on top of other windows option. If the Auto-hide option is selected, then click to deselect it.

Remove It!
If you have moved the Taskbar and you want to return it to its original location at the bottom of the screen, then click, drag, and drop it back to the bottom of the window.

TELNET CLIENT:
Connect to a Telnet Server

If your office network allows you to connect remotely — such as from home or from another external location — and supports the use of Telnet, then you can use the Telnet client to communicate with your office network. Telnet is a network communications environment where server software that is installed on the primary network computer allows users with the Telnet client software to log on, access files, and work.

Windows XP supplies the Telnet client for you, along with a Telnet server that you can set up if you want to use it.

Unlike most Windows programs where you point and click, Telnet works only from the Command Prompt. Through your available network or Internet connection, you must use valid Telnet commands to launch and run the client, connect to the network, and perform your work. You also need access information for the Telnet server, which is usually available from the server Administrator.

See also>>

Command Prompt

Telnet

Command Prompt

① Obtain your Telnet logon information from your network Administrator.

② Click Start.

③ Click All Programs.

④ Click Accessories.

⑤ Click Command Prompt.

The Command Prompt window opens.

⑥ Type **telnet**.

⑦ Press Enter.

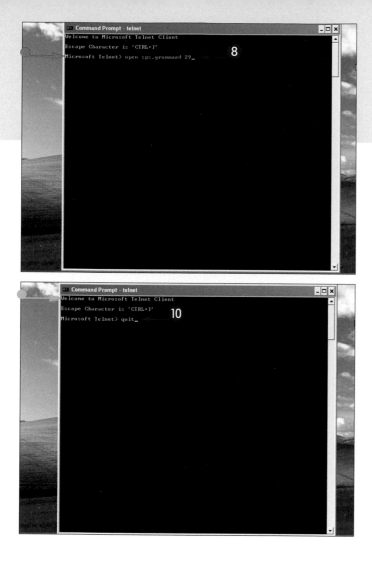

The Command Line changes to read Microsoft Telnet.

8 Type **open *hostname***, where *hostname* refers to the name or address of the Telnet server to which you need to connect.

9 Press Enter.

An on-screen message appears, reporting that you have connected to the server.

10 When your work is complete, type **quit**.

11 Press Enter.

The Telnet client closes.

TIPS

Did You Know?
Type **help** after you load the Telnet client to see a list of Telnet commands and how to use them. To view the status of your Telnet connection, type **status**.

Important!
If you have never used Telnet before and are unfamiliar with Command Line operations, then the Help and Support Center can assist you. Type **Telnet** in the Search text box and press the arrow. A list of Telnet-related articles appears. You can read about Telnet commands, troubleshooting tips, and more.

More Options!
You can also set up your own Telnet server if your system meets the basic requirements. This way, others can connect to your server to work and share files.

TEMP FOLDER:
Locate and Manage the Temporary Files Folder

You may not realize that Windows maintains a Temp folder to store temporary files that are created as you work. It is important that you manage this folder, because otherwise, it can become so full that it can actually limit your available disk space and affect your system performance. An overflowing Temp folder can also cost you time when you perform searches, run Disk Defragmenter, or use an antivirus scanner.

Keep in mind that not everything stored in your Temp folder should be deleted. Occasionally, an important

file may end up in there, so you need to review the contents of the folder before you delete files. For example, you may find copies of important files in the Temp folder that you can move back to their original folder if a crash or other problem causes you to lose the original version. Once you review the contents of the folder, you can use the Disk Cleanup tool to purge the remaining files.

See also>>   **Disk Cleanup**

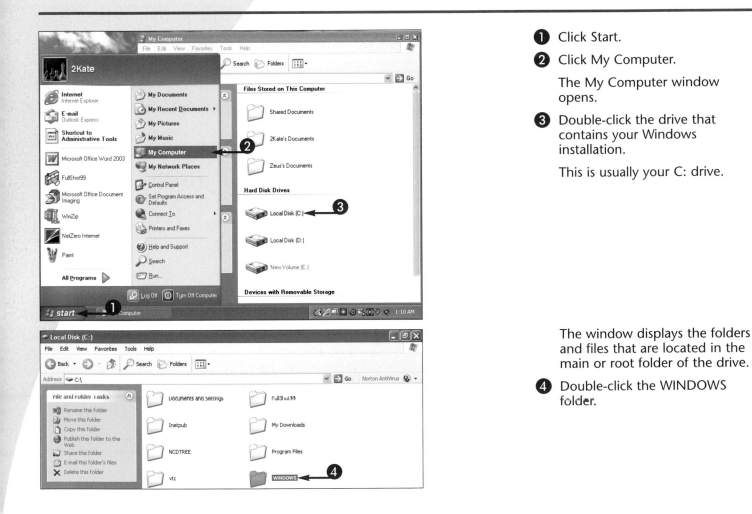

① Click Start.

② Click My Computer.

The My Computer window opens.

③ Double-click the drive that contains your Windows installation.

This is usually your C: drive.

The window displays the folders and files that are located in the main or root folder of the drive.

④ Double-click the WINDOWS folder.

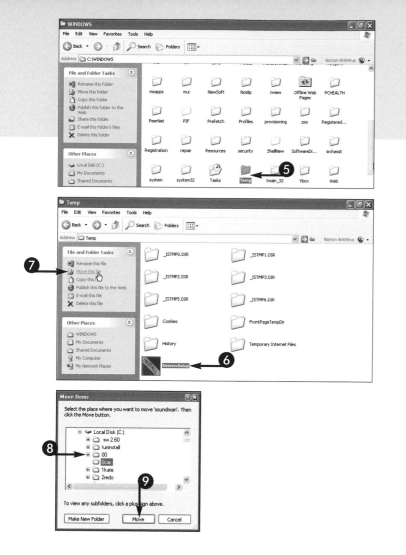

The contents of your WINDOWS folder display.

5 Double-click the Temp folder.

The contents of the Temp folder display.

6 Locate a file that you want to keep, and then click to select it.

7 Click Move this file.

The Move Items dialog box appears.

8 Click the drive or folder to where you want to move the file.

9 Click Move.

Windows moves the file to the drive or folder that you selected.

TIPS

More Options!

To purge the remaining files in your Temp folder, click Start, click All Programs, click Accessories, click System Tools, and then click Disk Cleanup. Select the drive where your Windows installation is located. From the Disk Cleanup window, click to select the Temporary files option. Click OK to start the cleanup process.

Try This!

If a file that you need to move is located in the Recycle Bin rather than the Temp or other folder, then you cannot use the Move command. Right-click the file that you want to move back to its original location, and then click Restore. The file is automatically moved from the Recycle Bin back to its original location in its original state.

TEMPORARY INTERNET FILES:
Clean the Internet Files Cache

Your system may contain thousands of temporary Internet files that are left behind as the result of browsing the Web. To prevent these files from clogging your system, you need to clean the Internet files cache on a regular basis. Windows stores these files in special folders, which you can easily purge.

If you do not regularly clean the temporary files cache, then you not only lose valuable disk space, but your disk management tools also take longer to run. You also increase the risk that your Web browser will experience difficulties when you navigate

between different sites on the Web. For example, you may discover that you can no longer press the Back key in the browser when you want to move back to your previous page.

Your temporary files may also contain programs or other files that can compromise your privacy, identify your passwords for others to find, or leave behind a computer virus such as an Internet worm.

See also>>   **Disk Cleanup**

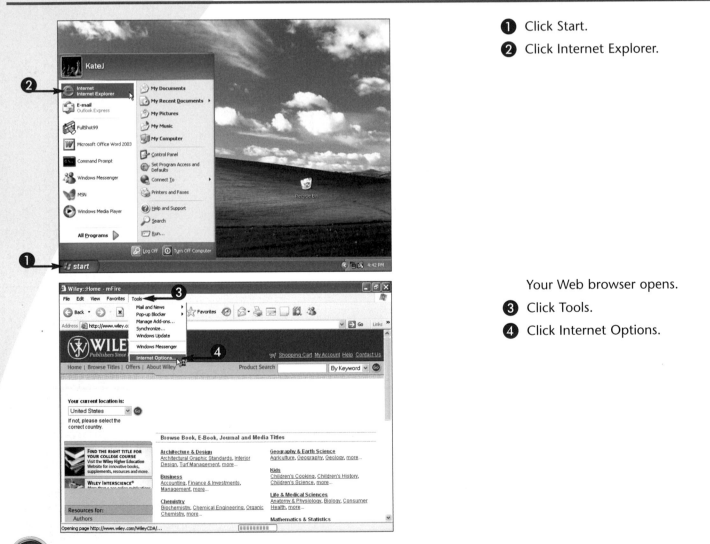

① Click Start.

② Click Internet Explorer.

Your Web browser opens.

③ Click Tools.

④ Click Internet Options.

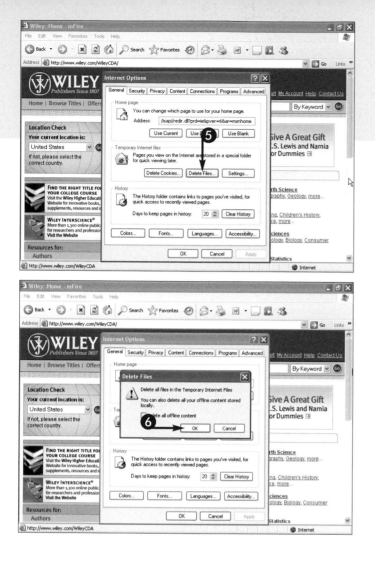

The Internet Options dialog box appears.

⑤ In the General tab, under Temporary Internet files, click Delete Files.

The Delete Files dialog box appears.

⑥ Click OK.

Windows purges the temporary Internet files.

TIPS

Did You Know?
When you run the Disk Cleanup tool, it also purges many of your temporary Internet files.

Important!
To maintain your privacy and to make it more difficult for others who access your computer to view where you have visited, you must also clear your Internet site history. To do this, perform Steps 1 to 4. Then, under History, click Clear History.

Remove It!
In the Delete Files dialog box that appears after Step 5, click to select the Delete offline content option to remove these files, as well.

Try This!
For best results, you may want to purge your temporary Internet files on a regular basis. If you browse the Web daily, then you should clean up the temporarily files at least once a week.

THEMES:
Add a Desktop Theme

When you want to customize your Windows desktop without spending time setting individual options, you can add a desktop theme to change the overall appearance. A theme is a package of files that create a specific look, based on a particular topic such as outer space or a safari. By default, Windows is configured with its own theme named Windows XP. You can use this theme or select an alternative choice.

In addition to appearances, some themes may also include customized sounds to replace the standard ones used by Windows. You can choose from the list of themes that automatically install with Windows, go online to search for more Microsoft themes, or download custom themes from any number of Web sites. You can use a Web search site such as Google or Yahoo to locate them.

You can also create your own custom themes. The Internet offers a great deal of information about how you can do this.

See also>> **Display Properties**

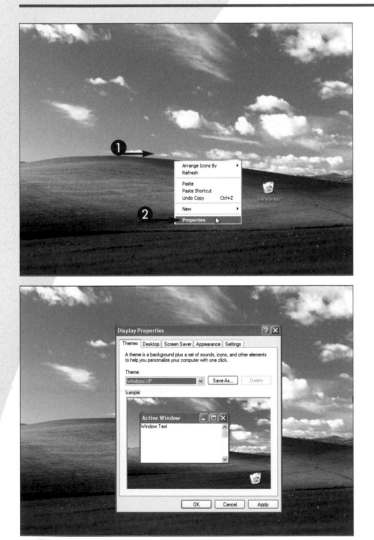

❶ Right-click an empty area on your desktop.

A sub-menu appears.

❷ Click Properties.

The Display Properties dialog box appears, displaying the Themes tab.

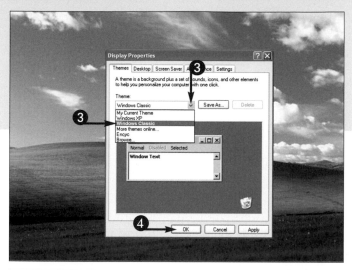

③ Click here and select a theme.

④ Click OK.

Windows applies your theme to the desktop.

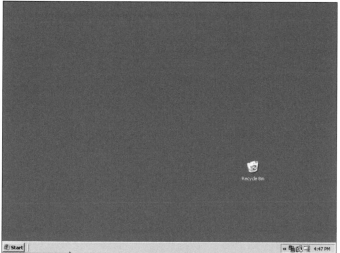

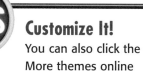

TIPS

Customize It!

You can also click the More themes online option in the drop-down menu in Step 3. Through your live Internet connection, Windows connects to a Microsoft site where you can locate and download additional themes.

More Options!

If you download additional themes from the Web, then you can use the Browse option in the drop-down menu in Step 3 to look for these themes in your system.

T

THUMBNAILS:
Configure Folders to Display Thumbnails

You can configure your folders to automatically display small images — or thumbnails — of any graphics that they contain. This makes it much easier for you to locate a specific photo or drawing if you cannot identify it, based on the filename.

This feature is especially useful with stored pictures. When you acquire images from your digital camera or scanner, they are often saved with filenames that make them difficult to identify later unless you take the time to rename and organize them. Thumbnail

images can help you because they display a miniature version of the image directly in your folder view.

Once you configure this option, thumbnail images also appear when you perform a search through your system for photos. You can also view them when you access a recorded CD or DVD that contains photos or other images. Without this feature, you may have to rely on third-party imaging software specially designed to display graphics.

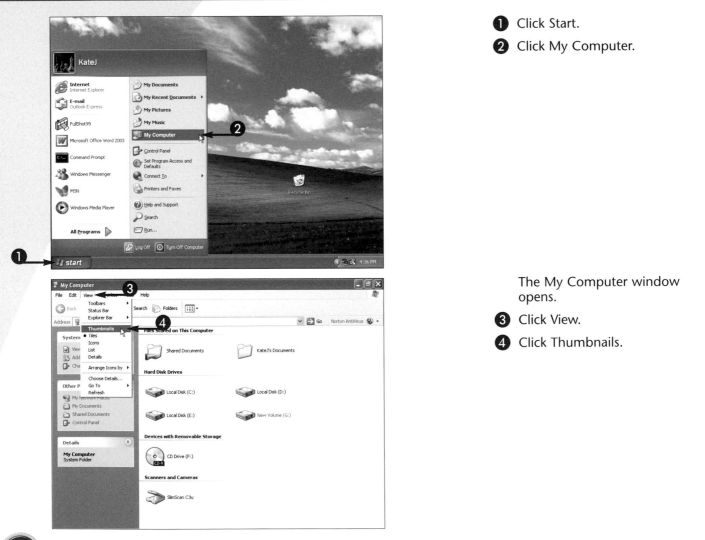

① Click Start.

② Click My Computer.

The My Computer window opens.

③ Click View.

④ Click Thumbnails.

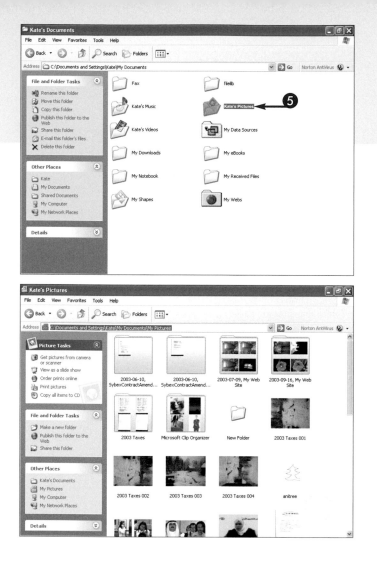

⑤ Locate and double-click the folder that contains your images.

Thumbnails of the images appear onscreen.

TIPS

Important!
In some situations, you may find it difficult to view thumbnails. For example, you may have limited memory installed or a low-quality video card, or you may be viewing folders that contain a large number of images. In these situations, you may find that the system slows considerably while it tries to display the thumbnail images.

More Options!
You can also set other options for how folders display their contents. Click Start and then click Control Panel. From the Control Panel, double-click Folder Options to view and select the options that you want.

Remove It!
To stop the display of thumbnails and return to another view, click View and then select Icons or another format that you want.

TROUBLESHOOT:
Use Troubleshooting Wizards

When you experience problems with your computer, you can troubleshoot to determine the cause of the problem and to resolve it. To do this, you can use one of the many troubleshooting wizards. These wizards are designed to ask you questions and to help you identify what is wrong with system components — such as your modem, printing, or network communications — as well as what needs to be done to correct the situation.

In the majority of cases, the wizards can provide you with valuable assistance before you call technical

support by helping you to narrow down the symptoms that the device displays. If you cannot fix the problem after you use the wizard, then you can consult the Help and Support Center. The Center may offer steps that help you to determine what may be wrong, even if it does not supply you with a solution.

See also>> Device Manager

Device Manager

① Click Start.

② Click Control Panel.

The Control Panel window opens.

③ Double-click System.

The System Properties dialog box appears.

④ Click the Hardware tab.

⑤ Click Device Manager.

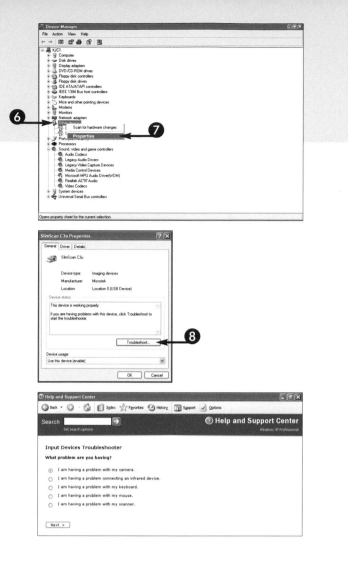

The Device Manager window opens.

⑥ Locate and right-click the device needing troubleshooting.

⑦ In the sub-menu that appears, click Properties.

The Properties dialog box appears for the device.

⑧ In the General tab, click Troubleshoot, if this button is available.

The troubleshooting wizard opens for the device.

Attention!

Not every device or feature has a troubleshooting wizard available. If you cannot locate one through these steps, then use the Help and Support Center to identify additional resources.

More Options!

If the troubleshooting wizard fails to help, then you may want to consult the Web site of the manufacturer or publisher of the device or software that does not work properly. This can often be more helpful than a call to the technical support line.

Try This!

If the problem is a device, then you may want to see if there is an available update for the equipment. This may resolve your problem. However, if the problem occurs right after a driver update, then you may want to roll back the driver.

TRUETYPE FONTS:
Add a TrueType Font

Although Windows has a number of fonts installed, you can add additional fonts at any time. Once you add a font, it becomes available to Windows applications as well as other programs, such as Microsoft Word, Web page editors, and desktop publishing programs.

TrueType fonts make up the majority of the available fonts in Windows. Free fonts, try-before-you-buy shareware fonts, and purchase-only fonts are available throughout the Web, as well as on disc at stores that sell software. Some of these fonts have

installation utilities that allow you to add these fonts automatically.

When you add fonts, you increase the number of custom display options that are available to you when you create documents such as catalogs, brochures, and Web pages. If you create your own published works regularly, then you will want to augment your font collection to include popular typefaces that are not already available in Windows. You can also add special-use fonts that create images in place of letters.

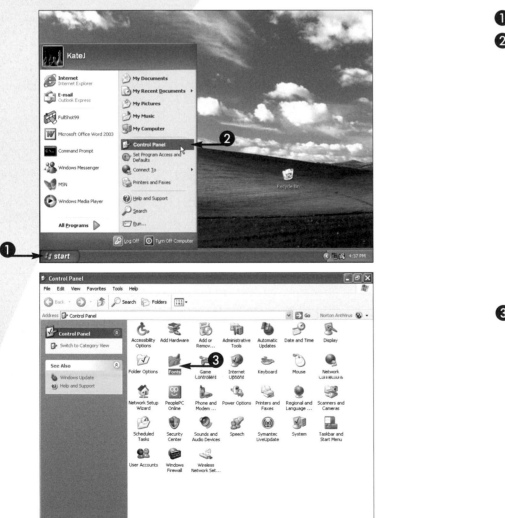

❶ Click Start.

❷ Click Control Panel.

The Control Panel window opens.

❸ Double-click Fonts.

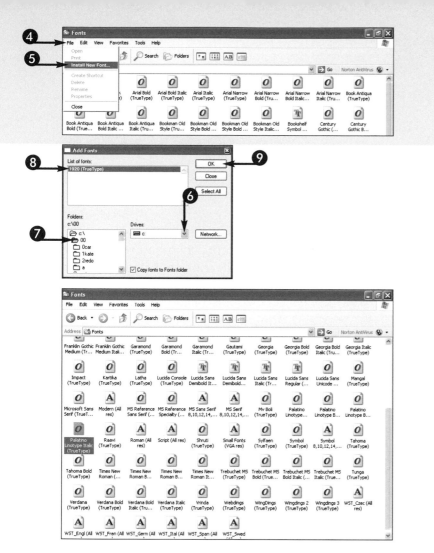

The Fonts window opens.

④ Click File.

⑤ Click Install New Font.

The Add Fonts dialog box appears.

⑥ Click here and select the drive where the new font resides.

⑦ Click the folder where the new font is stored.

⑧ Select the font from the list of available fonts.

⑨ Click OK.

The new font installs and appears in the Fonts window.

TIPS

Attention!
Stylized fonts can consume a lot of disk space. This becomes a problem when you add a lot of fonts, or if your disk space is limited. You should remove fonts that you do not use if your disk space becomes low.

More Options!
If you do not see a font that you have just installed, then click View in the Fonts window and click Refresh.

Remove It!
To remove an installed font, repeat Steps 1 to 3. When the Fonts window opens, locate the font that you want to remove, right-click it, and click Delete.

Try This!
Many fonts come in a ZIP archive, which ends with the .zip file extension. You must unzip these files before you can install them.

USER ACCOUNTS:
Check for Administrator Account Status

As an Administrator with the capability to grant and limit access to a computer or a network, you can create and manage user accounts with Windows. User accounts are central to how Windows XP organizes and handles different users who share the same system.

Even if you are the only user on your computer, when Windows XP installs, it prompts you to create an Administrator account, complete with password. This is the very first user account for your Windows computer. As an Administrator, you can now limit or change settings for users with lower status.

By default, Windows also creates a Guest Account that permits visitors to your home or office to access basic computer functions, such as Web browsing. However, the Guest account is extremely limited, and so you may want to set up a user account for a user who needs more access privileges.

See also>>

Guest Account

User Accounts

1 Click Start.

2 Click Control Panel.

The Control Panel window opens.

3 In the Control Panel section, click Switch to Classic View.

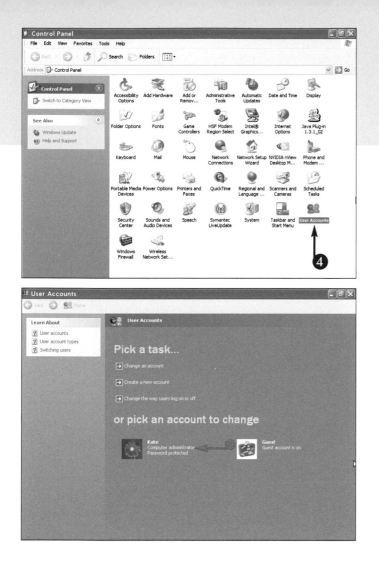

④ Double-click User Accounts.

The User Accounts window opens.

● The information beneath your user account name should identify you as a computer Administrator.

A computer Administrator can change information for just about any account or setting; a limited account holder cannot.

TIPS

Important!

For better security, as an Administrator, you can set up an additional account with which you only have limited privileges. You can then use this account to perform most of your work, and only use the Administrator account to do computer management activities. This reduces the chance that when you are logged on but away from your desk, another user can make unwanted changes to the system.

Attention!

For best security, all accounts should be password protected. Every password should also be changed at least every 30 to 90 days, and passwords should consist of a combination of random alphanumeric characters.

USER ACCOUNTS:
Create a New User Account

As an Administrator, you can set up new accounts for everyone else who shares your Windows XP computer. You can also specify whether each new account receives Administrator status. You should not allow more than two people to have this status.

If you allow a user Administrator status, then they can change almost anything on your computer. For example, Administrators are the only account users who can turn the Guest Account on and off, change the way that users log on or off, and turn Fast User Switching on and off.

If you set an account to limited status, it restricts what the user can do. You may also need to add a password to use with these accounts.

For optimal computer security, you can create a second account for yourself, with limited account status, which you can use for the majority of your work. When you need to perform computer management tasks, you can log in with your Administrator account instead.

See also>> Guest Account

User Accounts

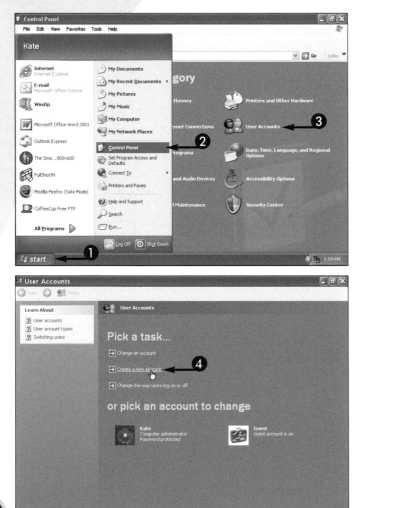

❶ Click Start.

❷ Click Control Panel.

❸ Double-click User Accounts.

The User Accounts window opens.

❹ Click Create a new account.

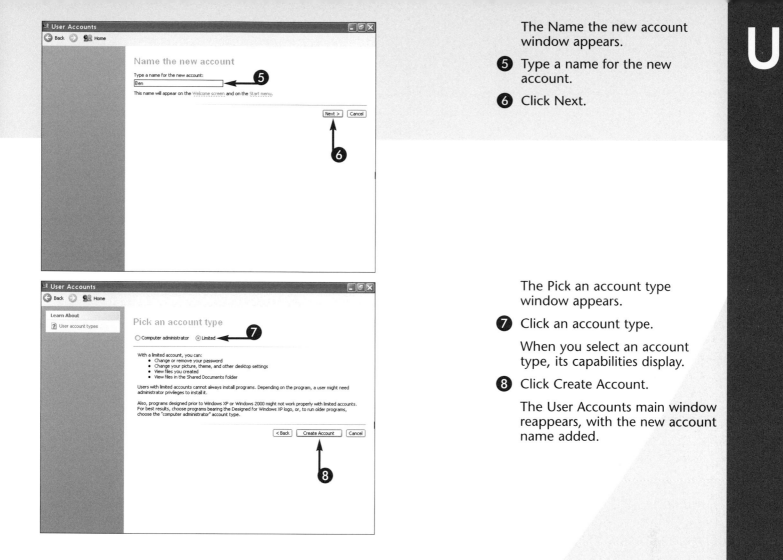

The Name the new account window appears.

⑤ Type a name for the new account.

⑥ Click Next.

The Pick an account type window appears.

⑦ Click an account type.

When you select an account type, its capabilities display.

⑧ Click Create Account.

The User Accounts main window reappears, with the new account name added.

TIPS

Attention!
It is important to create secure passwords and to keep them confidential. However, this is critically important with an Administrator account. Anyone who can access your Administrator account with your password has the power to change virtually anything on your system. Create the most secure password possible and do not write this password where others can find it.

Important!
There must always be at least one Administrator account on a Windows XP computer.

More Options!
You can go back at any time to change a user account from Administrator to limited, or vice versa; however, you must be logged in as an Administrator to do this.

USER ACCOUNTS:
Manage User Accounts

Wherever you have user accounts, you need to ensure that only those people who should be able to share a computer have access to it. This means that you should remove accounts for people who are no longer using the system. You should also create and change passwords for users who do not create their own.

You can also change another user's account from Administrator to limited, or vice versa. The main difference between an Administrator and limited

account type is that an Administrator can create, modify, and delete any account on the system, as well as specify how users log in, while a limited account type can only modify some aspects of an account. The limited account user cannot perform any changes to other user accounts, nor can they configure the system. You should usually limit Administrator status to two users.

See also>>   **Guest Account**

❶ Click Start.

❷ Click Control Panel.

The Control Panel window opens.

❸ In the Control Panel section, click Switch to Classic View.

❹ Double-click User Accounts.

The User Accounts window opens.

❺ Click Change the account type.

❻ Click the user's account name.

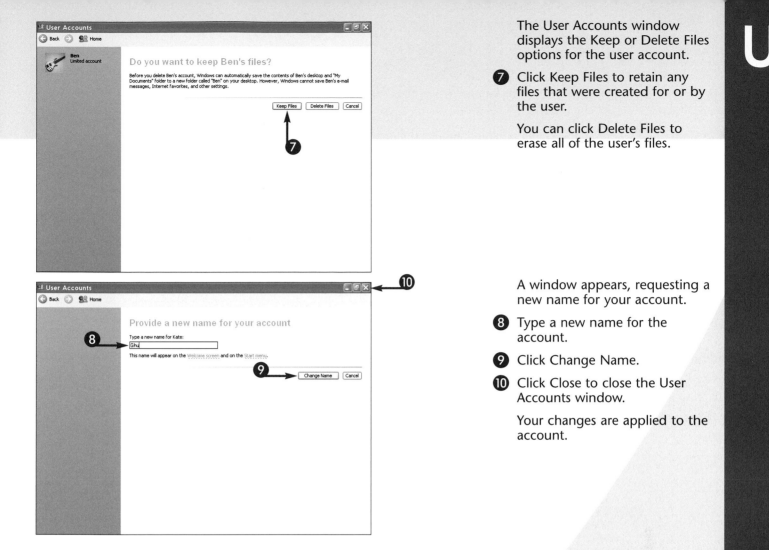

The User Accounts window displays the Keep or Delete Files options for the user account.

⑦ Click Keep Files to retain any files that were created for or by the user.

You can click Delete Files to erase all of the user's files.

A window appears, requesting a new name for your account.

⑧ Type a new name for the account.

⑨ Click Change Name.

⑩ Click Close to close the User Accounts window.

Your changes are applied to the account.

TIPS

Attention!
If you log in to change user account information and find that you cannot do this, then it is probably because you are logged in through a limited user account.

Caution!
You cannot delete the account that you are currently using. This ensures that an Administrator does not delete his or her Administrator account, which would be very serious.

More Options!
To change a user account name, follow Steps 1 to 4, click Change the name, type a new name, and then click Change Name.

Try This!
If users on your computer do not regularly change their passwords, then you can change these passwords as an Administrator and notify them of their new passwords.

USER PROFILES:
Create and Manage User Profiles

Although Windows can automatically set up user profiles, you can also create and manage user profiles manually. This allows you full control over what information appears in a user profile. This profile stores specific settings and preferences that each user on a shared computer configures in the course of setting their preferences.

When you set up specific user profiles, you can enable a user with a physical challenge to log in and use the computer differently, even when all other users log in through a standard interface.

You can also create a roaming user profile, which allows you to set up a special type of profile so that a user can sit down at a different computer on the network and work as they would at their own desktop. For example, as you log in, you would have the same settings and preferences recognized as if you were seated at your regular desk. These settings include desktop choices, screen resolution, mouse settings, program choices, and other unique preferences.

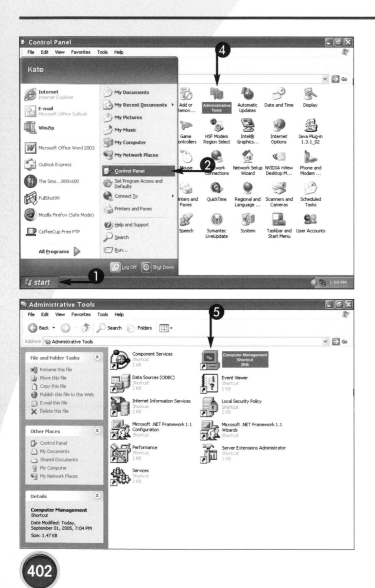

1 Click Start.

2 Click Control Panel.

The Control Panel window opens.

3 In the Control Panel section, click Switch to Classic View.

4 Double-click Administrative Tools.

The Administrative Tools window opens.

5 Double-click Computer Management.

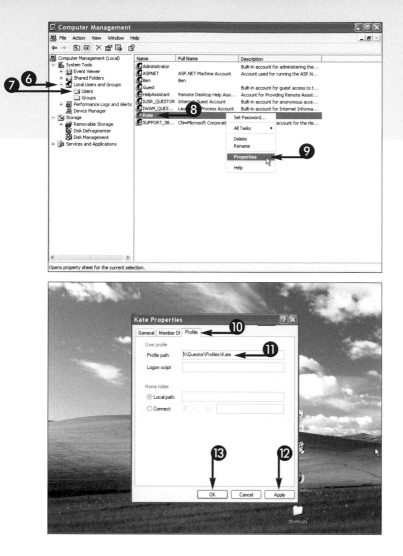

The Computer Management console opens.

6 Click the plus sign next to Local Users and Groups.

7 Click Users.

8 Right-click your user account name.

A sub-menu appears.

9 Click Properties.

The Properties dialog box appears.

10 Click the Profile tab.

11 Type the location of your user profile.

12 Click Apply.

13 Click OK.

Your User Account profile is changed.

TIPS

Attention!
Windows creates a basic user profile with settings when you set up your user account.

Try This!
If you need to set up user profiles specifically for users with physical limitations, then you should run and configure your system first using the Accessibility Wizard.

Caution!
If you do not know the proper address for your network or network server profiles folder, then consult with your network Administrator before you make any changes.

Attention!
You cannot access Administrative Tools from the Control Panel if you are not logged in as an Administrator.

UTILITY MANAGER:
Manage Accessibility Features

If you use Windows XP Accessibility features, then you should also use Utility Manager. This is a management tool that allows you to control the available Accessibility options in Windows. Utility Manager also allows you to avoid using the Accessibility Wizard.

Utility Manager is a control console that allows you to either check the status of, or stop and start, an Accessibility feature. Certain Accessibility tools are available through Utility Manager; these include Magnifier, Narrator, and On-Screen Keyboard.

You can use Utility Manager to tell Windows to automatically load one or more Accessibility programs as soon as Windows opens on the desktop after a start or restart. This feature is useful to those with a physical impairment, such as reduced eyesight or lack of hand movement, as well as other people such as parents, teachers, and friends who assist the disabled person to set up a computer with certain aids turned on and ready for use.

See also>>

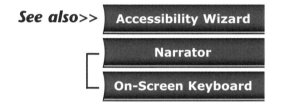

1 Click Start.

2 Click All Programs.

3 Click Accessories.

4 Click Accessibility.

5 Click Utility Manager.

The Utility Manager dialog box appears to inform you that if you launch Utility Manager from the Start Menu, then you cannot manage programs when you lock or unlock your system.

6 Click OK.

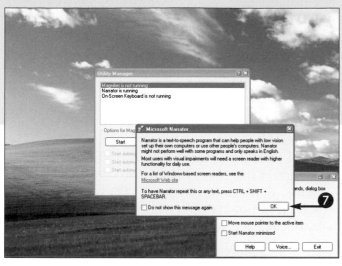

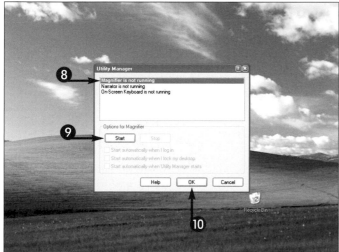

The Microsoft Narrator information window opens.

7 Click OK to close the information window.

8 In the Utility Manager dialog box, select a tool that you want to start.

9 Click Start.

To stop a program that is currently running, you can select it and click Stop.

The selected tool stops or starts, depending on the option that you chose.

10 To close the Utility Manager dialog box without making changes, click OK.

U

TIPS

Important!
You should log on as an Administrator for most of the operations that you perform with Utility Manager.

Customize It!
If you want one or more Accessibility tools to load automatically when you log in to Windows, then select the programs from the list in Utility Manager and click to select the Start automatically when I log in option. Repeat the steps and deselect this option to disable it.

Attention!
If you want full capability with Utility Manager, then do not open it through the Start Menu. Instead, on Windows-integrated keyboards that display the Windows flag keys — usually between the Alt and Ctrl keys — press the Windows flag key+U. Utility Manager opens without the limitation warning that appears after Step 5.

VIRTUAL PRIVATE NETWORKING:
Create a VPN Connection

Virtual Private Networking, or VPN, is a Windows XP feature that enables you to create a secure connection between your computer and a remote network. For example, if your office network supports incoming VPN connections, then you can connect your home computer to your office network through VPN to use file servers, printers, and other office network resources.

VPN uses encryption to secure the network traffic moving between your computer and the remote network. Windows XP supports two protocols, Point-to-Point Tunneling Protocol — or PPTP — and Layer 2 Tunneling Protocol — or L2TP. In general, L2TP

provides better encryption and is the recommended choice if your remote network supports it.

When you create a VPN connection, you must specify the IP address or fully qualified host name of the VPN server. You also must specify other options, such as whether Windows must dial a regular connection before attempting the VPN connection. You can modify these and other settings after creating the VPN connection.

Before you create the VPN connection, you must obtain the required settings from your VPN server Administrator.

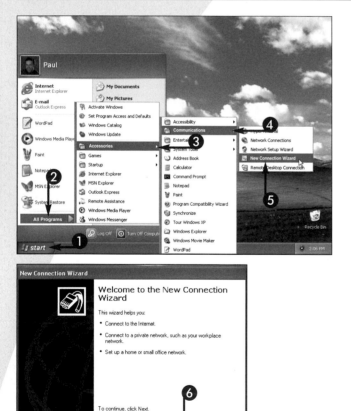

① Click Start.

② Click All Programs.

③ Click Accessories.

④ Click Communications.

⑤ Click New Connection Wizard.

The New Connection Wizard opens.

⑥ Click Next.

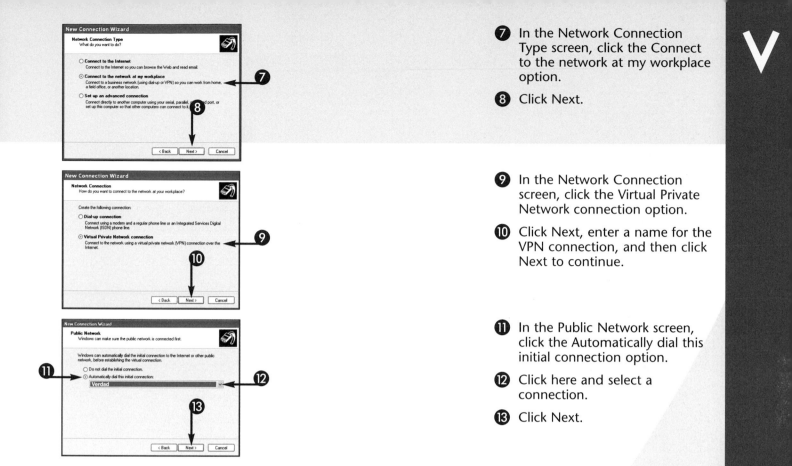

⑦ In the Network Connection Type screen, click the Connect to the network at my workplace option.

⑧ Click Next.

⑨ In the Network Connection screen, click the Virtual Private Network connection option.

⑩ Click Next, enter a name for the VPN connection, and then click Next to continue.

⑪ In the Public Network screen, click the Automatically dial this initial connection option.

⑫ Click here and select a connection.

⑬ Click Next.

TIP

Did You Know?

It is possible to create a VPN connection between two routers in order to connect two networks. In fact, many companies connect branch offices across the Internet using VPN. This enables these companies to share network resources more effectively and allows users easy access to the main network, while at the same time, saving the expense of a dedicated connection. If you telecommute, then a Windows VPN connection can be a great way for you to stay connected to your office. However, if you are working from a branch office, then a network-to-network VPN connection is probably a better choice.

VIRTUAL PRIVATE NETWORKING:
Create a VPN Connection (Continued)

When you create a VPN connection, you can specify an IP address or a fully qualified host name for the VPN server. If you specify a host name, then it must resolve to the IP address of the VPN server. Check with the VPN server Administrator if you are not sure what to enter.

After you create the connection, you can change authentication options as well as a variety of other properties. For example, you can choose between PPTP and L2TP, depending on what your server supports. You can also specify dial-up settings if the VPN connection uses a dial-up connection to the Internet.

While the default options for a Windows XP VPN connection work for most situations, you may need to change the protocols and other settings used by the VPN connection. You can modify these settings after you create the connection.

Although your network is probably secure, it is a good idea to also enable the Windows Firewall option for the VPN connection. The firewall protects your computer from potential threats.

⓮ In the VPN Server Selection screen, type the host name or IP address of the remote VPN server.

⓯ Click Next.

⓰ Click Next again.

⓱ Click Finish.

The Connect My Office Network dialog box appears.

⓲ To connect using the current settings, type your username.

⓳ Type your password.

⓴ Click Connect.

㉑ To change the settings, click Properties.

The Properties dialog box appears for the connection that you selected.

22 Click the Networking tab.

23 Click here and select either PPTP or L2TP.

● If you select Automatic — the default setting — then Windows attempts an L2TP connection; if that fails, then it attempts a PPTP connection.

24 Click to enable or disable the networking items that the connection will use.

25 Click the Security tab.

26 If your VPN server requires a pre-shared encryption key, then select the Advanced option.

27 Click IPSec Settings.

The IPSec Settings dialog box appears.

28 Click the Use pre-shared key for authentication option.

29 Type the required key in the Key field.

30 Click OK.

31 Click OK.

Your VPN connection is configured for the encryption key.

TIPS

Did You Know?

Although it is not difficult to set up a VPN connection in Windows, it does require the right settings. Make sure that you understand the requirements of your VPN server so that you can enter the necessary settings when you create the connection. The VPN server Administrator can help you if necessary.

Delete It!

You can delete a VPN connection as you would any other type of connection. To do so, open the Network Connections folder, click the connection icon to select it, and press the Del key. Click Yes when prompted to confirm the deletion. You can also right-click a connection icon and choose the Delete command.

V

VOLUME CONTROL:
Control Audio Volume in Windows

Although the speakers attached to your computer often allow you to adjust audio volume, and sometimes treble and bass levels, you can control volume and balance directly through the Master Volume window. This feature offers you dynamic control directly from your Windows desktop; you do not need to adjust the controls on the actual hardware.

From the Master Volume window, you can adjust the volume, the left and right balance of your speakers, and the settings for your CD drive, your microphone,

and other audio devices that you have installed on your system.

You can access the Master Volume window through a Speaker/Horn icon in the System Tray. However, some high-end audio cards replace this icon with a special icon that is specific to the software that you install along with the audio card. When you click this special icon, a more complex sound control panel appears that is specific to the type of soundboard that you have.

① Click Start.

② Click Control Panel.

The Control Panel window opens.

③ In the Control Panel section, click Switch to Classic View.

④ Double-click Sounds and Audio Devices.

The Sounds and Audio Devices Properties dialog box appears.

⑤ Click to select the Place volume icon in the taskbar option.

⑥ Click OK.

The Volume Control icon appears in the System Tray.

7 Double-click the Speaker/Horn icon in the System Tray.

The Master Volume window opens.

8 Click and drag the sliders to set the sound levels that you want.

9 Click Close when you are done.

Windows adjusts the volume levels, based on your settings.

V

TIPS

Did You Know?
To mute a particular sound option such as CD Audio, click to select the appropriate Mute option at the bottom of the Master Volume window.

Important!
If your Volume Control icon does not appear in the System Tray after you select the option in Step 5, then you may need to reinstall or update your audio card device driver.

Try This!
If you do not hear any sound coming from an audio device, check the volume control switches on the device and then check the Master Volume window to ensure that the device is not set to Mute. If it is, then click to deselect this option.

WEB PUBLISHING WIZARD:
Publish Files to a Web Server

With the Web Publishing Wizard, you can transfer files — images as well as documents — from your hard drive to a Web server where you can share them with others. This makes it much easier for you to collaborate with other people in a team, on a committee, or in a class. This is the simplest and most common technique used to share files today.

You can use the Web Publishing Wizard to publish pages and pictures to your Web site. You can also use it to share files on a group site such as MSN Groups, which provides free Web site space for sharing photos among family and friends.

You can use this wizard instead of FTP software or a Web management package such as Microsoft FrontPage. However, the wizard provides almost no options for management beyond the transfer of files from your system to the server.

See also>> [Web Publishing Wizard]

[FTP]

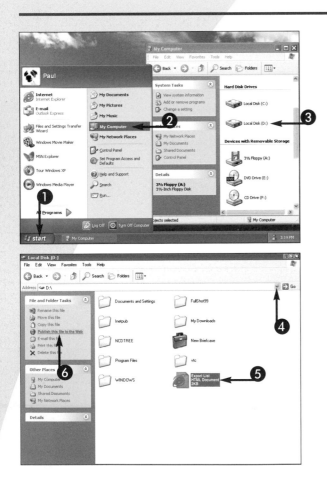

❶ Click Start.

❷ Click My Computer.

The My Computer window opens.

❸ Double-click the drive that contains the files or folders that you want to publish.

The window displays the contents of the drive that you selected.

❹ Click here and browse to locate your files.

❺ Click to select the file that you want to publish.

❻ Click Publish this file to the Web.

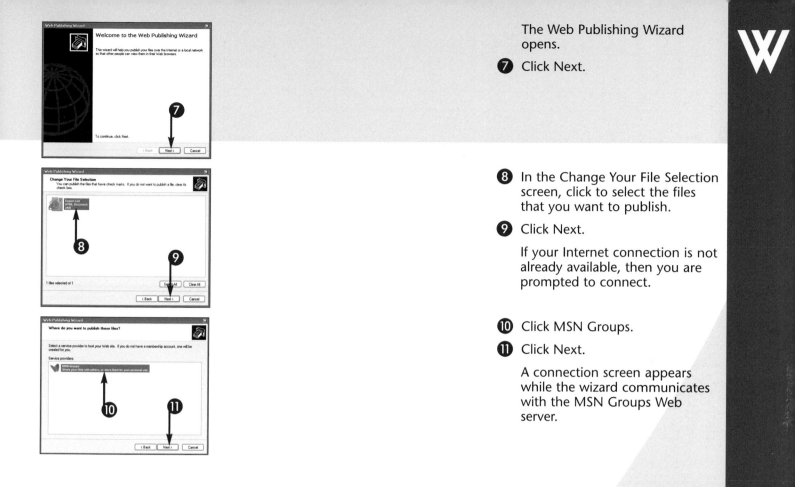

The Web Publishing Wizard opens.

7 Click Next.

8 In the Change Your File Selection screen, click to select the files that you want to publish.

9 Click Next.

If your Internet connection is not already available, then you are prompted to connect.

10 Click MSN Groups.

11 Click Next.

A connection screen appears while the wizard communicates with the MSN Groups Web server.

Did You Know?

After you first publish files to a Web server, a shortcut that points to the address for that server appears in your Favorites list of sites in Internet Explorer.

More Options!

By default, the wizard points you to MSN Groups, a free Web server. If you want to share files and folders to a different location, then you can set up a new connection in My Network Places. You can then use FTP or another Web communication program to publish your files.

Try It!

If you have just one or two files that you want to share with others, then it is usually faster to send these files as an attachment through e-mail. You can do this in Outlook Express.

WEB PUBLISHING WIZARD:
Publish Files to a Web Server (Continued)

When you choose to publish files and folders through the Web Publishing Wizard, Windows directs you to set up a free account in order to access their MSN Groups Web server service. This account allows you to set up a Web page, free of charge, in which you can transfer files to share with family and friends.

You do not require previous Web design experience to use this service. Here, the Web Publishing Wizard can serve you well because it is designed with MSN Groups in mind, which requires no design skills or major setup. You just choose the files you want to add to your MSN Group, the default setting in the

wizard. Once you have published your first files there, you can use the wizard again to publish more files to the same server with the same account.

MSN Groups allows you to publish documents, digital photos, scanned images, and other types of files that you want to share. You can then provide the address of your MSN Groups site to friends, family, and coworkers with whom you want to share your files. Keep in mind that the ability to publish in your group is limited to you and anyone to whom you provide your account information.

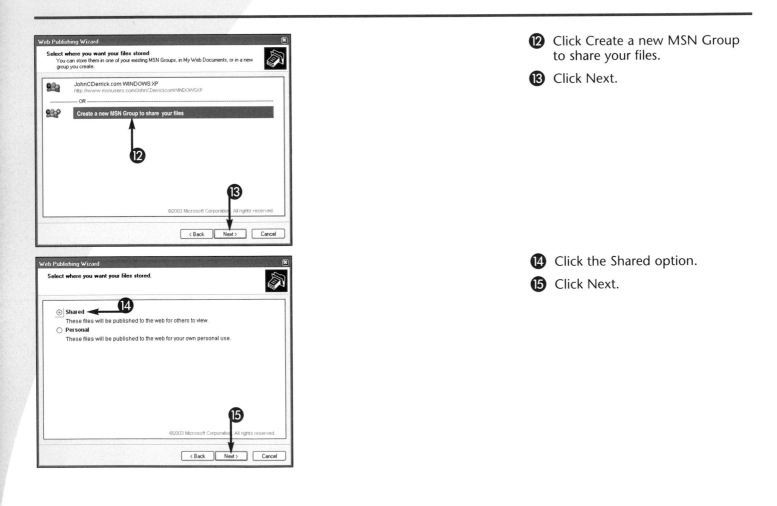

⑫ Click Create a new MSN Group to share your files.

⑬ Click Next.

⑭ Click the Shared option.

⑮ Click Next.

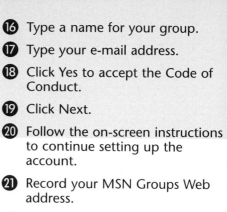

16 Type a name for your group.

17 Type your e-mail address.

18 Click Yes to accept the Code of Conduct.

19 Click Next.

20 Follow the on-screen instructions to continue setting up the account.

21 Record your MSN Groups Web address.

22 Click to specify whether you want your group to be listed in the MSN Groups directory.

23 Click Next.

The wizard transfers the selected files to your newly created space.

24 Click Finish to close the wizard.

TIPS

Attention!
Your MSN Groups Web address will look similar to this: www.msnusers.com/*mygroupname*. You will see the exact address as you finish the wizard. You should write it down for later reference, although a link for your site appears in your Favorites folder in Internet Explorer.

Did You Know?
As you set up your account on MSN Spaces, you should access the link to the Code of Conduct. Because you must agree to this code in order to create your group, you should understand exactly what you agree to uphold.

More Options!
You will also see a shortcut to your MSN Groups file share when you click Start and then click My Network Places.

WINDOWS CLASSIC FOLDERS:
Configure Windows for Classic Folder Interface

If you prefer the folder interface in Windows Classic mode to the more modernized Windows XP interface, then you can quickly configure your desktop to use Classic mode. The primary advantage is if you are already familiar with the old interface, then you can recreate and use it in Windows XP. Even if you have not used Windows in Classic mode before, you may find that Classic works best for you.

There are some differences in the availability of certain features between the two interfaces. For example, the Classic version does not have the left-hand task pane, and so you can see more folder content within a single screen.

When you change the Folder Options for the Classic style, you may want to check out some of the other available selections. For example, in the View tab, you can set various preferences for when you open a folder, such as whether system or hidden files display.

See also>>

① Click Start.

② Click Control Panel.

The Control Panel window opens.

③ In the Control Panel section, click to Classic View.

④ Double-click Folder Options.

The Folder Options dialog box appears, displaying the General tab.

5 Under Tasks, click the Use Windows classic folders option.

6 Click OK.

The Classic folders interface now appears in the My Computer window.

TIPS

Attention!
After you change to the Windows Classic folder interface, you cannot view the Control Panel in Category view. Only the Classic view is available because the Control Panel, like My Computer, is a type of folder.

More Options!
You can also access the Folder Options dialog box when you click the Tools menu in My Computer and Windows Explorer. This feature is also available in many other tools and folders.

Remove It!
If you no longer want to use the Classic folders interface, then you can always revert to the Windows XP style. To do this, repeat steps 1 to 3, and then click to deselect the Use Windows classic folders option.

WINDOWS FIREWALL:
Configure Windows Firewall

When you enable and configure the Windows Firewall, you set up a layer of protection that tries to shield your computer or network from intrusion that can put your system at risk. As its name implies, a firewall creates a barrier between your system and a network such as the Internet. You should not use more than one firewall on your system at any given time.

System intrusion can take many forms. One example is an Internet worm, which is a type of computer virus that can do many bad things, such as leave behind files that create an opening for others who

want to access your computer or steal your passwords. A worm can also send out copies of itself to the people that are listed in your Address Book. Other intruders, such as hackers, may also try to access your files or confidential information.

See also>>

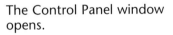

1 Click Start.

2 Click Control Panel.

The Control Panel window opens.

3 In the Control Panel section, click to Classic View.

4 Double-click Windows Firewall.

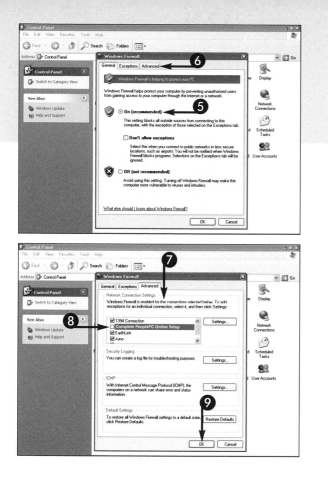

The Windows Firewall dialog box appears, displaying the General tab.

5 Click the On option.

6 Click the Advanced tab.

7 Review the listings under Network Connection Settings.

By default, all of these listings are selected.

8 Click to deselect any connection setting for which you do not want to enable the firewall.

9 Click OK.

Your firewall is now configured and enabled.

TIPS

Attention!
With the firewall operational, you may find it difficult to use Internet-ready programs that formerly ran well. To keep these programs or connections from being blocked by the firewall, you can add them to your list of exceptions, located in the Exceptions tab of the Windows Firewall dialog box.

Remove It!
If you have customized your Windows Firewall configuration and you want it to operate as it originally did, then you can restore the default settings. To do this, follow Steps 1 to 3 to access the Windows Firewall dialog box. In the Advanced tab, under Default Settings, click Restore Defaults.

WINDOWS FIREWALL:
Manage Exceptions

When you manage exceptions through Windows Firewall, you can control whether the firewall blocks certain programs or connections from accessing your system or the Internet. An exception is a program or connection that you want to allow so that it does not limit your ability to work or communicate. It is vital that you manage these exceptions so that your network communications are not blocked by the firewall. You can then tell the Windows Firewall how to handle these programs and connections properly.

For example, when you instant message with someone, you often create a short-term connection

between your systems. The firewall may block this connection unless you identify the connection as okay. You can do this by configuring the firewall, or when you receive a message from the firewall, asking if you want to block or unblock a connection or program.

See also>> **Windows Firewall**

Windows Firewall

① Click Start.

② Click Control Panel.

The Control Panel window opens.

③ In the Control Panel section, click to Classic View.

④ Double-click Windows Firewall.

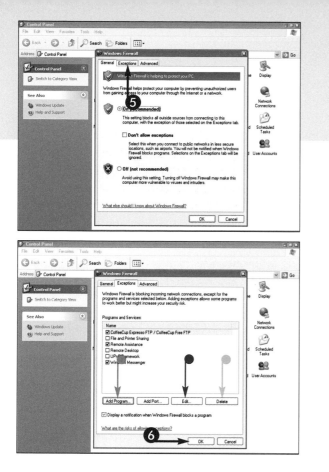

The Windows Firewall dialog box appears, displaying the General tab.

⑤ Click the Exceptions tab.

In the Programs and Services list, a check mark appears next to any items that are not blocked by the firewall.

● To add a program, you can click Add Program and follow the on-screen instructions to specify the application.

● To remove a listed exception, you can click the program and then click Delete.

● To modify details for an exception, you can click the program in the list and then click Edit.

⑥ Click OK.

Did You Know?

If you do not specify any exceptions, then Windows automatically notifies you if a program or service tries to use your Internet connection. You can then choose whether to block permanently, block for that session, or unblock to allow the program to run. As you make these choices, they are registered in the Exceptions tab.

Important!

For maximum security, you can choose not to allow any exceptions. To do this, repeat Steps 1 to 3. In the General tab, click to select the Don't allow exceptions option. Keep in mind that this option may make it difficult, if not impossible, to run at least some Internet programs, such as instant messaging and FTP software.

WINDOWS FIREWALL:
Temporarily Disable Windows Firewall

You may find that the Windows Firewall prevents you from communicating with a network or running a particular program. One possible solution is to disable the firewall.

If you want to temporarily disable the Windows Firewall, you can do this, although it is not recommended. Unfortunately, there is no halfway measure — the firewall must be either on or off. While the firewall is off, your system may operate under an increased risk of security threats and computer viruses such as Internet worms.

Two common reasons why people temporarily disable their firewalls are because they want to chat with friends or to transfer files without limitations. However, it is usually better to try to manage these programs by allowing them as exceptions than it is to disable the firewall, even for a short period of time.

See also>> **Windows Firewall**

Windows Firewall

---

① Click Start.

② Click Control Panel.

The Control Panel window opens.

③ In the Control Panel section, click to Classic View.

④ Double-click Windows Firewall.

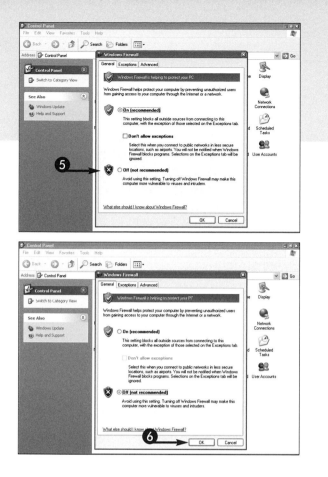

The Windows Firewall dialog box appears, displaying the General tab.

5 Click the Off option.

6 Click OK.

Windows disables the firewall.

TIPS

Attention!
To reduce your risk while the firewall is temporarily disabled, you should leave your antivirus software enabled, if you are using any. The antivirus software should be able to detect and isolate an Internet worm or any other type of virus that may appear.

Did You Know?
If you have Windows XP Service Pack 2 installed, then Windows Firewall is enabled by default.

More Options!
Just because you use the Windows Firewall does not mean that you do not need other forms of protection, including common-sense measures that limit your risk of exposure to threats. You should continue to run antivirus software and be careful when opening e-mail attachments or other files from any source, even a trusted one.

WINDOWS PICTURE AND FAX VIEWER:
Print a Photo

You can use the Windows Picture and Fax Viewer to view images and fax documents, as well as to perform other basic tasks. For example, you can rotate an image clockwise or counter-clockwise, view a series of images in rapid succession, or launch a picture editor. You can also print a copy of your digital photos or other graphic files to either a standard or photo-specific printer.

Before you print the photo, you can use tools in the viewer to add text, attach a note, or zoom in or out to inspect the image. You can even delete that image and move to the next image in the folder.

When you want to print an image, you can launch the Photo Printing Wizard. This tool guides you through printing options that optimize the quality of the print job for the photo. For example, you can choose the printer that you want to use along with the type of paper, such as special photo print paper.

See also>> **Windows Picture and Fax Viewer**

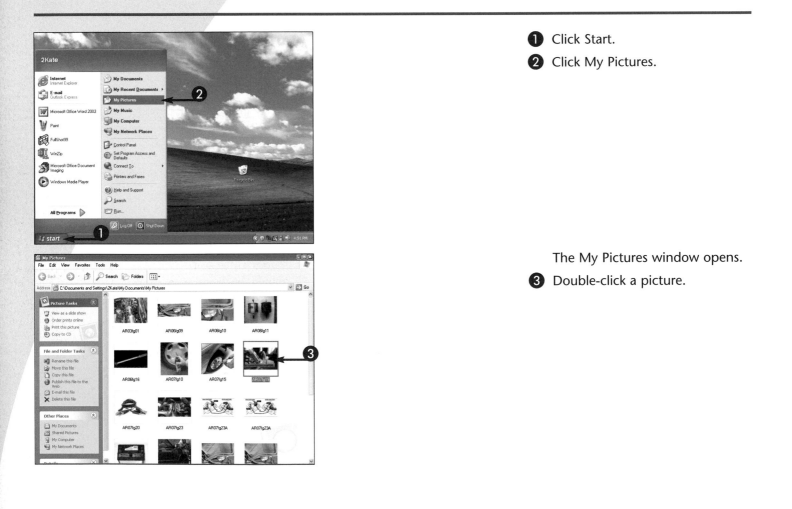

1 Click Start.

2 Click My Pictures.

The My Pictures window opens.

3 Double-click a picture.

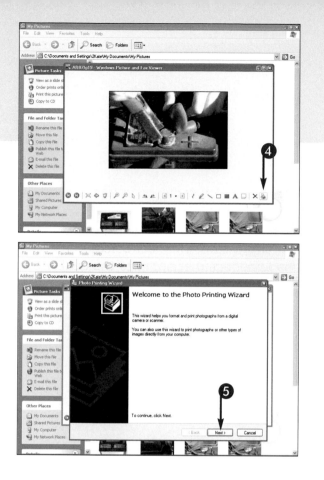

The Windows Picture and Fax Viewer opens, displaying the image.

④ Click the Printer icon at the bottom-right corner of the viewer window.

You can also press Ctrl+P.

The Photo Printing Wizard opens.

⑤ Click Next.

⑥ Follow the on-screen steps to print your image.

TIPS

Attention!
If you install a recent version of Microsoft Office, then your images and faxes may open by default through Microsoft Office Document Imaging rather than through the Windows Picture and Fax Viewer.

Customize It!
If you want, you can use a different program to view your images than the Windows Picture and Fax Viewer. Click Start and then click Control Panel. Double-click Folder Options. In the File Types tab, click an image file type and then click Change to specify a different program.

More Options!
To open an image or fax with a program other than the Windows Picture and Fax Viewer, right-click the image. In the sub-menu, click Open With and then select the program you want.

WINDOWS UPDATE:
Check for Updates Now

Even when you configure Windows Update to run automatically, you may want to check updates manually so that you can view and select update options. You can do this at any time through an update option that is pinned to the All Programs menu. You should do this on a regular basis to ensure that your system is up-to-date and to see what other optional updates are available.

A situation where this updating feature is useful is when you experience a problem with a program or

tool on your desktop. You are typically asked whether you want to report the issue, and you are then directed to a link. This link may then tell you to install a particular update file to resolve your problem. To download the file, you can run Windows Update manually.

See also>>

Automatic Updates

Windows Update

① Click Start.

② Click All Programs.

③ Click Windows Update.

You must already be connected to the Internet.

Microsoft Internet Explorer opens on your desktop and displays the Microsoft Windows Update Web site.

④ If prompted to do so, then click to install the ActiveX software that is needed to run the Windows Update feature.

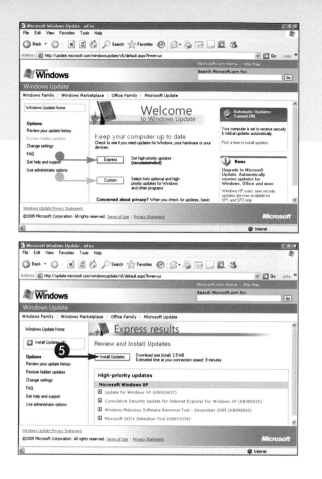

The Windows Update site determines which updates have already been applied to your system, and then produces a list of available updates that you do not currently have.

● You can click Express to view all of the recommended or high-priority updates for your system.

● You can click Custom to choose only the updates that you want.

The site checks your current update status.

5 Click Install Updates.

If an end-user license agreement, or EULA, screen appears, then you may be prompted to click an I Confirm button.

The update download commences.

6 Click OK when you are done.

You may be prompted to restart your computer for the updates to take effect. However, most updates allow you to choose Restart Later if that is more convenient.

TIPS

Customize It!
If you have not already activated Automatic Updates, then you can use the feature that is available at the right side of the browser window on the update site to enable automatic download and installation.

More Options!
If you use Microsoft Office, then you can use a feature similar to Windows Update to apply patches and drivers to your Microsoft Office software. Click Help in your Microsoft Office application and then click the link to Microsoft Office Online to learn more.

Remove It!
If you experience a problem with an update that you install, then you can remove it to see if this resolves the issue.

WINDOWS UPDATE:
Remove a Potential Problem Update

When you run Windows Update, Windows may replace important system files as it installs new versions. However, you may run the risk of serious problems because the new version may not be compatible with your system. If you notice any problems with your system immediately after an update, then you should suspect the update. You can remove the update to see if the computer returns to normal operation.

Not all Windows Update installations are of equal importance. Some of these updates are critical to your system, which means that you should download

and apply the update as soon as possible to avoid placing your computer at serious risk. However, the potential for incompatibility always exists. For example, an update to a modem or video driver may leave you unable to connect to the Internet, or it may adversely affect your display. In these cases, you can solve the problem by removing the update.

See also>>   **Automatic Updates**

Windows Update

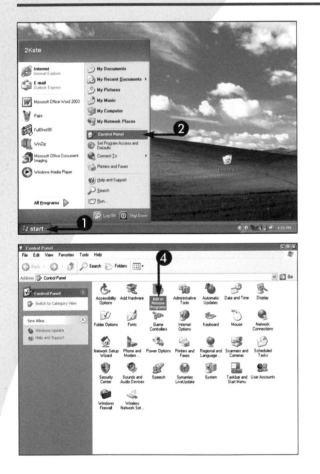

① Click Start.

② Click Control Panel.

The Control Panel window opens.

③ In the Control Panel section, click to Classic View.

④ Double-click Add or Remove Programs.

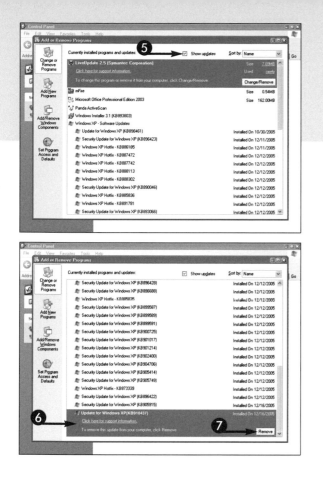

The Add or Remove Programs window opens.

⑤ Click to select the Show updates option.

The program listing expands to include all of the applied updates, along with their install dates.

⑥ Click the update that you want to remove.

⑦ Click Remove.

Windows removes the update from your system.

You may be prompted to restart your computer.

TIPS

Attention!
If the problem that you experience prevents you from starting up in Windows normally, then you may be able to launch Windows in Safe Mode. You can then roll back to a previous Restore Point by using System Restore.

Did You Know?
The files that are available from the Windows Update site include Windows patches, security updates, and drivers that are required for both Microsoft Office software, as well as Windows XP-compatible hardware.

Try This!
Because Windows Update can run automatically, you may not always know exactly what updates you have installed. You can find out in two ways. The first is through Add and Remove Programs in the Control Panel. The second is through the Windows Update site, where you can click the Review Your Update History option.

WIRELESS NETWORK SETUP WIZARD:
Run the Wireless Network Setup Wizard

If you have set up the necessary hardware for a wireless home or small-office network, then you can use the Network Setup Wizard to help you. You can run the wizard to detect and configure your equipment.

The Network Setup Wizard may work better than the software that ships with your wireless hardware. In fact, you should probably use the wizard, as the manufacturer's software may not be fully compatible with Windows XP.

After the Network Setup Wizard helps you to configure the hardware components, it can then enable them to communicate with the various workstations that make up your network. These hardware components can include a wireless access point, or WAP, as well as the individual wireless network cards that you install in each desktop computer or laptop.

See also>> Wireless Network Setup Wizard

Network Setup Wizard

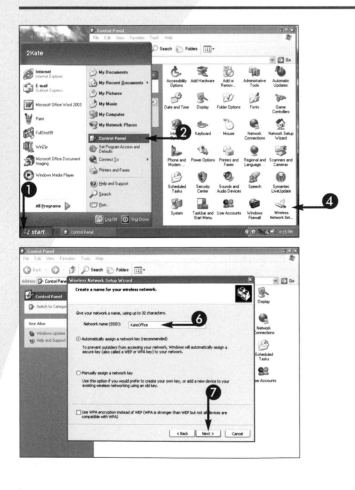

You should first follow the manufacturer's directions to ensure that the hardware is properly installed.

1 In Windows, click Start.

2 Click Control Panel.

The Control Panel window opens.

3 In the Control Panel section, click to Classic View.

4 Double-click Wireless Network Setup Wizard.

The Wireless Network Setup Wizard opens.

5 Click Next.

6 Type a name as a label for your wireless network.

7 Click Next.

430

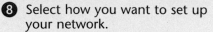

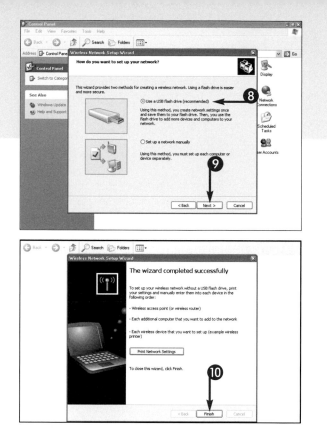

8 Select how you want to set up your network.

If you do not have a USB flash drive, then click the Set up network manually option.

9 Click Next.

10 Click Finish.

Your wireless network is now configured.

TIPS

Attention!

Before you run the Network Setup Wizard, you should carefully review the documentation that accompanies your wireless network equipment to properly install the devices. The wizard may not detect a problem with the hardware or its installation.

Did You Know?

The USB flash drive option in the wizard refers to an external hard drive that connects through the USB port of a desktop computer or laptop. This drive can be easily shared between different computers to make network setup simple and efficient.

More Options!

To learn more about setting up a wireless network, you can consult the Help and Support Center, which is available through the Start Menu.

WORDPAD:
Save a Document

WordPad is a basic word processor that allows you to format documents with installed fonts and print the files that you create. It also allows you to save those documents to your hard drive, where you can later retrieve them to read and edit.

One advantage to using WordPad is that it is fully compatible with Microsoft Word. In fact, it functions like a light version of a commercial word-processing program. This compatibility makes it easy to open WordPad documents in Microsoft Word and to save these documents in a way that retains all of the formatting when you import them into Word.

By default, WordPad saves your documents to the My Documents folder. However, you can change this to save any document that you create to a different folder, or even to save it to a different drive. You can also rename a document that you have already saved in order to store it with a new, more easily identifiable name.

See also>>

Save Dialog Box
WordPad

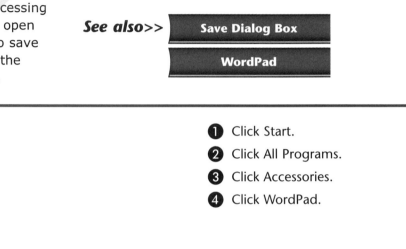

❶ Click Start.

❷ Click All Programs.

❸ Click Accessories.

❹ Click WordPad.

The WordPad window opens.

❺ Create a document.

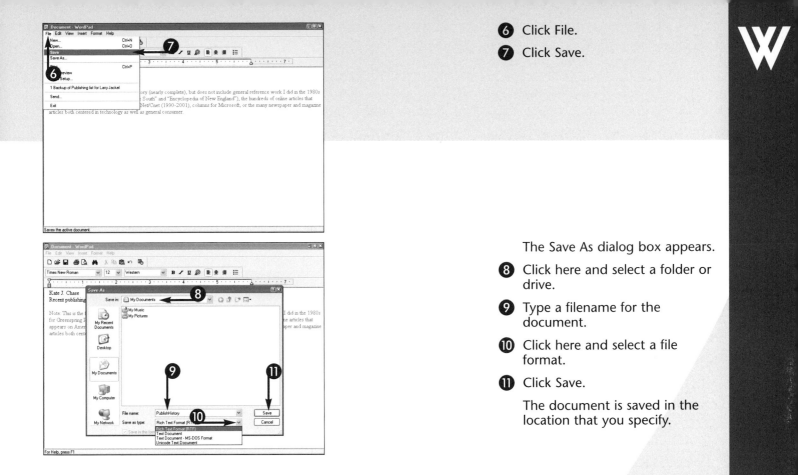

6 Click File.

7 Click Save.

The Save As dialog box appears.

8 Click here and select a folder or drive.

9 Type a filename for the document.

10 Click here and select a file format.

11 Click Save.

The document is saved in the location that you specify.

TIPS

Did You Know?

Once you save a document in WordPad for the first time, the Save or Save As dialog box does not reappear unless you click File and then click Save As. This allows you to save the document with a new filename or with a different format, such as .htm for Web pages.

Important!

By default, unless you specify a different format, WordPad files are saved with the .doc file extension.

More Options!

You can easily print your new document. To do this, you can click the Print icon from the WordPad toolbar, click File, and then click Print — or press Ctrl+P. The Print window opens, where you can select your print options.

ZIP FILES:
Use Compressed Archives in Windows

ZIP files are compressed file archives that collect several files together into one compressed file that takes up less disk space. Compressing files into an archive not only saves storage space but also reduces the amount of time it takes to send or receive files from a Web site or through e-mail. You probably already use ZIP files and may want additional ways to save space and work with these types of files in Windows XP.

Although you probably use a tool such as WinZIP to compress files before you send them out through

e-mail or store them on disks, or to unzip ZIP files that you receive, you can also create ZIP files in Windows. Windows treats these files—and ZIP files created by other means—as special folders. You can move less frequently used or large files into these ZIP files to save space. In addition, the Disk Cleanup tool in Windows offers ZIP file and folder compression as one of the choices to free disk space.

See also>> **Disk Cleanup Wizard**

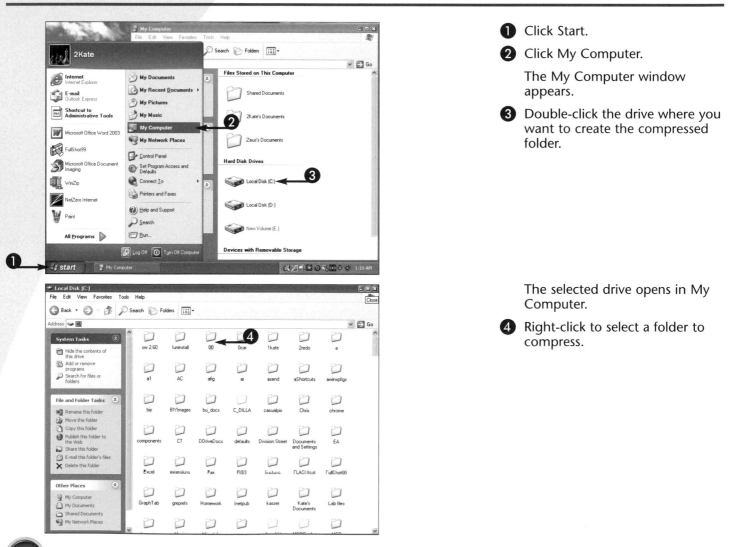

1 Click Start.

2 Click My Computer.

The My Computer window appears.

3 Double-click the drive where you want to create the compressed folder.

The selected drive opens in My Computer.

4 Right-click to select a folder to compress.

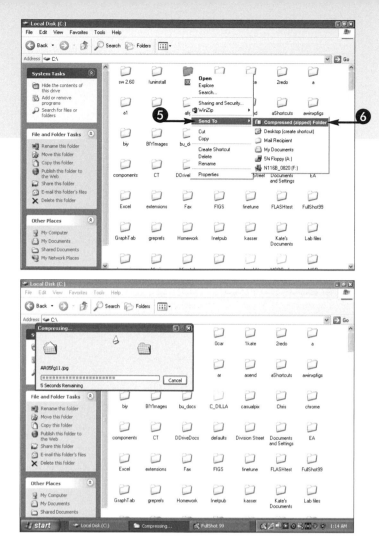

A sub-menu appears.

⑤ Click Send To.

⑥ Click Compressed (zipped) Folder.

The contents of the folder are then compressed into a zip format.

Note: Alternatively, you can right-click the Desktop (or in any other folder) and create a new, compressed folder when you click New and then click Compress (zipped) Folder.

Note: See "File and Folder Management" for instructions on moving files.

TIPS

Caution!

Whenever possible, do not store program files within a compressed file. These programs can take notoriously longer to start and open from a compressed folder. If you do need to store programs there, choose those programs or utilities you rarely, if ever, use.

Important!

Because the files you move to a ZIP file will be compressed and will take slightly longer to open than files you keep in an uncompressed folder, only store less frequently used files in a compressed folder.

Remove It!

If you want to delete the compressed folder you created, right-click the folder and click Delete. The deleted folder goes to your Recycle Bin and will be permanently removed when you empty Recycle Bin. However, if you have files within that folder, you may want to move them to another folder first.

Index

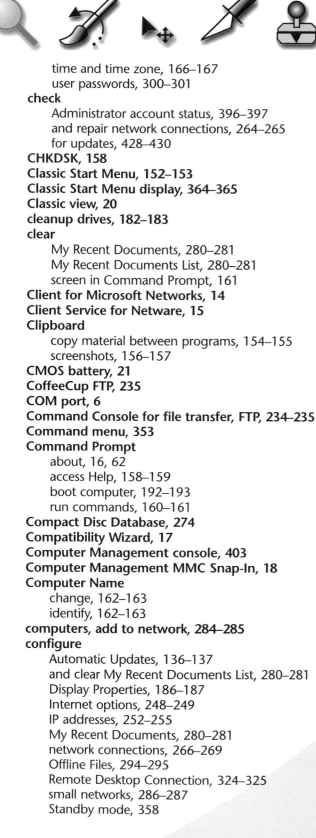

Index

Index

Index

Index